PHOTOSHOP LAB COLOR

The Canyon Conundrum

And Other Adventures in
The Most Powerful Colorspace

DAN MARGULIS

Peachpit Press

Photoshop LAB Color: The Canyon Conundrum and Other Adventures in the Most Powerful Colorspace

Dan Margulis

Peachpit Press

1249 Eighth Street
Berkeley, CA 94710
510/524-2178
Fax: 541/524-2221

Find us on the World Wide Web at www.peachpit.com.

To report errors, please send a note to errata@peachpit.com

Peachpit Press is a division of Pearson Education.

Trademarks

Notice of Rights

Disclaimer

ISBN: 0-321-35678-0
10 9 8 7 6 5 4 3 2

Manufactured in the United States of America.

Table of Contents

The Canyon Conundrum

The basic LAB enhancement technique is very powerful—but it always seems to be used on a single category of image.

LAB by the Numbers

A general description of how LAB is set up, complete with opponent-color channels, imaginary colors, and positive and negative numbers.

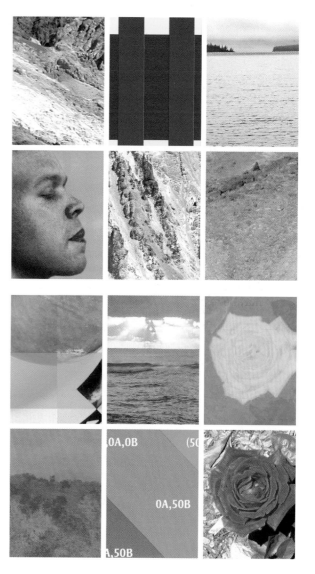

3

Vary the Recipe, Vary the Color

Choosing different angles for the AB curves—and making sure that Photoshop is properly configured.

4

It's All About The Center Point

How LAB defines neutrality—a zero is a gray—is the key to its color-enhancement potential

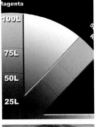

5

Sharpen the L, Blur the AB

Separate channels for color and contrast give LAB a decisive advantage in blurring. Often it's the best sharpening space as well.

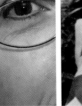

6 Entering the Forest: Myths and Dangers

Understanding LAB requires discarding bogus preconceptions—and being aware of real risks.

7 Summing Up: LAB and the Workflow

How LAB fits into your workflow depends on both your expertise and how much time you have per image.

8 The Imaginary Color, The Impossible Retouch

What happens when LAB calls for a color that isn't just out of gamut, but that couldn't possibly exist?

9

The LAB Advantage in Selections and Masking

With the A and B channels, we can create masks that seem to come out of thin air—or selections *of* thin air.

10

The Product Is Red but The Client Wants Green

The most convincing way to make radical color changes—or to match a PMS specification.

11

The Best Retouching Space

In complicated collaging, moiré elimination, adding color to selected areas, restoring older images, and painting, LAB has big advantages.

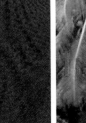

Command, Click, Control

Advanced LAB curves can drive objects away from one another without ever selecting them. It only requires a click of the mouse.

The Universal Interchange Standard

How LAB is (and how it should be) used to facilitate colorspace transfers, and to match PMS colors.

Once for Color, Once for Contrast

Some LAB techniques can translate into RGB—provided you separate color and contrast in your mind.

15

Blending With the A and B

Smashing channels that contain no detail into the L, which does, seems crazy—but it's extraordinarily effective at creating transitions.

16

A Face Is Like a Canyon

Introducing a powerful RGB-LAB hybrid, a recipe that dramatically improves the appearance and believability of almost all portraits.

Foreword

The book you are holding in your hands is the most deeply advanced, inspiring, insightful, maddening, awesome, demanding, and illuminating educational effort—in any media format—ever created for Photoshop.

While this proclamation might sound a bit overstated, there is no doubt in my mind that it's also decisively true. It's a gift from one of the deepest thinkers in the imaging industry, one that will be as relevant in a hundred years as it is this very moment. It's a way to begin thinking about Photoshop as so much more than just a collection of interface implementations, tightly coded algorithms, marketing decisions, and business machinations. The soul of the machine is revealed in granular detail, and stepping into the atomic structure of Photoshop is something that is all of a sudden not only possible, but almost inevitable.

Paradigm shift has never seemed so appropriate a term as it does in describing this book. The trees rejoice at its publication, and you should rejoice at the bravery and progressive approach of the Peachpit folks in publishing and distributing it—and at the tireless efforts of Dan Margulis.

I'll repeat. The trees love Dan Margulis.

Trees everywhere breathe an oxygenated sigh of relief at the publication of this noble and desirable work, primarily due to their frustration and fear, their reluctance to submit their firm flesh to the pointless pulp publishing of Photoshop books that have no purpose, no reason to exist outside of the profit motive. There are more than a few books that fit this general category, written by professional writers looking to capitalize on the vibrant market for all things Photoshop. These books are tailored around specific versions of the software, lack any meaningful insight or originality, are obsolete within months of publication, and are a waste of precious resources, of both human and arboreal species.

And so, bad Photoshop books literally rob us of one of the most essential elements of life, the oxygen that washes over our ravenous lungs, nourishing us, the crisp, fresh oxygen of the countryside, which we so desperately crave in the centers of dirty, grimy cities. Trees are sad whenever they are sacrificed in vain, wasted on meaningless musings on the Quick Mask mode, or the misguided merits of the Brightness/Contrast abomination.

This book is not one of those sinful wastes.

* * *

As you can probably tell, Dan is one of my heroes, a designation I do not bestow lightly. To prove it, I'd like to tell you about some of the others.

My father, Louis Biedny, one of the most creative humans I've ever known, always drilled into me the importance of having the intellectual and emotional clarity to choose heroes carefully, and only after significant consideration and reflection. As a result, it always seemed to me that the idolization of sports figures or television celebrities never made much sense. Such folks don't possess much of a potential to contribute anything lasting, and are quickly forgotten.

From the time I first considered the role of heroes in my life, music has provided a rich source of pleasure and inspiration, as well as spiritual growth and a better understanding of the world, and cemented Mozart, Beethoven and the Beatles in my heart and soul as cultural heroes.

Leonardo da Vinci and Albert Einstein were natural candidates for the roles of scientific heroes, and have since been joined by Nikola Tesla, Bob Moog, Leon Theremin, and other deep thinkers, inventors, and creatives in my virtual shrine of innovative thought. Salvador Dali and René Magritte form the core of my artistic ideals, Isaac Asimov stands large in my mind as the bastion of integrity of the written word, and Noam Chomsky's radical thoughts on politics and the dynamics of human language formed the admittedly—actually, proudly—leftist bent of my own political beliefs. The thought of spending an hour, a day, or a year talking with any of these individuals is as invigorating and exciting as the first blush of love, but unlikely to occur, as most of them are long since departed or simply not accessible in any kind of personal way.

I've also had the amazing good fortune to meet and befriend some of my primary technological heroes, including Ted Nelson, Roger Dean, and Todd Rundgren. In the Photoshop universe, John and Tom Knoll, the program's original developers, were the two first heroic figures I encountered. Their efforts have affected the history of the evolution of computer graphics in ways we don't yet fully comprehend or appreciate.

Because of John's support and encouragement (as well as his invaluable recommendation to management), I moved from New York City to lovely Marin County in early 1991, to work at the infamous Industrial Light and Magic special effects facility. John was the primary source of all of my earliest Photoshop knowledge, and opened my mind to the possibilities of using it to create the highest-end imaging work one could imagine, the pursuit of realistic visual portrayals of fantasy in motion pictures.

The Calculations command has remained one of my main go-to tools, thanks to the hours spent looking over John's shoulder and engaging him in conversation about his surrogate software offspring. John has since become a hero to legions of imaging fanatics, as well as science fiction aficionados worldwide, as the special effects visionary behind the magic of the last few *Star Wars* films.

I consider Dan Margulis to fit right in to my pantheon of heroes. I've been fortunate enough to meet him, speak to him in the flesh, and even call him friend, a rare pleasure and honor. He's really the only Photoshop expert I currently look up to as a mentor, and certainly the most capable Photoshop author I have ever read. The combination of his deep understanding of technical matters and his eloquent, amusing, and engaging writing style provides an unparalleled opportunity to learn meaningful ideas in a realistic, pragmatic context. His seminal *Professional Photoshop* books served as the foundation for my deeper understanding of color correction theory and practice, and have helped me gain a better foothold in my own area of Photoshop fascination, channels and masking techniques.

For years, I have recommended his writings as some of the most important information available for advanced Photoshop training, particularly in regard to color correction and color channel theory and practice. And I'll qualify that recommendation, in that the only other significant source for channel knowledge has been my *Photoshop Channel Chops* book, out of print and, oddly, one of the most collectible computer trade books ever. I'll tell you this: *The Canyon Conundrum* means that if I ever update *Channel Chops*, and assuming that I devote an entire chapter to discussion of LAB, that chapter will consist solely of a picture of the cover of this book. No need to improve upon perfection.

Still, when I first heard about Dan's project, I was surprised by the declared topic—was it possible, let alone wise, to devote an entire tome to a single colorspace, let alone a seemingly obscure and specific one? Just the idea of writing books about colorspaces seems beyond the scope of any type of sane, rational behavior. In a world with over 500 Photoshop books, how can Dan be crazy enough to devote an entire title to an esoteric subdiscipline like LAB?

Dan has discovered, by means and methods steeped in no small amount of mystery and mystique, the myriad of secrets and awesome power buried in LAB. He has used the raw energy of his mind to convey a whole new way of looking at images, and how to make them better in the most significant ways, to truly enhance their clarity and color, to make those images tell a better story. There's nothing gratuitous about the techniques revealed here, no sparkly sequins or pixelated pap.

*   *   *

The Canyon Conundrum is nothing less than an entirely new and original toolbox for the resourceful Photoshopper. You know who you are: memorization of strings of menu commands doesn't cater to your thirst to know how Photoshop works. The only thing that will quench it is discovery of the "why" of how a specific technique or approach delivers a certain result.

Even so, Dan has taken the time to accommodate folks simply looking to press the right buttons by the way he's arranged many of his early chapters into two discrete, yet related, segments. Early on, he suggests that you may wish to read just the first parts, and delve into the second parts of those chapters only if you're seeking a deeper understanding of the principles being discussed.

This is the only time I'll suggest that you ignore Dan, and read every single word he has written, regardless of location within the chapter. All of this book (with the exception of this introduction) is useful content, and worthy of your consideration, even if the author offers some of his effort as a tangential detour. There is definitive meaning in Dan's madness, and if you think he's sometimes showing off, well, it's for your own good anyway.

I'll assume that you are the kind of person who, by the fact that you're reading these words, is open to the notion of "no pain, no gain," and who is not afraid to confront the limits of your own current level of knowledge and understanding. There's no reason to be ashamed if some of the material in this book feels overwhelming at times. *The Canyon Conundrum* is unlike any other Photoshop book that has come before it, even compared to Dan's previous outings, and is meant to really push your mind to new extremes.

You're not likely to master the information in this book in one or two sittings. Like a truly powerful meme, these ideas need time to settle into your brain, to germinate, take root and flourish. Thankfully, Dan has deployed his rather unique sense of humor to the task of making the medicine sweeter, a true accomplishment. Dan could have easily earned his living as a comedy writer, although that would have been a tremendous loss to current and future generations of digital artists and color correctionists.

Something else needs to be addressed at this junction, and it's a bit more of a base issue: Dan is not likely to make a financial killing from this endeavor, certainly nothing along the lines of the books that are sold on the basis of their weight. There is nothing quick and dirty about *The Canyon Conundrum* (I like to think of it as "Slow and Clean," which is a vastly superior approach to learning), and for this, we will all thank Dan in the future. Or feel free to go up to him and pass your gratitude along personally when an opportunity presents itself, if you are lucky enough to attend one of his seminars or rare public appearances.

While I wish that this book were bundled with every single copy of Photoshop, I recognize that it's far too much to absorb for many decent folks. Still, the idealist in me wants to imagine a world where everyone who uses Photoshop wants to know this much about a tool they use so often.

What this is also not is a book solely addressing color correction, unlike most of Dan's previous offerings. This is an exploration that shows sides of the author that surprised me. In my first reading of the draft, a grin came to my face at Chapter 9, which discusses the usefulness of LAB for making selections and masks. Even though my own knowledge of channel structure is fairly comprehensive, I found new wisdom awaiting me in this chapter, nicely rounding out my own prior techniques involving using LAB to isolate specific tonal ranges. The retouching techniques covered in Chapter 11 are nothing short of astounding, and well outside of reasonable expectations of the potential usefulness of LAB.

*   *   *

During the weeks I read the draft chapters that Dan was sending out, I found myself literally meditating over some of the tougher material before I'd fall asleep late at night. Needless to say, there were more than a couple of dreams (or were they nightmares?)

involving Dan's great-great-grandmother, endless vistas of neutral density rock formations, bright green Corvettes, and lots of other eccentric imagery springing from the pages you're about to absorb. Calm, collected sleep is overrated anyway, and I'm glad I was given the opportunity to read this stuff early on.

After spending quality time with this masterpiece, I can honestly say that I'm a better Photoshop user, a better imaging enthusiast, and a better thinker. My own work will never be the same, and I owe Dan so much for the creative expansion, the deeper appreciation of Photoshop and LAB color that his words have helped catalyze for me. I hope that this foreword serves as appropriate payback for the many times that I've learned from Dan, and perhaps you've even found it of some use in getting prepared to become part of this gang, those of us who want to understand Photoshop better than the rest of the world does.

Simply stated, welcome to the most advanced Photoshop book ever conceived. Revelation is yours for the taking, thanks to Dan and his *Canyon Conundrum.*

David Biedny
New York, June 2005

Introduction

If you wish to succeed in a supervisory position, graphic arts or otherwise, here's some invaluable advice: try to follow a weak act. If the previous manager was a fool, any successor will look very good. Otherwise, watch your back.

The truth of both statements has been amply demonstrated several times during my career. I was always a hero to my staff when my predecessor was an idiot; always a goat when he wasn't. So, you can understand my concern at this point. Instead of following a weak act, I get to follow David Biedny, one of the legendary figures in Photoshop history. Worse, I get to disagree with a lot of what he says.

David's *Photoshop Handbook* was not merely the very first Photoshop textbook but one that became a bible to serious users, back in the days of Photoshop 2. His lectures at the Seybold conferences and elsewhere were the highest-rated in the industry. His 1998 book *Photoshop Channel Chops* (written with Bert Monroy and Nathan Moody) is still so influential that today acquiring a used copy will set you back more than $150, in spite of the fact that it employs Photoshop 4 terminology throughout!

Also, David's background is not writing but heavy-duty production: difficult retouching and special effects for some of the world's most recognizable clients. Therefore, unlike most Photoshop educators, he is a power user—and a top-level power user at that.

So much for the flattery. Now, the problem. As his foreword indicates, David has read pre-publication drafts of this book thoroughly. What he takes four pages to say can be summed up quickly. Like most people at the top of the field, he was aware of the power of LAB and was making some use of it himself. Then he started reading this book, flipped out, stayed up half the night reading it and dreamt about it after he fell asleep, continued this pattern over several days, discovered a lot of new techniques, figured out where his workflow was deficient, developed an understanding of why things work out the way they do in LAB, and wrote a foreword declaring this to be the deepest educational material ever prepared for Photoshop.

I am not sure that this sequence of events exactly encourages those considering buying this book. He says that he had to reread certain parts several times before grasping what was going on. If a top predator like David finds the going to be that tough, where does that leave you, me, and the rest of the world?

That working in LAB often is spectacularly better than any alternative is no secret among professionals. It is also no secret that working in LAB can be quite complex. The surprise is how much of it is accessible to beginners.

Example: shortly before the publication of this book, my wife and I spent three weeks in Italy with a group of friends. Like any other tourist, I shot a lot of pictures, mostly bad. I was unfortunately co-opted into printing up a set of around 60 of these pictures for other members of the group.

These other members are not Photoshop users, but they have a vague idea of what I do for a living and several of them have gone to the trouble of Googling me. That's why the assignment was so unwelcome: these people didn't know what to expect other than prints that were much better than they could shoot themselves. Also, they didn't understand that if I treated each one as if it were a full-page magazine ad, it would take me several days.

Inasmuch as the book project had me under deadline pressure, I welcomed this new assignment about as much as I would have the news that I needed root canal. As I only could afford to devote about an hour to the project, I did all the image prep in LAB, using the basic techniques set forth in Chapters 1, 3, and 4. They wouldn't have been appropriate for every image if more time had been available, but when time is short, LAB gives by far the biggest bang for the buck, and is more than sufficient to make photo lab personnel gasp at the vibrant colors that have been engineered into the set.

I believe that many people face this type of predicament and are looking for the sort of quick solution that LAB offers. I believe that somewhat fewer people have the priorities of David Biedny or would like to be as good at Photoshop as David is.

The Eye of the Beholder

Although mainstream, LAB is still bleeding-edge, so there isn't any consensus on what parts to use. By and large, current use falls into three areas: using simple moves like those described in the first few chapters to intensify color; sharpening the L channel; and using LAB to rescue extremely poor originals.

Of these, only the first is a real home run for LAB. In the other two, LAB often does a marginally better job than the other alternatives, and usually quicker. But we could live without it.

There is a whole world of LAB that is not so widely known, and which offers really, really better results than any other method—particularly if you're good at Photoshop. Note David's comments about retouching, which is his field, not mine. He calls Chapters 9 and 11 "astounding" and says "my work will never be the same."

Now, David is as good as it gets in said speciality. If he says he's seeing revolutionary possibilities, that's pretty eye-opening. Fur-

thermore, you and I probably don't fully grasp all of what he sees in these chapters—he's drawing on a whole body of experience and figuring out on the fly how he could have done specific jobs better and/or faster with LAB. You and I may just see possibilities; he sees dollars.

Similar reactions occur when people who are specialists in face work see the techniques of Chapter 16, or those who specialize in "impressionistic" shots such as undersea photography see the AB blending of Chapter 15. Fixing pictures is just not all that exciting a profession, when you come right down to it. Yet experts sit there with their mouths open and/or gasp at what LAB can do.

Consequently, there were two possible scenarios for this book. Many people want to know how to use LAB and want to get into the workflow quickly. They do not care so much about the why as the how. They buy a book on the assumption that the author knows what he's talking about and are willing to take his advice at face value. I could write a book for such people at around a third the size of the present volume.

That kind of book, however, would never satisfy David Biedny, or any other person with ambitions of becoming a Photoshop expert. Read David's foreword again, and you'll detect an extreme skepticism toward Photoshop books.

It is correct that most such books are not written by persons who are themselves experts in the use of the program. That doesn't make their work worthless. However, David and all those who would like to be as good as he is won't accept what an author says just because the author says so. Also, it is their desire to take the ball and not just run with it, but do things with it that the author never dreamed of. I have no doubt that David is going to do that in the retouching field.

Such persons require a more fleshed-out presentation than would be necessary to satisfy the first class of readers. David and his ilk don't buy into unsupported claims that a certain method is better than the one that they're used to—they want a discussion of why. This is unfortunate, because it sometimes takes one page to describe how to do a thing in LAB and eight pages to explain why the alternatives are not as good.

The Structure of the First Chapters

I teach small classes on color correction for a living. It gives me a good idea of what people in the trenches actually think, and how they approach learning. I am quite confident of the existence of many open-minded people who are willing to give things a try to see if they work, without demanding justification for every step of the process, like David does.

The two-part structure of the first six chapters is an attempt to cater to both groups. The first halves of these chapters, taken together, constitute the brief LAB book that I talked about writing a few paragraphs ago. They are about Photoshop technique only. They don't assume a whole lot of Photoshop knowledge. They establish that certain methods work without explaining why. When I claim that LAB is the best way of doing certain things, I don't take time out to discuss the other options. Only a rudimentary knowledge of Photoshop is required, and I try to spell out how each command is used.

The second halves of these chapters can be read or not as you choose. David is quite strong that you should read them. You can make your own choice. The water starts to get deep in Chapter 7, when we drop the pretense of having advanced and beginning sections. I wouldn't say that the rest of the book is impossible for the inexperienced user; I try to explore the concepts in plain English, not some pseudo-academic Photoshop jargon. On the other hand, David says that he had to read some sections several times. You can always go back to the first halves later.

You also have several options on how to approach each chapter. The enclosed CD contains most of the book's original images (in a few cases, the owners have requested that they not appear in digital form), usually at a lower resolution than shown in the text. If my explanations aren't clear, or if you doubt them, you may wish to turn to the CD and see if you can duplicate what I'm talking about.

Also, almost all chapters have "Review and Exercises" sections. The exercises are a kind of homework; the review questions are answered in the book's "Notes & Credits" section, beginning on Page 351.

How to Know What Works

My classes give me a major advantage in figuring out what works and what doesn't. If I run across an image that I think is really hot for LAB, I can assign it to a group of advanced users, with no instruction except to make the image look better. I enter the competition myself, and then the fun begins, as the preconceptions may or may not go out the window.

I first suggested the idea of using LAB in image manipulation at a trade show in 1985, before Photoshop even existed. I first began to use it seriously in 1994, but at that time I believed that its strongest points were essentially the same laundry list I recited earlier: resurrecting extremely poor images, unsharp masking, and manipulating the L channel in workflows where speed is the main priority.

LAB still does those things, and they're all covered here. I no longer think, however, that these are LAB's main attractions. Effective substitute methods exist. I found this out the hard way, when students were able to reproduce certain work that I had assumed required the use of LAB, sometimes getting better results than I had.

On the other hand, in certain kinds of retouching, and certain classes of image, canyons among them, I've watched as many as several hundred students try different methods, and only those who use LAB wind up with a competitive picture at the end. Furthermore, we have post-mortem discussions after we compare each other's work, where those people who used LAB comment on whether they think it helped a little, a lot, or not at all.

The experience of watching others succeeding with some uses of LAB and getting mediocre results with others gives me a unique perspective and makes many of the assertions in the text more reliable. When an author says that Task A can be best achieved by the use of Command B, all it means in principle is that the author personally has not figured out a better way to do it. In this book, when I say that Task C works better in LAB than elsewhere, not only have *I* not been able to locate an alternative, but neither have a whole lot of other people who were trying hard to find one.

The Work Behind the Scenes

The idea that LAB is only for bad images is shattered by the examples in this book. There are some howlers, to be sure, but most of them are shot by professional photographers; any deficiency in the original is likely to be the fault of the environment. Where LAB shines, however, is in adding believability to images that are already reasonably good.

For this reason, the idea that such a book might be in the works aroused great interest, not just among book publishers, but among serious photographers and other Photoshop users. As to the first group, the book was held up more than a year by litigation that need not be discussed further. The second group provided generous support for the project. which you'll see in nearly every chapter, in the form of particularly instructive images.

When I run across pictures that I think are especially interesting, I ask the photographers for permission to use them in print.

Also, I sometimes ask publicly for help in finding particular kinds of images.

In addition to the people who gave permission for single images, there was another even more generous group—a group that gave me access to lots of pictures, sometimes entire libraries, telling me to use whatever I liked. Some photographers went to the effort of burning me multiple CDs, knowing that I might not even use any of the images at all, because they supported the idea of this book. If you think that the images herein are appropriately chosen, please join me in thanking the people who gave me several images to choose from—including those people whose work never made it into the final product. Let us tip our hats to the following: the Atlanta Falcons Football Club; David Barr; Jim Bean; Michael Benford; Hunter Clarkson; Mike Demyan; Fred Drury; Jason Hadlock; the Knoxville News-Sentinel; Mark Laurie; David Leaser; the National Aeronautics and Space Administration; Mike Russell; Marty Stock; Lee Varis; and Michael Vlietstra.

The third group, however—the group not limited to photographers, but of anyone interested in the project—made a much bigger contribution, at least by proxy.

Publishers usually hire a technical editor to go through books like this one, hoping to ferret out errors in Photoshop usage as well as forcing the author to write more clearly. That wouldn't work well here. No individual can represent the broad spectrum of potential readers. Concepts with ramifications that are obvious to David Biedny may slip right by an intermediate user. Explanations of how LAB features work make a lot of sense to an editor who already knows something about it, but possibly not to the many readers who never have ventured into LAB at all. Yet a technical editor who knew nothing about LAB would have quite a struggle with this manuscript.

Rather than go that route, I asked my Applied Color Theory online discussion group for help. I requested volunteers to "beta-read" the manuscript—to go over each chapter in detail and report back to me, on a deadline schedule, as to how it could be improved.

Because of how much work would be involved for no pay, I expected only a few responses. I got 70, many with essays attached on why the person wanted to do it.

Cutting this down to a manageable number was no easy feat. I had hoped to limit the group to six, but wound up with seven who I hoped would represent the interests of you, the reader. Understanding that almost everyone in the group wears at least two hats, here's how they shook out:

- Two expert LAB users, two advanced Photoshoppers who had not used LAB previously, two people who do not use Photoshop full time but find it helpful in their work, and one beginner/hobbyist.
- Two professional photographers, one supervisor of a service provider that accepts work from the general public and always has to output it in CMYK, another such supervisor who always outputs in RGB, one academic, one professional editor, and one professional programmer.
- Two people I know personally, three that I had corresponded with but never met, and two who were strangers to me.
- Two people who teach Photoshop to others, three people with backgrounds in the hard sciences, two with a background in fine art, and one color-blind individual.
- Residents of the Eastern, Southern, and Western United States; Eastern and Western Canada; Bulgaria; and Finland.

This international group took its work very seriously. My posterior is still somewhat sore from all of the kicking that it took, much to your benefit, because a lot of unclear material has been rewritten, certain technical errors have been corrected, and a couple of remarks that were unusually tasteless even for me have been extirpated.

From time to time in this book, you'll see the beta readers mentioned by name, when they disagree with something I've said or suggest a different approach that I haven't tested myself. I'd also like to name them here, because they deserve so much of the credit for getting the book to this form. They are Les De Moss, André Dumas, Bruce Fellman, Timo Kirves, Katia Lazarova, Clarence Maslowski, and Clyde McConnell.

The Good News and the Bad News

Two other professional editors had at the manuscript, one for money and one for love. For Peachpit Press, Elissa Rabellino found a host of ambiguously written sentences and other sloppinesses in the course of shaking her head about writers who not only think that they know more about printing than the publisher does but also have more confidence in their own understanding of how the English language is written than that of *The Chicago Manual of Style*. Cathy Panagoulias, on the other hand, has been married to me too long to imagine that there is any chance whatever of my agreeing not to split infinitives, start sentences with numbers, or end them with prepositions. However, vast experience in these matters imbues her with an instinctive sensitivity to when I am going over the top, if not a notably diplomatic way of pointing it out to me.

Having this extraordinarily large and diverse group of readers means that I'm pretty sure how this book will play out with the world at large. There was some dispute about the efficacy of the "easy parts," the first halves of the first six chapters. Nobody could tell whether my suggestion that a person could read them as a unit and skip the second halves would actually work, since all these people had read the second halves. David Biedny thinks no, I think yes.

But with respect to the rest of the book, there was unanimity: very worthwhile, but large amounts of concentration required. Everyone echoed David's comment that more than one reading is needed.

David, of course, was already using LAB, so he had a good idea of what he was getting into. If you haven't had such experience, you may be interested in the reactions of the two beta readers who were proficient in Photoshop but didn't know LAB.

One, after going through the retouching chapters that David commented on, remarked that he was quite confused after reading them once, but "On second read, my reaction: a second-grader can do this! Epiphany after Epiphany!"

At the end of the final chapter, he continued, "My second-grade understanding of LAB has already saved hours of workstation time, eliminated most hand-made selections and produced final prints that knock off the socks of not only my clients—but me. I almost feel guilty that such effusive praise follows such easy effort, so I lie about it."

The second wrote, "Dan, there is a point in a book so much on the cutting edge as this one. We can always take comfort in knowing that although we could not understand the meaning of everything you said on first and second readings there is still another and another reading to bring us closer to understanding it all. There is also the monetary aspect, being able to keep on getting more and more out of this book without having to pay additional money!"

No Pain, No Gain?

This, then, is the choice and the challenge. You can make LAB as easy or as difficult as you like. Stay on the easy side, and you'll have little trouble producing more vivid and life-like color images. Go for a little more pain, and the rewards become greater. LAB offers much better retouching, easier selections and masks, and extraordinarily effective channel blending opportunities. And it does get faster the more you use it.

If you wish to approach this book the way David Biedny does, with a high degree of skepticism, I hope the book will dispel it for you as it did for him. And I hope that your ideas about how to proceed further with LAB will be at least as ambitious as his.

If you want to approach it the way I do, as a reliable way to get much better-looking pictures in much less time, I hope that you won't have to go through nearly as much agony as David suggests. Anyway, you probably don't have the time for it. If you're like me, there are several cards full of digital pictures waiting to be printed—and waiting for us to apply the simple LAB moves that will make them look so much better.

The Canyon Conundrum

The Canyon Conundrum

LAB has a reputation for enormous power, yet virtually all reference materials that advocate its use illustrate its capabilities with a single class of image. This chapter introduces the basic LAB correction method and explains why it is so extraordinarily effective—if you happen to have a picture of a canyon.

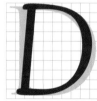

Deep in Death Valley, land of desolation and summertime heat in the high 120s, a narrow canyon holds several lessons about color, photography, human perception, and a powerful digital imaging tool.

Parts of the clayish soil contain mineral deposits that create striking color variations, especially when the light hits just right in the late afternoon. The effect allegedly reminds some people of a painter mixing up the tools of his trade.

So, it's called "Artist's Palette," a considerable stretch. These dull tints have about as much to do with those found on the palettes of Renoir or Rembrandt as this book does with animal husbandry. But nothing seems great or small except by comparison. It's such a shock to encounter green or magenta dirt that it seems absolutely blazing next to the monotony of the surroundings. People stand and stare at Artist's Palette for hours, seeing subtleties that cameras can't record and imagining brilliant colors that cameras don't think are there.

We can leave aside the philosophical question of whether the reality is these dull colors that the camera saw in Figure 1.1A, or the comparatively bright ones conjured up by the infinitely creative human visual system. The fact is, if this picture is a promotional shot or even something for a nature publication, the original isn't going to fly. Anybody would prefer Figure 1.1B, which was created in approximately 30 seconds in LAB.

When I first wrote about LAB, in a 1996 column, I used a canyon shot

Figure 1.1 This Death Valley canyon is noted for its strangely colored clay. Green soil like that on the right side of this photograph is so unusual that people remember it as being greener than what the camera saw. Canyon images are often used to illustrate the power of LAB correction (bottom).

from Capitol Reef National Park in Utah. My book *Professional Photoshop* goes around 100 miles to the south with a shot from Canyon-lands National Park.

Another Photoshop book illustrates its LAB section with a shot from Bryce Canyon National Park. A third uses a scene from Grand Canyon National Park, and a fourth a canyon from the Canadian Rockies. And author Lee Varis has a scintillating LAB exercise, reproduced here in Chapter 16, that brings out the best in a canyon in North Coyote Buttes, on the Arizona/Utah border.

Start to detect a pattern?

Yes, indeed. LAB does really, really well with canyons. And you don't even need to know how it works to make the magic happen; the approach to canyons is simplicity itself. Figure 1.1B isn't the best we can do in LAB (we'll be revisiting this image in Chapter

4, treating it in a slightly more complex way) but it's much better than any comparable moves in RGB or CMYK, and even if you could match the quality in some other colorspace it would take far longer.

When I wheeled out that first canyon shot in 1996, I likened LAB to a wild animal: very powerful, very dangerous. That label has stuck. Use of LAB is now widespread among top retouchers, but a huge fear factor limits the techniques they use it for. Most of those who claim to be LAB users are only doing what's described in the first five chapters here, missing out on much magic.

You can't blame them for being satisfied with what they've got, because those limited LAB tools can make an extraordinary difference in image quality. They are also so simple that beginners can enjoy their benefits.

I hope, and the publisher hopes harder, that people with limited experience will learn enough to dramatically improve their pictures. On the other hand, some of what follows either is unbearably complicated or suggests methods that only power users can fully appreciate. For the best of reasons, it isn't customary for Photoshop books to cater to novices and simultaneously include material that leaves experts cursing in frustration until they re-read it for the eighth time. Special handling is clearly required.

The Rules of the Game

Each of the first six chapters is divided into two parts, readily identifiable by a change in typeface. If you're just trying to get into working with LAB as quickly as possible, you can skip the second part of each chapter, which is more analytical, and can be somewhat difficult to follow.

Figure 1.2 *Like Figure 1.1, this image features colors that are possibly accurate, yet too subdued when taken in the context of the scene. This canyon is called "Yellowstone" for a reason. The yellowness of the canyon walls should be played up.*

For efficiency's sake we will bypass two customary procedures. First, a few paragraphs ago, I did something that I find exceedingly irritating when other authors try it. I asserted that a certain way of doing things is better than the customary alternative, and expected you to take it on faith. Yet, if I had stopped to prove that straight LAB correction indeed yields better results than RGB in canyon images, there would have been an eight-page detour.

So, in the interest of speed, the first half of each chapter concentrates on the how, not the why. I will say things that might be labeled matters of opinion without stopping to prove they are so. Take my word for them if you like; if you'd rather not, they are backed up in the "Closer Look" section.

Also, the first halves don't assume much Photoshop expertise. I try to give simple explanations of each command being used. The second parts play by no such rules, and often dive right into techniques familiar only to a sophisticated audience. And they don't offer many explanations of Photoshop basics.

LAB is always an intermediate step. Files must be converted into it before the fun begins and out of it afterward. Almost everyone will be converting into LAB from an RGB file. When finished, some will convert back to RGB and others, needing a print file, will go to CMYK. For the time being, it doesn't matter which; we will assume for convenience that it goes back to RGB. Your definitions of RGB and CMYK in Photoshop's Color Settings dialog don't matter yet, either. We're now ready to tackle some canyons.

A 30-Second Definition of LAB

It would take a wheelbarrow to carry every way of defining color that's been propounded in the last century. Our current LAB is one of the most prominent, an academic construct designed not just to encompass all conceivable colors (and some that are imaginary, a fascinating concept that we'll explore at length later, notably in Chapter 8), but to sort them out in a way that relates to how humans see them.

The version of LAB used in Photoshop was born in 1976, child of a standards-setting group called the International Commission on Lighting and known by its French initials, CIE.

There have been several close relatives. We need know nothing about them, but color scientists feel that we should use a more precise name for our version. They call it CIELAB or L*a*b*, both of which are a pain to pronounce and maddening typographically. Photoshop calls it "Lab color," but the name has nothing to do with a laboratory: the L stands for luminosity or lightness; the A and

Figure 1.3 *A more vivid version of Figure 1.2, prepared using the LAB recipe of this chapter.*

B stand for nothing. The name should be pronounced as three separate letters, as we do with other colorspaces.

We need not concern ourselves with LUV, LCH, xyY, HSB, XYZ, or other color definitions (at least until Chapter 13), because Photoshop fully supports only three: CMYK, LAB, and RGB. Pretty much everybody has to use either CMYK or RGB; increasingly people are being called upon to use both.

All printing is based on CMYK, although most desktop color printers either encourage or require RGB input. Web, multimedia, and other display applications require RGB files. Commercial printers want CMYK. But LAB files are usually unwelcome, except in Photoshop, Photo-Paint, and other specialized applications. A few raster image processors (RIPs) for printing devices also claim to be able to handle LAB, but gambling that they actually do is a sport for the dedicated player of Russian Roulette.

Although LAB is a distant relative of HSB, which has been used as a retouching and color correction space on many high-end systems, such as Quantel's Paintbox, nobody thought that people would be perverse enough to use LAB for such purposes in Photoshop. Instead, it's there as a means of expediting color conversions.

The language of color is notoriously imprecise. If you work in RGB, $255^R0^G0^B$ defines pure red. Unfortunately, there's no agreement as to what *pure red* means. Anybody needing to know exactly what kind of red you intend would have to find out what your Photoshop Color Settings are, because there are different definitions of RGB, each of which has its own idea of what constitutes red. There is, however, only one Photoshop LAB.

If you wish to order a car in a different color than the model you test-drove, it won't be sufficient to say you want a red one. Before accepting your money, the dealer will insist that you look at a swatch book to make sure you get the red you expect. You won't hear anything about LAB, but the supplier of the vehicle's paint will, if you complain that the color doesn't match and the car manufacturer agrees with you. It wouldn't do for

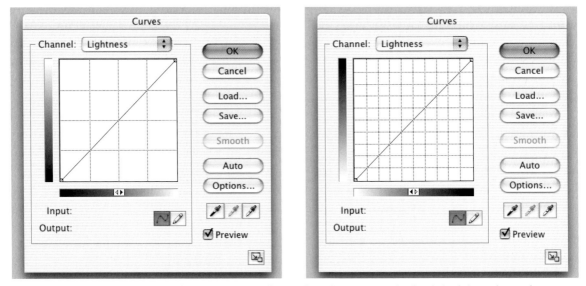

Figure 1.4 *Photoshop defaults (left) look slightly different than the curves in this book (right). In the gradient at the bottom of the grid, note that the LAB default has darkness at the left (in agreement with the Photoshop RGB default), but this book uses lightness at the left, which is the default for CMYK and grayscale images. To reverse the orientation, click inside the gradient bar below the grid. Also, the default uses gridlines at 25 percent increments, whereas the book uses 10 percent intervals. To toggle between the settings, Option– or Alt–click inside the grid.*

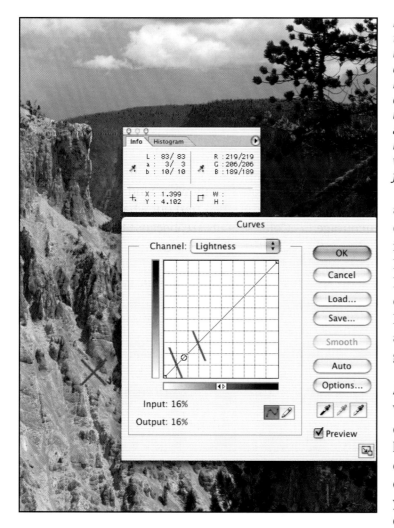

Figure 1.5 Measuring the lightness range of the interest object. After the file is in LAB, call up the Curves dialog and, with the Lightness curve open, click and hold the mouse over an important part of the image. A circle appears on the curve, indicating the value of the point underneath the cursor. If you move the cursor around the interest object with the mouse button still depressed, the circle will move with it. The tonal range of the canyon walls falls between the two diagonal lines.

artwork that represents that color, you'll be getting the LAB information as well, just as Photoshop gets LAB values from Pantone, Inc., that enable it to construct the PMS (Pantone Matching System) colors that are the de facto standard in the graphics industry.

Assembling the Ingredients

We will start with, shockingly enough, a canyon. You can follow along with the image on the enclosed CD, or you may use one of your own, provided that you think you understand why canyons make such great LAB fodder. Regrettably, there's more to life than canyon shots. And just as LAB does extremely well on certain classes of image, it does poorly on others. Much of this book is aimed at showing how to distinguish such images.

the manufacturer and the paint supplier to scream and wave swatch books in each other's faces. They specify LAB values, plus a tolerance for how far off the paint can be. In the event of a dispute, they whip out a spectrophotometer and measure its color.

If the manufacturer hires you to produce

If you do choose to use your own image,

Figure 1.6 The LAB curves that produced Figure 1.3. Note how the L curve has been made steep in the area indicated in Figure 1.5. The A and B channels have also been steepened, by rotating them around the unchanged midpoint.

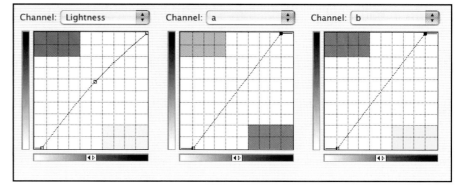

Figure 1.7 *In LAB, unsharp masking must be applied to the L channel only, and should be evaluated with the screen display at 100% view. The numbers shown here can be used as defaults, but better results can be had by customizing them to the specific image.*

Also, it appears to be just the kind of image we're looking for, needing a color boost nearly as badly as the Artist's Palette of Figure 1.1 did. The canyon walls here are slightly off-gray. Not nearly enough, however, considering that the most famous national park in the world bears the name of that particular color, for this is a picture of the Grand Canyon of the Yellowstone.

The following recipe for bringing out the colors that are hidden in such images will be refined considerably in coming chapters. But to get started on making something more convincingly yellow, like Figure 1.3, make yourself a copy (or a duplicate layer) of the RGB original if you think you'd like to have something to compare your work to afterwards.

Next, Image: Mode>Lab color. The picture should look no different, but the identification bar at its top should now read Lab rather than RGB.

Call up the Curves dialog with Image: Adjustments>Curves (keyboard shortcut: Command–M Macintosh; Ctrl–M PC). If you've never worked in LAB before, the Photoshop default treatment of lightness-to-the-right is probably still in effect. Although there's no technical advantage either way, this book uses lightness-to-the-left, so you should probably change over now by clicking inside the gradient bar at the bottom of the curve, as shown in Figure 1.4.

three types should be avoided. First, the image should not contain colors that are already brilliant or highly saturated. Second, it shouldn't have an overall color cast. If you think that the Figure 1.1A is too gray or too blah or whatever, fine, but if you think it's too blue, you won't be able to fix it without reading Chapter 4. And third, nobody should have applied unsharp masking yet.

Figure 1.2 seems to qualify. It hasn't been sharpened; there's nothing even close to a bright color in the canyon, and the clouds appear to be white, not some goofy hue that would indicate a cast.

Also, the default curve box has gridlines at 25 percent increments, a little coarse for serious work. Option–click (Mac; Alt–click PC) inside the box, and the grid changes to 10 percent increments.

Having made these cosmetic changes to the interface, we proceed to the recipe.

A Canyon Correction, Step by Step

• Click into the word *Lightness* above the curve grid and change it to *a*. Move the top right point of the curve one gridline to the left; that is, a tenth of the way toward the left axis. Move the bottom left point one gridline to the right. The two points must be moved an equal amount, because the resulting curve needs to pass over the same center point as it did originally.

• Without clicking OK, switch over to b, and apply the same changes. In both channels, we're making a steeper line by, in effect, rotating it counterclockwise around the center point.

These two moves are the ones unique to LAB, the ones that drive colors apart from one another in a way that other colorspaces can't equal. What comes next could be done elsewhere. So, stop now, click OK, and return to RGB if you must—but you should really leave the dialog open, and try to complete the magic in LAB.

The following two steps can be modified to taste if you're comfortable with curves and/or sharpening settings.

If you've never worked on the A and B channels before, then you've never worked on anything like them before. On the other hand, if you know how to apply curves to a grayscale document, then you know how to apply them to the L. We'll discuss the concept further in Chapter 3, but it boils down to this: the steeper the curve, the more the contrast. Your task is to make the part of the L curve that encompasses the canyon steeper than the rest.

• Before clicking OK, switch to the Lightness curve. Move the cursor back into the picture over part of the canyon, and click and hold. While the mouse button is depressed, a circle appears on the curve, indicating where the point under the cursor is located. Still holding the mouse button down, move the cursor to various parts of the canyon, and note the range where the circle is moving. In Figure 1.5, I've inserted red lines to indicate where on the curve most of the pixels representing the canyon are located. That area of the curve has to be made steeper. Sometimes we do this by inserting points where my red lines are and lowering one while raising the other. Here, I simply raised the center of the curve, as shown in Figure 1.6.

• Apply the curves by clicking OK in the dialog. Now, display the L channel only, either by highlighting it in the Channels palette or by using the keyboard shortcut Command–1 (Mac; Ctrl–1 PC). Then, Filter: Sharpen> Unsharp Mask. If you are familiar with how the dialog in Figure 1.7 works, you'll have a good idea of what numbers to enter. If not, enter Amount 200%, Radius 1.0 pixels, Threshold 10 levels, understanding that better results will be possible after you've read Chapter 5. Hit OK and compare it to the original. If satisfied, return the image to RGB if that's what your workflow needs, or convert it to CMYK, as I did for this book.

Finding Color Where None Exists

The first two steps established the color variation that gives LAB its reputation for realism. The third added snap, and the fourth sharpness. If you are considering how this might have been done in RGB or CMYK, the bottom line is that Steps One and Two aren't easy to duplicate. Step Three happens to be easier for LAB in this particular image, but in other images there's no advantage. Step Four is sometimes better done in LAB, although this time it could be done equally well elsewhere.

But working in LAB is fast, fast, fast. Once you get the hang of it, it should take about a minute to get this kind of result with a canyon image. Let's try another.

Figure 1.8 comes from a substantially nas-

tier clime than Yellowstone. It's Anza-Borrego Desert State Park, one of the hottest places in the world. Located in Southern California just a short way from Mexico, it enjoys summer temperatures that rival Death Valley's. Rainfall is a pitiful inch or two each year.

Such conditions aren't exactly conducive to plant life. The scraggly ocotillo in the foreground at right will wait patiently for five years or so for enough winter rain to permit it to blossom into orange and green splendor. The rest of the time, it sits and awaits developments, clothed in a brown as drab as the background. This canyon was cut not by a river, but by repeated flash floods, because when the rain does fall, the ground is too parched to absorb it.

When you or I visit such an area, we don't find it particularly colorful but we certainly see more than the monochromatic mess that any camera would. Whenever we look at a scene of substantially the same colors, our mind's eye breaks them apart, creating different levels of brownness in the rocks that artificial instruments

Figure 1.8 The desert image at top shows the lack of brilliant colors and the shortness of range that suggest an LAB correction. Bottom, after a literal repetition of the steps that produced Figure 1.3.

such as cameras lack the imagination to envision.

In other colorspaces, it's rare to apply exactly the same move from one image to the next. But with the speedy LAB recipe, it's more thinkable. Figure 1.8B was produced by a literal repetition of the steps that produced Figure 1.3. The result is the same: dramatically increased contrast and color variation, in a way that as far as I know can't be achieved in RGB.

Customizing the recipe to this image yields a marginally better result, as shown in Figure 1.9. The changes are two.

First, the AB curves are twice as steep as they were in the Yellowstone example. That is, rather than bringing the bottom and top endpoints in by one gridline, the curves shown in Figure 1.9 are moved

Figure 1.9 A second corrected version uses the curves shown below, increasing the color variation by bringing the corners of the A and B curves in by twice as much as in Figure 1.3.

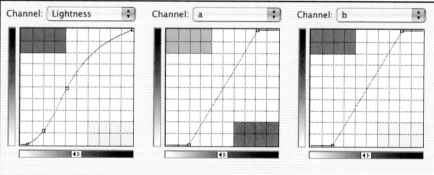

twice as much. There's no right answer as to how much to steepen these curves, but it does make sense that this image should have steeper AB curves. The Yellowstone image was too flat, but it did have some color variation. Figure 1.8A is pretty close to a sepiatone. The function of the AB curves is to bring out the colors. This picture needs such surgery a lot more than the Yellowstone image did.

Second, a slight improvement is possible in the L curve. The two canyons were just about the same darkness. The Anza-Borrego canyon occupies a slightly smaller range, so the curve could be made a bit steeper. But the Yellowstone L curve works acceptably.

A River Runs Through It

Finally, having run out of canyons, we'll move a few miles to the south of Figure 1.3, onto the shores of majestic Yellowstone Lake. Figure 1.10A was taken in early morning, with uninspiring lighting and a bit of fog.

In addition to great canyon work, LAB melts fog like a blowtorch does butter. Again, we'll show a version (Figure 1.10B) made by exact repetition of the procedure that created Figure 1.3. For the customized version (Figure 1.10C), instead of doubling how far we took in the AB curves, as in Figure 1.9, it's tripled—the top and bottom points have each moved in three gridlines.

How much to steepen the curves is a subjective call. The four originals we've looked at exhibit varying degrees of colorlessness. Personally, I feel that the Yellowstone Canyon image starts off better than the others and needs less of a boost; the Death Valley picture is second best; the Anza-Borrego shot is next; and the worst of all is this Yellowstone Lake image. As the originals got less colorful, I made the AB curves steeper, always remembering to make them cross the same center point on the grid.

There is, of course, no reason why you have to agree with the foregoing assessments. You can choose steeper angles for some or use the same one each time. And please remember, this is the first chapter, discussing the most basic move. This recipe permits an amazing variety of modifications.

The L curve is somewhat different here than in the other examples we've looked at. The steep area is a bit longer, because the lake has a fairly long range—parts are light, and parts get almost to a midtone. All three of the canyons fell in a very short range, both for contrast and color.

Figure 1.10 *Top left, this original needs an extreme steepening of the AB curves to bring out color. Bottom left, a version done exactly as in Figure 1.3. Below, a customized version using the curves at right, in which the AB endpoints are brought in three times as much.*

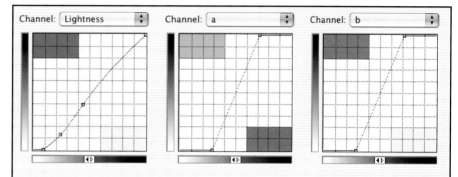

Which brings us back to why authors use canyon images to illustrate the power of LAB. The recipe works extremely well—provided the subject is a canyon, or something with the same characteristics. By the same token, you should now be able to imagine the type of image in which the recipe would probably *not* do so well.

These canyon shots have all featured subtle colors. What if they aren't so subtle? This recipe makes all colors more intense. If the original colors were brilliant, LAB is highly effective at rendering them radioactive. And it is no coincidence that the most important parts of all four images so far have fallen into a relatively small range of tonality (darkness). That isn't the case with all or even most pictures, and if it isn't, these L curves won't work.

And that's the basic LAB correction, minus explanations of why LAB works or how it's structured. If you want that now, skip ahead to Chapter 2. If instead you'd like a more technical explanation of why we like color variation and why the best way to get it is in LAB, keep going, remembering that the second halves of chapters assume much more Photoshop knowledge than the first halves do.

And a final reminder, once you're done with your LAB maneuvering: few output devices accept LAB files, and few programs outside of Photoshop will display them. So, convert the file back to RGB, if you're going to post it on the Web or send it to a desktop or other printer that requires RGB; or convert directly to CMYK for commercial printing, as I had to throughout this book.

Review and Exercises

NOTE: Answers to this section, which appears in every chapter, are found in the "Notes & Credits" section of this book, commencing on Page 351.

✓ Why is it important that the images we've worked with so far not start out with any obvious color cast? What would probably have happened if they had?

✓ The images in this chapter are obviously selected to portray LAB in its best light. What do they have in common? What types of images would you suspect might not be appropriate for LAB?

✓ What is the impact of making the AB curves more vertical?

✓ What do you think would have happened if, instead of making the AB curves more vertical by rotating them counterclockwise around the center point, we had done the opposite, making them more horizontal by rotating them clockwise?

✓ Do you understand how LAB keeps color and contrast as separate items? If in doubt, try redoing some of these moves, once in the A and B channels only, and once in the L channel only.

✓ Have you verified that your curves display darkness to the right as in Figure 1.4? If they don't, click into the gradient bar underneath the curves grid to reverse it.

✓ Try this method with some of your own images, or redo some of these images. Try the effect of steepening the A and B by different amounts, which we'll be discussing in Chapter 3.

Michel Eugène Chevreul, a French chemist, anticipated LAB correction by a century and a half in his seminal 1839 work, *On the Law of Simultaneous Contrast of Colors.* He tried to describe something that is even today indescribably complex—the propensity of the human eye to break colors apart from their surroundings. The effect had been known to some extent by the ancient Egyptians, and in the 15th century Leonardo da Vinci indicated that he understood it. Three hundred years later, the brilliant German poet Johann Wolfgang von Goethe expounded on it, and it took less than a century thereafter for Chevreul to fully flesh it out.

Everybody is familiar with examples like those of Figure 1.11, which are often described as "optical illusions." The term implies that a human observer would have one opinion as to whether certain colors or even sizes were the same, and a machine (including, *bien entendu,* a camera) would have another.

Simultaneous contrast is an old survival instinct, dating from the prehistoric days when our ancestors were obliged to forage for food in the forest, as they could not go to McDonald's. Unfortunately, granted that we are forced to be hunters and gatherers, the design of our bodies leaves much to be desired. We don't run very fast. We aren't particularly strong. We don't fight well. We can't climb trees easily. We don't have good senses of smell or hearing. We don't see well at night. We have impeccably designed hands, and what might be described, at least until recent years, as superior intelligence, but still, we stack up poorly in comparison to, say, a tiger.

Darwin advises that when a species has an advantage that enables it to survive, that advantage gets selected for and therefore magnified over time. Start with an animal that can reach certain edible leaves that others can't, because its neck is longer; give it a few million years and you get a giraffe.

Figure 1.11 The surroundings influence human perception. Above, are the two red objects the same color, or is the bottom set lighter and more orange? Below, are the two magenta circles the same size? Humans and machines would disagree on the answers to both questions.

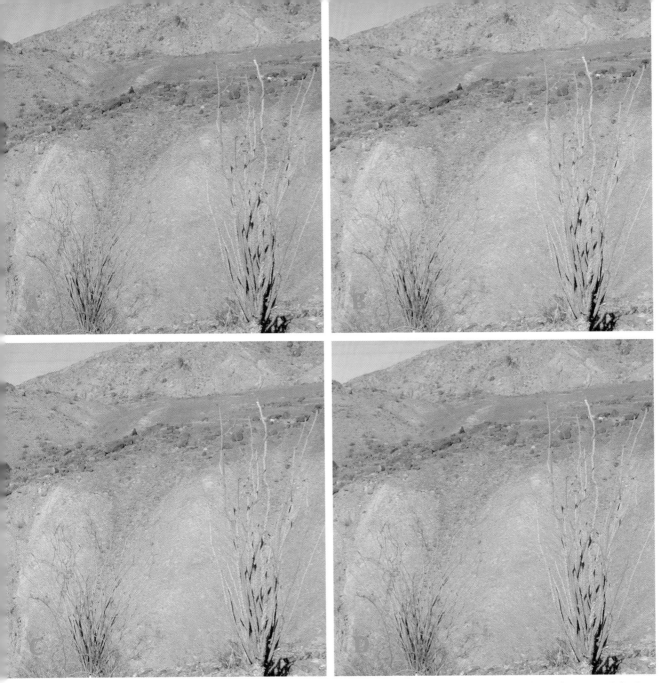

Figure 1.12 *Four methods of boosting color. Top left, steepening the AB curves only and not touching the L. Top right, in RGB, boosting saturation with the Hue/Saturation command. Bottom left, the application of a false profile, Wide Gamut RGB when the picture is nominally sRGB. Bottom right, RGB curves applied in Color mode.*

With ourselves, the same rule applies. One of the few physical advantages we enjoy over other animals is that we see color better. Other animals, it has been proven, don't live in a black-and-white world, but they can't see nearly the range of color variation that we do.

Our prehistoric ancestors were therefore able to peer into a forest and distinguish things that weren't exactly green. Such objects might well be something that would make them a fine breakfast, whereas a tiger would look at the same scene, see nothing but green, and leave hungry and irritable.

This highly useful ability to differentiate a color from its surroundings became, we presume, more refined as the millennia went by.

Scientists don't yet understand whether it's a function of the brain, or the eyes, or a combination, but they do know what we all do: that colors change depending upon the background.

When the things that we're looking at are as gross as the vector objects in Figure 1.11, it doesn't matter that they're being printed on a page with other irrelevant visual information. But in every other image in this chapter, the color changes quite subtly. Under those circumstances, the rest of the page baffles our visual systems. If we were actually in Anza-Borrego, we would be surrounded by brown everywhere we looked, and evolutionary factors would force us to see variation. The setting of this book, however, does not surround Figure 1.8 with brown but rather with a lot of nasty white space. Consequently, the printed rendition looks tepid.

We have to respond. LAB is the best alternative because it emulates how humans see things much better than any other colorspace. To understand why, let's reconsider the Anza-Borrego shot. But before doing so, another reminder that you have entered the for-experts area, and that you can proceed safely on to the next chapter if the following discussion doesn't interest you. Also, while the following isn't highly technical,

in later chapters this section can get rather murky, particularly since in some cases the text anticipates stuff that hasn't been introduced or explained yet.

The beginner's recipe of this chapter increases color variation by moves in the AB channels; it hikes contrast by a move in the L; and it adds sharpening. These last two items can be duplicated in other colorspaces, although probably not as quickly. The color-variation issue, though, is tougher. Here's the challenge: leaving aside sharpening and contrast, how would we achieve the desired variation in color, if we had never heard of LAB?

I can think of three alternatives, which we will compare not to Figure 1.8B, which introduces the irrelevancies of sharpening and detail enhancement, but to Figure 1.12A, which differs from the original only in that the AB curves have been steepened as they were in Figure 1.8. Its three opponents are

• **A saturation boost** while the file is still in RGB, using the Image: Adjustments>Hue/Saturation>Master slider. Hue/Sat is more than ten years old and not especially precise. In comparison to steepening the AB curves, it's prone to emphasizing artifacts of such things as JPEGging,

Figure 1.13 *An extreme boost in colors highlights the smoothness of the AB-only correction, magnified at left. At right, an attempt to match the brilliance in RGB with Hue/Saturation creates artifacting and a significantly lighter file.*

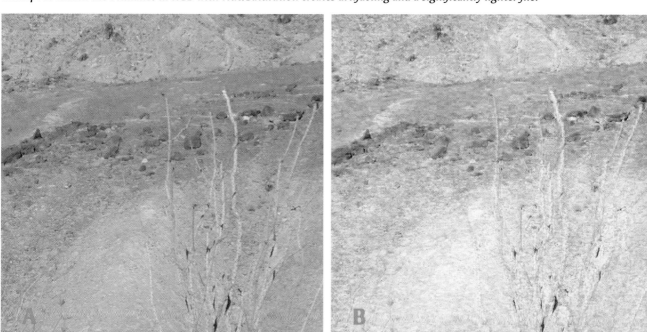

Figure 1.14 *When the A and B curves have different angles, LAB produces a result that's not analogous to any tool in RGB. Left, the original. Right, after applying an A curve that is three times steeper than the B. The L channel is unchanged.*

and it has problems differentiating colors in objects that already have a pronounced hue. But the biggest problem is that the Saturation command actually affects lightness as well, unlike the AB channels.

Magnified sections of exaggerated moves using both methods illustrate the problem: Figure 1.13A moves the AB curves in by four gridlines, or twice as much as in the original correction. Figure 1.13B was done in RGB with a +80 boost in saturation. The two overall color sensations are about the same, but the Hue/Sat version is far lighter than the LAB alternative. The differentiation between the ocotillo and the background is wounded. The red rocks are also too brilliant, and artifacting is beginning to show up in the background.

These weaknesses are muffled in the less psychedelic Figure 1.12B. Still, the unwanted lightening hides the ocotillo—and we're only comparing Hue/Sat to the very simplest LAB move. Let's consider two more competitors.

● **A false profile.** This involves redefining RGB as something more colorful. This book assumes

for convenience that your default RGB working space is sRGB. If it isn't, you can use Edit: Convert to Profile (Photoshop CS2; Image: Mode>Convert to Profile in Photoshop 6–CS) to move the file into sRGB. And once you have an sRGB file, you can Edit: Assign Profile>Adobe RGB (Image: Mode>Assign Profile in Photoshop 6–CS) for a significant boost in color, or (as in Figure 1.12C) assign Wide Gamut RGB for an even bigger one. The Assign Profile command doesn't change the file, but the next time there's a conversion to another colorspace, the result will be more vivid.

A false profile avoids the artifacting of the Hue/Saturation command and seems to me the best of the three alternatives. Unfortunately, it's also the least flexible. The images we've seen so far all took the same basic correction, but the angles of the AB curves were different in all four. If you're trying to use false profiles for more vivid color, you have only two alternatives without a completely unreasonable effort. If any of the other three versions aren't quite right in your mind, they can be adjusted. With Figure 1.12C you pretty much have to take it or leave it.

Also, there's none of the introduction of subtle hue variation that LAB does so well, and relatively bright colors are intensified more than duller ones, which is undesirable. So, on to the third alternative.

- **Curves in Color mode.** In RGB or CMYK, one could establish a duplicate layer, try to apply curves that would intensify the color, and then change the blending mode of the top layer to Color, thus preserving the detail of the bottom layer. First of all, it isn't always possible to do so. Trying to get the same yellowish soil that the AB curves created would be extremely difficult. More persuasive, it's an experts-only move. At least my first two alternatives are accessible to nonprofessionals. This one can easily introduce nasty casts, and should be undertaken only by somebody with a good knowledge of color-by-the-numbers and of how to structure curves.

Going Too Far, and Then Coming Back

The above discussion demonstrates that the AB moves so far, in addition to being faster, have a slight technical superiority to the logical alternatives. However, those who study LAB are looking for magic, and the puny advantage that these last trials have shown scarcely qualifies.

But, who cares? So far, we have looked only at the simplest possible application. Granted, steepening the A and B curves is the fundamental move on which all further progress is based. But it's rare that the moves in the AB are identical, as they are in this chapter. And when they're not, all these RGB alternatives that produced credible competitors vanish.

For example, the sand in Anza-Borrego has a distinct yellow tinge. The AB curves and the Saturation boost both accentuate it. My personal opinion is that the yellow isn't that attractive and that I would prefer a reddish brown. Therefore, if I were doing it to please myself, I wouldn't make identical moves in the A and B as previously shown. I'd move the A curve in three gridlines on both sides (as in the Yellowstone Lake shot) and the B curve by only one gridline, as in the

Yellowstone Canyon image. These two moves would produce Figure 1.14B.

To steal a little of Chapter 2's thunder, the A channel governs a magenta-green axis and the B a yellow-blue one. I am choosing to accentuate changes in the magenta-green A. Almost nothing in the picture is green, but certain things, notably the large rocks, have a strong magenta component. The soil in the canyon walls is really neither: some parts are very slightly magenta and others slightly green. All, however, are decidedly yellow as opposed to blue.

My move therefore enhances all yellows slightly, not as much as in Figure 1.12A. Some yellows get slightly warmer, more magenta; others get slightly colder, more green; and still others are simply more yellow. Things that clearly favored magenta more than green are affected strongly, and driven more toward red, as the magenta component gets pushed three times as hard as the yellow. So there's a variety of hue changes, as well as a general increase in saturation. The rocks are driven sharply away from the yellowish dirt.

All these shifts and countershifts in hue can't be emulated by any RGB or CMYK procedure that I'm aware of. No command outside of LAB allows certain yellows to move toward green and certain others to move toward magenta while some don't move at all.

Figure 1.14B is therefore deceptively simple. It looks so natural that one has to assume there would be some way to emulate it in RGB, as Figures 1.12B, C, and D emulated Figure 1.12A.

But there isn't.

If you're still in doubt, the next exercise should dispel it. The purpose of Figure 1.15B is not to offer an artistic impression of a man from Mars, but rather to illustrate how AB curving is the only way to get certain results. The L channel wasn't touched. The image was created by AB curves that are simply straight lines made as steep as possible. Both cross the center horizontal line well to the left of where they originally did. The left side is the negative side, the cool-color side.

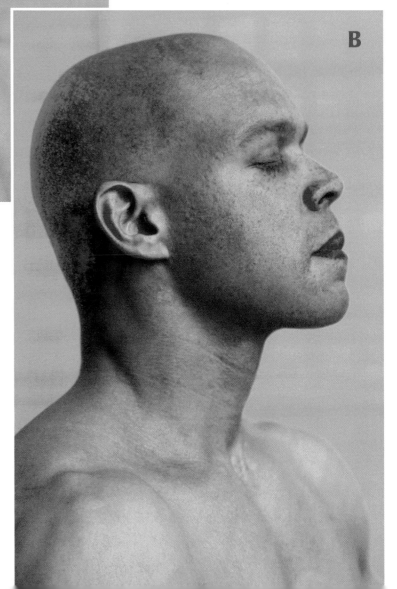

A

B

You are told that you have to produce something that looks like Figure 1.15B, because that abstract look is exactly what the client wants. How do you proceed?

If you don't know your LAB, probably you proceed to punt. The change isn't possible, because we are making similar reds go in wildly different directions. No other colorspace allows us to make some reds blue and nearly indistinguishable reds orange. Yet if we know LAB, the changes take less than a minute.

It would be understandable to protest that the challenge is ridiculous, because nobody in their right mind would ever ask for anything like Figure 1.15B.

If you concede, however, that it can't be

Figure 1.15 The original, above, looks like a sepiatone. The man at right appears to come from another planet. In fact, this version was created in LAB by modifying only the A and B channels.

The image is therefore being forced toward green and blue, but the curves are so steep that certain parts of the man's skin get redder in spite of it. Thus, the weird effect of having some skin turn violently more red while other parts become phosphorescent cyan.

Suppose that you are given the original file for Figure 1.15A and a printed copy of this page.

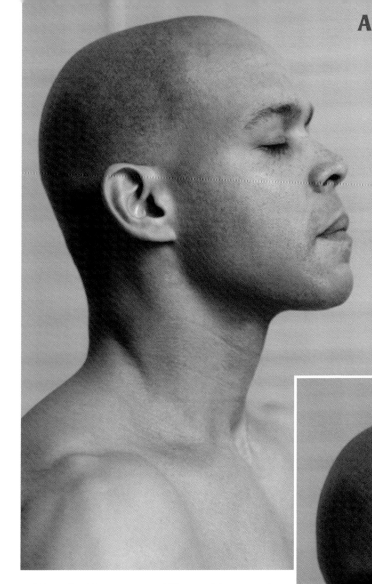

A

optical-illusion graphic of Figure 1.11, or lips against a slightly duller fleshtone. Studio models are heavily made up exactly because the photographer desires to create this type of apparent contrast—redder cheeks, redder lips.

Figure 1.16 *Assigning a false profile of Adobe RGB, left, increases saturation but does nothing to create color variation. Below, Figure 1.15B is applied to the original at 18% opacity (inset).*

B

achieved without LAB's ability to drive certain occurrences of a given color toward red and others toward green-blue (cyan), there's a small problem. If only LAB can produce Figure 1.15B, then only LAB can produce Figure 1.16B, which is Figure 1.15B applied to the original image at 18% opacity. And Figure 1.16B is something that a client might very well ask for, because there is very attractive color variation in the face. The background, which is nearly the same color as the face in the original, suddenly becomes more yellow. The lips are much redder than in the original, which is the way we want it, because that's what the human sense of simultaneous contrast sees. We break things away from their surrounding colors, whether gross variations as in the

To give us some idea of why alternatives are unsatisfactory, Figure 1.16A is analogous to Figure 1.12C. It strives for brighter color through the assignment of a false profile, in this case Adobe RGB rather than sRGB, prior to conversion to CMYK for printing. It's an improvement, yes, but the picture is still monochromatic. There's no music in it.

The last exercises are not intended to be final corrections. In real life, I'd do plenty more to this last image and assume you would as well. However, those other moves don't require LAB. Therefore, I've left them out, so we can see in pure form the LAB move that the other colorspaces can't duplicate.

Also, don't spend too much time trying to figure out how 18 percent of Figure 1.15B could possibly produce Figure 1.16B. The drastic AB curves have forced certain colors not just wildly out of the CMYK gamut, but beyond the capability of a monitor to display them. On the printed page, we're trying to approximate colors that are unimaginably vivid, particularly in the lips and the forehead. Photoshop has to improvise in these cases, and beyond knowing that the lips are some kind of bright red and the forehead some sort of bright cool color, Figure 1.15B isn't particularly informative. It's only when we start reducing the opacity that we get an accurate idea of what's occurring.

The super-steep curves that did it aren't shown, not because we're short of space, but as a shot across your bow, a warning that things may start to get difficult. You should really be able to visualize what the curves look like at this point. If not, return to this exercise after getting to Chapter 4, and it should be a piece of cake.

Finally, the question arises of why we are deliberately brightening all colors, beyond what is actually found in nature. Granted that LAB is the way to do it, why do it in the first place?

I could give an answer, but Chevreul beat me to it:

> *Correct, but exaggerated coloring* is almost always more attractive than absolute coloring; we also cannot hide the fact that many who experience pleasure in seeing how colors have been modified and exaggerated in a picture, would not feel the same pleasure from the sight of the real thing, because the actual variations in color that the artist exaggerates would not be prominent enough to make themselves felt.
>
> Anyway, the eye's apparent desire to be overwhelmed by exciting colors is basically analogous to our preference for prominent flavors in what we eat and drink; which comports with the comparison I've previously made between the pleasure we derive from vivid colors (forgetting all other characteristics of the object presenting them) and the pleasurable sensation of agreeable flavors.

The Bottom Line

This chapter introduces the simplest LAB move: a recipe for boosting contrast, sharpening, and enhancing all colors. The recipe is limited, notably in its inability to deal with originals with obviously wrong colors.

Nevertheless, the recipe is the foundation for the more complex moves that make LAB magical. It's technically a better way to enhance color than trying to do the same thing in RGB, allowing us to create color variation in a more natural-looking way. And it offers the possibility of driving apart colors that are so similar that RGB can't separate them without making a selection in Photoshop.

2

LAB by the Numbers

The structure of LAB is frightening: opponent-color channels; a zero in the middle of a curve; negative numbers for cool colors and positive numbers for warm ones; colors that are well outside the gamut of any output device. And outright imaginary colors, ones that don't and couldn't possibly exist anywhere but in the mind. But there's logic behind the lunacy, and with practice the system is easy to use.

adical alternatives show up from time to time in politics. Usually they are harmful, occasionally appealing, but rarely do they solve all problems at once.

In recent years in the United States, two such radical alternatives actually became governors of populous states. One was a professional wrestler, the other a bodybuilder/actor. Each has much in common with LAB: great physical strength, a certain intuitive simplicity and ability to express things in a way that human emotions respond to, and a whole lot of baggage that one would rather not hear about.

LAB has the advantage that if we don't like what it has to offer, we can ignore it and stick with the old reliables. But to understand what it has to offer, we need to understand the logic under which it works, which is no mean feat.

* * *

The biggest problem in attempting to teach almost anything about imaging is that around half the world learns how to work in RGB and is deathly afraid of CMYK, thinking that it's some kind of black art instead of just RGB with a black channel attached. The other half learns CMYK first, thinks that RGB is for simpletons and that working in it is akin to performing brain surgery wearing boxing gloves. Both sides thereby miss a host of opportunities that work better in one space than the other.

Such colorspace chauvinism is particularly galling in that RGB and CMYK are exceedingly similar. If you know how to work in one, you already know how to work in the other. The one that's really different is LAB, as Figure 2.1 demonstrates.

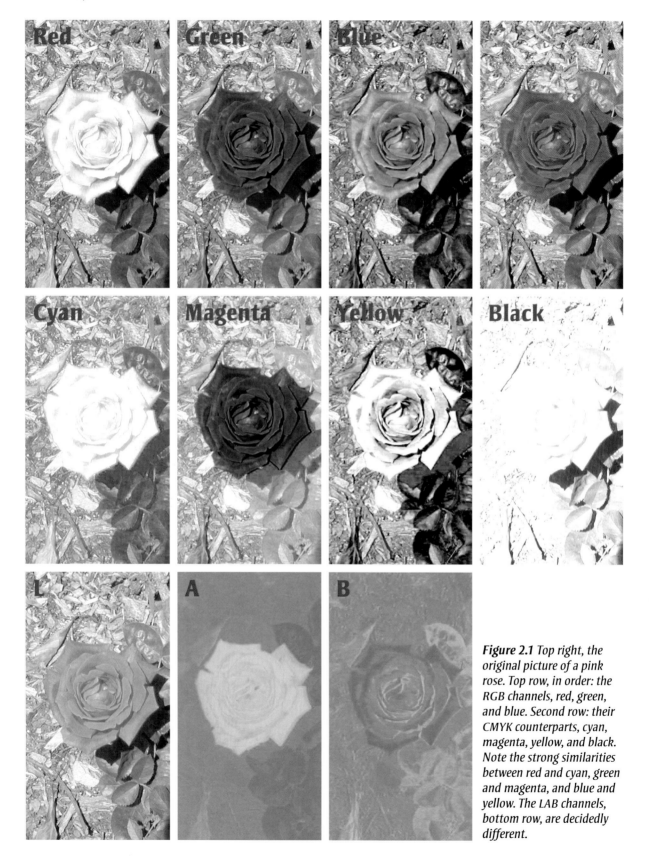

Figure 2.1 *Top right, the original picture of a pink rose. Top row, in order: the RGB channels, red, green, and blue. Second row: their CMYK counterparts, cyan, magenta, yellow, and black. Note the strong similarities between red and cyan, green and magenta, and blue and yellow. The LAB channels, bottom row, are decidedly different.*

Three Pairs of Channels

At top right is the composite color image of this flower. There are identical-looking versions in all three of the colorspaces that Photoshop fully supports. The ten channels are arranged in three rows. From top to bottom, they are RGB, CMYK, and LAB. There's a striking relationship between each RGB channel and the CMY one directly underneath it.

In the magenta channel of CMYK, the flower is quite dark, because we need a lot of magenta ink to make it, and in CMYK, the darker a channel is, the more ink we get. The leaves are much lighter, because magenta ink kills green.

In RGB, the lighter a channel is, the more of that color of light is supposed to be hitting our eyes. Little, if any, green light should be doing so in the middle of a magenta flower. Hence, the flower in the green of RGB is as dark as it is in the magenta of CMYK. For the same reason, the leaves are about equally light in both channels. The magenta and green aren't identical because of such tiresome factors as dot gain, ink impurities, and the presence of a black channel, but still it's as easy to see their relation as it is to see the ones between red and cyan and blue and yellow.

The radical concept of LAB is to separate color and contrast completely, followed by a most unusual way of defining color. Even once you get the general idea, there are complications, exceptions, and nonobvious ramifications.

All channels in RGB and CMYK affect both color and contrast. In LAB, all the contrast goes into the L channel, all the color into the A and B. Consequently, the L is easy to understand, because, since it's colorless, we can think of it as a black and white version of the color photo, although for technical reasons the L is a bit lighter than a black and white would be. The A and B, which are color only, make zero sense to the casual observer.

If an image has no color at all—that is, if it's a black and white—the sensible thing would be blank A and B channels, right? Not in the weird world of LAB. If there's no color, the A and B have to be *gray*—a pure, 50% gray. The further they get away from gray—the more they move toward white and/or black—the more colorful the image gets.

The two are termed *opponent-color channels*. When the A is a lighter gray, it contributes magenta, but a darker gray represents green. And the lighter or darker it is, the more intense the color.

From that, you might surmise that the A channel's flower would have to be almost a white, since it would be hard to find an object more magenta and less green. But again, LAB has a trick. It is designed not just to encompass all the colors that we can print, put on film, or display on a monitor, and not just colors that are too intense for any of these media, but colors that are so intense as to be beyond our conception: imaginary colors, colors that couldn't possibly exist.

We'll get to the official LAB numbering system in a moment, but for now let's think of the A channel as though it were a grayscale image, with possible values from zero to 100%. A 50% value is neither magenta nor green; anything lighter favors magenta and darker favors green.

Treating the A channel as a grayscale, the rose's magenta is only about a 25%—in other words, about halfway as magenta as LAB can ask for. The dull green of the leaves is 57%, only slightly higher than the 50% that would denote something neither magenta nor green. And the background isn't gray, either. It's biased toward magenta, but it reads only 48% or 49%, just a point or two away from the neutral 50%.

Although the shapes are blurry, we see the flower as a light object and the leaves, just barely, as dark ones in the A channel.

In the B channel's opponent-color scheme,

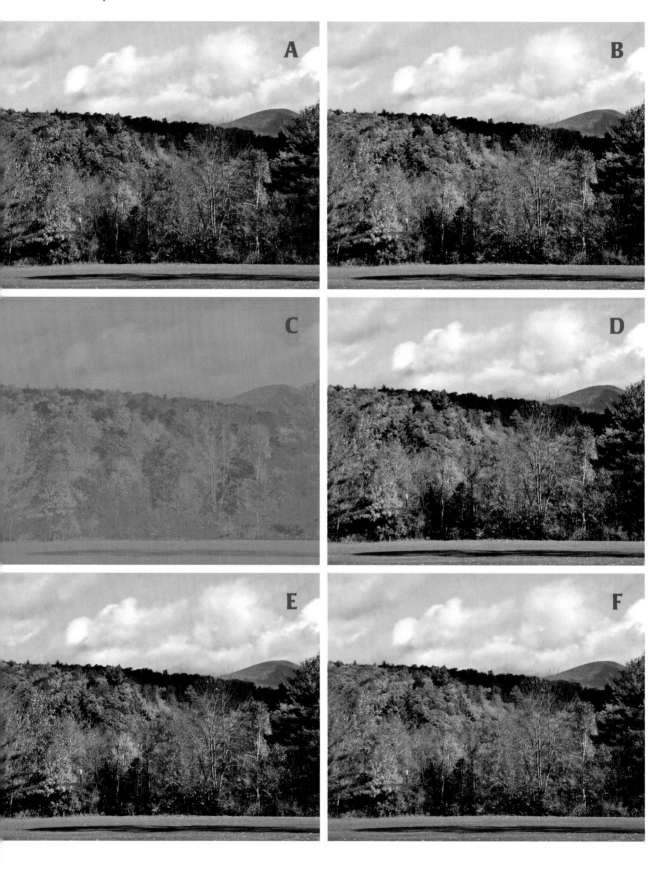

light grays represent yellowness, dark grays are blue, and a 50% gray is neither. Inasmuch as nothing in this picture can be described as either yellow or blue, the B is subtler than the A, but it plays an important role in modifying other colors.

In the A channel, the flower is pretty much all of one darkness, but in the B, the edges are darker than the center. So, even though the B is much less intense than the A, it's helping create a different hue on the edges of the flower than in its center.

How we would describe that change in hue depends on how hoity-toity opponent-color we want to be about it. A person off the street might say, the flower is more purple around its edges and more red in the center.

An LAB aficionado would probably say the same thing, but would actually be thinking: the flower is always the same in its magenta-as-opposed-to-greenness; but it's more blue-as-opposed-to-yellow at its edges and more yellow-as-opposed-to-blue at the center.

In every category of image, this type of subtle variation in hue is critical to making the color believable. LAB establishes hue variation better than any other colorspace.

Now, let's do the exercise in reverse, starting with a normal image and examining what happens when certain LAB channels are weakened or omitted.

The Role of Each Channel

Figure 2.2A is the original autumn scene, and Figure 2.2F is a dirty trick with a lot of ramifications for future magic. The other four show the function of the channels by eliminating them one at a time. Or, rather, by weakening

Figure 2.2 Top left, the original. The next four show the effect of drastically reducing tonal variation in one or more. Top right, both the A and B channels are suppressed. Center left, the L only. Center right, the A. Bottom left, the B. The version at bottom right is the original with the A channel inverted, reversing the relation between magenta and green.

them severely. If I eliminated the A and B altogether by changing them to 50% gray, the picture would become a black and white. So, instead, in Figure 2.2B, I wiped out four-fifths of their variation. In the next three versions, I did the the same to a single channel at a time.

The ugliest version is doubtless Figure 2.2C, the one with the devastated L channel. When all luminosity contrast is gone, clouds are gray, not white, and autumn foliage is a color swatch in which individual trees can't be discerned. But the version with almost no color isn't much better. The interesting ones are those using only one of the color channels, because they tell us a lot about how each hue is constructed.

When the A channel is AWOL, magentas and greens are impossible. For that matter, so are cyans, which probably doesn't cause you much lack of sleep, and reds, which are colors we can't live without. A red occurs when both A and B are lighter than 50%. In Figure 2.2D, with the A almost nonexistent, the central trees and the grass are the same color, which is disconcerting given that one used to be red and the other green. But both were, and are, more yellow than they are blue.

An LAB person always needs to think in terms of what the secondary AB channel must be. For example, in Figure 2.2A, do you think that the sky should be more blue, or yellow? That, of course, is a stupid question. Naturally, the B channel is supposed to be darker than a 50% gray, because that's how you make things blue. But now, the secondary question: admitting that blue is the dominating color, should the sky be more green, or more magenta?

Figure 2.2E gives the answer, which you should squirrel away into your storehouse of knowledge. Skies almost always fall to the green, not the magenta, side of blue. And here's another one to remember, a lesson from Figure 2.2D: grass, and anything else that grows, is always to the yellow, never the blue, side of green. Notice how Figure 2.2E's grass seems bluer than that of the original, Figure 2.2A. This is not because it was shot in Kentucky, but rather because it has no B channel to introduce the yellow component that the grass needs.

Finally, to change the original into Figure 2.2F, I selected the A channel (either by Command–2 Mac, Ctrl–2 PC, or by clicking the A icon after opening the Channels palette), and did Image: Adjustments>Invert. That is our first real piece of magic, because if you can somehow transport yourself to an imaginary planet with orange grass, purple skies, and green leaves in peak autumn foliage season, you must admit how persuasive Figure 2.2F is. Everything seems to fit in place. Unless you know that the colors are impossible, the illusion is undetectable.

The structure of the AB channels makes such trickery possible. The key is the definition of neutrality as 50% gray. The clouds in Figure 2.2F are just as white as they were in Figure 2.2A. Originally, they were neutral: neither magenta nor green, neither yellow nor blue. So, both AB channels had them at or near 50%, and inverting 50% doesn't change anything. The inversion affects only things that have color, whether slight or significant. As we saw when the B was suppressed in Figure 2.2E, the sky in the original tends slightly toward green. Inverting its A channel makes it tend slightly toward magenta, which is why the sky is purplish in Figure 2.2F. And in the original, most of the trees are red—heavily magenta as well as yellow—meaning that inverting the A makes them become heavily green.

It's high time to cease the impossibly verbose references to magenta-as-opposed-to-green and start using real LAB numbers. The value that we've been referring to as 50% gray is fundamental. It is expressed, in the weird language of the AB channels, as zero. Things that are lighter than 50% gray are

given positive values, the maximum being +127; things darker than 50% are negative, with the maximum –128.

This is the sort of news that makes people throw the mouse in the air and pray to whatever deity watches over graphic artists to deliver them into some more comprehensible discipline, such as differential equations. However, now that we're this far, you'll have to admit that there's a logic, however radical, however perverse, at work. Positive numbers always indicate warm colors: magenta, yellow, red. Negative numbers are cold colors: blue, green, cyan. And a zero is no color at all, a neutral.

By setting zero midway between the two opponents, we get an easy reference as to how colorful an object is: the further it is from zero, the more colorful. For example, in Figure 2.1 the flower averages around +65 in the A, while the leaves above it are in the neighborhood of –15. You don't need to know what exact colors are being called for to realize that the flower has to be more colorful than the leaves are.

It can be very convenient to represent all whites, blacks, and grays with a single number that doesn't depend on the values found in any other channel. Imagine a picture that's full of colors known to be neutral, but of different darknesses. A man wearing a tuxedo would qualify. The shirt would be white to light gray; the jacket, tie, and pants dark gray to black.

If we were working such a picture in RGB, every channel would have a big tonal range, because every channel contributes to lightness and darkness. That's unfortunate, because in RGB, neutral colors happen when all three channels have equal values. Many, many points would have to be compared channel-to-channel to be sure that the values were approximately equal in all three, regardless of the darkness.

In LAB there is no such problem. The A

Figure 2.3 *Colored bars are superimposed on an otherwise neutral (0^A0^B) image. Top left, the values are plus or minus 25 in the A and B. Top right, they are ±50, and bottom left the bars are ±75 in the A and B.*

The Easiest of the Three

After the complications of the AB, the L channel is relatively easy to understand once you get used to its being backward in relation to its close relative, a grayscale image. In the L, a value of zero is absolutely black, and 100 absolutely white. The L is slightly lighter, and higher in midtone contrast, in comparison to what we would get if we went Image: Mode>Grayscale, but for now it's enough to know that the lower the value, the darker.

The L doesn't have negative numbers. As the A and B do, there's a typographical problem in the LAB language that we're about to be speaking. Minus signs cause confusion, because people mix them up with dashes. Instead, we'll use parentheses to denote negative numbers when citing AB values. Earlier in this chapter, for example, we saw an object

channel should be just about zero throughout both the shirt and the tuxedo. If it is, we don't need to compare it with the B or anything else—the A is now known to be correct.

The idea of a fixed neutrality value of zero, independent of other channels, also makes certain kinds of color correction easier, as we'll see in Chapter 3.

that measured around $60^L(15)^A15^B$. Can you name what it was?

The 60^L suggests something in the middle range of darkness, probably equivalent to around a 50% gray in any other type of file. (Remember: the L channel is deceptively light.) The negative A reading tells us that the object is more green than magenta, and the positive B indicates more yellow than blue. AB values of plus or minus 15 aren't particularly high, so although the object has a distinct color, it certainly isn't unusually saturated or brilliant.

In short, the numbers describe a relatively dark, dull yellow-green. They are typical readings for the leaves in Figure 2.1.

For a final look at how the AB channels interact to construct color, Figure 2.3 is a grayscale image except for the four colored bars. Therefore, to use proper language. everything other than the bars reads 0^A0^B. Each of the four bars is a pure AB color: magenta, green, yellow or blue. The L channel is unaffected and would look like a grayscale still-life picture without any bars.

The three versions of the image use different values for the bars. Figure 2.3A starts with ±25. That is, the magenta bar contributes 25^A to whatever the L value is, the green bar $(25)^A$, the yellow bar 25^B, and the blue bar $(25)^B$. Figure 2.3B has the bars at AB values of ±50, and 2.3C at ±75.

Before we get to the bad news, note how these channels work in tandem to produce intermediate colors. In the top right corner, where the bars intersect and both A and B are positive, we get red. At the bottom left, mixing the AB negatives, blue and green, gives us cyan. At top left, mixing blue and magenta yields a purple, and at bottom right is a yellow-green that's closer to the color of most things that grow than a pure LAB green is.

These images—in their original LAB form, not the CMYK conversion that was needed to print this book—are on the accompanying CD. Open them, and they'll look very different from the printed page. Inasmuch as the printer of this book had difficulty acquiring opponent-color inks, I was obliged to supply CMYK files. And CMYK practicalities trump LAB theories much of the time.

The bars become more colorful as the distance from zero (neutrality) gets higher. Therefore, the bars in Figure 2.3C should be more intense than in Figure 2.3A. That much is true. But the bars theoretically don't affect contrast; the detailing in the two images should be the same. It's not. Under the magenta and blue bars, at least, the picture is distinctly darker than it was.

Certainly this is an artificial picture in the sense that the colors being called for can't possibly be right. Then again, so was Figure 2.2F, which was a lot more convincing.

That certain colors theoretically exist in LAB doesn't mean that we have the slightest hope of achieving them in CMYK, or even in RGB. Inability to print bright blues, particularly light, bright ones, is a notorious CMYK failing. But CMYK falls short in many other areas, particularly when colors are supposed to be very pure and yet either quite dark or quite light. It's a major issue. Remember: working in LAB is seldom the final step. The file almost always has to go back into RGB or CMYK at some point.

If the LAB file contains colors that the destination space can't reproduce, it takes a fair amount of experience to predict what will happen. The ability to create such colors is one of the big dangers—and big opportunities—of LAB. In the "Closer Look" section of this chapter, we'll dig deeper, but for now, we need to be careful when dealing with colors that exist in the warped world of LAB only.

In Chapter 1, we worked on canyon after canyon, having learned that canyons are a specialty of LAB. At this point, you should understand why. First, canyons have very subtle color differentiations that cameras don't pick up as well as human observers do. Steepening the AB channels is extremely effective in bringing them out. Second, canyons don't have brilliant colors: the colors in Chapter 1 are far less vivid than in, say, Figure 2.2. It would be difficult to enhance canyon colors so much that they couldn't be reproduced accurately in CMYK or RGB. Canyons are therefore very good things to hit with AB curves. Something like Figure 2.2 needs to be approached with caution.

You should now be able to identify colors using LAB terminology. Check that you can by going over the "Review and Exercises" section, which offers a quick quiz. If you pass it, you can move on to Chapter 3 if you like. The remainder of this chapter goes into more detail about what happens when LAB produces the unreproduceable, and more about why steepening the AB is a better way to emphasize color than attempting to do the same thing in RGB.

Review and Exercises

✓If you're working with an RGB file, how would you know whether a certain object will reproduce as neutral—that is, white, gray, or black?

✓How do you know that an object will reproduce as neutral if you are working in LAB?

✓Why are the A and B channels, when viewed on their own as they are in Figure 2.2, never white or black, but only various shades of medium gray?

✓How does the L channel, viewed alone, compare to a version of the file that's been converted into grayscale?

✓Which colors are denoted by positive and negative numbers in the A and B channels?

✓Refer back to Chapter 1. Match each item in the left column with its typical corresponding LAB value. (Answers in box on page 33.)

1. The sky in Figure 1.1A	A. $86^L 8^A (8)^B$
2. The lake in Figure 1.10C	B. $49^L (4)^A (10)^B$
3. The pinkish background of the Review box on page 14	C. $74^L 13^A 19^B$
4. The large magenta circles in Figure 1.11	D. $52^L 81^A (7)^B$
5. The African-American skintone in Figure 1.15A	E. $67^L (3)^A (30)^B$

A Closer Look

I once attended a lecture in which the speaker warned against using LAB because, he said, fully a quarter of the colors that LAB can construct can't be reproduced in either RGB or CMYK. Both premise and conclusion are wrong. The number of LAB colors that are out of the gamut of other colorspaces is more like three-quarters; and no, it's not an argument against using LAB, quite the contrary.

The quaint idea that LAB wastes only a quarter of its values comes from a faulty analysis of the AB channels, which run from values of −128 to +127. Commonly used variants of RGB can't achieve these extremes of color purity, but under certain circumstances they can get to about three-quarters of it, or ±90. CMYK doesn't even get that close, except for its yellow: the other three colors rarely get higher than ±70.

The killer is that phrase *under certain circumstances.* If we are told that a certain object is supposed to be *dark green,* or *dark red,* no doubt we can visualize such a color. But what does *dark yellow* mean?

Yellow has to be light to be recognizable. The most intense yellow in real graphic-artist life is found in CMYK, not RGB. It's 0^{C}0^{M}100^Y. Yellow is such a pure ink that solid coverage of it is beyond the gamut of most RGBs. It's rare to find CMYK colors that RGB can't reproduce, but yellow is the glaring exception.

In Photoshop's Color Picker (click on the foreground/background color icons in the toolbar to bring it up), if I enter 0^{C}0^{M}100^Y, I learn that it is "equal" to 95^L(6)^{A}95^B or 255^{R}242^{G}0^B. On your system, these values may vary somewhat if you aren't using the same CMYK and RGB definitions this book does, which we'll discuss in Chapter 3.

As we just discussed, however, the RGB values shown in Figure 2.4 don't really match the CMYK ones, because they can't—something that yellow doesn't exist in RGB. But LAB just yawns. It matches this yellow with 32 points to spare in the B channel, roughly a quarter of its possibilities, just like the man said.

95^B is therefore the maximum yellow-as-opposed-to-blue that can be equaled in CMYK. The rub is, we can only do that well at the extremely light value of 95^L. Any attempt to produce something lighter than that would have to use less yellow ink. Anything darker would have to employ extra inks that would contaminate the yellow. For example, 25^{C}20^{M}100^Y equates to 75^L(5)^{A}67^B. Now, the B is only about half its maximum value—and we're just a quarter of the way down the L scale of darkness. At 50^L, we can be no higher than 47^B without going outside the CMYK gamut. And at 20^L, the limit is about 28^B—not even a quarter of the maximum.

If it isn't light, it isn't yellow.

In CMYK and RGB, all colors operate in this fashion. They are most pronounced at a certain darkness level. Green is strongest at around 60^L, magenta at 50^L, and blue, the darkest of

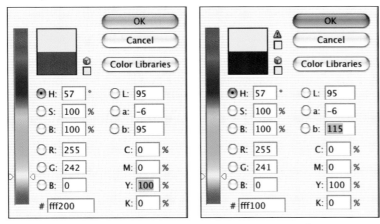

Figure 2.4 *The Color Picker displays equivalencies in four different colorspaces, but sometimes a match between them is impossible. At left, there's no warning that the solid yellow CMYK ink can't be reproduced accurately in RGB. Note, though, that it isn't even close to the B channel limit of +127. When the B value is increased, the yellow leaves the CMYK gamut as well, but this time Photoshop lets us know—there's a small alert icon just to the left of the Cancel button.*

all, at 40^L. A light rich blue is like a dark brilliant yellow, or a giant midget, or a rectangular circle.

Yet LAB permits us to ask for it.

Consider the yellow bar at the right of Figure 2.3C. Nominally it contributes 75^B to whatever's underneath it. But as we have just seen, such an intense yellow is only possible when the L is quite light—say, between values of 95^L and 85^L. Part of the center of the apple meets that description. Everything else that the yellow bar passes over is not merely out of CMYK gamut and undisplayable by any monitor. It portrays out-and-out imaginary colors—yellows that don't exist, couldn't possibly exist, and never will exist, such as the dark area of the plate where it intersects the lower edge of the yellow bar. That area should be around 5^{L}0^{A}75^B, and may be described as a brilliantly yellow dark black.

And now, the key question. Sooner or later, this file has to come out of LAB. What will happen to all these impossible, undisplayable combinations of color and darkness?

An Introduction to the Imaginary

When we translate an imaginary color out of LAB, we get a compromise—a compromise that doesn't match the original luminosity any more.

Figure 2.5 is Figure 2.3C converted to grayscale. To be more specific, it is converted to grayscale from the CMYK file needed to print this book, which itself had been converted from the LAB original. Had the conversion been done directly from LAB, there would have been no sign of the colored bars. But because of the intermediate conversion into CMYK, which had to bring certain colors into gamut, the compromises are readily seen.

Photoshop bravely fights the unbeatable foe by splitting the difference. The white plate gets darker where the bottom of the yellow bar surprints it. The dark leaf gets lighter where the yellow bar passes over it. And most of the apple stays about as it was.

The same thing takes place in reverse on the left side of the image. Very light blues aren't part

Figure 2.5 *If any of the versions of Figure 2.3 were converted into grayscale directly from LAB, there would be no sign of the colored bars. This grayscale version, however, was converted from the CMYK file from which Figure 2.3C was printed, not the original LAB file. During the separation process, Photoshop often changes luminosity values when it confronts colors that can't be matched in CMYK.*

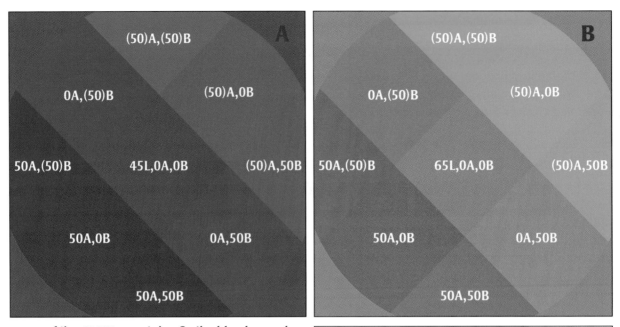

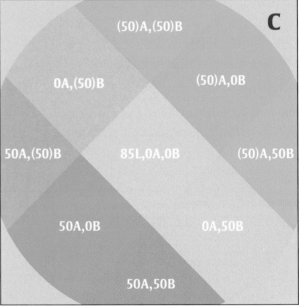

of the CMYK repertoire. So the blue bar makes a lot of things darker, taking a nasty bite out of the pear. Both the magenta bar and the red corner almost wipe out what's beneath them.

If you don't like the idea of darkening and lightening when we are supposed to be affecting color only, consider the alternative. Or, better yet, consider how you would reverse-engineer Figure 2.3C. Suppose you are given only the grayscale version of the picture, and a copy of the printed page showing the color bars, and asked to duplicate the look, using only RGB.

There would be no problem creating the shapes of the bars, but things would bog down thereafter, because RGB can't construct colors that are out of its own gamut. Without them, attempts to blend with pure color can't change the underlying luminosity, and if you can't change the underlying luminosity you can't get any kind of yellow at all where it overprints a white object such as the plate.

Therefore, if you're trying to colorize all or part of a document, LAB will give a smoother look that's hard to duplicate elsewhere. Smoother is not always better. If you're trying to turn a photograph into a duotone, LAB may give you more consistent color, but that's not a

Figure 2.6 The structure of LAB's channels is logical but often produces colors that can't be matched in other color-spaces. Each of the above had no lightness variation when in LAB, but conversion to CMYK has produced some.

big traditional selling point for duotones. Most people will prefer the higher-contrast ones made by a simple mode change. On the other hand, if realism is what you're after, the impossible colors of LAB can be a major ally.

Figure 2.6 shows how the A and B interact—and offers a strong reminder of how color and

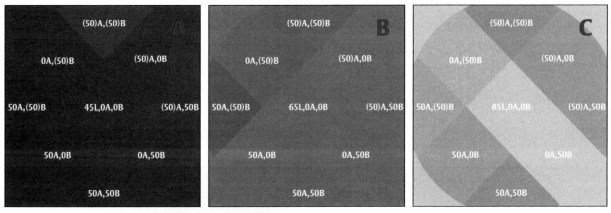

Figure 2.7 *The originals of Figure 2.6 had no variation in their L channels. When converted to other colorspaces their luminosity did not remain constant, as Photoshop tried to compensate for the inability to match certain colors. The effect is particularly visible in the lightest of the three versions, where every colored area except yellow has been darkened. These images were converted to grayscale not from the LAB originals, but from the CMYK print files.*

darkness can't be divorced altogether. Each of these graphics was constructed in LAB with a completely uniform L channel: 45^L, 65^L, and 85^L, from darkest to lightest. Covering it are the nine possible permutations of the values −50, 0, and +50 in the A and B. One of those nine produces gray. 0^A0^B. The other eight represent the four LAB primaries of blue, green, yellow, and magenta, plus the four LAB intermediate colors of cyan, yellow-green, red, and purple.

The lower right corner of Figure 2.6A demonstrates the truth of an earlier remark: if it isn't light, it isn't yellow. 0^A50^B, that's supposed to be yellow, and in Figure 2.6C, when 85^L is added, yellow is what I'd call it. If, instead, we use Figure 2.6A's 45^L, I'd call that color mushy brown.

That's not the only surprise here: one primary and one intermediate color aren't quite the hue that one would expect, or at least they aren't what I would expect if I had never heard of LAB.

$(50)^A0^B$ is supposed to be green. That's not what I'd call it. In all three of these images, *teal* is a better description. To be

considered green, I think that color has to move part or all the way toward the one at right center of each image, $(50)^A50^B$.

Also, 50^A50^B is supposedly *red*. This is a real orange-looking red to my way of thinking. Be

Figure 2.8 *Steepening the AB channels is the most natural way of adding extra color to the brightest area, a common need in sunset images like this original.*

aware that most real reds, other than human faces, need a higher value in the A than in the B.

As with Figure 2.5, I've made grayscale conversions of each of the three CMYK files that make up Figure 2.6, to show how Photoshop is adjusting the luminosity of out-of-gamut colors in a desperate effort to match the unmatchable. If these grayscale images had been generated directly from the LAB files, each one would be an even, solid, flat gray without any tonal variation in the colored areas. They weren't, and they aren't. Where colored areas break away from the gray background in the actual files, it's an attempt to compensate for something out of gamut. And, the lighter (greater) the L value, the more out-of-gamut colors there will be.

Photoshop can't figure out how to make a dark cyan, so it substitutes a lighter one, but that's the only questionable area in Figure 2.7A. As the background gets lighter in Figure 2.7B, the blue and purple patches join the fun.

When the object gets as light as 85^L, as it does in Figure 2.7C, almost nothing works. The yellow patch is the only one of the eight colored areas that hasn't been significantly darkened.

So, where the image is light, and the LAB file calls for it to be colorful as well, it's apt to get darker when it enters either CMYK or RGB. This sounds like a strong incentive not to let such colors occur in LAB in the first place. In fact, it's an incredibly valuable, if perverse, part of the LAB magic, one that can enable effects not otherwise thinkable.

So Hurry Sundown, Be on Your Way

In print, we can't manufacture colors brighter than blank paper. This is unfortunate when the image contains the sun or some other extremely bright object, and explains why so many photographers expend so much time and energy trying to get the best artistic effect out of their sunset shots.

A setting sun is a brilliant yellow-orange. That's the whole problem. In print, we only get to choose one of those two adjectives. Blank paper is the most

Figure 2.9 *This corrected version of Figure 2.8 was produced by steepening the AB channels by an equal amount. The L channel was not altered. Below, an enlarged look at the area around the sun.*

brilliant thing available to us. Add color, and it's no longer as bright.

Historically, those who enjoyed such limited success as is possible under these straitened circumstances have usually left the center of the sun blank but exaggerated the transition to orange around it, hoping to fool the viewer into perceiving a colorful sun. Any contrasting colors also get hiked.

Boosting colors by steepening the AB curves is technically better than any analogous move in RGB or CMYK. The advantage is never more clear than in images like Figure 2.8, as the following competing efforts demonstrate.

Figure 2.9 is the LAB entrant. It's nothing more than a repetition of the AB curves applied back in Figure 1.9 to the image of a desert scene. In the interest of a fair competition, one limited to color only, I did not touch the L channel. Also, I made sure that the A and B curves were identical, as no move in RGB easily duplicates the effect of different angles in the AB curves.

Figure 2.10 tries to achieve the same thing in RGB, using the master saturation control in Photoshop's Image: Adjustments>Hue/Saturation command. I was trying to match the general appearance of Figure 2.9, but couldn't come close. In LAB, most of the extra golden tone goes into the area around the sun, where it belongs. In Figure 2.10 it goes into the foreground beach. And the water winds up being too blue as well. We call them *whitecaps* for a reason.

The magnified versions highlight another major problem. As is common with digital captures in vicious lighting conditions, there's a lot of artifacting: strangely

colored noise, particularly in the clouds around the sun. The enlarged pieces show that Figure 2.10 is a disaster area in this respect, while Figure 2.9 is reasonable.

People who know their LAB recognize immediately that this is a case for blurring the A, and especially the B channel. We'll be discussing that topic in Chapter 5, but no blurring was done here. The simple straight-line curve in these two

Figure 2.10 *This version was produced in RGB, using the Hue/Saturation command. Although many colors have been exaggerated more than in Figure 2.9, the critical sun area is much less intense. Also, there is serious artifacting in the sky.*

color channels brought up the color variation without also bringing the defects out.

This picture exploits LAB's propensity to make impossible colors. In RGB, the brightest color is and must be a pure white, $255^R 255^G 255^B$, and any attempt to add color must also darken.

In LAB, where color and contrast live apart, pure lightness—100^L, in LABspeak—*can* be

---

The Bottom Line

The LAB way of defining color by two opponent-color channels is not exactly intuitive, but it makes eminent sense once you get used to it. Positive values represent warm colors: magenta in the A, yellow in the B. Negative numbers are cool colors: green in the A, blue in the B. And values of zero are neutral.

The L channel can best be understood as a black and white rendition of the document, although somewhat lighter. Its numbering system is the reverse of grayscale: 0 for darkness, 100 for lightness.

Many LAB formulations are out of the gamut of either CMYK, RGB, or both. On conversion out of LAB, Photoshop usually adjusts their luminosity in a futile attempt to match the color.

---

accompanied by a color value, even a totally obscene one. A value of $0^L 120^A 100^B$, for example, would be totally black but simultaneously more brilliantly red than a laser beam. I doubt that such color exists in real life, but LAB thinks it does, and can call for it.

Here, the demand—a color as brilliant as possible, but orange—isn't quite so unreasonable, but it's still asking for the impossible. Photoshop, scrambling to comply, splits the difference, adding a gradual move toward yellow and thus allowing some darkening. Figure 2.10 lacks the pleasing impact of Figure 2.9, because when working in RGB, we can't call for any colors that RGB is incapable of producing.

Using an imaginary color in LAB to enable an otherwise impossible effect in print is an idea that will be getting quite a workout in the following pages, particularly in Chapter 8. The idea that we should try to fix real pictures by adding imaginary colors that can't be seen or printed is, to put it mildly, a radical alternative. But, like most radical alternatives, it has an attractive side. I wish we could steer clear of the *other* side as easily with politicians as we can with LAB.

3
Vary the Recipe, Vary the Color

The simple, symmetrical curves of Chapter 1 are powerful, but they're just the beginning. By using different mixes of ingredients, LAB curving can become considerably more spicy, emphasizing certain colors more than others.

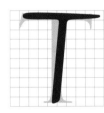

The best cooks never follow recipes, or at least not literally. A pinch of something extra here, a little bit of something not in the list of ingredients there, adjust the quantity of this, delete all mention of that, and presto, a culinary masterpiece, although when I do it, there always seem to be more carbohydrates in the result than the original recipe suggested.

It's that way with LAB, too. Chapter 1 presented the basic recipe, the fundamental method of using LAB to bring out the natural colors of an image. Because I was trying to assume that you had never been in a kitchen before and didn't know the difference between a truffle and a habanero pepper, the recipe was necessarily simple—and inflexible. Several contingencies could derail it, such as a cast in the original, the presence of brilliant colors, or a subject that was excessively busy in the L channel.

Now that we've had an introduction to how LAB operates and what its numbers mean, we're in a position to expand the recipe's usefulness. We can wipe out casts while enhancing other colors; we can exclude brilliant colors without formally selecting them or using a mask; we can choose certain colors for more of a boost than others.

Getting to that happy point requires some preparation of Photoshop settings, but before doing that, let's review the recipe. Figure 3.1 demonstrates LAB's knack of smashing its way through any kind of haze. The bottom version follows the recipe, and therefore is made up of four basic moves. We will now look at each in isolation, to see how the whole is greater than the sum of its parts.

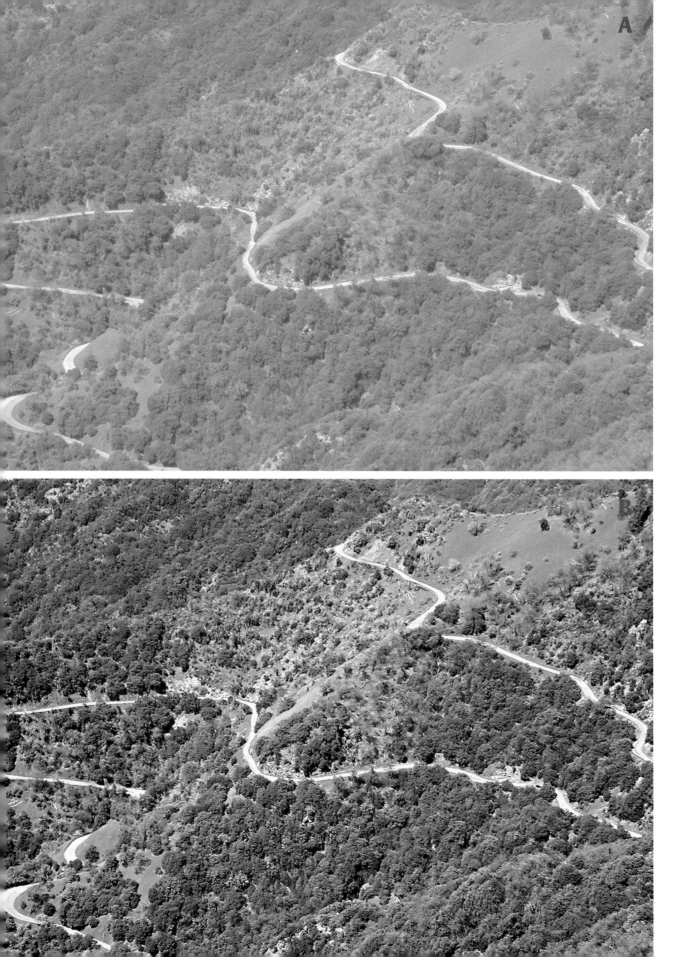

As we know, LAB, unlike RGB and CMYK, treats color and contrast as separate ingredients. Figure 3.2A has greatly improved detail in comparison to Figure 3.1A, but there has been no change in color because the A and B channels were left untouched.

The L curve that provided the extra detail was derived in the same way as in Chapter 1, by steepening the area of major interest. To find that area, I held down the mouse button and, with the Curves dialog open, ran the cursor across key parts of the image, which yields a moving circle that indicates the range in which the objects fall.

As with the Chapter 1 images, this very flat original falls in a narrow range. The part of the curve that affects that range can be quite steep, and the increase in contrast (Figure 3.2A) dramatic.

In principle, it would be nice to show a version with sharpening applied to the original image only. The result would be deceptive because, with everything so flat, the sharpening wouldn't be nearly as pronounced as it would be after the L curve was applied. Therefore, Figure 3.2B sharpens not the original file, but rather Figure 3.2A.

Both of these L-only moves repeat a sad story about images that are too dark, too light, or too flat: they also tend to be colorless. If a picture is too dark, merely lightening it won't make it acceptable, because it's almost always too gray as well. The same thing is happening here. A haze hurts not just contrast but color. By the time we reach Figure 3.2B, there's so much snap that the tepid colors look artificial. We need more vivid greens. The A and B channels will give them to us.

To get the final version (Figure 3.1B), I steepened the A and B curves by moving their endpoints three gridlines horizontally toward the center. This is almost exactly the same

Figure 3.1 (opposite) LAB excels at cutting through haze. The bottom version was prepared in much the same way as the canyon images of Chapter 1.

procedure as in Figure 1.10, the picture of Yellowstone Lake. Figure 3.3A shows how the picture would look if the curve were applied to the A alone without any change to the other two channels; and Figure 3.3B does the same for the B alone.

Three Channels, One Image

These four intermediate images are the ingredients. But, as with anything involving seasonings, the chef's good taste must come into play. Let's discuss some of the options, because there are some things about Figure 3.1B that I don't particularly like.

The L curve shown in Figure 3.2 is definitely of the right shape. It places the entire scene in a steep part, but opinions could vary as to how steep the slope should be. You may feel that it gives the image too much bite, in which case a less extreme steepening is called for. Or, you may wish to go further than I did, making the curve even more vertical. I wouldn't, because I think that the grassy areas are getting too light already, and that the trees are getting so dark as to be threatening to lose all detail.

Sharpening is the most irritatingly subjective item in all of color correction. We'll discuss some of the considerations in more depth in Chapter 5. For now, it's enough to say that you could sharpen this image more than I did, or less, or not at all.

As for the color changes, they're hard to evaluate without seeing them in conjunction with the move in the L channel. One way to begin, however, is with this question: if the choice is between hanging and poison (that is, between Figures 3.3A and 3.3B), which one would you choose?

If these two were the only choices, which I thank the gods of color they are not, I'd go with Figure 3.3A. Green is a pleasing hue in the context of this image. Yellow isn't.

Figure 3.1B is far better than the foggy original, true, but—at least to my taste—

some of the grassy areas at the center of the image seem too yellow. So, we could alter the recipe. All the images in Chapter 1 used different angles for the curves, but the angle was always the same in both the A and B channels. They don't throw us in prison for applying different ones, and that's what we might do here. We could use the existing curve for the A channel, but something milder, less vertical, for the B.

There's another option, too. Making the B less vertical tones down not just the yellow component of the image, but the blue also. Personally, I happen to like how the background has picked up a blue shade at its top right. If we wanted to preserve that increased blue but keep the yellow where it was, Chapter 4 will explain how to do it.

Expertise with the AB curves gives us enormous flexibility. Before we turn to their magic, let's verify our system settings.

Flight Check: The Photoshop Settings

As we get ready for serious curvewriting, we need to check that several Photoshop defaults are set up properly. Some of these settings require Photoshop 6 or later; others will work with any version.

• First, double-click the eyedropper tool. In the Options bar at the top of the screen, the default is Point Sample. That's no good. It means that when measuring a color, Photoshop will report the value of the single pixel that's underneath the cursor. Since a single pixel may well be random noise, a piece of

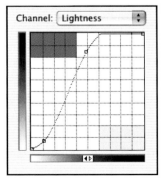

Figure 3.2 *Changes to the L channel affect contrast, not color. Above, the curve shown at left enhances contrast. Then (below) an application of unsharp masking to the L channel enhances focus.*

dust, or something else totally atypical, the measurement isn't reliable. Instead, as shown in Figure 3.4, set the preference to 3 by 3 average, which reports the average value of the nine pixels that surround the cursor. 5 by 5 average is also acceptable, but Point Sample is not.

• Next, check the Info palette itself (Window: Info), shown in Figure 3.5. Its top half can conveniently be configured to display two colorspaces simultaneously. A separate eyedropper controls each side. The left side should be left at its default, Actual Color, which means that it will read LAB for an LAB file, RGB if RGB, and CMYK if CMYK. Working with LAB numbers is not a walk in the park for the uninitiated, so you should set up the right side to read whichever colorspace you're most comfortable with. That way, you can refer to, say, RGB numbers, even though you're working in LAB.

You will doubtless think that I should be sent to an asylum for saying this, but after a while the LAB values will start to make more sense than either of the alternatives. I now have my own Info palette set to LAB on the right, no matter what colorspace I'm working in. Even though I've worked in CMYK for a very long time, the LAB values now make more sense to me—certainly more than RGB!

• While on the topic of equivalencies, here's an optional change. In Photoshop, LAB has a fixed meaning: your LAB is the same as mine. Our definitions of RGB and CMYK may not be. Therefore, if we each convert an LAB file to one of the other colorspaces, we'll get different results, unless your workspaces (Edit: Color Settings; Photoshop: Color Settings in certain versions) happen to match mine.

The subject of what definitions to use has generated more heat than its importance merits. It's off-topic for this book, because it has little impact on the question of when to

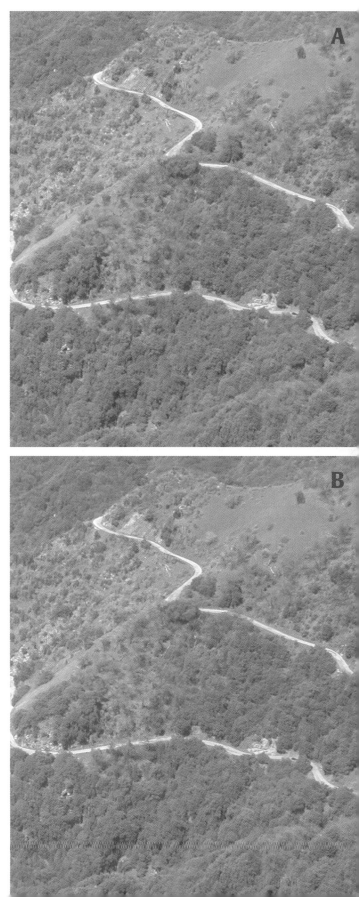

Figure 3.3 *Top, an image modified only by altering the A channel. Bottom, if the modification is only to the B.*

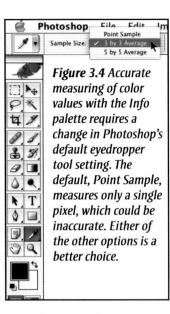

Figure 3.4 *Accurate measuring of color values with the Info palette requires a change in Photoshop's default eyedropper tool setting. The default, Point Sample, measures only a single pixel, which could be inaccurate. Either of the other options is a better choice.*

use LAB. However, we have to assume *something,* and it's going to be what's shown in Figure 3.6. These settings are chosen only because more people use them than anything else, and not because I approve of them, which I do not. If you are dead set and determined to follow the exact numbers shown here, make your settings match; otherwise, leave them alone and you won't miss much.

If you use these RGB and CMYK settings, your Info palette will report numbers similar to those of this book, although certain other settings may cause them to vary slightly. Otherwise, there will be differences in things like the equivalencies shown in Figure 3.5.

Also, from here on, I'm not going to waste space with a reminder every time the acronyms *RGB* and *CMYK* appear that they permit differences in definition. Unless otherwise stated, those acronyms mean the variants thereof specified in Figure 3.6.

• For converting between RGB and LAB, I prefer to use the Image: Mode>Convert to Profile (Photoshops 6–CS), Edit: Convert to Profile (CS2) command, with Use Dither unchecked. Although Convert to Profile can also be used to go into CMYK, I use a simple Image: Mode>CMYK instead.

The reason for dropping the dither is philosophical; I'm not sure it has any real-world impact. By default, when converting between colorspaces, Photoshop introduces a very fine noise, or randomization, hopefully so fine that nobody can see it, yet sufficient to wipe out any banding or posterization, of which phenomena noise is an enemy.

Since we commonly go back and forth between RGB and LAB (and therefore are applying the noise twice), and since there's often a sharpening or contrast enhancement in between that could conceivably aggravate it, I'm a bit leery of putting it in in the first place, although I think it's a healthy thing when going into CMYK. So, I'd use Convert to Profile, but I'd turn off the dither, as shown in Figure 3.7. Also, Relative Colorimetric is the correct Intent setting for most conversions; your system may have Perceptual as the default. In the current state of technology, it won't affect your conversions between RGB and LAB, but you should change it anyway. Once all these fixes are made, they'll be with you until you change them back.

• If you intend to use any automated adjustment command (Auto Levels, Auto Contrast, or Auto Color, all found under Image: Adjustments) or the eyedropper endpoint tools within the Curves dialog box, you need to reset their defaults, which are pure white and pure black. Instead, as shown in Figure 3.8, double-click the white eyedropper icon in the Curves dialog, and enter new numbers of $97^L0^A0^B$. Then, do the same with the black eyedropper, using $6^L0^A0^B$. These settings will take effect for every colorspace, not just LAB.

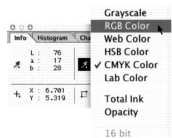

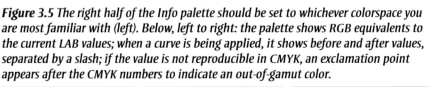

Figure 3.5 *The right half of the Info palette should be set to whichever colorspace you are most familiar with (left). Below, left to right: the palette shows RGB equivalents to the current LAB values; when a curve is being applied, it shows before and after values, separated by a slash; if the value is not reproducible in CMYK, an exclamation point appears after the CMYK numbers to indicate an out-of-gamut color.*

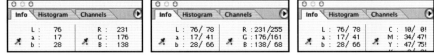

• Finally, a reminder that all curves in this book are shown with darkness to the right of the curve. It doesn't hurt to set it the other way, but you'd have to cope with shapes of the curves that are backwards in comparison to what's shown here. To change the orientation, click once in the gradient bar underneath the curve grid.

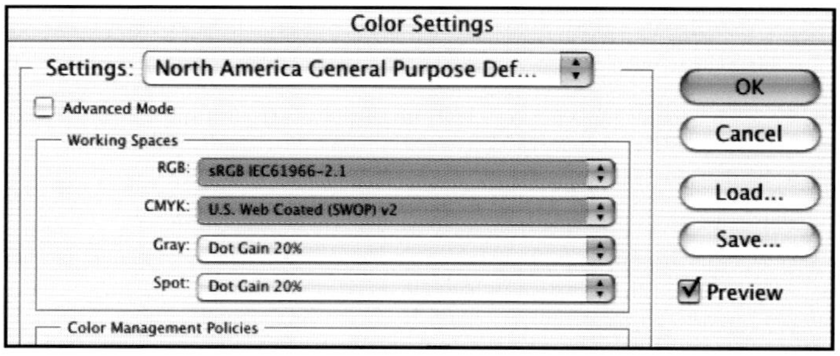

Figure 3.6 This book uses the above definitions of RGB and CMYK in computing color equivalencies.

The Recipe and Its Ramifications

Now that we're set up, and know the implications of the LAB numbering system, we can make more sense of the recipe and why and how it works—and we can also make its impact more specific.

The objectives of curve-based corrections in LAB are the same as they would be in any other colorspace: full range, no impossible colors, and allocation of as much contrast as reasonable to the main focus of interest. Let's consider these three points in turn.

• **Full range** means that the lightest and darkest significant points of the image get handled appropriately.

Most people call this step *setting highlight and shadow*. The task is a little more onerous in other colorspaces, where we generally have to be sure that the highlight and shadow are also *neutral*—in RGB, equal values in all three channels; in CMYK, equal magenta and yellow, a bit more cyan, with black irrelevant. In either one, if we decide that the highlights and shadows should be something other than neutral, we have to scratch our heads to come up with different numbers.

With LAB, which defines range independently of color, there's no such problem. If the L channel's numbers are good, you can set a

neutral highlight and shadow (or not) by establishing values of 0^A0^B in them.

On the other hand, there are workflow issues that don't exist in other colorspaces.

The strength of LAB is that it can make dramatic changes almost inconceivably quickly. If you have only one minute to fix an image, LAB gives the biggest bang for the buck. If you've got more time than that, there can be room for an argument, because LAB's strength is also a weakness.

Dramatic, instantaneous changes for the better, as in Figure 3.2A, are possible because the L channel is a bull, far more powerful than the black of CMYK, which is itself much more potent than anything in RGB. If there's something seriously wrong with contrast, the bull is strong enough to fix it, provided that you have a little tolerance for what may happen to the china shop of endpoints.

With one minute to fix an image, use LAB and hope for the best—with almost any original. If you have more time than that, first of

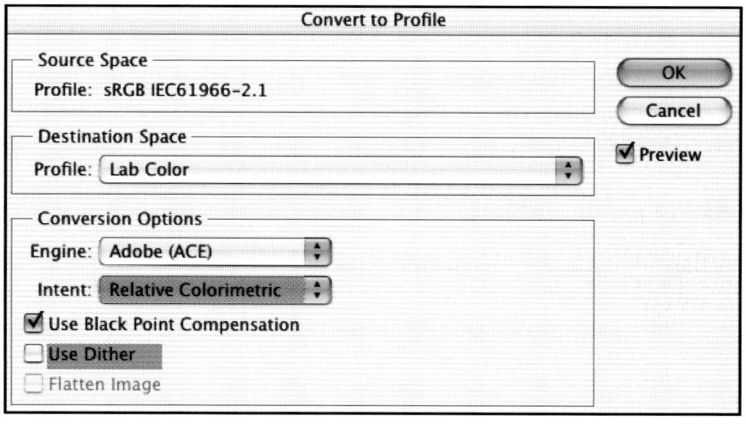

Figure 3.7 The Convert to Profile command permits easy moves back and forth between colorspaces. The highlighted areas should be changed from the defaults.

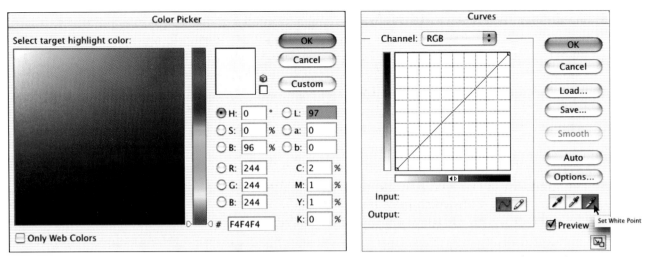

Figure 3.8 *The default endpoint settings should be changed to the values shown. To do so, double-click the Set White Point eyedropper (above right) and enter $97^L0^A0^B$ in the Color Picker. Then, set the black point to $6^L0^A0^B$ (below).*

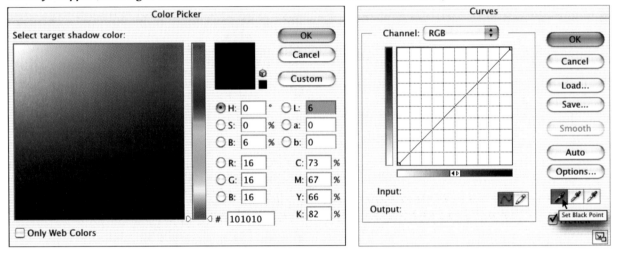

all there are a whole slew of images that RGB and CMYK will handle better. We'll discuss these cases in Chapters 6 and 7. But even if it's the type of image that LAB does well with, sooner or later it has to come back to RGB or CMYK for output. And when it does, it can almost always be made slightly better by optimizing the highlights and shadows in a way too delicate for a bull.

The real question is, therefore, have you budgeted time to finalize the correction in RGB or CMYK after you hit it in LAB? Because if you have, you should be more conservative with endpoint values. Blowing out highlights and/or plugging shadows is a disaster more easily accomplished in the L channel than by

any competitive method. If you're certain that you're going to be correcting in RGB or CMYK afterward, play it safe. Use 95^L and 10^L as your endpoints, and fine-tune later.

Lastly, remember that the purpose of endpoints is to maximize range while retaining highlight and shadow detail. If the lightest point of the image has no detail of any value, you may as well use 100^L for the light point. If you don't care whether the shadow plugs, you should use 0^L for the black.

• **No impossible colors** sounds easy, and sometimes actually is. If fortune is on our side, she provides something that we know ought to be a neutral color—a gray. If such an object is found, the recipe is like one for duck soup, much easier than in RGB and CMYK, where all channels interact in a more complicated way. But 0^A0^B is neutral, no matter what's up with the L.

Sometimes we find something that's approximately neutral, but we're not sure exactly. In Figure 3.1A, I'm not positive that the winding road is gray, but it certainly should be fairly close. Furthermore, we can rule out certain possibilities. I've seen roads that are gray, bluish gray, and brownish gray, but I'd sooner follow a recipe for jalapeño pepper ice cream than make the road greenish gray.

And we sometimes spot colors that can't be right. In Figure 3.1A, we know little about the exact color of the trees and the grass—except that they'd better both be some flavor of *green*. That means a negative A channel (more green than magenta), and a positive B, because all natural greens are more yellow than they are blue. In fact, we are so accustomed to greens being biased toward yellow that we might describe the top half of the A as being more of a teal than a green. Therefore, the B could actually be further away from zero than the A is, and we'd still buy the overall hue as a yellowish green. But if it's more than half again as far away, it's a greenish yellow, which isn't appetizing.

- **Allocation of contrast** was covered in Chapter 1. It's related to, but not the same as, setting range. The L channel curve has to establish light and dark points, yes, but beyond that it helps if it's steepest where the most important parts of the image live. It's not always possible. Often the image's entire range of tonalities is important, in which case there's nothing more to be done than establish the endpoints. Up until now, the images have been specially selected to avoid this inconvenience—each one has had the interest object in a small range, easily exploited in the L.

We'll move beyond that, and we'll move beyond canyons, too, ending this part with images of two subjects that not only strongly suggest LAB every time you see them, but demonstrate that the A and B channels should not always be handled identically.

LAB and the Greens of Nature

Photos dominated by greenery scream out for LAB. Cameras lack the sense of simultaneous contrast common to all human beings. When we see lots of similar colors in close proximity, we break them apart. Cameras don't, so we have to rely on a steeper A curve to avoid the flat look.

The thought process for any image starts with an overall gross assessment, without any numbers. Figure 3.9 is too dark, and there's not enough variation in the greens.

Next, a strategy meeting to decide how to attack whatever problems exist. The battle against Figure 3.9 requires no great generalship: we'll be fighting in LAB, because of its enormous tactical ability to drive a wedge between colors.

Summarizing the Setup Steps

Here's the executive summary of the steps you need to take before beginning to work with LAB in earnest. Fuller explanations of these steps are found in the text of this chapter.

- Be sure the eyedropper tool is *not* set to Point Sample.

- Configure the Info palette to read Actual Color on the left, and either RGB or CMYK on the right, whichever you're more comfortable with.

- (Optional) Change your color settings to the ones shown in Figure 3.6 if you wish to be able to access the same numbers when the book discusses translations between LAB and either RGB or CMYK.

- Disable the dither option in the Convert to Profile dialog, and verify that the Intent is set to Relative Colorimetric.

- Set the Auto Color endpoints so that they don't produce pure white and pure black.

- (Optional) Set the Curves dialog grid so that darkness is to the right and lightness to the left. If this is not done, the curves shown here will appear inverted.

Finally, a look at the existing numbers, to see if there's something nonobvious wrong with the existing picture. We look for things that we know or can surmise the colors of, and see whether the current values make sense. Most frequently, we're looking at the AB values only, but sometimes we're lucky

enough to know the L as well. For example, the top of the waterfall is the lightest significant object. If we assume that it's also white, we'd like to find a value of $97^L0^A0^B$. We put the cursor above at least three different points in the area, and mentally average the results to get an idea of how close we are. Here, remembering that parentheses denote a negative number, I find typical values of $89^L(1)^A(1)^B$. That's too dark, but the color seems fine—being off by only a point or two is inconsequential, and anyway these numbers are slightly green-blue, which surely might be right in this context.

The darkest significant area of the image, a deep shadow just above the waterfall, measures $9^L0^A0^B$, so close to the target of $6^L0^A0^B$ that we can leave it alone.

There are no known colors here, other than the trees themselves, which have to be some species of green. A patch to the right of and about a quarter of the way down the waterfall seems to be the yellowest part of the forest. It measures $60^L(20)^A35^B$; the darker, bluer leaves above it average $45^L(14)^A7^B$. Both are reasonable numbers, in keeping with the definition of natural greens developed in Chapter 2: strongly negative in the A, strongly positive in the B. They solidify our conclusion that there's nothing horribly wrong with the original color in this picture—it just needs to be pepped up.

The recipe calls for putting the steepest part of the L curve where the action is—

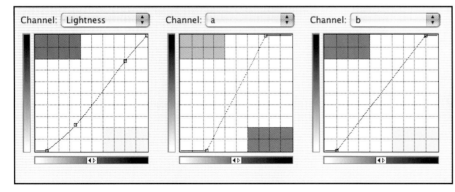

namely, the forest. Such a curve suppresses detail somewhat in the waterfall, which falls in the very lightest part of

Figure 3.9 *Images of greenery often need the A channel sloped more sharply than the B, as otherwise trees may become too yellow.*

the curve. That area has gotten flatter in the L curve, but the price is probably worth paying. The question is, what to do with the AB channels?

Figure 3.10B uses the same AB curves shown earlier in Figure 1.9, the shot of Anza-Borrego. However, I perceive it as too yellow in certain areas, and prefer Figure 3.10A, which has curves much steeper in the A than in the B, as shown in Figure 3.9.

You'll remember that I did almost the same thing with Figure 3.1. Indeed, emphasizing the green more and the yellow less is usually a desirable move with pictures of greenery—and one that can't readily be executed in RGB or CMYK.

If you're curious about the numbers, the extreme points of the forest that used to be $60^L(20)^A35^B$ and $45^L(14)^A7^B$ have become $73^L(37)^A44^B$ and $55^L(26)^A9^B$. There used to be 15 points of difference between the two areas in the L channel and now there are 18. There used to be 6 in the A and now there are 11; 28 in the B and now 35. These big changes create the separation between the two points that we were looking for, variation that RGB and CMYK can't find.

You can use different slopes for the A and B curves with any image, but greenery images are one of two major categories that really suggest a different approach. Greenery usually calls for more A than B. The other major category usually wants more B than A.

The Artificial Tanned Look

Just as we remember—or desire—forests to be greener than a camera sees them, so do we adjust our perception of the human face.

Every face contains what our society perceives as defects: wrinkles, blemishes, scars, and whatnot. So ingrained is our instinct to remove these in Photoshop that we often

Figure 3.10 Top, a version using the curves shown in Figure 3.9, which treat the A and B channels differently. Bottom, when the A and B curves are identical.

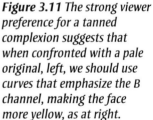

Figure 3.11 *The strong viewer preference for a tanned complexion suggests that when confronted with a pale original, left, we should use curves that emphasize the B channel, making the face more yellow, as at right.*

nowadays see pictures of 60-year-olds whose skin has been manipulated to be as smooth as that on the centerfold of *Playboy*. Without endorsing such an atrocity, one can agree that something should be done to tone down, if not eliminate, obvious aesthetic problems in a face.

Having voted in favor of revising reality by retouching, it's hard to make a case against doing it with color as well. We visualize people as being healthy; we associate health, perhaps, with outdoor activity; but for whatever reason we tend not to like overly pale or pink skin—even if that's the kind of skin the model has. The powerful preference for suntanned skin was first noted in print at least as early as 1951, by a Kodak scientist, David MacAdam. My own tests not only confirm it but go further: we tend to consider the suntanned skin more *accurate*. Some ten years ago, before digital photography became common, I ran tests with professional juries who were asked to determine whether a result in print matched the original film for color. I also used some ancient hardware to see how a machine felt about the same question. Man and machine tended to agree, except in fleshtones, where the humans consistently rated golden skin as being closer to the original than the machine believed, and in trees, where the machine persisted in believing that the original art's greens were dull, in spite of the popular vote that a more vivid green matched it better.

Our preference for suntanned skin is most pronounced in images of light-skinned Caucasians, who can roughly be classified as anyone with a natural hair color lighter than dark brown. Hence, we do the rainforest correction in reverse: the basic recipe, but a steeper B than A curve.

In Figure 3.11A, the lightest point known to be white is at the top of the woman's sweater. it averages $94^L(1)^A4^B$. There's no obvious dark point. The dark hair below the chin reads $23^L15^A10^B$ and the skin of the neck $82^L9^A12^B$. We prefer to measure skintone in areas other than the face because of the possibility of makeup that might throw our measurements off. And, in fact, the cheeks show up as pinker than the neck, with typical values of 12^A10^B at various values of the L.

This face is rather light, which isn't necessarily a problem. In fact, in Figure 3.11B the skintone has gotten somewhat lighter than in the original. The big issue is that the skin is pale and pink.

The L channel move lightens the shirt and the background in the interest of getting more snap in the woman's face. The A and B curves are both steepened, but the B much more, to emphasize the yellow component of the skin and hair, hopefully giving the complexion more of a golden feel.

You may notice a little extra trick here, an unadvertised departure from the recipe, caused by the annoying complication that the shirt didn't measure as neutral. Dealing with that issue will be the theme of Chapter 4, to which you may jump now if you wish. The next section of this chapter discusses why LAB corrections seem so realistic—because they work in a manner very like that of the human visual system.

Review and Exercises

✓ In Figures 3.2 and 3.3, which of the four separate moves appears to be the most significant? How would you have been able to predict this by looking at the original image?

✓ Make a new from-scratch version of Figure 3.1, on the assumption that the client has seen Figure 3.1A and comments that her only objection is that the grassy areas have become too yellow. However, she desires to retain the added blue effect in the background. How do you manipulate the B channel to accomplish this?

✓ What are the two categories of image discussed in this chapter that often require different slopes for the A and B curves?

✓ Why do we usually not want to set the endpoints of an image to their extremes, that is, to 100^L and 0^L?

A Closer Look

Politically insensitive jokes about vision deficiencies are exceedingly common in the publishing industry—normally with respect to visual (if not mental) impairments allegedly suffered by clients who offer certain questionable opinions about color.

Even the best of us can suffer this indignity. Once when I supervised a pressrun, the pressmen, offended by some of my decisions the previous time around, announced that the only reason I was being permitted to do it again was that Stevie Wonder had turned the job down and Ray Charles was out of town.

Calling other people blind is a frustrated reaction to what everybody knows: we all see color differently and therefore we all have different, sometimes radically different, ideas of what looks good.

One of the most irritating challenges we face today is determining what constitutes a visual match. So, without further ado, you are hereby assigned to make such a decision. In Figure 3.12, #1 is the original. Which of the other four do you think is the closest match to it? Which the worst?

This question isn't as weird as you might think, provided you visualize #1 as being held in your left hand while the rest of the book is held in your right. Say #1 is found in an annual report that uses much whiter paper than this book does, for example. In that case, we wouldn't be able to match it exactly. Nevertheless, we'd try to get close—and choosing the best way to do so is not as easy a call as this one appears to be.

I empaneled a jury of 12 to come up with the answer here and in several other sets of images. You probably won't agree with their verdicts, particularly (speaking of politically insensitive commentary) if you are female.

Justice may be blind, but this jury pushed the envelope. I decided to find out how bad it would be if clients were actually as visually impaired as many retouchers and printing firms claim. To that end, I empaneled a jury of the color-blind. And color blindness is almost exclusively a male phenomenon.

The Protanope-a-Dope Strategy

Color blindness is caused by a sex-related recessive gene. Men have only one of these genes, and the wrong one turns up around eight percent of the time. Women have two. If either one is normal, the woman has no problem herself, although if the other is bad, half of her male children will be color-blind. For the same reason, men are vastly more likely to be afflicted by the disastrous blood illness hemophilia. According to my wife, sex-related recessive genes also exist for dishonesty, shallowness, poor listening skills, and inability to keep a kitchen clean, although the scientific evidence to support her position is as yet inconclusive.

The term *color-blind* is misleading, because those afflicted have no problem seeing many colors. Plus, some individuals have more of a deficiency than others.

The overwhelming majority of the color-blind, including all members of my jury, are said to suffer from *red-green* color blindness. This, too, is a misleading term. *Magenta-green* is a more accurate description. I showed the jury the famous Kodak picture of Figure 3.13 and asked what color the woman's hat was. All but one responded "Brilliant red."

There are at least two categories (some say four) of magenta-green deficiencies. Part of my testing was a protanope-and-deuteronope-a-dope strategy aimed at finding which category each juror belonged to. It turned out that the class of deficiency played almost no role in the men's evaluations of the images.

If individuals with normal vision were evaluating Figure 3.12, I'd expect a unanimous vote for #3 as best match to #1, and #5 as worst match. I would also expect, but not guarantee, a decision that #2 is closer to #1 than #4 is. The color-blind jury, of course, felt very differently.

This was one of a series of similar comparisons, all produced in LAB. The black numbers were burned into each image so that they could conveniently be viewed on screen.

In each case, I created one alternative by horsing around with the L channel, while doing nothing to the AB. That version (#3 in this set) therefore matched the original for color but not for detail. If you're normally sighted, that's probably your favorite, because the color in all three alternatives is so abysmal. But we can't pretend that it actually matches.

There was always a second version (#4 here) where I flattened the A curve in just the same way that we've steepened it in every example so far. That is, the center point stayed the same, but instead of rotating the curve counterclockwise around it, I rotated it clockwise. This

Figure 3.12 *The question is, supposing that #1 is the reference image, which of the others is the closest—and which is the worst— visual match to it?*

Figure 3.13 *The common term for the affliction is the inaccurate "red-green color blindness." A group of such individuals nevertheless had no difficulty saying what color this woman's hat is.*

savagely reduced saturation along the magenta-green axis.

In a third version (#2 here) I flattened the A only half as much, but I also modestly flattened the yellow-blue B channel. And there was always a trick image, #5 here, that was meant to prove a point and about which I asked specific questions. The trick in Figure 3.12 is that #5 is identical to #4 except that the A has been inverted; that is, everything that tended toward magenta now tends toward green and vice versa.

The jury always hated the version that toned down the yellow-blue channel. If the colors of the image were relatively subdued, as in this river shot, the jurors tended to like the version that matched for detail but washed out the magenta-green distinction. In more brilliant shots, they started to abandon the version with the unchanged L in favor of the one with true colors. The only one in which the wrong-detail picture

decisively beat the magenta-green washout was this Kodak image, where the hat is apparently so red that even the color-blind take notice.

Since Figure 3.12 doesn't feature many bright colors, only three jurors voted for #3 as the best. Yet only three went for the normal winner, #4. The other six rated it an unusual kind of tie.

I asked for a description of the differences between #4 and #5. Half the jury replied that the two are identical. Five people saw significant differences, but only one offered a description reasonably similar to what a normally sighted person might say. The others made comments like "There is a saturation issue in the trees."

Those who thought there was something seriously messed up about #5, even without knowing what it was, naturally voted it as the worst. The other six did the conventional thing for the color-blind, choosing #2 as worst match.

Those who saw #4 and #5 as identical all voted the two of them as best match to #1. This makes sense. These people can't see the magenta-green component at all, so they completely ignored the flat-looking colors of #4. They only saw that #4 and #5 match the detailing of #1 and that #3 doesn't.

One of the most valuable attributes anyone working in the graphic arts can develop is the ability to predict how clients may react to certain images. Given what you know now about this color-blind jury, how do you think it felt about the Halloween image of Figure 3.14? Once again, image #1 is the reference version. You are supposed to say which of the other four matches it the best, and which the worst.

It Can't Be Put into Words

The variations here follow the same lines as before, with the numbers shuffled. Version #2 corresponds to #4 in Figure 3.12: the magenta-green component is sharply reduced by a severe flattening of the A. Figure 3.14's #3 is the equivalent of Figure 3.12's #3: the color is the same, but there's a slight change in the L, causing a variance in detail. The overall reduction in all color that was #2 in Figure 3.12 is #5 in Figure 3.14. #4 is the trick image, a specialized treatment of the A channel in which darker magentas, such as the man's jacket, were left alone, but softer colors, such as his face, were grayed out. And I asked for specific comments comparing #4 and #5 of Figure 3.14.

With a single exception, the jury made its normal choice for the best, splitting between #2 and #3. Version 5, with its diminution of the yellow-blue component that the color-blind see well, was, as usual, voted worst, but there were also several votes for #4 as worst, presumably from those who could see enough of the magenta component to have a serious issue with the man's face.

The group had a hard time evaluating the man's jacket in #4 and #5. Let me paraphrase some of their comments:

Figure 3.14 *Another challenge to the color-blind jury: assuming that #1 is correct, which of the other four is the closest visual match to it, and which the worst?*

- One is lighter.
- One is more saturated.
- One is punchier.
- One is browner.
- There's no difference at all.

As for the clown's costume, most of the jury correctly said that it was more yellow in #4. But, strangely, four jurors said that in #5, it had turned green.

Accordingly, if you're thinking of designing graphics with the color-blind in mind, you have to accept that there's a lot of variation in the group. These jury findings suggest that the best way to predict how a color-blind person would react to a picture is to convert it to LAB and apply the curve shown in Figure 3.15—the same curve that produced version #4 of the river scene and #2 of the Halloween image. Keeping that in mind, how do you think the jury voted in the simplest of all these sets, the vividly colored Figure 3.16?

The variant of #1 that uses this curve is #2, and that's the version that the color-blind think is a closer match than #5, which seems so obviously closest to the rest of us that we don't notice that its darkness doesn't quite match.

The jury always disliked anything that hurt the B channel, like #3 here, which is analogous to #2 in Figure 3.12 and #5 in Figure 3.14. I offered them a choice of poisons by generating #4, in which everything red has been wiped out (damaging the B channel as well as the A), while pure blues and yellows were left alone. The vote for worst match to #1 was a dead heat between these two versions.

Using Figure 3.15's curve is a good deal more accurate than just assuming that people are "red-green color-blind," or that they see a black and white world, but it has severe limitations, in that nobody has ever been both color-blind and normally sighted in the same lifetime. Thus, no eyewitnesses can be called.

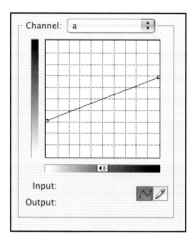

Figure 3.15 *The quickest way to approximate how a color-blind person might see an image is to apply this curve to the A channel.*

The conventional wisdom is that those who are deprived of one sense compensate by becoming more acutely sensitive in the others. Do we know how a symphony of Beethoven sounds to a blind person? Or whether deaf people are able to see things in Renoir that the rest of us cannot?

There was only one unanimous response to any of the questions. In an ocean shot, the water was not particularly vividly colored. I asked in which version it was the least blue. The question was difficult enough to stump some normally sighted persons. Every member of the jury nevertheless got it right. They appear to respond to blue at least as well as the rest of us do. Is it possible that they actually see it better?

Nobody has any trouble detecting that the clown's costume is less yellow in #5 than in any of the other variants in Figure 3.14. But what do you make of the strong minority sentiment that it's gone green? I myself don't see greenness, yet by measuring the numbers that make up the jacket, one can construct the argument that it is in fact more green. Can the color-blind be picking up a distinction that's too subtle for the rest of us? We can see colors that aren't even on their map, but is it not possible that the converse may also be true—that the green they are reporting is simply a color that's out of our gamut?

In that Kodak picture of Figure 3.13, are the color-blind just seeing a duller-colored fleshtone, or do they detect more yellowness as well? Do they see her hair as a brilliant yellow, rather than the mousy eyesore the rest of us perceive?

And What If God Is Color-Blind?

In 1994, in the first edition of *Professional Photoshop*, I showed examples of the work of a color-blind person who had been trained to correct images, by the numbers perforce.

That sideshow received more attention from readers than it actually deserved. But it was a measure of how we are fascinated by the way other people perceive things.

Some of us are fortunate enough to create images that need please only ourselves. But most professionals have to please a client, or a reader, or an art director, or somebody else whose preferences—and perhaps, whose ability to see certain colors at all—is in question. And everyone who has been there has found out the hard way about the consequences of these perceptual differences.

Granted, having a color-blind person evaluate your work is tough. If your client tells you that #2, #4, and #2 are the best matches to #1 in the river, Halloween, and hockey images, respectively, it can be a little disconcerting. Yet this is merely an extreme case of what happens every

Figure 3.16 *This image features more vivid colors than those found in Figures 3.12 and 3.14. How do you think the color-blind jury voted?*

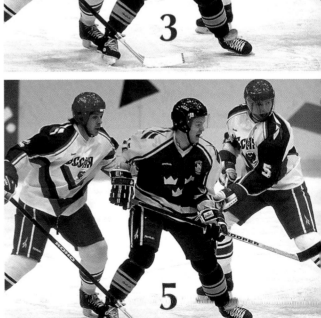

day in the real world. As people age, their corneas get yellower and they lose perception in certain shades. Also, many drugs, Viagra being a notorious example, affect color perception.

The questions listed just above the last subhead therefore are not just an academic matter. If people see color differently than we do, we can hardly blame them for acting on it. And who knows, perhaps they're right.

Having our own opinion about these matters is both natural and desirable, provided we don't take it too seriously. And, given the differences in human perception, we have to realize that

---

The Bottom Line

This chapter employs steeper curves in the AB channels, as in Chapter 1, but explores the possibility of having the two curves at different angles. The results are not readily duplicated in any other colorspace.

Pictures of trees and other greenery commonly benefit from having a steeper A than B. Pictures of Caucasian flesh, particularly light skin, usually become more attractive by emphasizing the B.

Enhancing color via the A and B channels looks very natural, because it approximates human visual response. A "color-blind" person, for example, is basically an individual who has limited or no ability to see the impact of the A, but is fully sighted with respect to the B.

---

the client is king. After all, in the land of the color-blind, the spectrophotometer isn't even the scullery maid.

At high noon in hell, when viewing conditions are the best, punishment is meted out to the unholy. Every color management consultant who has overhyped his technology or overrelied on the measurements of an artificial measuring instrument, is forced, day after day for all eternity, to argue and demonstrate the accuracy of his profiles—to a jury of the color-blind.

Perhaps it is all a matter of divine humor and spite. How do we know what is normal, and what is defective? Perhaps God Himself sees the clown's jacket as green, and has difficulty with magentas. Perhaps our own ability to distinguish these magentas and greens is a handicap, a cosmic joke, and not reality at all.

Fortunately, there's no need to decide this issue, not that it could ever be decided. We must merely concede that there is not necessarily a correct answer to the question of which version is the best match, just as there is not necessarily a correct answer as to which looks the best.

Magenta, green, yellow, blue. The wavelengths of light intrude upon us, enter our consciousness, trick us into thinking we see an absolute, laughing at us the whole while, knowing that for all the certainty we feel in our own perceptions, each of us is just a bit color-blind.

It's All About
The Center Point

The simple concept that a value of zero is a gray allows elimination of most color casts while pepping up colors at the same time. The center, or zero, point of the curve holds the key to correct color—and it allows separating the A and B curves into two halves.

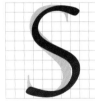

Some people just can't be happy with success. Michael Jordan was not content to be merely the greatest basketball player of all time. He wanted to play major league baseball as well, and invested a great deal of time and money trying to get it done. He was a fine fielder and a speedy baserunner. At the plate, however, in spite of his unquestionable athleticism, he never became more than an automatic out. Alas, he never figured out how to hit a curve ball. And so he went back to basketball.

There's some danger that the same may happen to you, if you're good at RGB and aspire to be good at LAB as well. We've taken some practice swings in Chapters 1 and 3, with some tempting glimpses of potential and tremendous raw power.

Chapter 1, however, was the equivalent of batting practice. Fast ball down the heart of the plate every time, canyon after canyon. Under those circumstances, even Michael Jordan was able to hit the ball out of the park with regularity.

Chapter 3 put the fast ball in different places and encouraged hitting it into different locations. Nevertheless, the idea was the same. Build the color variation, accent the detail, add sharpness. Again, severely limiting the type of pitch that we are exposed to.

We will now study two more varieties of image that may be thrown at us. First, everything we've seen so far has come in at the same speed: the colors may have been flat and listless, but there haven't been any obvious casts that our recipe would exaggerate. Second, we've always wanted to intensify colors. That leaves out the breaking ball: the image in which we want to intensify certain colors and not others.

Figure 4.1 *LAB excels at eliminating casts while simultaneously boosting colors. The corrected version moves strongly away from blue overall, yet the onion-shaped domes on either side of the tallest tower are distinctly bluer.*

We'll work on both types of image in this chapter, starting with the elimination of color casts, which requires that we identify certain colors as being wrong from the outset. That can be difficult, unless we are favored by the presence of a known color, ordinarily something neutral—like snow or ice. Prepare to get cold.

What Should Be Gray?

The brooding Trinity monastery at Sergiev Posad, 50 miles from Moscow, is the Russian Orthodox Church's equivalent of the Vatican. Reverend Sergius of Radonezh, who founded it in about 1340, played an important role in the consolidation of Russian power. Its historical importance is so immense that even the officially atheistic Bolshevik party named it a national landmark in 1920, and Stalin left it alone during his reign.

Figure 4.1A also illustrates another important attribute of Russian history: winters that are notoriously hostile not just to invading armies, but to photographers. The image is so lacking in velocity that we have to think of LAB to liven matters up. If we use the same curves seen so far, however, the thing will become even more unbearably blue-green than it already is.

All previous images have been easy because they were neutrally correct. Translated into lay English, that means that any areas that are supposed to be white, gray, or black are reasonably close to being just that. Retranslated for denizens of the LAB world, it means that these white areas measure reasonably close to 0^A0^B, which is how LAB defines neutrality.

Figure 4.1A is so obviously messed up that it tempts us to start swinging before the pitch arrives. Proper procedure is to take a few practice cuts, by measuring several points. This is particularly so when trying to assess neutrality; not every point we look at will be 0^A0^B. Some may appear neutral but should properly be blue, others red, and so forth. But our suspicions will be confirmed if *all* the points in nominally gray areas turn out to have cold values—negative numbers in the A and B.

That's how it turns out. The lightest significant point of the image is at the center of the snow nearest to us. I found this out by using the Image: Adjustments>Threshold command described in the box below.

The average of several points in that light area is $79^L(10)^A(5)^B$. The darkest significant point is under the bridge at left. Its average reading is $27^L(6)^A(15)^B$.

Interpretation: the endpoints should be more like 97^L and 6^L. So, the highlight is much too dark and the shadow much too light, and the image is very flat.

Colorwise, the AB readings show a green cast in the highlights, since in the lightest area the magenta-green A channel is considerably more negative than the yellow-blue B. In the shadow, the cast is apparently more of a blue-green.

The White Point and the Threshold

Before applying curves, we need to find the lightest and darkest points in the image. In Figure 4.1B, it's clear not only that the snow is the lightest part, but also that its lightest area is in the center of the image. Yet when working with something as flat as Figure 4.1A, it's often hard to pick out the light point.

Many people like to find light and dark points by using the Image: Adjustments>Threshold command. This command changes the image into two colors only, black and white. A slider controls where the break takes place: everything lighter than the slider point becomes white and everything darker black. To find the darkest points of an image, therefore, open the Threshold command and, with Preview checked, move the slider to the left until almost all the image is white. If there's any difficulty recalling what areas the dark parts now represent, click OK and then toggle back and forth between the original and the Thresholded image with Command–Z (Mac, Ctrl–Z PC). Reverse the procedure to find the lightest part of the image.

There must be some limited sunshine right above the tower in the center of the walls, because the sky seems to be darker and bluer at the edges of the image than it is at the center. On the right side, it reads $67^L(10)^A(10)^B$; at center, it's a lighter $75^L(8)^A(9)^B$. Other objects of interest: the wall itself averages $65^L(7)^A(7)^B$, and the golden dome of the 1770-vintage clock tower checks in at $55^L(6)^A4^B$.

Like Russian politics, these numbers can be hard to analyze, but the general trend is clear: the picture is too blue and too green simultaneously, but the green factor is worse. Is that what you would have guessed just by looking at Figure 4.1A?

Moreover, not just the detail, but the color is hopelessly flat. Notice that all the measurements fall between $(6)^A$ and $(10)^A$, a range of only five points. The B channel has a 15-point range, but that's understandable in context. The sky must be at least slightly blue, because its B value is more negative than the snow's. The golden dome logically has to have a big yellow component, so we expect a big positive B value.

The A, on the other hand, should have a narrower range, because there's nothing in the image that seems to have a particularly green or particularly magenta bias. But one way or another, both A and B need drastically increased contrast, and they both need to move toward warm colors, meaning toward more positive numbers.

The trick is figuring out how far to go. This opponent-color business is hard. Something that's less green in LAB is simultaneously more magenta. The walls are less green than the snow at the outset, but they both have negative A values.

Both being green seems improbable, but we have to pick an alternative. Walls neutral and snow slightly green? Walls slightly magenta and snow neutral? Or walls quite magenta and snow slightly magenta?

The answer—and mine is, the walls should be slightly magenta and the snow neither magenta nor green—will govern how we handle the key to any successful AB curving: the center point. Every AB curve done so far in this book has kept it constant: we rotated the curve counterclockwise, making sure that it continued to pass through the center of the grid. That's what we wanted, because until now all neutral colors have been approximately correct. We therefore wanted values of 0^A0^B—which are what's at the center point— to remain constant. But that isn't what we want now. Anything that's 0^A0^B in Figure 4.1A must be warmer, and should therefore be positive in both channels. We know this, because we know that objects that *should* be approximately 0^A0^B, like snow, are in fact negative in both channels.

And so, the curves can't go through the center point. Instead, they need to pass to the

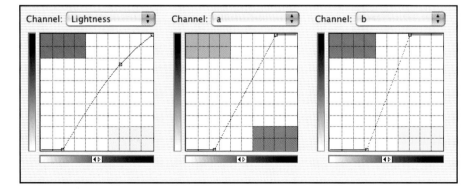

Info	Histogram	Channels
L :		R :
a :		G :
b :		B :
X :		W :
Y :		H :

#1	L : 67/ 78		#2	L : 55/ 60
	a : -10/ -2			a : -6/ 5
	b : -10/-15			b : 4/ 21
#3	L : 79/ 97		#4	L : 65/ 75
	a : -10/ -2			a : -7/ 3
	b : -5/ -2			b : -7/ -7

Figure 4.2 The curves used to produce Figure 4.1B. Note that the A and B curves both pass to the right of the center point, forcing the image toward warmer colors. Left, the Info palette shows numbers for critical areas of the image before and after the application of the curves.

Channel: Lightness   Channel: a   Channel: b

right, in the direction of warmer colors, away from green and toward magenta, away from blue and toward yellow. The only questions are how far to the right, and how steep.

Figure 4.2's curves leave the snow slightly on the cool side—typical values of $(2)^A(2)^B$. That's not intentional; I just couldn't get them all the way to 0^A0^B while retaining the straight-line shape. With images this weak and grainy, we can't expect to achieve perfection the first time, in LAB or elsewhere. So, if the format of this chapter didn't require me to stop here, I would take the image into RGB or CMYK and do further work.

It is, however, hard to imagine how we could have gotten even close to where we are now without using LAB. There's almost no color variation in Figure 4.1A, but the ultra-steep B curve of Figure 4.2 has provided quite a bit. The golden dome has gone from $55^L(6)^A4^B$, nearly neutral, to a healthy $60^L5^A21^B$, which is on the orange side of yellow, not the green side. More impressive, look halfway down the bell tower. It's framed by two of the onion-shaped domes of the 16th-century Assumption Cathedral behind it. Those start out bluer than the sky, at $47^L(6)^A(23)^B$. One would think that, with the whole picture moving sharply away from blue, they would lose color. They would, too, if this correction were done in any other colorspace. Precisely the opposite occurred here. They're now a regally blue $48^L6^A(48)^B$.

Summing up: the contrast-enhancing move in the L curve was introduced in Chapter 1, as was the general idea of steepening the A and B curves while keeping them in straight-line form. The notion of using different angles for each of the AB curves derives from Chapter 3, and pushing them away from the center is the novelty.

To verify that we can hit this change of pace again if we need to, we will leave the winter of the world's largest country to get even chillier in the world's second largest.

Its Fleece Was Green as Snow

Québec winters get every bit as nasty as the Russian variety, and so, apparently, do the shooting conditions, which would doubtless be blamed either on acid rain from the province's southern neighbor or discriminatory policies on the part of its western one.

Figure 4.3A isn't as bad as the Sergiev Posad image, but it still needs a big color boost. This time, the cast isn't bluish green, but rather greenish yellow.

The typical values are $88^L(4)^A13^B$ in the foreground snow; $91^L(3)^A14^B$ in the large icy tree at right center; $83^L(7)^A9^B$ about halfway up the sky, which gets slightly bluer higher up. These positive numbers in the B channel confirm the huge yellow cast. After all, the sky is now, ridiculously, more yellow than it is blue. It needs a negative value in the B. Also, as all the A numbers are negative, everything has a green tinge.

Before figuring out how to deal with what may be charitably called the color of the image, we get to take a cut at the contrast issue, which is a fat one right down the middle of the plate. The left side of the rock is basically one big reflection, which retouchers call a *catchlight* or *specular highlight.* Since such areas contain no detail at all, instead of going with a normal highlight of 97^L or so, we blow it out completely. The lower left corner of the curve moves to the right, until the Info palette reads a pure white, 100^L. Then, since the foreground trees and the sky are both light objects, we increase the slope of the curve in the light (quartertone) area to increase the contrast between them as much as possible.

Back to the color. We need to move away from green and toward magenta, so the A curve must pass to the right of the center point, as it did in Figure 4.2. In the last image's B, however, we were trying to push away from blue and toward yellow, and this time we need to do the opposite. So, the B

Figure 4.3 This winter scene lacks color generally but also contains a yellow-green cast. The corrected version creates a bluer sky and greener trees, and burns out the catchlight in the rock.

curve now needs to pass to the *left* of the center point.

Both AB curves have to get much steeper if there's to be any color in this image at all. Exactly how steep, and which of the two should be steeper, largely depends on how blue you want the sky to be. There's no right answer, but my curves are shown in Figure 4.4.

0ᴬ0ᴮ Isn't the Holy Grail

Trying to force absolute neutrality into areas that are only relatively neutral is a tactic that strikes out many color corrections. The icy tree, for example, is one of the things you might think should be set to 0ᴬ0ᴮ. So might the foreground snow. However, they can't *both* be. They don't measure the same color in Figure 4.3A, so they certainly aren't going to be the same after we've applied curves that are designed to enhance color variation. If we make the tree 0ᴬ0ᴮ, the snow will be on the blue-green side of gray, because its AB values are both lower than the tree's. But if the snow is set to 0ᴬ0ᴮ, the tree will be on the red side of gray.

It's also permissible to have neither one be neutral. Green is a really ugly color for snow, and anyway it makes sense to me that the icy parts of the tree could be slightly red, if the bark behind them is partially visible. So, I think we need to push the A away from green and toward magenta, and that we shouldn't stop until the snow reads 0ᴬ. I'm not sure that we need be so doctrinaire with the B.

New York children are taught to beware of yellow snow, but probably their mothers are thinking of something at least as yellow as Figure 4.3A. I wouldn't want that in an image, either. Slightly yellow, now that's a possibility. When I first tried correcting this image, I went for perfectly neutral, 0ᴬ0ᴮ snow. Doing that made me think the picture looked too blue, so I backed off. Instead of $88^L(4)^A13^B$, it's $91^L0^A6^B$: not green at all, but a little less than half as yellow as it once was. I suspect that the presence of a slightly red object as large as the icy tree forces our eyes into seeing the snow as more blue than Photoshop's Info palette believes.

Of course, if you want the snow absolutely white, you could just move the B curve farther to the left. Similarly, if you disagree with my decision to make the A curve steeper than the B (I was trying to make the background trees greener, and didn't want a super-blue sky), you could reverse it.

More interestingly, if you wanted to handle blues and yellows as separate items, rather than as equal partners in a single B enhancement, you could do that, too. It's one of the great attractions of LAB— but it requires a bit more complexity. In every image we've done so far, the "curves" in the A and B channels have actually been

Figure 4.4 The curves used to produce Figure 4.3B. This time, the B curve passes to the left of the center point, to move away from blue and toward yellow. Left, the Info palette during the application of the curves.

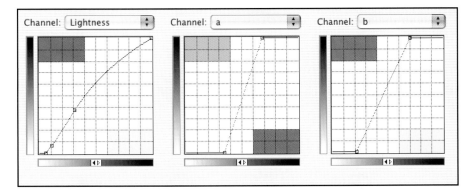

A

B

Channel: Lightness   Channel: a   Channel: b

straight lines, albeit at odd angles. They don't have to be, provided we remember that it's all about the center point.

A Walk in the Park

Heading almost due south from Québec lands us in a place with nearly as much significance in American history as Sergiev Posad has in Russian. Boston Common remains as beautiful an urban parkland as it was in Revolutionary days. To keep it that way, we're likely to want to increase color intensity, particularly in the greens and blues.

We won't be able to do a whole lot with the L channel. Unlike the last two originals, Figure 4.5A has a full range: the whites are white and the blacks are black. We may want to lighten the image slightly to give more range to the horse and rider, which are relatively dark, but that's about it.

Before steepening the AB curves, we need to think about the center point. The huge color casts of Figures 4.1A and

Figure 4.5 Applying the normal steepening curves to the AB channels of the top image causes the horse to become quite red.

4.3A are absent, but there's nothing obviously gray that we should be examining to see whether there's a cast at all. Instead, there are a slew of things that should be in the neighborhood of gray—but not necessarily completely missing all color.

Remembering that a perfect gray is 0^A0^B, that negative numbers represent green and blue, and positive ones magenta and yellow, let's check numbers. We needn't bother with the L values, which are irrelevant to whether something is gray. Also, we avoid looking at things that are nearly white or black, because they *can't* get very far off 0^A0^B.

We don't know for a fact that any of the following items actually should be gray, but they all need to be close, and perhaps we can detect a pattern. Here goes. Blaze on the horse's forehead: $(3)^A0^B$. Walkway just inside the open gate: $(2)^A2^B$. Column just outside the fence: $(2)^A2^B$. Trooper's hat: $(1)^A4^B$. His shirt: 0^A1^B. Street: $(3)^A(4)^B$. Plastic garbage bag at lower right: $(6)^A(16)^B$. Blanket underneath the saddle: $3^A(7)^B$.

We can start by forgetting the last two items. They may look gray, but they can't be, particularly the bag. With everything else so close to zero, those big B–negative numbers indicate that the objects must be navy blue.

Everything else is negative in the A, meaning it's all slightly biased toward green. I seriously doubt that it should be that way, and would

therefore move the A curve very slightly to the right of the center point, away from green and toward magenta.

The B readings seem more plausible. I'll buy that the street is supposed to be a bluish gray; everything else is either neutral or slightly yellow. So, we leave the center point alone, and produce Figure 4.5B.

The background looks better, but all I have to say is, that's a godawful stupid-looking horse. Horses are supposed to be brown, not orange. In Figure 4.5A, he averaged $51^L25^A39^B$—substantially yellowish red, yet not absurdly so. That got changed to $54^L46^A56^B$, totally out of hand.

What's needed is something like Figure 4.6, which intensifies the cool colors—note how the grass is greener and the sky bluer than in

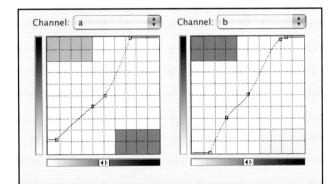

Figure 4.6 The AB curves of Figure 4.5 are modified by adding a center point to each and forcing the top half to be steeper than the bottom. This enhances cool colors while holding warm colors roughly constant.

Figure 4.5A—while not permitting drastic changes in the warm ones. To achieve it requires making real AB *curves*—not just angled straight lines.

Each curve has a top (cool) and bottom (warm) half, but to exploit them separately we need to take care with the center point.

So far, we've never actually clicked a point into the center of the curve grid, because there was no point in doing so: straight lines are easy to maneuver through any arbitrary center point we might choose. But now, that approach has to change. At least in the A, the bottom half of the curve needs to be flatter than the top, so that the magenta component doesn't get punched up as much as the green.

The A curve of Figure 4.6 looks very foreign to anyone accomplished with curves in RGB, CMYK, or grayscale. In those colorspaces, one would never do anything like what's happening in the lower left corner. Otherwise, anything that used to be a pure white would become darker, annihilating contrast.

In the A channel (and the B likewise), we yawn at such considerations. This curve shape merely means that 127^A, which is about as frequently seen in the real world as a batting average above 1.000, will become something like 110^A, which is no more common than a seven-run homer. You don't have to worry about these areas of the curve, because they're far out of the gamut of anything you'll ever output to, and even if they weren't, they cover brilliant reds and yellows, of which there are none in this particular photograph. The only areas of real concern in the bottom half of the curve fall in the first two gridlines beneath the center.

Each gridline is worth roughly 25 points in the A or B. So, the point one gridline down from the center point covers the horse, which started at 25^A. Since that point doesn't change from its original position, the magenta-as-opposed-to-green component of the horse won't change either.

The B curve in Figure 4.6 is a variation on the same theme. There's a point in the middle to prevent anything that was 0^B from changing to something else. The top of the curve is very steep, to accentuate the blues. The point two gridlines below the center covers the horse, preventing it from getting more yellow. As to why the bottom quarter of the curve hooks to the right, as opposed to the A curve, which hooks to the left, that question can be left to the philosophers. Nothing in this picture is more yellow-as-opposed-to-blue than the horse is. Therefore, provided that there's an equine locking point, it won't matter whether the lower left point is found higher up, more to the right, or on the moon.

A Horse Is a Horse, of Course, of Course

The move in this Boston Common scene—adjust the center point, adjust each half of the curve—is so fundamental to working in LAB that I'll end this section with a hanging curve ball: an image that's handled in almost exactly the same way.

Figure 4.7A is a better original than Figure 4.5A was, but otherwise is a horse of the same color, minus the horse, of course, of course. Trying for more intense blues and greens is a noble objective that has been achieved in Figure 4.7B, at the horrific cost of blinding the viewer with ridiculous reds.

Now that we've seen the wrong way to do it, it's up to you to do it the right way. There's no need to show it here, because the raw image is on the CD. It would be handled in much the same manner as Figure 4.6. That is, the AB curves would be divided in half, and the cool colors emphasized while the warm ones would stay close to their original values. I'll make some quick observations about how to do it, and terminate this part of the chapter

Figure 4.7 (opposite) It may seem tempting to try to enhance the greens and blues in the top version, but using standard straight-line AB curves creates radioactive reds (below).

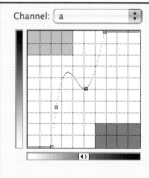

Figure 4.8 *A "correction" of Figure 4.7A that goes overboard in reducing the impact of the reds. Below, the AB curves that created Figure 4.7B. Left, the weirdly humped A curve that was substituted to produce the image above. The L channel is untouched in all three versions.*

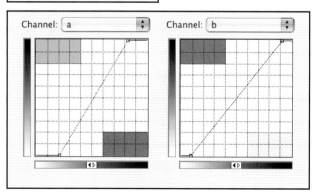

with a move that produces an even worse result than Figure 4.7B, if possible.

The brightest part of the house is $99^L 0^A 0^B$. Straight above the third red column is a cloud whose lightest area averages $98^L (8)^A (6)^B$. The column itself checks in at $80^L 29^A 13^B$. The deepest shadow, in the greenery to the left of the house, averages $5^L (3)^A 0^B$.

Interpretation: the house values sound right, but we don't really know. The clouds are greenish-blue, which seems highly doubtful. The columns are whatever they are. Knowing their values is helpful only insofar as we prevent them from becoming intensely red by planting appropriate holding points on the AB curves. And the shadow, slightly green, seems appropriate for the middle of a grove of trees.

Getting the right balance is an exercise left to you. You should probably leave the L channel alone. Important parts of this picture are light, dark, and everywhere in the middle, so we can't isolate them in the L. We therefore can't add contrast by steepening the affected part of the L curve, because the *entire* curve would be involved.

Figure 4.8 is a fanciful effort that shows what happens if you go several miles too far in suppressing the bottom half of the A channel: you can not only tone the red objects down, but actually turn them green.

It's also an advertisement for the second half of the book, because it reveals magic, LAB's sensational ability to make gross color changes in isolated areas without need for a selection or mask. Sure, you don't really want to have both the columns and the magenta plants in the foreground turn green. But suppose the unsupposable, that you did. Doesn't Figure 4.8 do it in a natural way? How would you do this in RGB, if you had to?

While that question hangs unanswered, you can read more detailed information on drawing color inferences in the "Closer Look" section, or, if you prefer, jump right ahead to the sharpening and blurring of Chapter 5.

Review and Exercises

✓ Prepare a new, from-scratch version of Figure 4.3, on the assumption that the client wants a bluer sky but does not want the foreground to get too yellow.

✓ Revisit the Death Valley image of Figure 1.1. All the colors were enhanced, which was probably good for most of the subject, but it made for a rather blue sky. Prepare a new version, applying a different curve to the B, that prevents the sky from getting as blue as it did in Figure 1.1B.

✓ Explain, in terms of positive and negative values in the A channel, how the curves of Figure 4.8 are turning the red objects in the image green.

✓ Starting with Figure 4.7A, prepare a curve in the B that turns the sky yellow. (Hint: it has to look like an inverted V.)

✓ How is the Threshold command used to locate light and dark points prior to writing curves?

A Closer Look

All images in this chapter depend on drawing the correct inferences about original colors. Previously, we were content to assume that everything was basically sound and that colors merely needed to be intensified. In the real world, images often have casts, sometimes slight, as in the Boston Common image of Figure 4.5A, sometimes gross, as in the two winter images in this chapter. Analyzing the AB values is often easy (after all, snow is normally white, and therefore somewhere in Figures 4.1 and 4.3 we need to find 0^A0^B, a value conspicuous by its absence in both), but sometimes it takes a bit of head-scratching. In the tropical image of Figure 4.7A, how did we know to choose the clouds as the reference white, rather than the building?

The answer has a lot to do with how digital cameras usually handle images, and offers an important lesson about workflow, not to mention a good segue into the gamut issues of Chapter 8. After discussing it, we'll have a look at a pair of even tougher judgment calls.

The White Point That's Not White

For over 500 years, graphic artists, with the notable exception of professional photographers of the late 20th century, have realized that using a full tonal range is indispensable for quality reproduction. In practice, this means that every work, with certain rare exceptions, has to have some significant area that's roughly as light as it can be while still holding detail, and a similar dark endpoint. The step of ensuring that such a point exists is often called *setting highlight and shadow*, or *setting the white and black points*. Whatever it's called, if the step is omitted, the picture can't be competitive. My classes regularly see well-known photographers, Photoshop experts, get thrashed by relative beginners because they don't realize the importance of setting these endpoints. And no wonder: back in the dark ages, when digital files only came into being when somebody scanned film, the photographer didn't have to worry about it. The scanner operator set the endpoints, and the photographer never even knew it was important.

Today, there's no scanner operator. It's *our* job now, but if we're not careful, a machine will set the endpoints for us. Photoshop's Auto Levels, Auto Contrast, and Auto Color commands attempt to do so, each in a slightly different way. Beginners frequently get good results with them, although professionals tend to shy away.

Consumer-level digital cameras are designed to give amateurs professional-looking results. Since amateurs don't realize that setting endpoints is essential, the camera does it for them. This is a great thing for those who have no idea what endpoints are good for, a dubious blessing for those who do.

Human scanner operators had their foibles. However, they could usually be trusted to determine whether the lightest point of an image was white or some other color. Many modern cameras, as well as the Auto Levels command, take the if-I-am-a-hammer-then-you-are-a-nail approach and force whiteness and blackness somewhere in the picture, no matter what.

Doing so may not be a conscious decision, but rather a result of a gamut limitation that's been referred to before and will be more fully explored in Chapter 8. Namely, in RGB and CMYK (but not, weirdly, LAB), absolute brightness is always white. The very act of adding color to it also darkens. Yet, if the endpoints are set extremely dark and extremely light, the picture becomes very high-contrast, which a lot of people like. In Figure 4.7A, a raw digital capture, the endpoints are 99^L and 3^L, more extreme than the 97^L and 6^L that I recommend in Chapter 3. In print, much of the house is blown out, because that 99^L was converted to, in many cases, $1^C1^M1^Y$ or something similar, difficult for presses to hold. Similarly, if the file had gone to RGB, the white areas would be around $253^R253^G253^B$.

Therefore, it's almost inconsequential to our

analysis of the picture that the light parts of the house measure as white, 0^A0^B or something very close. They measure that way because they can't measure anything else, granted how light the camera has decided to make them. Instead, we need to look at slightly darker areas to determine whether the picture is neutrally correct. It's not—but we'll get to that in a minute.

Figures 4.1A and 4.7A don't have this problem, because they weren't shot digitally. If they had been, instead of being images with severe casts, they would have been images with severe casts except in their lightest points, which would have been white.

An interesting experiment is to apply Image: Adjustments>Auto Levels to these two pictures. The following are likely to be your findings:

● The pictures look better afterward. The casts are cut roughly in half.

● But they still don't look as good as the versions that were generated with AB curves applied to the original, flat images.

● Furthermore, if you're looking to achieve something better than Auto Levels can give, you're better off forgetting the Auto Levels version and working with the original.

● On the other hand, there's much to be said for layering the Auto Levels version on top of the original at 50% opacity or so (or using the Edit: Fade command immediately after Auto Levels to reduce its impact). Either of these moves will increase contrast without wiping out the cast in the highlights and shadows—and may make subsequent correction easier.

The foregoing digression has workflow ramifications for those who force highlights and shadows into their images with a considerably more sophisticated crowbar, Photoshop's Camera Raw.

Camera Raw, introduced during the reign of Photoshop 7 and now significantly improved, requires a raw capture—not a JPEG—from certain brands of digital camera. It is strikingly analogous to the old-fashioned way of doing things: Camera Raw is the drum scanner, you are the operator. In a strange way, both are analogous to curving in LAB. And the same piece of advice applies to all three.

If your workflow is such that you truly intend to make a final file (or nearly so) without further correction, then obviously you shoot for perfect endpoints, whether using drum scanner, Camera Raw, or LAB.

If not, however, you should be more conservative. Particularly, in Camera Raw, adjusting the Exposure setting lets you

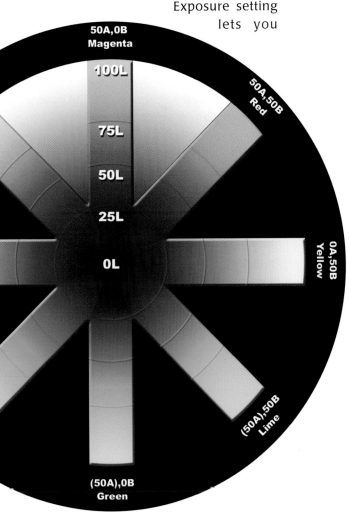

Figure 4.9 *The four primary and four secondary colors in the LAB channel structure.*

set the lightest point of an image to an arbitrarily bright level. Generally speaking, lighter is better, but if you go so far as to eliminate the natural color of the light area because you've made it impossible to fit within the RGB gamut, then it may look better for the moment, but it will be a pain to fix later.

A Tour with Eight Stops

Making the decision about the center point in LAB is like evaluating casts in any other color-space: we assume that everything is fine, until we discover colors that can't possibly be right, whereupon we apply corrective measures.

If you're accustomed to working in RGB, you probably think in terms of six colors: the three primaries, plus their three intermediate neighbors—between red and green is yellow; between green and blue is aqua (cyan); between blue and red is light purple (magenta). In addition to looking at near-neutral colors for evidence of a cast, an RGB expert knows, for example, that human skin is always red, but if it isn't exactly red then it's always to the yellow, never the purple side of red. Similarly, trees are green, but always to the yellow side, never the cyan.

Those accustomed to CMYK use a slightly different syntax that involves the same six colors in the same neighborhood arrangement. Red is seen as not just living between, but as a combination of, yellow and magenta colorants, and so forth.

LAB, however, has *four* primary colors, meaning that we have to be aware of eight different possibilities. The job is made more complex because the names usually given to the eight points on the star don't always correspond with the names we'd use ourselves for various colors. Plus, as the AB values get further and further away from zero, sometimes the color that they purport to describe changes, even if the ratio of the two channels stays the same. Finally, just to keep us amused, three of the points are wildly more important than the other five.

With these cautions in mind, let's commence the tour, for which a new guide appeared after the chapter was drafted. Beta reader Les De Moss was seeing enough potential in LAB that he felt he needed to make a better visual aid for his own work. He kindly offered it up for the book (and for the CD, so that you can have it on-screen as he does). It is gratefully reproduced here as Figure 4.9.

Les wrote, "Since reading the manuscript I've run into more 'canyon conundrums' than I can count. An entire series of aerial photos for [a large national realty firm] shot during the gray-brown-death of winter (sans snow) were all handled in LAB with great success. I am fortunate in that most of the images that hit my workstation are for clients who specifically request my work and are willing to pay for the time required. So unlike those in a one-minute correction environment, I have the luxury of jumping in and out of LAB/RGB/restroom as needed."

In Figure 4.9, the four primary colors are found at the ends of the horizontal and vertical bars. Our departure point is the top, and the tour proceeds clockwise.

- *Stop 1: A and B both sharply positive.* The first stop is also the most important one, because it defines the color we know as *red.* All human faces are red, and so is most Caucasian hair, because brown is a species of red. A host of other objects that are extremely important in photographic work are also red. When the B is the more positive of the two, it's an angrier, yellower red. When the A is more positive, it becomes a more sedate color. Human faces, except for the lightest-complexioned individuals and small children, have a more positive B. Red roses are more positive in the A.

- *Stop 2: A near zero, B sharply positive.* The sign at this station says *yellow,* but most of us would think of it as slightly reddish. A big B plus 0^A is a good color for blond hair. A banana has to have a slightly negative A to compensate for the redness. So does 100% yellow ink in CMYK, which is about the yellowest thing we can manufacture, at $95^L(6)^A95^B$.

- *Stop 3: A sharply negative, B sharply positive.* This is a critical area, because it defines almost everything that grows. Les uses the word *lime* to describe the color, which is close enough.
- *Stop 4: A sharply negative, B near zero.* The sign says *green,* but the advertising isn't enough to get any business. Anything that you and I would call green will have a heftily positive B. When the B is near zero, the color is more like what might be called *teal.* And that's a color we just don't visit very much. I can only think of one image in this book that uses it, a car we'll be working on in Chapter 10.
- *Stop 5: A and B both sharply negative.* If you liked the original Sergiev Posad image of Figure 4.1A, you'll be interested in this stop. But cyans are rare in nature, outside of water in a tropical setting. The pool in Figure 4.7 is cyan. Good luck finding another example.
- *Stop 6: A near zero, B sharply negative.* Here are found all things blue, so it's a most important stop. Bear in mind that blue is a weak area in most output devices, especially printing presses. Also, when blue is important to an image, a cyanish blue is usually preferred to a purplish one. Therefore, in most cases we prefer a slightly negative A to accompany the strongly negative B. A slightly positive A helps when trying to achieve the color known as royal blue.
- *Stop 7: A sharply positive, B sharply negative.* Eggplants, grapes, "red" wine, and precious little else live here in the purple/violet zone.
- *Stop 8: A sharply positive, B near zero.* These are magentas, a common color in flowers but not in many other objects.

Finding the Impossible Color

We close with three examples of how to identify a cast, and how far to go in correcting it. We've already seen the first one—Figure 4.7A. The cast may not have been obvious, so let's reexamine the picture. Certain components may seem plausible, others conceivable, still others out of the question. When we have this information, we're in a position to act.

We've already found that the endpoints are so extreme—99^L and 3^L—that anything much different from 0^A0^B would have been impossible in the original RGB file. Therefore, we pay no heed to the brightest area of the house or the darkest areas in the trees.

And, with the exception of these endpoint areas, the L value is also irrelevant. We're looking only at color, and the L doesn't have any. So, from now on, just the AB values concern us.

The color of the house's columns is irrelevant, too, because we have no clue what it should be. In other words, we may not know much about the specific blue of the sky, but we certainly know it can't be orange. The columns appear to be some kind of red, but we have no information suggesting that they couldn't be more orange or more purple.

Here, then, are some key areas, with comments as to whether they make sense. The values are always averages of several readings in the same area.

- *The sky.* Left side, $(5)^A(35)^B$; center $(8)^A(25)^B$; right side $(4)^A(33)^B$. All these combinations are acceptable: they're all just to the cyan side of blue, exactly what we'd expect in a sky. The center appears slightly less blue, and more cyan, than the sides. This natural variation also makes perfect sense. The entire sky would have to be a radically different color before we could conclude that it was wrong.
- *The lightest parts of the clouds.* Right side, $(7)^A(7)^B$; large cloud above left side of house, $(8)^A(6)^B$. Light parts of clouds are usually white, but it's certainly possible that they're picking up some of the background sky—but if they did, they'd be blue, not cyan, not greenish cyan. Therefore, the B values don't seem happy but they're at least conceivable. The A is definitely wrong. It needs to be closer to zero.
- *The trees and lawn.* Trees on both right and left sides average $(20)^A34^B$. The lighter parts of the lawn average $(14)^A22^B$. Again, just what we expect: midway between yellow and "green." These numbers are a bit more yellow than usual,

Figure 4.10 *It's hard to evaluate this original, because the face is potentially correct and the background color is unknowable. This woman's hair, however, isn't dark enough to be black or light enough to be blond. Therefore, it must be brown—but it measures as neutral. This is the telltale sign that the image has a cast favoring the colder colors.*

so we should try to avoid tilting toward an even more positive B. For the time being, though, we have no reason to doubt these numbers.

- *The pool.* It's $(27)^A(17)^B$, on the green side of cyan. I could accept that it might be even greener, depending upon lighting and how much chlorine is in the water; but I also could see it more blue. So, again we can't conclude that anything is wrong.
- *The concrete walkway around the pool.* I'd guess that it should be neutral, but if it's anything else, it's probably a warmer color. And, some concrete is a bluish gray, although I doubt that here. The current value is $(3)^A0^B$—a *greenish* gray. I think that's impossible.
- *The roof.* This type of tropical roofing is distinctly orange. Here, it's 23^A30^B. As the B is more

positive than the A, it is in fact on the orange side of red. Maybe the A should be even higher, or the B lower, but we can't prove it.

- *The reddish plant in the foreground.* A poinsettia might be a bright red—A and B equally positive. All other plants tend more toward magenta, like the 30^A20^B found here.

The foregoing discussion makes image analysis seem like a bigger deal than it is. In real life, experienced people wouldn't look at all of these areas, because they would know that only certain places have the potential to be problems—usually near-neutral colors. The idea of measuring the sky to see whether it's too green sounds good, but another way is to simply open one's eyes. The clouds and the lip of the pool are another story. No matter how good our monitors are, we can't evaluate these colors accurately. A phenomenon known as *chromatic adaptation* causes our eyes to adjust to the light that's hitting them—and makes us perceive things that are nearly gray on the monitor as being gray in fact. That's why we need to check the Info palette.

The Whole Is More Than the Two Halves

As previously advertised, I'm not going to provide curves for Figure 4.7A, but here's how to proceed. The A curve should look like the lower right quarter of a circle. It should pass not through the center point of the curve grid, but to the right of it, eliminating the negative A in the clouds and the lip of the pool. It needs to climb steeply in the top half because even if we didn't want the trees to be greener, the center-point move has pushed them toward magenta, and we need to compensate. And it needs to be relatively flat in the bottom half, because if everything that's red gets intensified, the picture will look like it does in Figure 4.7B, which is to say, ridiculous.

The B curve might look just like the A. Its bottom should stay relatively constant because otherwise the greens and reds will get too yellow. Maybe you should move the center point to the right, so as to eliminate the blue component of the clouds, but maybe not. You have to decide what looks best. Similarly, you must make a decision as to whether to steepen the top half of the B curve as much as the A. It will depend on how much you want to intensify the blues of the sky and pool.

Good luck with that image. Let's move on to another, one that represents one of the most significant areas of imaging.

Human faces are not ordinarily thought of as being like canyons. Nevertheless, they share the critical element that makes canyon corrections so successful in LAB: a short range in all three channels. Unlike canyons (and, for that matter, almost any other kind of picture), in faces we usually aren't enthusiastic about bringing out details, for fear they're skin imperfections that the subject would not be keen on emphasizing.

Like canyons, however, we invariably want to bring out color variation. Just as we wanted to see variation in the color of the soil of Figure 1.1—variation that a camera doesn't see—we want to break apart the colors of the face in Figure 4.10, letting us imagine rosier, healthier cheeks, and redder lips, than the camera picked up.

As there are few other important colors, we can get by with simple straight-line AB curves. The question is, should they pass through the center point? Which numbers should we examine to find out?

We have no clue about the color of the background. The face, being red, needs to be positive in both A and B. Faces can occasionally have equal AB values, but not this one. How do we know that?

I've never met this woman, so I don't know her hair color. Nevertheless, even if the color of this original is all wrong, the hair is too dark for her to be a blond. Only people with light hair have complexions light enough for the A and B to be equal. For everyone else, the B is higher.

The typical reading in the arms and neck is 10^A12^B, a little more neutral than usual. But the model seems to be in shadow, which could explain it. We don't put much faith in readings in the face itself because she is wearing makeup, which could disguise the measurements.

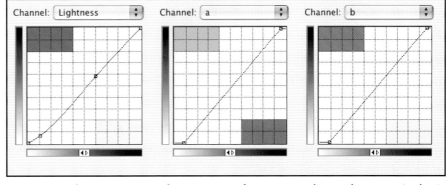

Figure 4.11 *These curves move the image away from green and toward magenta in the A channel, away from blue and toward yellow in the B.*

Figure 4.12 (opposite) Top, a copy of the same original that opened the book as Figure 1.1A. Bottom, after application of the more complex set of curves at right.

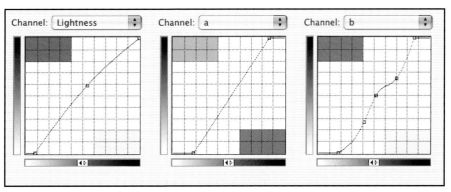

Similarly, we guess that the dress is black, but we don't measure it on the shoulder, because it's thin enough that we could be picking up the skintone underneath it. Lower than that, we find $15^L0^A(4)^B$, not quite black, but a very dark blue. It's suspicious, but not strange enough to assume that it's wrong.

The dress is significantly darker than the hair, though, which gives us another clue. I noted before that this woman can't possibly be blond. If the hair is lighter than the dress, then it can't possibly be black, either. And she is clearly too young to have gray hair.

If the hair isn't yellow and it isn't black and it isn't gray, then it has to be some kind of brown. Brown is a red—positive values in both A and B. But the B value must be higher—even if she's what is inaccurately called a *redhead*. Hair always has to fall to the yellow side of red, never to the magenta side.

In the lightest areas of the hair on the left of her face, I find typical values of 1^A6^B. On the right side it's 0^A2^B. That's the impossible color that makes it mandatory that the curves not cross the center point. If it is

Figure 4.13 This reduced-size version, split between Figure 4.12B (left half) and the earlier correction, Figure 1.1B, shows that failing to compensate for the neutral color produced a cast, an overly cool image.

The Bottom Line

When an image has a cast, we can still use straight-line AB curves to accentuate colors. The cast can be eliminated by making the curves pass not through the center point of the grid but rather to the right or left as needed.

The center point is also critical when trying to accentuate one side of an AB curve more than another. Provided there's a holding point to protect the center, it's easy to write a curve that accentuates greens but suppresses magentas, for example.

Deciding whether an image has a cast is probably the most difficult task in color correction. It involves taking several measurements of each significant area of the image and deciding whether the current values are plausible.

true, the hair is no more magenta than it is green, and that simply cannot be. Yet, if we make the A value higher, we have to do the same to the B, because it can't be that the hair is more magenta than it is yellow, either. There is some question as to how far to the right of center the curves have to pass, but you can make that call yourself. The curves that made Figure 4.11 are one possibility.

The Return of the Canyon Conundrum

This concludes a multiple-chapter study of how simple steepening curves work in LAB. Now that we are more familiar with inferences about color and with different shapes, it makes sense to revisit the very first canyon we worked on. So, back to Death Valley, to see if more nuanced methods can get a better result.

Figure 4.12A, therefore, is an exact copy of Figure 1.1A. Back then, it was an impressive display of LAB's ability to drive colors apart. However, we took for granted that the original picture was neutrally correct, because we hadn't covered what to do if it wasn't. We will now examine whether that assumption was warranted.

Remember that this is a most peculiar picture: a shot of clay soil with improbable patches of green and purple, visible on the right side of the image. Right below the purple is a largish patch that looks kind of white. It averages $88^L(4)^A(4)^B$. A similar area on the left is $88^L(6)^A(2)^B$.

In 99.997 percent of all pictures, finding cyan or cyanish green dirt would end the discussion: we would hit the curves right away. But here, when certain parts of the soil are known to be green, we have to keep looking.

The sky is $73^L(3)^A(36)^B$, barely on the cyan side of blue, very normal values for a clear sky. The highest background hill, however, is suspect. Its top reads $62^L2^A3^B$, reddish, but just below it is what seems to be a purplish stripe at $61^L1^A(1)^B$. Furthermore, the foreground ledge, which I would take to be some kind of yellow, is actually

$80^L0^A1^B$, measured at around the same horizontal location in the picture as the top of the hill.

I don't buy any of this, except for the sky. All these near-neutral colors need to get warmer, which is to say more positive in both A and B. Those suspiciously green patches of soil have now been exposed as the frauds they are.

The center points must move to the right. There's no correct answer as to how far, but my best guess is that the above-mentioned green soil is actually gray. So, the curves in Figure 4.12 push it to 0^A0^B.

And, there's one last twist. This image is supposed to advertise the very unusual greens and purples in the soil. You may feel, as I do, that an overly blue sky would detract from these subtle hues. So, I used the B curve to suppress the blue side. Figure 4.12B's sky is therefore more purple than Figure 1.1B's, because the magenta-green A channel plays more of a role. If you don't like the effect, you could modify my curves to keep the sky as blue as it was, or even make it bluer.

Figure 4.13 is reduced so that we can get a better feel for how the techniques shown here differ from those of Figure 1.1. In evaluating, remember that each half used the same L channel. You may feel that the left-hand version is too purple. I don't. I think it's unlikely, however, that we'd disagree about the right half. It's too greenish blue for sure. The only question is how far to go toward the left half. And fortunately, LAB leaves that decision to you.

Similarly, you may not approve of the purplish sky in the left half. If you'd like to keep the same purple hills but pair them with the blue sky found in the right half of the image, all you have to do is use the curves of Figure 4.12, but omit the point in the B curve that's suppressing the blue. More magic! Just as we could "select" the red plants of Figure 4.7 and turn them green, we can "select" this sky and turn it whatever color we want, without any mask, without any magic wand, path, or lasso.

5

Sharpen the L, Blur the AB

Focus is a question of luminosity variation, not color. Noise often is color only, with little change in luminosity. Separate channels for color and contrast make LAB the first choice for blurring imperfections away, and often the best choice for sharpening as well.

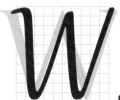orking in color in LAB, some would have you believe, is like rocket science: a discipline of its own, requiring extensive study, difficult to comprehend, full of potentially explosive hazards.

Certain parts of it, however, are no such thing. They're easy, powerful, and more effective than doing the same things in CMYK or RGB. Many people blur or sharpen in LAB, even if they don't feel comfortable with it otherwise. The reasons LAB has horned into this particular area of people's workflows are not exactly rocket science, but to help us out in uncovering them, my friends at NASA's Johnson Space Center have donated Figure 5.1, a picture of, yes, a rocket scientist.

Photographs taken in subpar lighting conditions have always had problems with noise, but the noise in film is as the Wright Brothers' airplane to the Galileo spacecraft in comparison to that of today's digicams. Indeed, I am convinced that certain camera manufacturers have squadrons of engineers whose sole job it is to ensure that the blue channel of each capture should be covered with random pixels to the point of near-obliteration, as shown at high magnification in Figure 5.2A.

This picture is loaded with such garbage, which the cognoscenti call *noise,* not just in the blue channel, but in the more important red channel. The noise would provoke some image technicians to launch one of Photoshop's many blurring filters, any of which may tone down the damage and all of which will harm contrast if applied to any channel in RGB or CMYK.

The space-age method of eliminating the colored noise is to convert the image to the colorspace that keeps color and contrast in separate compartments. The B, which governs the blue versus yellow component, almost always has the most noise, but Figure 5.3 shows that the A (magenta versus. green) has quite a bit as well.

The noise was so all-pervasive that I couldn't use a big enough Filter: Blur> Gaussian Blur without destroying every color transition in the image. Instead, I tried Filter: Noise>Dust & Scratches, with an appallingly large Radius of 7 in the B and 4 in the A.

That sufficed. And having thus separated the noise stage from the image capsule, I reentered the RGB atmosphere. The resulting blue channel in Figure 5.2B is almost celestially crisp in comparison to its predecessor.

The Second Stage Is Sharpening

Blurring, blending, or even retouching the A and B works wonders in a variety of noisy environments, and as the principal weapon against prescreened originals—which are only a more extreme version of Figure 5.1.

It should be made clear up front, however, that many users get unduly frazzled by seeing *any* kind of noise. The yellow channel of CMYK, the blue of RGB, and the B of LAB don't have nearly as much impact on the picture's detail as other channels do, so we can get away with a lot, although certainly not as much as in Figure 5.2A.

Nevertheless, blurring the A and B is so much more effective than any other known method that it has to be part of the arsenal of the serious retoucher.

The corollary of blurring the A and B is sharpening the L. It, too, has become entrenched in the professional community, although sometimes for the wrong reasons. It first became widely adopted in the early-to mid-1990s, before digital photography and before anybody owned a desktop scanner capable of professional-quality work. A new technology called Kodak Photo CD seemed to offer considerable potential at an attractive price. The color quality was fine, but the big knocks against the technology were that the images were too soft and lacked weight in the quartertone.

LAB seemed to offer the perfect solution. There was no need for AB maneuvering. Instead, everything was applied to the L only: a quick curve to darken the quartertone, followed by sharpening, normally with Filter:

Figure 5.1 *At Mission Control in the Johnson Space Center, the lighting conditions may be just what the director of flight operations needs, but they're tough on digital cameras. This image is full of colored noise.*

Sharpen>Unsharp Mask, occasionally with more primitive methods.

If you weren't in that field of work back then, it's hard to imagine the state of the world. Apply a curve to a large file, and you could go out for a sandwich while Photoshop processed it. Try adding even a single layer to such a file, and you'd have time to add a bottle of wine plus dessert, and the progress bar would still be humming along by the time you staggered back to the office.

I thought at the time that there were two main reasons why sharpening the L became so popular. First, it appeared to be technically superior to sharpening in RGB, because it eliminated color shifts, the L having no color capable of change. Second, in the days of turtle computing, LAB's quickness was a very big deal. It's less strain on the system to sharpen one channel as opposed to three, particularly when standard computers have 8 megabytes of RAM and extra scratch disks cost $1,000 per gigabyte.

As the years went on, both factors vanished, or they appeared to. First, people became aware of a workaround that would prevent color changes when sharpening in RGB: a blending mode called Luminosity, which could be accessed in one of two ways.

The easier, if less flexible, approach is to apply Edit: Fade>Luminosity immediately after sharpening in RGB. A safer approach is to Layer: Duplicate Layer, do the sharpening on the top layer, and then, in the Layers palette, change the mode to Luminosity.

Second, computing power ceased to be an issue; nowadays, unless the file is extremely large, the sharpening is almost instantaneous.

Figure 5.2 *The blue channel of the RGB file that created Figure 5.1 is loaded with digital noise (above). Trying to eliminate it in RGB or CMYK often causes a loss of detail. Below, a new blue channel that was created by converting the file to LAB, applying the Dust & Scratches filter to the B channel, and then reconverting the file to RGB.*

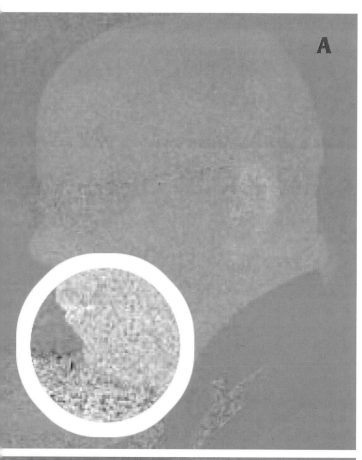

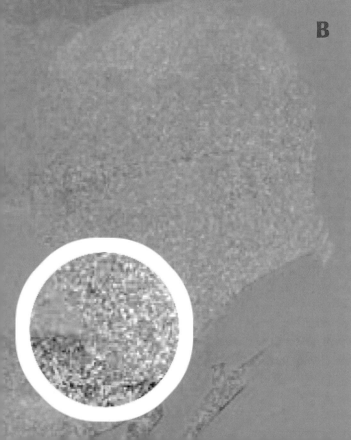

Figure 5.3 When Figure 5.1 is converted to LAB, noise is apparent in the A (above, greatly magnified) and B (below) channels. The areas within the circles have had a curve applied to make the noise more obvious.

Therefore, one would think that people would be less inclined, as time went on, to sharpen in LAB. Yet online groups featured a substantial number of users who stubbornly clung to the idea of sharpening the L because they said they got better results. I thought this claim of superiority was an old wives' tale, personally.

In the graphic arts as in life, old wives can be smarter than old husbands think. It turns out that L sharpening *is* sometimes better. It almost always beats a straight sharpen in RGB. In most cases it's equivalent to RGB/Luminosity, but a lot of times it yields a superior result. It's better than sharpening overall in CMYK, although some images are optimally handled by sharpening individual CMYK channels.

In the second half of this chapter, we'll go into why all this is so. For the moment, we'll stick with basic principles. Blurring to reduce noise works so much better in LAB that it's worth converting out of RGB to do it. I am not convinced that it's worth converting to LAB if you plan to do nothing but sharpening there; but if you are already there and plan to sharpen the image overall, LAB is where you should do it.

Selecting a Single Channel

Sharpening and/or blurring are sometimes applied to the entire file. Frequently, however, they have to be applied only to certain channels, particularly in CMYK. In LAB, the operative word is not *frequently* but *always*.

To limit yourself to a single channel, the keyboard shortcut is (and before going on, please read the box on the opposite page) Command plus the number that corresponds to the channel. In LAB, Command–1 would select only the L, Command–2 the A, and

Command–3 the B. Command–~ (tilde character; U.S. English keyboards only) restores the composite image, while the tilde minus the Command shows the composite image while leaving only the single channel active.

The sure way of seeing what's going on is to bring up the Channels palette (Window: Channels). The eye icon beside each channel indicates that we can see it; if the channel is also highlighted, we can work on it. Usually, we either have one channel highlighted (right side of Figure 5.4) or all of them, but occasionally we need to work on two channels simultaneously, as in the left half. To accomplish that, we Shift–click on the right of the name of each channel we wish to work with.

Figure 5.5 is a sobering reminder of how difficult rocket science is. These decorations were placed at the entrance to the Johnson Space Center on the occasion of the disintegration of the shuttle Columbia, with the loss of all its crew. What we see is heavily cropped. The entire uncropped image is too sad to print here: the wreaths and other memorials extend hundreds of feet away from the sign.

The picture is useful first as a reminder that Photoshop is not the most important thing in life, and second because it shows several sharp transitions between colors, such as when the brightly colored flags butt the background. We'll take a close look at what happens when we blur the AB and, later, when we sharpen the L.

The left half of Figure 5.4 shows the A and B channels active, the L unavailable, but the entire image visible. With that setup in the Channels palette, I hit Figure 5.5A with a Gaussian blur, Radius 3.0, thus blurring only the AB. The result is Figure 5.5B, which looks nearly identical to Figure 5.5A.

Now, a 3.0-pixel blur is not what one would call subtle. To prove it, I changed the palette to the setting on the right of Figure 5.4,

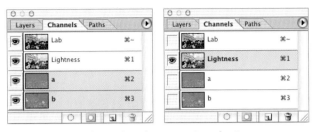

Figure 5.4 *The Channels palette permits selecting one or more channels for alteration while other channels are locked. The eye icon indicates that a channel is visible on screen; the highlighting shows that it is open for alteration.*

On Keyboard Shortcuts

Photoshop operates almost identically on any platform. Keyboard shortcuts using the Macintosh's Command (Apple) key are accessed by the Ctrl key under Windows; the Windows Alt is Option in Mac parlance. Starting now, only the Mac sequence is given. That's how I've been doing it for more than ten years.

In early 2005, caving in to political correctness, I changed over in my magazine articles and in early drafts of this book to what seemed to be the more equitable Command/Ctrl and/or Option/Alt whenever those keys were referenced.

It didn't work. Macintosh users wrote in saying I didn't know my shortcuts. The Macintosh has a Control key that has nothing to do with the Windows Ctrl. They were reading my Command/Ctrl to mean Command *plus* Control. Back to the drawing board.

Out of ideas, I presented the problem to my Applied Color Theory list and asked for suggestions. It was clearly a hot-button item. The topic drew about 60 responses and a lot of acrimony. Knowing that both topic and author can be difficult to follow, the group's consensus, with some dissent, was that anyone who has trouble translating keyboard shortcuts in their head is probably reading the wrong book. I agree.

Five years ago, most readers would have been Mac users, but I suspect that today Windows holds the majority. I would therefore use the Windows shortcuts, except that Ctrl is ambiguous to the Mac side, whereas Command is unambiguous to Windows users. So, until now I've given both sets, but in the interest of readability only the Mac shortcuts are in use hereafter.

In view of the controversy, the entire Applied Color Theory list thread, including my own comments, is on the enclosed CD in this chapter's folder.

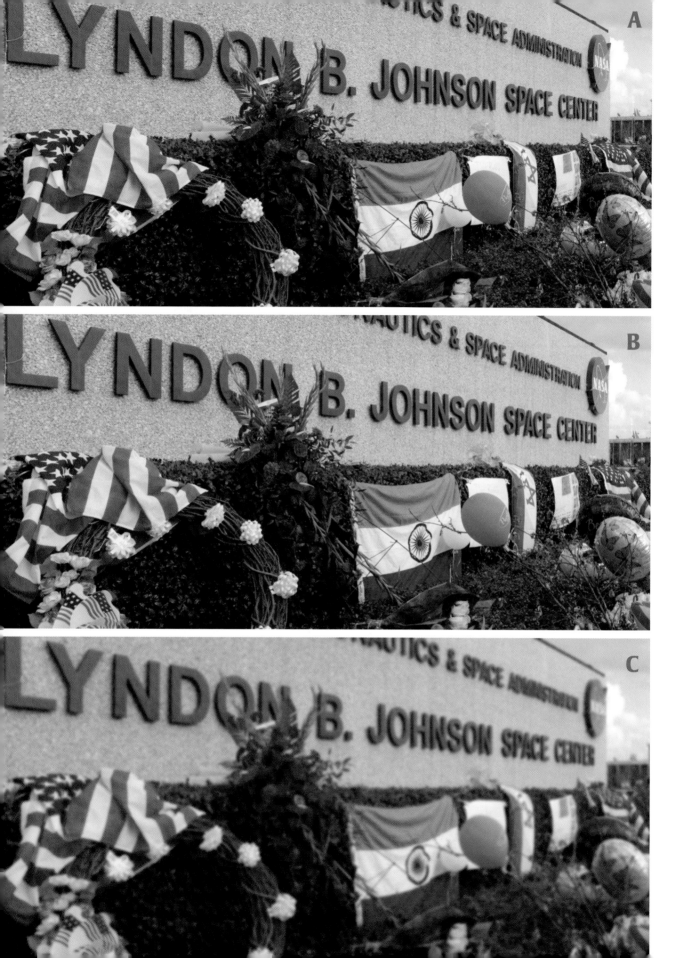

making only the L channel active, and annihilated Figure 5.5C with the same big blur.

Yet the effect in Figure 5.5B is so subtle that the image size has to be tripled (Figure 5.6) before it becomes obvious that there was any change at all. At that magnification, we can see that originally there was orange mottling in the red stripes. The blur has substituted a more uniform red. As against that, look closely and you will see a slight pink halo outside the edge of each stripe, bleeding into areas that used to be white or even bluish white.

At the actual size of Figure 5.5, neither the corrected mottling nor the undesired pink fringing is even visible, so this would be an example of an image I wouldn't bother to blur, unless there were extenuating circumstances—such as having to print it at a larger size than originally planned, or if the original was a lot flatter than this one, and thus might need more aggressive correction.

Photoshop CS2 Launches a Winner

Retouching and correction technique doesn't change much over the years. Photoshop 3, released in 1994, revolutionized workflows by introducing layers, which are critical to many of the moves shown in this book.

While I haven't busted out my copy of Photoshop 3 to check, to the best of my recollection almost every trick you have read or will read about here could also have been done in that ancient program. There are only three exceptions I can think of.

Figure 5.5 (opposite) The A and B channels can take a lot of blurring without obvious ill effects. Top, the original, at a resolution of 225 pixels per inch. Middle, a version in which the A and B were Gaussian blurred at a Radius of 3.0 pixels. Can you tell the difference? The bottom version shows what happens when the same blur is applied instead to the L channel.

Figure 5.6 Enlarged versions of Figures 5.5A (top) and 5.5B show the impact of the AB blur. Note the slightly fuzzier edges.

Photoshop 6 (2000) introduced the Convert to Profile command, which I've been recommending but which we could surely live without. Far more significant was the introduction in Photoshop CS (2003) of the Shadow/Highlight command, which we will discuss at length in Chapter 7.

In 2005, Photoshop CS2 added another advance. Filter: Blur>Surface Blur is a better solution to some of the problems we've just looked at. For those using CS2, this filter should be the first choice for blurring the A and B. As it is not adequately documented elsewhere, I'll describe how it works.

Blurring, regardless of what filter you use, is ordinarily aimed at getting rid of noise in relatively flat areas, such as a sky or a person's skin. The problem is that the noise helps define areas of sharp transition, such as the edge of the woman's glasses in Figure 5.7A. In fact, adding a form of noise to such transition areas is a principal function of the Unsharp

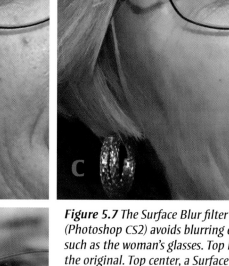

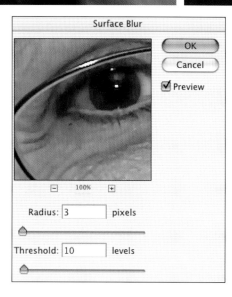

A

B

C

D

E

Figure 5.7 *The Surface Blur filter (Photoshop CS2) avoids blurring edges such as the woman's glasses. Top left, the original. Top center, a Surface Blur of Radius 3 pixels, Threshold 10 levels. Top right, increasing Radius to 10 strengthens the effect on the skin. Bottom left, increasing Threshold to 25 blurs the hair. Bottom center, increasing Threshold to 75 starts to wipe out detail in the earring and the eye.*

Mask filter that we'll discuss momentarily.

The Surface Blur filter attempts to recognize, and avoid blurring, edges. Unlike Gaussian Blur, which has only a Radius setting, Surface Blur has a Threshold. It's used to compare each pixel in the blurred and unblurred versions. If the difference is more than the Threshold, the blur is disallowed. Consequently, the higher the Threshold, the more powerful the effect, which is confusing to veterans of the Unsharp Mask filter, whose Threshold does the opposite.

Smoothing an older woman's skin is a common request, but it usually requires more hand work than we would really like. Showing a composite-color segment of a face makes explaining the filter's function considerably easier than looking at an A or B channel, so we'll revert to RGB for this example.

The larger the object, the higher the Radius that any blurring filter needs. If it hadn't been cropped so brutally, this woman's face would fill the entire page. Even a Radius of 3—Surface Blur, regrettably, doesn't yet work in tenths of pixels—seems conservative. In Figure 5.7B, it's joined by an equally conservative Threshold of 10. There's mild softening of the skin, and, to a lesser extent, the hair.

When Radius moves up to 10 in Figure 5.7C, the smoothing effect is more pronounced, as the blur reaches out to grab larger imperfections.

Figure 5.7D increases Threshold to 25, wiping out much of the detail in the hair without softening the face all that much further. But note that the eyebrows, glasses, and earrings have still not felt the bite of the blur, and they don't until we raise Threshold to a huge 75 in Figure 5.7E. If we had been using the Gaussian Blur rather than the Surface Blur filter, those objects would have been at risk from the get-go.

While Surface Blur is a big step forward, a couple of warnings are in order. First, it's compute-intensive, taking significant time to run, particularly on a large file. Second, we usually have to put it on a duplicate layer at less than 100% opacity. Look at the obtrusively uniform skintone in the last three versions of Figure 5.7. The filter tends to obliterate all distinctions rather than soften them. We'd want to move slightly back in the direction of the original texture.

Having thus learned how to protect edges, let's move on to the filter that enhances them.

A Small Step for a Man

Sharpening, or, to use the technical term, *unsharp masking,* is an artificial method of creating apparent focus. It's needed in most images, not because photographers are congenitally incapable of providing a properly focused product, but because the output process messes things up.

If this were a perfect world, the transition between the white and red stripes would always be razor-sharp. If this were a vector graphic created in Adobe Illustrator, and the stripes were absolutely horizontal or absolutely vertical, we'd have a chance. But here, they're diagonal and curved, most awkward for people who work with rectangular pixels. To make a diagonal line, we have to arrange those pixels in a stairstep pattern. Magnify the file enough, and the stairstepping becomes painfully obvious. But even at normal sizing, the stairstep pixels must be neither red nor white, as otherwise the effect would be too noticeable. Instead, these edge-defining pixels are pink, a compromise known as *anti-aliasing.*

Figure 5.8 is a sharpened version of Figure 5.5A. It also includes a magnification with

When and How to Blur: Some Tips

Before picking one of Photoshop's many blur options, we have to decide whether blurring is really necessary. The best way, in my view, is to examine channels while the file is still in RGB. Noise in the blue channel (or B in LAB, or yellow in CMYK) has to be quite pronounced before it will be noticeable in print. If the damage is elsewhere, we need to be more aggressive.

If you're planning extensive repair work on an overly flat image, blurring the AB is more attractive, because anything that enhances the image may well enhance the noise. Similarly, if the image may be printed at a large size, more than its resolution suggests, the AB blur may be needed—compare Figures 5.5B and 5.6B.

For those using Photoshop CS2 or higher, the Surface Blur filter is the tool of choice. For others, the Gaussian Blur filter works well with a Radius of 3.0 pixels or less, but sometimes that isn't enough to suppress the noise. At such times, the Dust & Scratches filter may be needed. It won't create the obvious fringing that a huge Gaussian blur would, but it also can eliminate more color variation than we would like.

Using other blurring filters is an idea that may have merit but one that I haven't explored enough to be able to offer an opinion, other than to say that I see no point in using Despeckle. Median or, especially, Motion Blur may have more promise.

Usually, the A and B channels need to be blurred separately. The B is much more prone to noise, and thus usually requires a bigger blur. There are exceptions, however.

Figure 5.8 *Application of the Unsharp Mask filter creates the impression of greater focus. At left, the secret: where two edges meet, the darker of the two (the red stripes here) gets even darker; the lighter edge becomes even lighter.*

the sharpening exaggerated so that we can see what's going on behind the scenes. At normal size, it just looks better focused, which is the whole point of unsharp masking.

The magnified version gives away the secret. The stairstepping is still there, but it's hidden by a trick. The edge of the red stripe is made darker, and the edge of the white stripe is made lighter. Hence, more contrast, a more decisive and believable transition.

Proper use of Filter: Sharpen>Unsharp Mask, the primary focusing tool, is a subject that could take an entire book. This isn't the one. My *Professional Photoshop* series offers a more in-depth explanation. Lots of variations exist, such as separating the darkening and lightening actions of the filter onto separate layers, sharpening through a mask, or Filter: Sharpen>Smart Sharpen (Photoshop CS2 or later only), which permits a bit of both. All such methods work in LAB, often better than in other colorspaces.

All sharpening must occur in the L channel only. Try to sharpen the A and/or B, and the results will be, shall we say, interesting. The idea of unsharp masking is to accentuate detail, not to throw in psychedelic colors. You can't change colors by working in the L.

Back in Figure 1.7, I suggested a default setting for USM: 200% Amount, 1.0 Radius, 10 Threshold. Default values are always conservative. There's no such thing as an image that looks too focused, but there is such a thing as one that looks oversharpened; the trick is to adjust the numbers to achieve one while avoiding the other.

The dialog settings adjust the *halos,* the darkening and lightening of the edges so apparent in the inset of Figure 5.8. The higher the Amount, the darker and lighter the halos. The inset and the main picture weren't sharpened at the same settings; the inset used a 500% Amount to make the halos obvious. That value would have made the main image, which uses only 300%, look clunky.

Adjusting Amount is straightforward. A common mistake is to try to evaluate the effect from a monitor set to display the image at the wrong magnification. So, before making a judgment on Amount, adjust to 100% magnification on screen, or use the command View: Actual Pixels.

The Radius setting governs the width of the halos, not their lightness and darkness. The main image of Figure 5.8 uses a Radius of 1.0 pixels, but the inset exaggerates the effect with a 5.0 value. Higher Radii wipe out detail. Note how smooth the texture is within the halos, in comparison to the unaltered areas of the stripes.

The key to picking the right Radius is deciding whether to accept that loss of detail. If the flag were the only thing in this picture, a higher Radius might be in order, there being so little detail in the stripes to begin with. But large, featureless halos surrounding each letter in the highly textured sign wouldn't look too good, particularly if those halos were white.

The Threshold setting controls noise. The higher the Threshold, the more it restricts sharpening to areas of big transition, such as between a white and a red stripe. In the inset of Figure 5.8, which uses a zero Threshold, the interiors of the red stripes show more action than might be desirable. Nevertheless, the original image isn't particularly noisy. For the main image, with its lower Amount setting, I used a zero Threshold as well. Choppier-looking originals need higher Thresholds. The Threshold reduces the intensity of sharpening even in the big-transition areas, so a higher Threshold often needs to be accompanied by a higher Amount.

We Have Liftoff

Accurate control of sharpening settings is one of the distinguishing marks of the successful retoucher. If the image is destined for CMYK, it sometimes pays to hold off sharpening until it gets there. The usual reason would be that the image is dominated by a single color. In such cases, sharpening the two weak channels in CMYK usually works out better than either attacking the L or sharpening all channels in RGB. For example, pictures of forests are best sharpened in the black and magenta channels of CMYK—if that happens to be possible in your workflow. Pictures like the Johnson Space Center shot we've just been working on, full of different colors, are best sharpened overall, or in the L. Also, if you're planning to take the file into CMYK eventually, and are planning to do any kind of major work there, you should hold off on the sharpening until it's finished.

High Radius, Low Amount

The L channel often can accept an alternate method of sharpening: the Unsharp Mask filter with a very high Radius and a very low Amount. The Radius setting could be anywhere from 7 to 20 pixels, as opposed to normal values of around 1.0. The Amount is always less than 100%, as opposed to much greater values with conventional sharpening.

The two methods of sharpening aim at different targets. Conventional sharpening emphasizes edges; hiraloam (*high Radius, low Amount*) sharpening gives shape. Certain noisy images that can't profitably be sharpened conventionally benefit from hiraloam.

Some users try to emulate the hiraloam look by creating a duplicate layer, setting mode to Overlay, and applying Filter: Other>High Pass. In addition to being more cumbersome, it's not as flexible, as there is no Threshold setting, and it's difficult to evaluate the effect of different Radius values.

A full discussion of hiraloam sharpening is beyond this book's scope, but it should be noted that it tends to work better in the L than in RGB. If you'd like to experiment with the technique yourself, I'd suggest starting with a portrait shot. Bring it into LAB, and, with the L channel active, apply Filter: Sharpen>Unsharp Mask at settings of Amount 500%, Radius 15.0, Threshold 0. This will look hideous, but it will show whether the Radius is correct. Look for a value that will emphasize the eye and cheekbone structure. Too high, and the entire face will lighten. Too low, and it'll just look silly. When satisfied with the Radius, reduce the Amount to around 50%. Hiraloam sharpening doesn't leave as many obvious artifacts as conventional sharpening does, so it's fairly safe to use at any point in the process.

To sum up what this chapter has shown, if an image has too much colored noise, it pays to take it into LAB and use some kind of blurring filter on the A and B channels. Sharpening gets a more equivocal recommendation. Some people make trips into LAB specifically to sharpen the L. If that's the right thing to do, it would only be on a minority of images: in most, an overall RGB sharpen would be just as good. However, an L-channel sharpen is better enough of the time that if you have decided to use LAB anyway, that's where you should do the deed.

[To that, beta reader André Dumas comments: "I tend to disagree. As a photographer I find that sharpening the L is almost always better, but if the photo has to go to CMYK, then I might also like to do some sharpening on the individual channels. Why not include this alternative here also?"]

Fair enough, but I'll take it further: if you're going into CMYK and are a real sharpening hound, one devious method is to make *two* LAB copies, sharpen one but not the other, convert both to CMYK, and substitute the unsharpened black channel for the sharpened one. Then you can attack *that* black, avoiding the hassle of resharpening something that LAB has already put artifacts into.

If you don't feel like exploring the why of all this, this chapter has served its purpose. If you would like to see some comparisons and know the technical nitty-gritty behind why LAB outperforms RGB in these areas, it's coming right up. If you can live without that information, jump ahead to Chapter 6.

Review and Exercises

✓You are about to open a new RGB image for the first time. You don't know what it's a picture of, or who took it. Which channel probably has the most noise? Assuming that you're right, if you convert the image to LAB, which channel will pick up most of the noise?

✓What major *negative* consequence of using the Gaussian Blur filter on the A and/or B is avoided by using the Surface Blur filter introduced in Photoshop CS2?

✓In the Unsharp Mask filter, what is the difference between Amount and Radius?

✓What defect in RGB sharpening is avoided by sharpening the L channel instead?

✓If you must sharpen in RGB, how would you avoid a color shift?

✓From the book's CD, open a copy of Figure 1.10, the image of Yellowstone Lake. Experiment with sharpening the L using a high Radius (>10 pixels) and a low Amount (<100%), and compare it to a more conventional sharpen with Amount>300% and Radius around 1.0 pixels.

✓Open three of your own pictures that have very different subjects. Convert to LAB, activate the AB channels only, and Filter: Blur>Gaussian Blur at a 4.0-pixel Radius. Is the effect visible in some but not all? If not, adjust the blur setting until it is. Then explain what prevented the blur from being visible in the image(s) that didn't seem to be damaged.

A Closer Look

Figure 5.9, dredged out of my backups, is the very first image I used in print to advocate sharpening the L, back in 1996. It exhibits the same kind of strong edges found in the Johnson Space Center image. The break between the red uniform and the greenish background is just as decisive as the one between the red and white stripes of the flag. There are similar strong breaks between the skin and the background, and the skin and the uniform.

Figure 5.10A is an L-only sharpen, using the same exaggerated settings as in the inset of

Figure 5.9 *This image, with its strong transitions in color areas, was used as a sharpening demonstration in a 1996 article.*

Figure 5.8: 500% Amount, 5.0 Radius, 0 Threshold. Figure 5.10B employs the same settings, but is sharpened overall in RGB.

Sharpening overall actually sharpens each channel individually, which unleashed a cascade of spectacular defects in Figure 5.10B. In the green channel of RGB, the uniform is dark, but the background is light. Therefore, the sharpening produces a dark halo just inside the uniform and a light halo just outside it. The red channel is light in the uniform, dark in the background. The haloing is reversed, lightening the edge of the uniform, darkening the edge of the background.

This combination of darkening and lightening produces a bright blue-green halo around the uniform, exactly the sort of thing that gives unsharp masking a bad name. Worse, the same thing happens where the young woman's neck meets the uniform. Green skintone may be appropriate when NASA encounters Martians, but it's not an attractive choice for human beings. Furthermore, when a photographer feels that the subject is not wearing enough makeup, the indicated procedure is to hire an artist to apply more, not attempt to correct matters with unsharp masking. Here, the sharpen has added eyeliner and lipstick.

Figure 5.10A has none of these defects. It can't, because the L can't change color. And therefore, it's a better sharpen. But we need to compare it against a third, more sophisticated, alternative.

Making RGB Behave Like LAB—Almost

As indicated in the first half of this chapter, Photoshop offers two ways to sharpen outside of LAB while limiting color change. First, and most flexible, we can create a duplicate RGB layer and sharpen there. Then we change the layering mode to Luminosity, which—in theory—picks up the color from the bottom layer and the detail from the top, creating—in theory—the same effect as sharpening the L of LAB. A simpler way to land in the same place is to sharpen in RGB and immediately Edit: Fade>Luminosity.

A

Either of these methods would produce Figure 5.10C. No question, it's better than Figure 5.10B. But is it really as good as Figure 5.10A? If this were a normal sharpen at a normal size, probably yes. Yet at this extreme magnification, we can see hints of problems.

The level of detail in the hair and eyes is better in the LAB version. The overall feel of the face is a bit lighter and more agreeable. The top of the uniform takes on a natural darkness in the LAB version, but is an eerie bright red in the RGB/Luminosity attempt.

The biggest difference is in the lightest areas of the skin. In Figure 5.10C, the ears are completely blown out—no dot at all on the printed page. Figure 5.10A, which otherwise has lighter skin, has the ears pink, as you would expect them to be. Blown-out ears may not be as big a defect as the green neck of Figure 5.10B, but they're nothing to be happy about, either.

Figure 5.10 *Greatly magnified, these images highlight sharpening defects. Top left, a version sharpened in the L channel of LAB. Bottom left, when using the same settings for an overall sharpen in RGB. Bottom right, when the RGB sharpen is faded to Luminosity mode.*

B

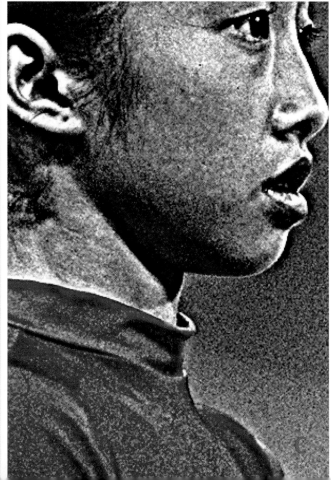

C

How did this happen? How could a method chosen specifically to *retain* color have managed to lose it in the ears and add it in the uniform's collar?

In preparing to write this chapter, I selected around 30 images on random subjects that seemed to pose different sharpening problems. I sharpened one copy of each in the L channel, and once with the same settings using RGB/Luminosity.

Around half the pairs were so close as to be indistinguishable. Not pixel-for-pixel identical, certainly, but so close that when I pasted one on top of the other, I had to increase the screen magnification to at least 200% and toggle back and forth to verify that I hadn't pasted the same image on top of itself by mistake.

On the other hand, around a quarter of the images were slightly better in LAB (this first example would be one of them), and around a quarter were markedly better. One was better in RGB, but that's unusual enough for us to ignore.

Two unrelated factors make LAB sharpening work better. If neither is present, RGB/Luminosity sharpening should work just as well. If you see that those items *are* present, however, it may pay to head for LAB. We'll have a look at one real-world image of each variety.

Houston, We Have a Problem

In the next two examples, we'll compare sharpening the L to the same settings applied in RGB, followed by a reversion to luminosity. In view of Figure 5.10A, there's no point in discussing overall RGB sharpening without that reversion.

Figure 5.11 is the easier of the two examples. Each version was sharpened at settings of 500% Amount, 1.5 Radius, 0 Threshold. Figure 5.11B, the LAB version, is superior, and Figure 5.12B shows why. At high magnification, we see that the sharpening halos in the area behind the

Figure 5.11 *The hand lettering in the original, top, poses a sharpening problem. The center version was sharpened in the L channel, the bottom version using identical settings in RGB, reverted to Luminosity mode.*

Figure 5.12 Enlarged versions of Figures 5.11B (LAB sharpen, left) and 5.11C (RGB/Luminosity sharpen, right) reveal a quality problem. The halos in the background at right have become a distracting white, as Photoshop could not create a yellow there without changing the area's luminosity. The LAB version retains the yellowness of the background.

large red letters are white. On a yellow background, this makes no visual sense.

Those areas went white for the same reason that the young woman's ears went white in Figure 5.10C, and for the same reason that LAB curves were so much more effective way back in the sunset image of Figure 2.8. Gamut considerations dictate that extremely light pixels are always white in RGB and CMYK. The initial sharpening drove those halos to be as light as they could possibly be. If they're that light, they can't have a color associated with them. Luminosity mode tells Photoshop to restore the original yellow, an impossibility. That's asking Photoshop to construct, in RGB, a color that doesn't exist in RGB.

If the action takes place in the L channel, the flight path is different. The yellow background starts at an average of $96^L(6)^A40^B$. Sharpening the L creates light and dark halos, just as it does in RGB. And, naturally, it doesn't take much lightening to get to the maximum of 100^L.

We have just entered the realm of the imaginary color. The file calls for $100^L(6)^A40^B$. There isn't any such spacecraft, at least not in RGB or CMYK. It demands to be as bright as a pure white, yet strongly biased toward yellow.

When confronted with imaginary colors, Photoshop splits the difference. So, we get a yellow, not as yellow as the rest of the background, and we get lightening halos, but not so light as in the disagreeable Figure 5.12B.

A Burst of Gamma Radiation

LAB also has a sharpening advantage in an entirely different category of image. The explanation is complicated.

First, however, let's verify that the advantage exists. Figure 5.13 is the original; the two competing versions are both sharpened at settings of 500% Amount, 1.1 Radius, 0 Threshold. The LAB version, Figure 5.14A, has a more attractive sheen to the leaves, particularly when viewed at high magnification.

Figure 5.13 Palm trees present a sharpening problem because of their fine leaves.

Figure 5.14A appears lighter than Figure 5.14B, but it's not because LAB magically lightens images during sharpening. Remember, Figure 3.10B, another LAB sharpen, came out *darker* than its RGB opponent. As we'll see in the next chapter, you can translate images back and forth between RGB and LAB hundreds of times, and, provided nothing else was being done to the image along the way, you'd never be able to tell the difference on the printed page. So,

Figure 5.14 Two competing sharpened versions of Figure 5.13, done with the same settings. On the left, the L channel sharpen appears to produce a lighter image than the version at right (RGB sharpening faded to luminosity). The magnified sections below show a more attractive sheen in the leaves in the version done in LAB.

something specific to Figure 5.13 causes the image to get lighter when sharpened in the L channel as opposed to RGB/Luminosity.

While Figure 5.14A is slightly better, I don't find the difference particularly compelling, certainly not enough so to warrant a lengthy technical explanation. Unfortunately, understanding why there's a marginal LAB advantage in sharp-

256 Levels per Channel

Varying number systems, some based on 256 values and some on 100, mislead some people into thinking that there are gross incompatibilities between channels that are in different colorspaces. Not true: you can paste the cyan of a CMYK file directly into the A of LAB if you are sufficiently foolhardy.

Every pixel in every channel is defined by eight bits of digital storage space, eight markers that can be set either to zero or one, two possibilities per marker. If you look at two markers, there are four total possibilities; look at three, there are eight; at four there are 16; and so on. With eight bits, there are 256 total possibilities, 256 levels of tonality.

If you're wondering why RGB values max out at 255, it's because zero is a legal value. If 256 were allowed to occur, it would constitute the 257th level of gray. This also accounts for the asymmetry of the AB channels, where the cool colors can get to values of −128 but the warm ones only to +127: since zero is an acceptable value, there are only 255 other possibilities left over.

Those with a printing background either can't count up to 256 or are not inclined to throw away a lifetime of experience dealing with percentages, so Photoshop reports information about CMYK and grayscale files in values of 0 to 100—as it does with the L channel. Nevertheless, each of these channels still has 256 possible values; Photoshop merely rounds the result before reporting it to us.

We also have the option of doubling the size of our files by using Mode: 16-bits/channel, which gives the theoretical possibility of 65,536 levels of gray, although still reported to us on the same 0–255 scale. I don't recommend using it inasmuch as repeated testing has shown no practical impact on quality; however, there's no harm in it, other than the impact on file size.

ening is key to understanding why there's a huge LAB advantage in blurring, which is key to understanding why LAB is a superior retouching space. So, here goes.

It all starts with the realization that many different definitions of "RGB" are possible. This book uses one called sRGB, currently the most common definition. But, supposing we had to describe sRGB to somebody who had never heard of it. What information would we need to convey?

At a minimum, five things. Three are obvious. We need to explain what we mean by *red, green,* and *blue,* because those three words mean different things to different people. One way to clarify is to use LAB numbers. The word *red* is ambiguous. The numbers $54^L81^A70^B$ are not. Those numbers define, in fact, the red of sRGB— that is, $255^R0^G0^B$. Other RGBs use different numbers. In the relatively vivid Adobe RGB, for example, $255^R0^G0^B$ equates to $63^L90^A78^B$.

The fourth category is white point, which describes what a value of $255^R255^G255^B$ really means: pure white, or some off-white? This setting has no bearing on anything in this book, so I propose to leave it alone.

The fifth setting, however, is the key to Figure 5.14. In almost all variants of RGB, equal values in red, green, and blue make a neutral color. Therefore, $128^R128^G128^B$ is a gray. The question is, how dark? Each channel is halfway between its maximum and minimum possibilities of 255 and 0. Is the result half as dark as pure black? In whose opinion, a machine's? And if it's a human's opinion, whose?

The answer to these stimulating questions is the *gamma* setting. A gamma of 1.0 would mean that the midpoint is exactly halfway between the two extremes, in the opinion of a machine. Most color theoricians don't like that structure. They feel, correctly, that human beings perceive more contrast in dark things than in light ones. Therefore, at a gamma of 1.0, the difference between $200^R200^G200^B$, a very light gray, and $195^R195^G195^B$ will be perceived as a smaller difference than between, say, $100^R100^G100^B$ and $95^R95^G95^B$. This heinous lack of *perceptual uniformity*, in their view, justifies a fudge factor. The midpoint, they feel, should be defined as a darker gray than the machine would like. Therefore, values darker than $128^R128^G128^B$ will be packed closer together than before, and those lighter will be further apart. More values are now being devoted to portrayal of dark colors and fewer to light colors.

We will delve deeper into this topic in Chapter 13. For now, all we need to know is, the higher the gamma, the darker the midpoint. Plus, we need to know that almost everyone uses one of two gamma settings: 1.8, which is the traditional Macintosh setting, or 2.2, the traditional PC setting. sRGB and Adobe RGB both employ 2.2.

Apple RGB, another variant, uses a 1.8 gamma. In it, $128^R128^G128^B$ is equal to $61^L0^A0^B$. In sRGB, with its

larger fudge factor, it's a darker $54^L0^A0^B$. Think about these two numbers, and a surprising secret comes slithering out from under a stone.

Neither of these two artificially darkened RGB midtones is as dark as 50^L.

The Clues That L Sharpening Is Better

The L's darkness values don't strictly correspond to the gamma model. Extreme highlights and shadows get shortchanged. The L channel could never look exactly like a grayscale version of an RGB file, no matter what gamma setting was in place. Nevertheless, it is approximately as

Figure 5.15 The encoding of the L is strange. Its midpoint is interpreted as being rather dark, so the channel itself has to be lighter than one might expect. Top row: the L, left, is lighter than a grayscale conversion of Figure 5.13, right. Bottom row: the original red, green, and blue channels, all of which are darker than the L.

dark as an RGB file would be with a gamma of 2.6 or 2.7.

Because the interpretation of the L is so dark, its contents have to be lighter than one would expect. Figure 5.15 shows that the L is not merely lighter than a grayscale conversion, but also lighter than any of the RGB channels.

The impact on sharpening is complex. In RGB, we're sharpening each of the three channels separately and then averaging their values. In LAB, the averaging comes first, then the sharpening. So, it's not surprising that the results are slightly different.

In almost all images, including this one, averaging the values first is a plus. The original red channel is so dark that it's difficult to sharpen, and the original blue is revolting. Sharpening them accomplishes nothing. However, when they're averaged together with the green channel during the conversion to LAB, the resulting L channel gets a larger range in the trees than any of the three RGB channels—particularly when we recall that the L has to be made lighter anyway, to compensate for its higher "gamma."

I almost yielded to temptation and, for the first time in my writing career, included a histogram with this image, something I always avoid for fear of creating the inference that I think histograms have any value in color correction. This histogram would have shown that the trees occupy a significantly larger range in the L channel than in the green, and a vastly longer range than in either the red or the blue. That longer initial range makes for a more believable and visually pleasing sharpen.

Look for this type of midtone-to-shadow contrast as an invitation to take a trip to LAB for sharpening. Imagine an image of a model with long hair. It needs to be sharpened carefully to avoid bringing out unwanted facial detail. Yet hair always wants to be sharp.

Success with such a picture requires a grasp of the Threshold function within the Unsharp Mask filter, but it doesn't necessarily need LAB. Weirdly, it depends on what color the hair is.

If the hair is blond, sharpening in RGB/Luminosity might knock some of the yellow out of it, as it did in Figure 5.11C. But it might not.

If the hair is a light brown, we'd probably see no difference at all between sharpening the L and RGB/Luminosity.

Change the model's hair to dark brown or black, though, and it's a different story. Now, the target is dark enough for the LAB advantage to manifest itself. Sharpen the L in this one, and the hair will get an attractive softness that RGB won't provide.

Aficionados of the Image: Adjustments> Shadow/Highlight command introduced in Photoshop CS will discover that its shadow-end manipulations work better in LAB than in RGB, for the same reasons. There'll be an example showing how and why in Chapter 7.

The Blur Is Not Just an Average

The LAB sharpening advantage, when it exists at all, is pretty marginal. The blurring advantage is huge. And, it's an advantage that gets magnified as the correction proceeds, because, as explained in the box on the next page, we tend to do our blurring early in the process.

Suppose you need the color that's halfway between a bright green and a bright red. I'm not talking about laying green ink on top of red ink, which would make a muddy mess, but rather about something halfway between the two.

It seems clear that the answer needs to be some kind of yellow. Red and green aren't opposites; magenta and LAB's "green," which is really more like teal, are. Red and real green share a yellow component, and therefore the midway point should be some kind of subdued yellow, not a brilliant one, because a brilliant yellow would be lighter than either parent.

Let's try this operation first in RGB, then in LAB, by putting a green layer on top of a red background at 50% opacity. In figuring out what comes next, Photoshop does a straightforward, yet undesirable thing: it averages the two. If the bottom layer is the brightest possible red, it's

$255^R0^G0^B$. The green layer is $0^R255^G0^B$. The two average to $128^R128^G0^B$, and that's what Photoshop gives us, much to our sorrow.

Suppose we convert these same colors to LAB and do the averaging there. The red comes in at $54^L81^A70^B$. The green is $88^L(79)^A81^B$. The average, therefore, is $71^L1^A75^B$—a much different and much better result than what RGB got. $128^R128^G0^B$ translates to LAB as $52^L(9)^A56^B$, which is simultaneously too neutral, too green, and, especially, too dark. The LAB averaging would translate back to RGB as the much lighter $201^R171^G0^B$. And, for CMYK chauvinists, the LAB averaging would yield $24^C27^M100^Y1^K$, but the RGB method a mightily muddy $51^C36^M100^Y13^K$.

How does such a travesty happen? How does the RGB blend come up with a color that's not only too greenish gray, but also darker than either of the two colors between which it's supposed to be splitting the difference?

There are two culprits. First, averaging RGB values is a recipe for grayness. That's why the colors are more neutral than LAB's version. But the bigger blame falls on the gamma adjustment. On a scale of 0 to 255, 128 sounds like it would be in the middle, but, thanks to gamma, it isn't—it's much darker. So, adding the two channels together to get $255^R255^G0^B$ and then dividing by two doesn't work. Plus, Photoshop overemphasizes the green component of the blended color, which is why its averaged version turned out ten points lower in the A channel than the version done in LAB.

A couple of computer-generated graphics should make clear the magnitude of LAB's advantage in blending colors. Please keep in mind that what you're about to see applies to all manner of retouching, not just blurring. So far in this book, we haven't had to mix colors with one another, but in professional retouching, we have to all the time, and doing it in LAB is always better.

We'll start with an extension of the red-green blend problem, only we'll add pure blue to the mix. We start with a layer of three vertical stripes at 50% opacity over a layer of three longer horizontal stripes. It doesn't pertain to blurring just yet, but be patient.

Figure 5.16A has the two layers in LAB. Figure 5.16B is exactly the same unflattened file, but in RGB. So, the needed averaging is done by two different methods. And in Figure 5.16B all of the intersection squares are obviously too dark, in addition to being the wrong color.

Figure 5.16B is so rancid that Photoshop offers a partial fix. In the Edit: Color Settings dialog (Photoshop: Color Settings in certain versions), when More Options (Photoshop CS2) or Advanced Mode (Photoshops 6-CS) is checked, the option illustrated in Figure 5.17 becomes available. It tries to compensate for the RGB gamma

Blur Early, Sharpen Late

Blurring and sharpening are two sides of the same noisy coin.

Blow up any digital picture, and you'll see some evidence of artifacting, or noise: pixels that seem out of place next to their neighbors, making the effect appear less smooth.

In moderation, noise is a good thing. The Edit: Fill command lets us build, for example, a perfectly uniform, perfectly smooth blue sky. But it won't look as natural as a real photograph of a sky, in which the noise introduced by the camera creates a feeling of action and authenticity. Sharpening is little more than the controlled application of noise in a way that emphasizes transition areas.

Too much noise, though, is a bad thing: it makes the picture look harsh, jagged, and unnatural. And it's rather difficult to know how much is too much. It's entirely possible that one might wish to blur and sharpen the same image.

The two steps should come at different times in the process. If a picture seems to need a lot of work, it's best to do any needed blurring immediately. If not, the later correction is apt to emphasize the noise and make it harder to remove.

For the same reason, sharpening should be postponed until the image is nearly finished. Otherwise, further correction might emphasize the sharpening halos so much that they become obtrusive.

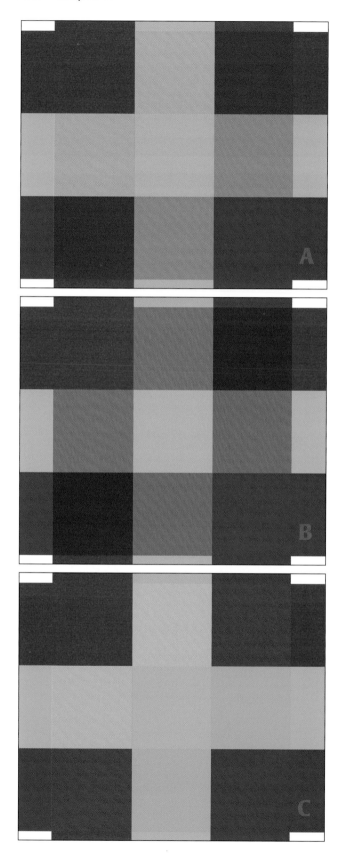

during blending, so that we won't get the unreasonably dark blends we've been talking about and seeing so far. By default, the option is disallowed, but if we turn it on, we get Figure 5.16C from the same file that produced Figure 5.15B.

It's an improvement, but it still isn't as good as Figure 5.16A, because it's stuck with the overly green color. In evaluating it, remember that we're hoping for a smooth look in every horizontal and vertical line, not just the ones that are green. In Figure 5.16C, the center horizontal green stripe is nice and smooth, but the vertical red and blue stripes look like some animal has taken a bite out of their center third.

Furthermore, as interesting as the 1.0-gamma experiment is, it doesn't work unless we're doing a straight blend. When doing something more on point—like blurring the file—the setting has no impact. That leaves LAB with a devastating edge in blurring colored noise, as the next example makes clear.

Again we start with a bunch of colored squares, and again the object is to remove some of the distinction between them, without obliterating the image. Figure 5.18A is pure color variation, since there is a constant value of 65^L.

Figure 5.18B is done in LAB. It's a Gaussian blur, Radius 20.0 pixels, applied to the AB channels only. (The image resolution is around 140 pixels per inch.)

Figure 5.18C is a false blip on the radar screen, something that looks useful but isn't. It's the original file converted to RGB and then, on a duplicate layer, blurred at the same 20.0-pixel Radius. It looks like it might be competitive to the LAB version, but regrettably, it's disqualified before the race begins.

Working in LAB offers considerable flexibility

Figure 5.16 *LAB is more accurate at blending colors than RGB, due to a superior method of averaging. In each case, three vertical lines of pure RGB red, green, and blue are intersecting three longer lines of the same color, at 50% opacity. Top, when the file is blended in LAB. Middle, normal RGB settings. Bottom, RGB with Color Settings set to 1.0 gamma, as in Figure 5.17.*

Advanced Controls

☐ Desaturate Monitor Colors By: [20] %

☑ Blend RGB Colors Using Gamma: [1.00]

Description

Blend RGB Colors Using Gamma: Controls the blending behavior of RGB colors. When enabled, RGB colors are blended using the specified gamma. A gamma of 1.00 is considered to be "colorimetricly correct" and should result in the fewest edge artifacts. When disabled, RGB colors are blended directly in the document's color space; this behavior matches the algorithm used by most other applications.

Figure 5.17 Photoshop's Color Settings have an option (only available when More Options or Advanced Mode is checked) aimed at avoiding some of the problems of Figure 5.16B. It compensates for the gamma of the user's RGB, rendering more accurate color.

in blurring the AB channels, but we have to avoid blurring the L, unless we want to jettison a lot of detail. In RGB, we can't just blur the channels, either, because they contain both color and contrast information, and the whole picture would wind up a blur, not just the noisy parts.

Therefore, we can't use Figure 5.18C as is. We have to restore detail by using the opposite of Luminosity mode, which is Color mode. If the top layer is set to Luminosity, Photoshop combines its detail with the color from the bottom layer. If it's set to Color, it does the reverse, taking the color information from the top and blending it with the detail from the bottom layer. We can also do this more simply and less flexibly, with Edit: Fade>Color immediately after the blur.

Either way, though, we get Figure 5.18D. If the objective is to deemphasize the variation, well, it's better than the original. But it's not even orbiting the same planet as the LAB version.

Blurring the AB is therefore always better than RGB/Color, but, somewhat like sharpening the L as opposed to RGB/Luminosity, the advantage can seem small. Unlike sharpening, however,

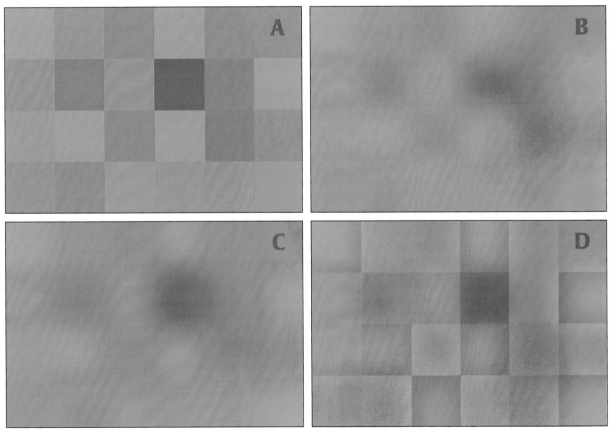

Figure 5.18 Blurring in LAB is much superior to blurring in RGB in Color mode. Top left, the original. Top right, Gaussian blur, 20 pixels, applied to the AB channels. Bottom left, the same blur in RGB, Normal mode. It can't be compared directly to the LAB version because it would affect detail as well as color, unlike the AB blur, which doesn't change the L. The top right version needs to be compared to the one at bottom right, where the RGB blur is faded to Color mode.

which typically is done at the end of the correction process, blurring is usually done right away. Any inadequacies in the blur are likely to be magnified down the line.

Computer graphics like Figures 5.16 and 5.18 prove their points, but we should end with a real image, albeit a horrendously noisy one, one that's probably familiar to readers of my columns and of *Professional Photoshop*, and one that in fact had to be corrected for use in a live job.

The RGB/Color blur, Figure 5.19C, is no doubt an improvement on the calamitous original. But it doesn't come close to the smoothness of Figure 5.19B, the AB blur. There are two main reasons for the superiority.

First, the mottling in the background to the right of the man's face is worse in Figure 5.19C, because it's trying to blur the red noise of Figure 5.19A into a green area. That's not working well, for the same reason Figures 5.16B and 5.18D didn't: blended colors in RGB come out too dark and too green.

Second, Figure 5.19B benefits by the presence of imaginary colors in the LAB file, which give the same smoothing effect seen earlier in sharpening examples such as the yellow sign of Figure 5.11. It's particularly beneficial in the face, which is full of black noise in the RGB but not the LAB version. Those spots started out at 0^L, and perforce 0^A0^B. The blurring of the AB, since it didn't touch the L, produced something like $0^L50^A50^B$, which is roughly described as the imaginary color that's brilliantly red

Figure 5.19 *An incredibly noisy, yet real-world, picture, top, demonstrates the superiority of the AB blur (center). The RGB/Color mode version, bottom, doesn't handle the red-green noise well.*

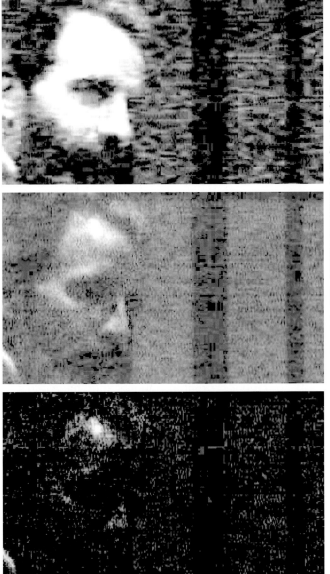

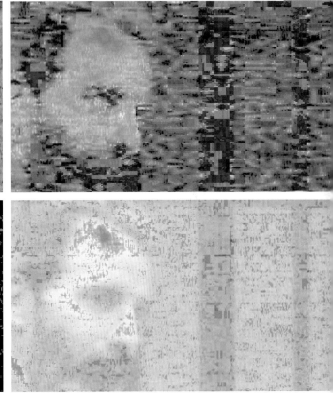

Figure 5.20 *Different kinds of damage call for different remedies. The relation between the red of RGB (top left) and the A of LAB (middle right) is clear. The jagged lines are too large for a Gaussian blur. The Dust & Scratches or Surface Blur filters are better choices. RGB's green and blue channels (center left and bottom left) show noise similar to that of the B channel (bottom right). In all three channels a Gaussian blur is appropriate.*

but simultaneously as dark as black. On conversion into another colorspace, Photoshop tries to preserve some redness, and the only way it can do so is to lighten, which is just what we want.

Similarly, white areas in the skintone are being filled. Extremely light areas have to be white in RGB or CMYK, but not in LAB.

Because of the different character of the noise in each channel, I used two different noise-reduction methods. The jagged patterns in the red and A channels of Figure 5.20 can't be blurred out with either the Gaussian Blur or Surface Blur filter, so I used Dust & Scratches at a Radius of 15 pixels. I Gaussian blurred the other three channels at an 8.0-pixel Radius. The resolution of Figure 5.19 is 72 pixels per inch.

The Blurring Problem in the Digital Age

This provocative discussion of blurring has become ever more significant in the age of digital cameras and challenging originals. We've always had to deal with grainy originals, but the advent of this colored noise with little change in the underlying luminosity is a fairly recent development—one that is stumping a lot of people.

Here are just some of the categories that can exhibit noise-related injuries best treated by surgery on the AB.

● Images shot in low lighting conditions.

● Sports photography, and other action shots requiring fast exposure.

● Underwater photography. With the camera

being inundated by light of a single color (namely, blue), colored noise is quite likely.

• Images that have been compressed to a point that may affect reproduction quality. The JPEG algorithm, which is what most people use for compression, wisely is less faithful to the color of the uncompressed original than it is to its detail. Blocklike artifacts may start to appear in the RGB channels. But if the JPEGged file is converted to LAB, the artifacts will live not in the L channel but in the AB, where they can easily be taken out.

• Older originals, where the emulsion has seen better days.

• Many of today's digicams create inappropriate color fringing, sometimes called *chromatic*

The Bottom Line

Sharpening the L channel and/or using some type of blurring filter on the A and B are major attractions of working in LAB.

Sharpening the L channel rather than an overall sharpen in RGB or CMYK sometimes is more effective, particularly if there are objects that are both light and colorful, or when the main focus of attention is darker than a midtone.

Blurring the AB is markedly superior to either using Color mode in RGB or trying to make the blur in an RGB working space of gamma 1.0. The LAB method of blending colors is more accurate and results in a more natural appearance. The digital age often provides images that are full of colored noise, for which AB blurring is the best solution.

Sharpening is best saved for near the end of the correction process. When blurring is necessary, it's usually done early.

---

aberration, where edges of two unlike colors meet. Photoshop's Camera Raw plug-in has a setting to control it (if you happen to have a file from one of the cameras that Camera Raw supports), but working the AB is a more elegant and effective solution.

• Images that lack sufficient resolution. Nowadays the question of how much resolution is enough doesn't always have a clear answer. However, every now and then some nitwit asks us to download a 128K JPEG from the Web and print it as a full page in a magazine, or even as a quarter page. When there isn't enough resolution, the picture looks grainy and jagged, and the colored spots seem as big as the squares in Figure 5.18—until we knock them out of the AB.

• And, the biggest-ticket item of all: the pre-screened original. Images that have already appeared in print consist not of continuous tone but of interlocking patterns of cyan, magenta, yellow, and black dots. That's colored noise if ever colored noise existed, but unfortunately it can't be doctored very much because it comprises all of the contrast in the image. Leave the noise alone, and the image will moiré when reprinted, but blur it in RGB, and detail will vanish. Taking the file into LAB and blurring the AB will solve most of the problems. We'll go through the process in more detail in Chapter 11.

Finally, we should realize that the countdown to a new style of retouching is underway. If all you have to do is use a painting tool such as the rubber stamp or healing brush at 100% opacity, it won't make any difference what colorspace you do it in. Anything more complex than that involves mixing two colors. In the space age, we know what colorspace does it best.

6

Entering the Forest:
Myths and Dangers

As with many a fearsome-looking, misunderstood monster, a mythology has grown up around LAB. That some of these myths are easily debunked shouldn't blind us to seeing the real dangers of cuddling up to the ogre too closely. This chapter sorts it all out.

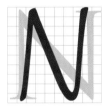ot all that very long ago, there lived at the edge of a great forest two beautiful young children, brother and sister. As children are wont to be, they were insatiably curious. One day they told their mother that they had decided to go for a walk deep into the green forest, where they would study firsthand the phenomenon of simultaneous contrast.

"Don't do it," the mother warned. "An evil witch lives there, and her principal joy in life is tormenting children. She has green skin, purple hair, and a big wart at the end of her nose. If she catches you, she will dip you in butter and batter, jam you into an oven, and bake you into gingerbread, which she will then feed to wolves."

The two protested, but the mother told them that if they didn't stop whining, when their father got home he would make them wish that the wicked witch had gotten them instead.

After she stalked out of the room, the two children huddled. "I think it's a crock," said the boy. "I don't believe in witches, especially not in ones that sound like somebody has been trying to color-correct them in LAB without knowing what they're doing. Skintones must always be positive in the A and B, and the most beautiful hair color is yellow, just like yours."

"I just Googled it," the girl replied, "and there've been no wolves in that forest since 1541. Furthermore, wolves, being carnivorous, don't eat gingerbread in the first place."

Early that evening, suitably emboldened, the two stuffed some gingerbread into their pockets and snuck off into the forest. No sooner had it gotten dark, however, than the little boy was set upon by muggers. Discovering that he had only gingerbread and no cash, they bashed

Figure 6.1 This image is a poor choice for LAB enhancement. The entire tonal range from white to black is important, the colors are bright already, and there's no need to separate them from one another.

his head with a blunt instrument, knocking him senseless.

The little girl started running at the first sign of trouble, but she tripped over a root, went flying, and was knocked unconscious herself. The gingerbread in her pocket drew no wolves because there had been no wolves in that forest since 1541; it did, however, attract the attention of three hungry and ill-tempered bears, who mistook the girl for another golden-haired child who had recently stolen their porridge. They dragged her to their den, set her to work in the kitchen, and told her so many blond jokes that she wished that the wicked witch had gotten her instead.

The boy was aroused the following day by attorneys for the muggers, who were unemployed photographers, and for their insurance company. The bashing instrument was an old Hasselblad (one of the better uses one could think for it in the digital age), but the insurance company wanted to be reimbursed for its original purchase value plus interest, as it had suffered irreparable injury as a proximate result of the little boy putting his

head in the way of its graceful arc. Also, the boy was handed a Summons and Complaint, which informed him that the muggers were suing him inasmuch as they had suffered extreme mental anguish resulting from seeing pain on the face of someone so young and innocent-looking. By the time the legal proceedings were over, the boy wished that the wicked witch had gotten him as well.

Moral: Mothers often give good advice, even when they don't know what they're talking about.

More Than Once Upon a Time

Fairy tales are a time-honored way of dealing with the unknown, particularly an unknown of a threatening nature. That we sometimes hear perceptions about LAB that are completely wrong shouldn't blind us to certain drawbacks that do exist, such as, if you start color-correcting skintone without knowing what you're doing, you're likely to get something that looks like the wicked witch.

The function of this chapter, therefore, is to go over some of the myths—tempered by a discussion of some of the real dangers, and how to avoid them.

MYTH: LAB, once understood, should be your primary workspace. As we will discuss in Chapter 7, it's no myth if you're pressed for time. LAB yields dramatic, if imperfect, results much quicker than any alternative.

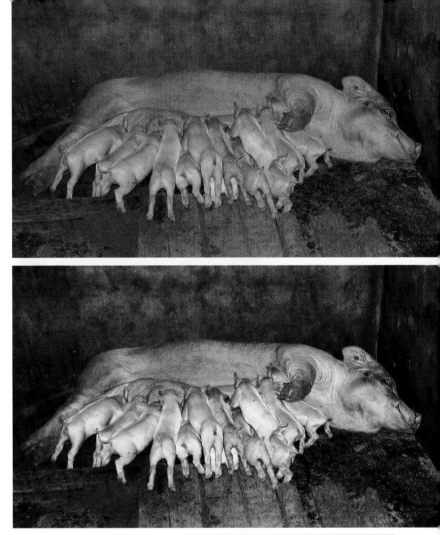

Figure 6.2 The entire interest area here consists of objects very close in color and darkness—objects that are light pink. Such images are ideal for LAB because curves (below) can be tailored to bring out snap in these tiny ranges.

If you've just taken a family trip, have a hundred photos that you want to print, and are willing to spend an hour or two adjusting them but not a day or two, you can't beat LAB. And for complicated retouching, LAB is the colorspace of choice, as it is when some type of blurring for noise reduction is desirable.

However, LAB's strength is also its weakness. Curves and other Photoshop moves have a much bigger impact in LAB than elsewhere; therefore it can be rather clunky to work in, especially the L channel.

To see why going into LAB shouldn't be automatic, compare Figures 6.1 and 6.2. One of them is a picture of Photoshop authors getting ready for the next release of software; I leave it to you to figure out which. But there should be no dispute about which one should be corrected in LAB.

Figure 6.1 has every

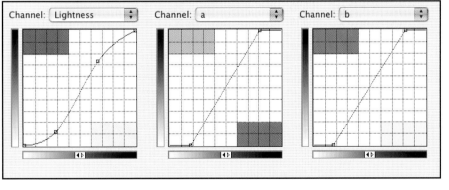

warning sign one could ask for against the use of LAB. We can't isolate the interest area in the L, because everything from the whites of the uniforms to the blacks of the tires is important. We don't need brighter colors, which is a normal reason to head to the AB; and we certainly don't need to drive these primary colors further away from each other than they already are. I'm not saying that

the picture is perfect as it stands, only that LAB offers no attraction in fixing it.

On the other hand, every factor that makes canyons easy pickings for LAB is present in Figure 6.2. We're concerned only with a very short range of colors, to wit, pinks. Anything we can do to drive the pinks apart (read: the A channel) will have a big impact. Plus, in Figure 6.1 we couldn't afford to have the

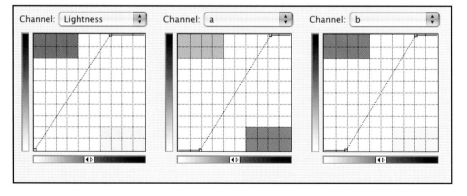

shadows plug (otherwise we'd lose the tires), but in this picture we don't care what happens to the background wall. So, we twist the L curve for a massive contrast boost to the hog and shoats.

DANGER: Overuse of the L. Such muscle-flexing moves in the L channel are tempting in extremely weak images like the dimly lit Spanish hotel of Figure 6.3A. It seems so enticing to grab the top end of the L curve, swing it to the left until the darkest shadow reaches 7[L], and steepen the AB curves to brighten the colors, achieving Figure 6.3B, which is a less impressive improvement than it appears.

Images that are much too light are usually also too gray. The very act of correcting tonal range in RGB, however, often also saturates colors. Figure 6.3C is the simplest fix of all, the Image: Adjustments>Auto Levels command. I don't like how it eliminated the yellowishness in the light part of the image, but it's certainly in the same league as the LAB correction.

A better approach is not to waltz with a hippopotamus. The L is insanely powerful, but it lacks the fancy footwork needed to avoid plugging the shadows.

Assuming we wanted the colors boosted, we might try the curves of Figure 6.3B but move the L curve only half as much as is shown. That

A

Figure 6.3 When the original (above) is grossly lacking in contrast, it's usually weak in color as well. Curves like those below can make a big difference (opposite, top left) but in fact are not much better than doing the correction with Photoshop's Auto Levels command (top right). A better way is to use the curves below but with the L curve steepened only half as much. This leaves the shadow too light (bottom left), but a light shadow is easily managed in CMYK (bottom right).

leaves us with Figure 6.3D, good color but very flat. At that point, we can exit LAB and make the shadow elsewhere. Since I had to get to CMYK anyway for this book, I got Figure 6.3E by applying a curve to the black channel that looked a lot like the L curve that made Figure 6.3B.

MYTH: The best way to convert a color image to black and white is simply to use the L channel.

Figure 6.4 *Converting a color image into black and white requires analysis of each channel of the original. Right, a version created by blending channels of the original, left.*

Jessica Rabbit, a prominent color theoreticienne, has explained: "I'm not really bad. They just draw me that way." Her wisdom describes the difference, such as it is, between the L channel and a file produced by direct conversion to grayscale.

In the "Closer Look" section of Chapter 5, we discussed the concept of gamma. The L, I explained, may *look* light, but Photoshop *interprets* it as considerably darker. Therefore, the L is almost always lighter than any of the RGB channels, and definitely lighter than a direct conversion to grayscale from RGB.

Neither is the best way to convert color into grayscale. The key to believability is to find areas of color contrast and convert them into luminosity contrast. That obscenely deep sentence gets a full exploration in a couple of chapters of *Professional Photoshop*. The executive summary is that we search for channels with attractive features in certain areas, and then blend them together by one means or another, typically Image: Apply Image, or Image: Adjustments>Channel Mixer. Such methods produced Figure 6.4B out of the RGB original, Figure 6.4A.

If you're not interested in channel operations, then you have to choose between Figure 6.5A, the L channel of Figure 6.4A, and Figure 6.5B, a direct Mode: Grayscale.

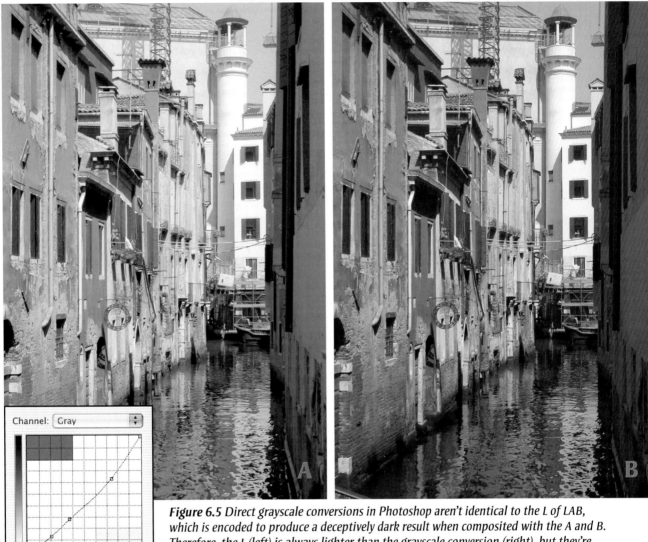

Figure 6.5 *Direct grayscale conversions in Photoshop aren't identical to the L of LAB, which is encoded to produce a deceptively dark result when composited with the A and B. Therefore, the L (left) is always lighter than the grayscale conversion (right), but they're based on the same original luminosity information. The inset curve would transform the grayscale version into a near-duplicate of the L channel.*

Both versions use a weighted average of the RGB channels: in rough terms, six parts green, three parts red, one part blue. The L channel, however, is lightened during the conversion to LAB, but it has all the characteristics of Figure 6.5B. Apply the curve inset into Figure 6.5A to a grayscale conversion, and you'll get what you would have gotten had you converted to LAB and taken the L.

When images have a lot of detail in the lightest areas, we tend to prefer the grayscale conversion. In the remaining images, we like the L better, which means we like it better most of the time, as witness all those who swear that the best black and white is a copy of the L.

It's interesting to consider that all the color-matching algorithms seem to suggest that the direct grayscale conversion must be better, but human beings regularly prefer the L channel. We can leave that problem to the philosophers. Neither version holds a candle to Figure 6.4B.

Figure 6.6 Top, left to right: the red, green, and blue channels of Figure 6.4A. Left, after channel blending that emphasized the role of the blue channel at the expense of the red, the image has become very green. However, this image converts into Figure 6.4B, a more desirable black and white.

For the record, here's a quick summary of how it was done. Figure 6.6 shows the original red, green, and blue channels of Figure 6.4A. Noticing that Figure 6.6A, the red, had less snap than either of the other channels, I used Image: Apply Image to replace it with the blue channel. I used Darken mode, which does not allow any pixels to get lighter. Darken mode is irrelevant in the buildings of this image, which are always darker in the blue anyway. However, the sky was somewhat darker in the red channel than in the blue, and I wanted to stop it from getting lighter.

Then, noting that the blend had made the image darker as well as more contrasty, I applied a separate curve to the green channel, lightening the lighter area and thus increasing contrast in the water. At that point, I had Figure 6.6D, which looks absurdly green. Fortunately, if we are producing a black and white version, nobody is going to care what the color image used to look like. This one converts directly into Figure 6.4B.

MYTH: One can load the L channel as a mask for an RGB or CMYK document without having a copy of the image in LAB.

Most readers can safely ignore this topic, but it is of conceivable interest to inveterate mask-hounds, and appropriate to discuss now because it's closely related to the exercise we just went through.

We haven't used selections or masks yet in this book. They'll rear their ugly heads at the end of Chapter 7 and get a full treatment in Chapter 9. Most people overuse them. Be that as it may, there are times when complicated selections are needed. Often we start by copying an existing channel as an additional, non-printing channel that can later be loaded as a selection. This permits us to edit the new channel as needed before we load it.

We can also load an existing channel as a selection. The usual excuse for doing so is that we want the mask to be based on the darkness of the image, without distortions based on its color. If we open the Channels palette and Command–click on the composite RGB line, Photoshop will create and load such a selection. On an American English keyboard, Command-Option–~ (tilde character) does the same thing.

This action is often described as *loading a luminosity mask,* from which some infer that Photoshop has generated an artificial L channel and loaded it as the selection.

Not so. In an LAB file in Chapter 7, I needed such a mask, so I used Command-Option–1. *That* loads the L channel as a selection. The RGB business described earlier doesn't. It loads a grayscale conversion. It's the difference between using Figure 6.5A and 6.5B as the mask.

The difference may be significant, more likely not. But there's actually a hidden danger. Sometimes people try for identical results on different computers. Suppose that you and I are working on identical RGB files, and we never intend to convert them to any other colorspace. Provided our definitions of RGB agree, we should be able to execute the same commands on our two systems and get precisely the same results.

And so we would—provided we never load a luminosity mask. For that to work, our definitions of grayscale would have to match as well.

DANGER: Layers aren't computed in the same way in LAB. When a file with more than one layer is converted from one colorspace to another, Photoshop asks whether we want to flatten (merge all layers) first. Usually, that's the wise move. Adjustment layers (layers that consist only of a single instruction, such as a set of curves) won't survive the transition to LAB in any case.

But any layer is a potential problem, because unless it is in Normal mode at 100% opacity, it will be evaluated differently in LAB. We saw several examples of this, all in LAB's favor, at the end of Chapter 5.

Worse, certain blending modes aren't supported in LAB at all. For example, if you have a layer in RGB that's set to either Darken or Lighten mode, if you refuse to flatten the image during conversion, the layer will reset itself to Normal mode. Multiply and Screen modes theoretically work in LAB, but not anything like they do in other colorspaces. Setting the A or B channel to Multiply actually is the same as setting it to Overlay mode.

On the other hand, Color and Luminosity modes work in all colorspaces, but they usually give best results in LAB. In principle, you should only flatten layers that are in those two modes once you have gotten to LAB. Unless, of course, as you watch the file appear to change colors when you make the transition, it seems to you that the previous look is more like what you want. Which brings up:

MYTH: Working in RGB or CMYK on a separate layer in Luminosity mode gives all the power of LAB. The idea is correct up to a point, but it becomes inaccurate when the lightest and/or darkest areas of the image are supposed to be colorful. In that case, working in the L channel will give better results. The prime example is in sharpening. In Figure 5.11 we saw how RGB/Luminosity sharpening introduced ugly white halos into a background that was light yellow, whereas sharpening just the L did not.

In Figure 6.3E, even if you could achieve

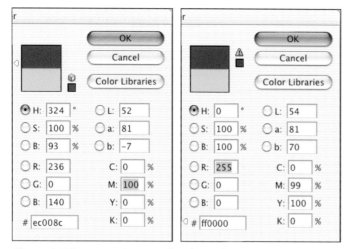

***Figure 6.7** Some texts incorrectly refer to the A channel as "red-green" rather than magenta-green. Left, the equivalent of solid magenta ink coverage in CMYK shows up almost entirely as a large positive value in the A. Right, the equivalent of pure CMYK red equates to a B channel nearly as positive as the A.*

approximately the same look in RGB/Luminosity, you couldn't retain the attractive yellowness around the light fixtures. LAB can. Those yellows are temporarily out of both the RGB and CMYK gamuts. When brought into one of those colorspaces they stay yellow, but they can't be originated except in LAB.

MYTH: The A channel should be described as red-green rather than magenta-green. This misconception lurks even in the best academic textbooks. Plus, the medical profession persists in referring to a common male vision deficiency as "red-green color-blindness." I noted the error in the 1999 edition of my book *Professional Photoshop 5.* Since then, "magenta-green" has generally been accepted as a more appropriate description of what goes on.

Figure 6.7 should resolve any doubts. If the A is really a red channel, then converting a pure RGB red, $255^R0^G0^B$, into LAB should result in a big positive number in the A and about 0^B. It doesn't; we get $54^L81^A70^B$.

If the A is a magenta channel, then pure CMYK magenta, $0^C100^M0^Y$, should convert into LAB with a high A value and near 0^B. It does; $52^L81^A(7)^B$ to be precise.

DANGER: Misunderstanding the effect of extreme AB values. This is a bigger threat to those needing to end with a CMYK file than it is to those who output in RGB, but it's insidious enough that everyone needs to be on the lookout.

Going from RGB to CMYK gracefully is one of the most difficult, image-specific tasks in the graphic arts. The problem is what to do with colors, chiefly pastels and bright blues, that aren't achievable in CMYK. There are few easy solutions.

That problem, fierce as it is, can be a walk in a brightly lit forest compared to what happens if you're not careful in LAB, which can construct "colors" that are not just far out of the gamuts of both RGB and CMYK, but that don't exist at all.

The second halves of Chapters 1 and 5 allude to, and Chapter 8 will emphasize, the idea of using these imaginary colors for fun and profit. Meanwhile, if you're doing such weird things to the AB that such colors are appearing (or, rather, not appearing: your monitor can't display them, either), you shouldn't convert directly to CMYK. If imaginary colors are in use, and you want to get something that looks like what you see on your screen, you have to, believe it or not, convert to RGB first and only then to CMYK.

Just as counterintuitive: if you bring an area into imaginary-color territory with moves in the AB channels, contrast will be hurt. In a picture of a face, the skintone may measure 20^A20^B, a red; the colorless L being irrelevant. If you push that to 40^A40^B, the red will be overpowering, but if that's what you insist on doing, fine. Go to 80^A80^B, however, and not only will it be an unprintable color, but detail will be lost even though you haven't touched the L, where all detail supposedly resides. During the inevitable conversion to another colorspace, Photoshop will sacrifice contrast in a futile attempt to retain the impossibly brilliant red.

MYTH: Converting to LAB hurts the image. I usually work with classes of seven students, but once or twice a year I demonstrate various tricks to larger groups. I prefer the more intimate setting. Photoshop moves look easy when an experienced person is making them. If there's a computer in front of you and you try to duplicate the expert's moves, they turn out not to be quite so simple. Worse, a lecture on color correction isn't exactly like an action thriller as far as holding attention goes. So, the jokes have to be better than mine usually are to avoid widespread episodes of snoring in the audience.

There is one happy exception. The lectures that formed the foundation for this book were called *The Magic of LAB* for a reason. Certain of the things LAB does—we haven't gotten to them yet; they're in the second half of the book—are so astonishing to experienced people that they occasionally gasp and break into wild applause.

On just one such happy occasion, I was drinking in the adulation and thinking of a new career in public speaking, when a questioner furiously began waving his arm in the back of the hall. When I called on him, he sputtered, "But—but—doesn't converting to LAB *damage* the image?"

The simple answer to this question is no; but giving it misses the point. The real response should be: you've just seen a move that achieved a dramatic improvement in quality in a way that the rest of this audience thinks is impossible using conventional methods. So, why do you care whether there was "damage" or not? The issue isn't whether converting to LAB is dangerous, it's whether the final result is better than the original, and if so, whether you can think of another way to have done it without the use of LAB.

Discussion of whether there's "damage" if we pointlessly move back and forth from LAB without changing anything is so boring and inconsequential that it's been consigned to the "Closer Look" section. The bottom line is, no, no damage occurs in taking a color photo from RGB to LAB and back.

Bear in mind, though, that an LAB file may be altered to include colors that RGB can't retain. Therefore, if you start with an RGB file and convert it to LAB and then back, no problem; but if you engineer such colors into your LAB file and then move it to RGB, there will likely be a shift.

Also, all colorspace conversions, and particularly conversions into LAB, are a bad idea for computer-generated graphics, such as Photoshop gradients. Banding can occur if the gradients lose their smooth transitions. The problem is most commonly seen when rich blue gradients are created in RGB and then converted into CMYK, which is blue-poor. The proper approach is to convert first, and then construct the gradient in CMYK.

MYTH: LAB is the only accurate way to specify known colors, such as those of the Pantone Matching System, or of a product where exact specifications are provided.

If you want to convey a precise color to someone else, several methods are available. Giving them the Photoshop LAB numbers is one of the safest. Unlike RGB, it can't be misinterpreted, and unlike LUV, xyY, and XYZ, alternative academic colorspaces that also express colors unambiguously, LAB is fully supported in most Photoshop operations.

Unfortunately, it's one thing to convey the color accurately in terms of numbers, and quite another to agree that those numbers are what we want to achieve on the printed page. We rarely get to deal with flat colors exhibited under laboratory lighting and evaluated by clients with spectrophotometers. If we did, and somebody had given us desired LAB values, we'd want to match them.

The problem is, we may not be *able* to match them in print. And even if we can, we may not *want* to. No press, no desktop printer, can make a brilliant blue without using custom inks. Viewers have unconsciously accustomed themselves to this sad reality, and adjust printed blues in their minds to seem more vivid than they actually are. If there's a relatively subdued blue in a printed image, a spectrophotometer and a human being won't agree on how blue it is.

DANGER: Few other programs support LAB. If you want to save a file in JPEG format, the normal compression standard for posting on the Web and suchlike, you won't be able to do it in LAB—the format doesn't support it. You'll have to convert to RGB first. Even if there were such a thing as an LAB JPEG, posting it on the Web would be a bad idea: nobody's browser would know how to read it.

LAB is also off limits to a number of other file formats, such as Scitex CT, PICT, and Targa. It's legal to save in TIFF, PDF, or EPS formats, but you're really taking a hike right into the wicked witch's kitchen if you do. Stick with Photoshop (.psd) format for LAB files. Simple prudence dictates naming them something that will warn the wolves off, like IMG100_lab_wkfile.psd.

TIFF is the normal file format for output. If somebody else sees a TIFF, they're likely to think it's printable. They'll be in for a rude shock if they try to place it in QuarkXPress or Adobe Illustrator, both of which choke if you ask them to swallow an LAB TIFF. You can place the file successfully in Adobe InDesign CS or later, and attempt to output it. You can rely on that attempt being successful about as much as you can rely on a wolf to have peaceful relations with a chicken. Some output devices may handle it; others will certainly reject it, or worse.

Many users have been burned by placing LAB pictures in PDF files, the native format of Adobe Acrobat. When they print, sometimes they come out as negatives, sometimes they come out with weird casts, sometimes they're blank, and on rare occasions they even come out correctly.

It's one thing to enter a forest where a monster is reputed to live, and another to walk up to something that looks like a monster and spit in its eye. Save your LAB files for Photoshop use only.

Review and Exercises

✓ How does the L channel differ from the single channel created by Mode: Grayscale?

✓ When we have a layered file in RGB, why is it usually necessary to flatten it before entering LAB, and under what circumstances should you consider not doing so?

✓ Choose ten of your own images on a variety of subjects. Identify the two that you think LAB would be best for—the ones with, for example, short ranges in the interest objects, or a need for enhanced colors. Also, identify the two for which you think LAB has the least to offer.

✓ With one of your own images in LAB, open the A curve and move the center point sharply to the right (magenta) side, until the file becomes horrifically pink. Click OK, and toggle back and forth to the original. Try to ignore the color change. Notice how much *detail* appears to be lost in the wildly colored version. This is the big danger of creating out-of-gamut colors in LAB.

✓ Why is it unwise to convert colorspaces when a file contains a computer-generated gradient?

A Closer Look

Writers are notoriously sensitive about others doing violence to their prose, none more so than the irascible poet, swordsman, romantic, and color theorist, Cyrano de Bergerac. A friend suggests that Cyrano's play might have a better chance if he enters into a business partnership with an influential cardinal.

> DE GUICHE. He's not a bad writer himself.
> He'll edit only a line or two.
> CYRANO. Out of the question, Monsieur.
> My blood curdles at the thought
> Of changing a single comma.

Cyrano's belief in the immutability of his own prose is an excellent introduction to a discussion of a recurrent myth, that converting into LAB somehow damages image quality.

To that, there are two replies:

* It doesn't.
* If it did, it wouldn't matter.

The second, being pure logic that even the maniacal Cyrano would approve of, is easiest to justify. We've now seen several ways to improve images using LAB. If you agree that the images actually are improvements, could you have achieved similar results without the use of LAB? If not—if they're better now, and they couldn't have been made that good any other way—then qu'est-ce que c'est this word *damage?*

As for the first, I was given to understand in 1996, from several persons claiming to be authorities on Photoshop, that converting to LAB even once would inflict "catastrophic" damage on the innocent image. It's not obvious what this means, but a likely guess would be, if you convert to LAB, you can never get back to where you started from.

Why anybody would want to do that, I don't know. The whole point of going to LAB is that we *don't* like the current image. But, shrugging my shoulders, I offer Figure 6.8. One copy (it should be as obvious as Cyrano's nose, some say, so I will not bother to identify which is which) is an original professional image, appearing here at 250 pixels per inch. The other has been converted to LAB, and then back to RGB.

And back again to LAB, and back, and back. 25 trips to LAB, 25 trips back to RGB. Because there could be defects or artifacts that aren't apparent at 100% magnification (Figures 6.8A and 6.8B are at the correct size for the image's resolution), I've also provided blowups of three different areas of the two images, including one of the critical green channel in the face area.

Similar demonstrations in the past have been met by commentary to the effect that the disastrous effects of the conversion to LAB only occur during the *first* conversion, and that repeatedly converting the same file over and over proves nothing, but that if it were converted at several points during the correction process, then, mor-bleu, quelle abomination!

While disposing of that, I want to deal with two other myths. First, it has been asserted that bad things happen if you work in a big-gamut space like LAB without being in 16 bits/Channel mode, which doubles the size of all files and adds several irritating steps. Second, it is alleged that the effect is particularly pronounced when the modifications are extreme, and even more pronounced when there is a series of modifications rather than just one or two.

Everything humanly possible has been done with the next example to incorporate the kinds of things that are supposed to provoke these problems. The original data quality is good. The bottom half is a digital capture, the top half is scanned film of a scene of different character.

Unlike Figure 6.8, where we took a good original and threw it back and forth 25 times, this time we have to make large changes to the file, just as the myth requires. Also, instead of doing it all in one move, I catered to the myth by dividing it into seven smaller moves. Furthermore, I've thrown in conversions to and from LAB after each step. Since the file is in a different state

each time, these are seven of the catastrophic first conversions.

Figure 6.9, which continues with enlarged pieces in Figure 6.10, has four versions.

The start point, which is not shown, is a 16-bit RGB file, which had been artificially lightened to enable a series of darkening moves. As you can see by the cast, I wasn't particularly interested in color fidelity, because it has no bearing on the present topic. The claim is that the damage will show up as excessive noise.

The test image consists of two halves. Both images were professionally shot; the top half is scanned film, the bottom half a digital capture.

These four versions came about as follows:
- 1. The seven sets of corrections were applied to the 16-bit original in 16-bit RGB. This is the politically correct approach. The file was only converted to 8-bit for printing, as printers cannot accept 16-bit files.
- 2. Same as above, except the file was converted to 8-bit immediately and all corrections were applied in that mode.
- 3. Same as #1, except after each of the seven steps, the file was converted to 16-bit LAB and then back to 16-bit RGB.
- 4. Same as #2, except after each step, the file went to 8-bit LAB and then back to RGB.

As with Figure 6.8, all variants are in a random order. If you care to guess which is which, the answers are in the "Notes & Credits" section starting on Page 351.

Personally, although I don't know whether it will be visible in print, if the proofs are accurate I think I could take a flyer about three of the five versions of Figure 6.9. But the difference is slight, we're looking at single channels at high magnification, and anybody who has to do corrections this extreme has many other

Figure 6.8 One of these images is the original. The other has been converted into LAB and back into RGB 25 times. Opposite page: magnifications of key areas at 200%, 300% (green channel only), and 400%. In each case, the placement of the two versions is random. Can you tell which is which?

things to worry about than bit depth and conversions. As for Figure 6.8, I state categorically that the two versions are identical for any conceivable professional purpose.

And Why Not Look, If You Please?

A boring bystander is unfortunate enough to be confronted by an enraged Cyrano, who imagines the man is staring at his nose.

> CYRANO. What do you think? Is it not a
>   phenomenon?
> THE BORE. But I knew better than to look!
> CYRANO. And why *not* look at it, if you
>   please?
> THE BORE. I was…
> CYRANO. Does it disgust you?
> THE BORE. Monsieur…
> CYRANO. Perhaps you do not like its color?

At the close of the scene, the bore is lucky to escape by being smacked on the side of the head rather than being run through with an épée. A good cuffing might do wonders for his counterparts in the Photoshop world, those who are so certain of their ground that they know better than to look.

And now that we *have* looked, and know the correct answer, it must be conceded that sometimes the theory seems so obviously true as to render any alternative inconceivable. This is a compelling example. How can moving to LAB *not* cause damage? We're throwing away (so they say) a third of the colors!

Translation: the original RGB file consists of three channels, each of which has 256 possible values, or *levels of tonality*. If we consider two channels simultaneously, each of the 256 values in the first channel has 256 more possibilities in the second, for a total of 65,536 possibilities. If we add a third channel, each of these 65,536 has 256 more, for a grand total of 16,777,216 possible combinations.

I don't know how many distinct colors are in the original version of Figure 6.8, but it isn't 16,777,216. For example, there's no bright yellow

anywhere. $210^R 210^G 40^B$, which is a fairly subdued greenish yellow, isn't likely to be found. And neither is anything with higher red, green, or both, coupled with an equal or lower blue.

If you agree, 86,756 possible colors have just fallen on their swords. Pastel blues, brilliant greens, and all cyans are also among the missing. Plus, there may be some luck of the cards. $50^R 50^G 10^B$ might easily be found in the woman's jacket, but there's no guarantee that even a single pixel will have exactly that value.

Some programs can analyze exactly how many discrete colors such a file contains, but I don't own one. My guess is that in this image it's a lot more like 10 million than 17 million.

But now, let's take it into LAB for the first time. There should be around 256 values in the L, granted. But there won't be anything like that in the A or B. With no really brilliant colors in the image, it would be surprising to see values more than ±50 in the AB channels. So, there are maybe 100 values in each one, tops.

Having just said goodbye to 14,217,216 colors, it only gets worse. As the L gets closer to its endpoints, the AB possibilities are sharply reduced. By the time we're at 5^L or 95^L we may be down to only 20 real possibilities in each AB channel.

To be generous, let's shortcut a lot of arithmetic and estimate that for each L value there are 60 possibilities in the A and B. If that wild guess is exactly correct, there are 921,600 possible colors in the LAB version. Since it isn't, let's call it a million. And we estimate that the RGB picture contains 10 million colors. We are throwing 9 million of them away by converting, no?

This is much worse than the advertised loss of

Figure 6.9 These two images, one digital, one from film, are joined in one file. Originally they were quite light, but instead of correcting in one pass, this drastic change was done in seven separate steps. In one version, all steps were done in 16-bit RGB; in another, 8-bit RGB; and a third and fourth were done in 16-bit and 8-bit respectively, but after each of the seven steps, the file was converted into LAB and back into RGB. On the opposite and next two pages, the four versions are shown in random order. Can you tell which is which?

Figure 6.10 *Views of the four versions of Figure 6.9 at various sizes. Left to right, the magnifications are 200%, 250%, 400%, and 500% (showing the green channel only).*

a third of the colors. We've lost nine-tenths of them! Surely, it is madness to suggest that converting into LAB is safe!

A great theory, seemingly irrefutable. And yet there's Figure 6.8, big as life, laughing at us, demonstrating that there's no loss at all, not even after 25 conversions to and from LAB.

When the Impossible Happens

This book assumes that our RGB is the variant known as sRGB, a choice of convenience, not an endorsement. Many professional photographers believe that sRGB is unduly limiting. Its definitions of the primary colors are relatively dull. Those who subscribe to this criticism generally prefer the definition Adobe RGB, which permits more brilliant colors at the expense of some subtlety. A few feel that Adobe RGB isn't wide-gamut enough and use an even more brilliant definition.

An Adobe RGB user who wishes to work on a file that was prepared for sRGB has to convert it, using Image: Mode>Convert to Profile, just as we LAB users need to convert out of whatever our own RGB is to do our thing.

So, here's the challenge. Suppose Figure 6.8 was prepared not by converting sRGB to LAB to sRGB 25 times in a row, but rather by converting sRGB to Adobe RGB to sRGB 25 times. How much closer to the original version would it be than the image with multiple LAB conversions?

Adobe RGB is certainly a much closer relative to sRGB than LAB is. It does waste a certain amount of real estate on colors that don't exist in sRGB, but still, if there are 10 million distinct colors in the sRGB version of Figure 6.8, I'd have to suspect that there would be 9 million in an Adobe RGB version. So it *has* to be less damaging to convert to Adobe RGB than to LAB—right?

Wrong.

If you do this test—and I have—a most perplexing thing occurs. The multiple-LAB conversion is closer to the original than the multiple-Adobe RGB version is. None of the three versions can be easily told apart, at least I can't, but we can apply statistical measures to verify that the impossible is indeed true.

This is becoming surreal, and we haven't even hit the clincher yet. Create a new RGB file. Choose a couple of unlike colors for Foreground and Background Colors, activate the gradient tool, and create a vignette. Make a copy of the file. Convert it to LAB, and then back to RGB. Hideous! Banding in several areas.

Seems fairly conclusive—but then again, there's Figure 6.9. Tortured almost beyond belief, converted again and again, when it's a real picture and not a computer-generated gradient, all four versions are so close as to be indistinguishable for any practical purpose.

Every logical way of looking at it suggests that the LAB versions have to be much worse than the RGB originals. But they aren't. Therefore, something about the reasoning is incorrect; it only remains to figure out what part.

Faced with things I don't understand, I find it useful to curse at the monitor. If that fails to resolve the problem, Armagnac, or on extremely rare occasions a cigar, may make an appearance to help the thought process along. I forget how much of this was necessary ten years ago, when I first tried to figure out how there could possibly not be a visible loss when going to LAB. Anyhow, there are two basic answers:

1. In mathematics, the symbols $+$ and $\times$ do not mean the same thing.

2. In a photograph, the blood does not curdle at the thought of altering a single comma.

Of Salaries and Pixels

Numbers make excellent servants, poor masters. An overweening and unwarranted belief in the power of their precision has been the hallmark of those who cry data loss every time there's a minor move in the image.

John Jones makes $50,000 per year. How much does he make per week?

A computer programmer would answer, is it a leap year, or not? A statistician would answer, about $1,000.

Someone who thinks that converting to LAB is damaging would answer, $958.9041095890.

We need clarification. Does what we have been told really, literally mean that he makes $50,000.00, not a penny more or less, in the course of one non-leap year? Or is $50,000 merely shorthand for somewhere between $45,000 and $55,000? Or between $49,000 and $51,000?

Knowing as little as we do, the statistician's answer is correct. It really sounds like $50,000 is some kind of rough estimate. Any answer more precise than $1,000 a week makes an unwarranted assumption about the reliability of the data. $958.9041095890 sounds ever so much more authoritative, and so impresses some Photoshop authorities that they call the $1,000 answer "quantization error." In fact, from the statistical point of view, it's far more accurate than making unwarranted assumptions about how many significant digits we start with. Anything other than the first digit after the dollar sign is a random number, for all we know now.

The same analysis applies to digital images. Cameras and scanners do not return perfect data. We should have more confidence in the reliability of midtone captures than those of extreme lights and darks; in less saturated rather than brilliant colors; in the green channel rather than either of the other two. But in any case, the very act of capturing the image has introduced unwanted variation.

Even if the data is very good (and how would you prove that it is?), it can never be fully reliable. Suppose you own the finest camera or scanner in the world. You claim that it's capable of resolving 1,000 different levels of gray, and that a certain pixel measures 437, and that's the correct value, period, amen.

The response is, how can you be so sure? The device is actually trying to juggle a lot more than 1,000 values, and it's doing some rounding. What 437 really tells us is that the pixel measures somewhere between 436.51 and 437.49. But is the device actually that good? Because if

it's off by as much as .02, it could conceivably be reporting something as 437 that actually should have been rounded to 436 or 438. And if you say yes, the device is really that good, I'll ask whether it's good enough to know the difference between 436.4999999, which rounds to 436, and 436.5000001, which should be reported as 437; and I'll keep adding decimal places until you give up and admit that it's theoretically possible that 437 is not technically the correct value.

Back in the real world, the results are reported on a scale of 0 to 255, or 256 values in all. We use this scale because 256 happens to be the number of possibilities that can be described with eight bits of computer data. That is, a single bit is either on or off, yes or no, 0 or 1. Two bits give us four possibilities: 00, 01, 10, and 11. Three bits permit eight, since any of the above four two-digit numbers could be followed by either a 0 or a 1. Each time a new bit is added, the possibilities redouble. Four bits allows 16, five 32, six 64, seven 128, and eight 256.

All modern capture devices nominally use more bits. They may think they're getting 1,024 values, or even 4,096. The question is whether the numbers are particularly accurate. Some people are so buffaloed by arithmetic and so in awe of any kind of measurement by machine that they forget to ask it.

No computer program can verify whether a given pixel is correct. We have only our gut feelings as to how accurate the capture is. My own is, I don't think any devices can make accurate real-world captures in more than thousandth-part increments, and that's only under the very best conditions at certain levels of lightness. If it's a digital capture taken in relatively dark conditions, I don't think the camera gets even close to 256 accurate values. Under better conditions, I think most cameras record accurately to within a level of the ideal, particularly in the critical green channel. That is, if the camera records 128^G, I doubt, but don't rule out the possibility, that 126^G or 130^G would have been more accurate. A difference of one level, that's another story.

Of Translations and Transfers

Cyrano never exactly said any of the things quoted so far. He couldn't have—he was speaking French. What you've read is a translation, a restatement of what he said, just as an LAB file is a translation, a restatement, of the RGB one.

Cyrano says, *"Mon sang se coagule."* The first two words can be matched exactly in English: *my blood*. The second two are harder. The cognate *coagulates itself* doesn't carry the proper sense. I vote for *curdles,* but would accept *runs cold* or *congeals.* The three choices are not identical, but equivalent for all practical purposes.

Now, suppose someone without access to the original text retranslates *my blood curdles* back into French. The first two words would be restored to the original *mon sang,* for sure. There are several possibilities for the third—all just as good as the original to everyone except Cyrano, whose blood curdled at the thought of changing a single comma.

If we retranslated the entire play, from French to English and back again, each phrase would compare to the original in one of the following ways:

- Identical.
- Worse.
- Equivalent.
- Better.

The phrase we've been discussing would be partially identical, partially equivalent. The chances are that much of the rest of the play would be worse, because there really is loss in certain translations. (On the other hand, a book of the collected speeches of George W. Bush might well read better if it were translated from English to Russian and back again.)

The point is, identical is not only unlikely, but it isn't even desirable, provided the retranslation is equivalent or better. And so it is with color files. Around two-thirds of the pixels in the version of Figure 6.8 that was translated 25 times in and out of LAB are identical to the original. The remaining third could conceivably be worse than the original—but conceivably some are just as

good, and others may even be better. We just don't know. Unless the pixels fall outside of our range of uncertainty, which is always at least one level, to insist that they match the original exactly is to go to the last hundred millionth of a cent when your margin of error is a thousand dollars; to announce that your blood curdles at the thought of changing a single comma.

And that's the fundamental difference between photographs and computer-generated art, one that renders the test of a gradient being converted to LAB pointless. In gradients, the change of any comma would indeed be blood-curdling.

A Photoshop value of, say, 127, is an approximation, if it's a photograph. Maybe if this were a perfect world, with infinitely precise cameras, its real value would be 126.67289, which rounds to 127 but can go to 126 instead without any worries. In our world, the range is considerably wider, so 126 might well be not just equivalent to but better than 127.

But if it's a gradient, then the correct value in a perfect world is 127.00000. Any change is by definition wrong. If the retranslation doesn't come back identical, then it's worse. Better and equivalent are no longer possibilities.

If a whole row of pixels in a gradient jumps by two levels rather than one, it's visible, even though in a normal photograph, a two-level variation can be seen by the naked eye about as frequently as Halley's Comet.

Theorizing that converting to LAB causes damage and attempting to prove it by converting a gradient is circular reasoning. It assumes that a single value is uniquely correct, tests a method that is sure to change it, and then concludes that the method is inaccurate. It is a statement that *my blood curdles* is the one and only correct way to translate Cyrano's phrase and that any other phrase is data loss.

Incidentally, the problem of gradients in conversion is by no means limited to LAB. Many people face needless frustration when they prepare gradients (particularly blue ones) in RGB for files that are eventually going to CMYK. This begs for banding or other evil consequences. Gradients should be created in the same color-space as the output device—in this case, CMYK.

The Most Useful Statistic

An architect planning to build something in a strange city needs to know what temperatures are likely to be encountered, so that appropriate heating and air conditioning systems can be ordered. The information that the average noon-time temperature in my New Jersey home town is around 53 degrees Fahrenheit would not be enough for that purpose. That average tempera-ture is similar to that of Kansas City, Missouri, which, not being close to any ocean, has more extreme heat and cold. Yet summer days where I live are frequently hotter than in San Juan, Puerto Rico, which has a much higher average temperature overall. As a matter of fact, Fair-banks, Alaska, is sometimes as hot as San Juan in the summertime.

The average temperature is not as important as how much it fluctuates. And the architect would need something better than all the tem-perature records of the last few years. For exam-ple, I don't recall noontime temperatures of higher than 95° in the last five years. However, around 15 years ago, it hit a ghastly 106° and stayed there for several days.

The supremely important statistic known as *standard deviation* would have informed the architect that such a heat wave was possible, even if the only records available were for the last two years. The concept applies whenever there are many data points clustered more or less uniformly around a mean value, as the weather is. If the mean is 53°, we're equally likely to find 63° as 43°; less likely but still equally likely to find 73° as 33°, and so on.

I haven't gathered the data or done the arith-metic, but I'm going to estimate that the stan-dard deviation in my home town is around 14°, and the cities mentioned above as follows: Kansas City, 17°; San Juan, 5°; Fairbanks, 24°.

High standard deviations are generally bad things. If you had to choose which of these cities to live in based solely on their climates, you would certainly choose them in the order of lowest standard deviation—even if you don't know precisely what standard deviation means or how it is computed.

In fact, almost everything having to do with process control in the graphic arts amounts to a struggle to reduce the standard deviation, because variation is bad and variation is what the standard deviation measures. For example, the printer of this book, whose presses are run by mortals, sometimes prints jobs lighter or darker than his average. I am hoping very hard that his standard deviation is low and that this book will fall close to the mean when printed.

Once enough data exists for a standard devi-ation to be computed, it can be used to predict the likelihood of various events. For example, the variation of noontime temperatures over the period of a year is likely to be slightly less than six times the standard deviation, meaning in my case that the hottest day is around 80° hotter than the coolest. Fairbanks, I am given to understand, has the highest standard deviation of any major city—around 140° difference be-tween the coldest and hottest days. I can also learn from the standard deviation that my town does occasionally have days in the 90s; that something on the order of the 106° heat wave is apt to occur every 20 years or so, and that a reading of 115° would indicate that either the thermometer is broken or the weather recording station is on fire.

The Odds Are Against It

As you may have conjectured, standard devia-tion can also be part of image analysis. Like the histogram, I consider it worthless as an aid to image manipulation. Neither can tell us about the visual quality of an image as accurately as our own eyes do.

Both are, however, sometimes helpful in try-ing to figure out why something is happening that we don't understand, like, for example, why converting to LAB is safe when logic seems to dictate otherwise.

To learn how close the two halves of Figure 6.8 are, I applied one to the other in Difference mode. This blend, which can be done in several ways, creates a black file, except in pixels where the two images aren't identical.

For an RGB image, Photoshop offers six different sets of statistics to accompany the histogram, in locations that vary with the version of Photoshop. The most important stats are those for the green channel and for luminosity, which is a weighted average of red, green, and blue. Photoshop reports that in the green channel the mean variation between the original of Figure 6.8 and the version that went in and out of LAB 25 times is .15 levels and the standard deviation .36; in luminosity the numbers are .10 and .30.

Let me offer, er, a translation. The numbers indicate that the variation is approximately equivalent in impact to the soft noise or dither that Photoshop by default inserts every time an image is converted from one colorspace to another. If you didn't know that Photoshop does so, you're not alone—it's undetectable, useful,

and harmless. (If you're going to be converting files 50 times, though, you should turn it off, as I did for these tests.)

Further, if these numbers are correct, around 80 percent of the pixels in the two green channels are identical, and essentially all others are one level apart. Variation of two or more levels would occur, if at all, less than one time in every 5,000 pixels.

Also, remember that we never see individual pixels except on the monitor. When the image is printed, there's always an averaging process to convert the original pixels into the form that the output device requires. This is true regardless of how the image gets printed. In the case of this book, the press requires halftone dots, tiny blobs of cyan, magenta, yellow, and black ink. Each dot is calculated by averaging, usually, the values of three or four pixels. Take a loupe to either half of Figure 6.8, and if you have a few weeks to spare you'll be able to count some 2.7 million halftone dots, averaged down from around 7.5 million pixels in the CMYK Photoshop file.

What would it take for us to notice roughness, any degradation in quality? I'd say, a dot, not a pixel, that varied from its proper value by at least two percentage points. Although printing dots are usually referred to in terms of percentages, they in fact are constructed on a 256-level scale, just as pixels are. Two percentage points equals five levels.

But let's be ultra-conservative and say that a dot might be detected if it were only two *levels* larger or smaller than it should be. Being that it's camouflaged by three other correct dots of different colors that are intersecting with it to some extent, it would be almost impossible to see, but let's theorize that we are going to edit the file so drastically that the difference might show up later.

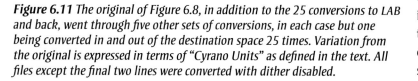

The Torture Test: 25 Times Back and Forth
(All variations from original are expressed in Cyrano Units; lower is better)

sRGB to	Red	Green	Blue	Lum
LAB	1.62	1.16	1.71	0.95
ColorMatch RGB	1.68	0.65	0.49	0.09
Adobe RGB	3.96	0.88	1.99	3.18
Wide Gamut RGB	8.45	12.80	3.66	9.12
LAB (w/dither, 1 conversion)	2.62	2.13	2.82	1.38
LAB (w/dither, 25 conversions)	9.50	7.67	10.04	3.37

Figure 6.11 The original of Figure 6.8, in addition to the 25 conversions to LAB and back, went through five other sets of conversions, in each case but one being converted in and out of the destination space 25 times. Variation from the original is expressed in terms of "Cyrano Units" as defined in the text. All files except the final two lines were converted with dither disabled.

Now, let's try to figure the odds of this rogue dot ever showing its long nose. I will skip over considerable arithmetic here in favor of approximations. The precise odds can't be calculated because of irritating complications such as the fact that the data isn't truly randomly distributed around the mean, and that the presence of one incorrect pixel sharply increases the odds that one of its neighbors will be also. So, I will use the traditional prepress technique of the fudge factor. I will assume that one in every 300 pixels varies from the original by two levels.

Cutting to the swordfight, the only sure way to get a two-level variation in the dot is to have four pixels forming a square, all being either two or more levels lighter or two or more levels darker than the mean.

The odds against either event occurring are approximately 65 trillion to one.

A much more reasonable scenario would be to take a cube of nine pixels. If any four of them were rogues, *and* if there weren't any rogues of the opposite persuasion to cancel their effect out, then it's fairly likely that a two-level variation might occur in a certain halftone dot. The odds against this happening are a much more modest billion and a half to one against.

And remember, even if it happened, you almost certainly wouldn't notice, particularly if it happened in the red or blue channel. And it assumes far too many rogue pixels. In fact, it assumes that the standard deviation is twice as high—like it would have been, if these repeated conversions had been into Adobe RGB rather than LAB.

The Tale of the Tape

Given these tiny variations, the two halves of Figure 6.8 are identical for all practical purposes, and to the extent they vary, nobody can prove which one is better. But what level of variation might actually cause a problem?

Disgracefully little research has been done into the vital issue of the handling of images that have been converted 50 times, an omission I propose to remedy here by offering the following formula: three times the standard deviation plus half the mean. As the inventor of this new standard, I get to name it; and in honor of this chapter, it is hereby dubbed the Cyrano Unit.

If the reconverted version varies from the original by less than two Cyranos, the files run a statistical dead heat. Between two and three, there's a case to be made that the original is better, but it won't make any difference. At values of three in the green or luminosity sets, somewhat higher in the red and much higher in the blue, it becomes conceivable that problems may develop later; at four it becomes probable; and at five it's a definite pain. (The stats labeled RGB and Color are not important.)

Not content with converting a file to LAB and back 25 times, I tried the experiment with four other settings. The results are summarized—in Cyranos—in Figure 6.11, which brings us back to the flabbergasting observation that we get closer to the original if we convert to LAB and back than to Adobe RGB and back.

I also tested conversions into ColorMatch RGB, which covers a smaller gamut, and into Wide Gamut RGB, which, as the name suggests, is huge, as big as LAB itself. Unsurprisingly, the smaller the gamut being tested, the closer the post-conversion file was to the original. The ColorMatch RGB version was slightly closer than its LAB counterpart. In its green channel, 19 of 20 pixels were identical to the original.

The Adobe RGB version isn't quite as close, particularly in the red channel. In fact, let me earn the price of the book by offering an important tip: before commencing work on a file, don't convert it to Adobe RGB 25 times and back. With LAB and ColorMatch RGB, go for it, if you've got a lot of time on your hands. But not Adobe RGB.

The Wide Gamut RGB version is the worst of the lot by a large margin. A lot of people would have thought that the LAB file would have had the same kind of grim numbers. It didn't happen. Let's discuss why.

The Plus Sign and the Times Sign

These three RGB definitions are more alike than different. The red channel in one is very similar to that of another, except the narrower-gamut one will show more contrast. It has to, because it needs to have a lot of action at the extremes if it hopes to match the brilliance of colors that the wider-gamut RGB produces routinely. Therefore, any object occupies slightly more space in the narrower-gamut RGB. It may take 11 levels to portray something for which the wider-gamut one only needs 10, which becomes awkward when converting between the two. With only ten steps in the original, we can't go from 1 to 11 in ten steps of 1.1, as we'd like to. We have to take single steps—except that somewhere along the line there will be one dubious double step. And if we go from 11 to 10 steps, we can't spread the damage among all eleven: ten will get their normal variation and one will vanish. That's potentially the birth of a rogue pixel.

This effect, where the very similarity of the file structure hampers the conversion, is absent in LAB. There's a mild correspondence between the L and every RGB channel, but it's heavily disguised by the impact of the AB, which have as much in common with the RGB channels as the poetry of Edmond Rostand has with that of Eminem. The A and B have disturbingly long ranges between steps, but since the steps don't correspond to anything in RGB, the effect is distributed more uniformly.

That the RGB channels are intact also explains the mystery of how LAB appears to dump nine-tenths of the possible colors without destroying the image. When the RGB channels are sound, it doesn't matter how many colors are missing, because they'll show up sooner or later. That the LAB file doesn't have millions of distinct colors merely means that certain combinations of RGB values are impossible—temporarily. If you have 150^{R}160^G, then perhaps 170^B may not be a possible companion; you'd have to go to 171^B or 169^B. The value 170^B exists in the file, just not in conjunction with the other two.

If that's an unsatisfactory state of affairs, there are lots of ways to restore millions of colors very quickly, such as:

- Gaussian blur at .1 pixel radius.
- Rotate the image 5 degrees and then rotate it back.
- Upsize the image by one pixel and then downsize it again.
- Make a copy of the file, convert it to LAB, reconvert it to RGB, and apply it to the original at 50% opacity.

In fact, just about any move you make to a single channel will create tens of thousands, if not millions, more color possibilities.

Fortunately, you can save all of the above quackery for the next time some nincompoop complains that your histograms look too ugly. A file that merely is missing a lot of color combinations is no cause for worry. There may have been less than a million distinct colors in the LAB version of Figure 6.8, but there are millions and millions now that ink has hit paper. There would have been millions had we output it on a desktop printer, and there are even millions when we open the file and look at it on screen.

No output process uses the red channel as is. Even a desktop printer that appears to be taking RGB data is converting the incoming file to CMYK. And the cyan channel, although similar to the red, has been heavily munged. Its center has been lightened, and to some extent it's been blended with the previous blue channel. The previous limits on combinations with other channels no longer apply, and the millions of colors are shown to be, like Cyrano orchestrating the courtship of Roxane from underneath her balcony, there all the time, temporarily hidden in the shadows.

A Bit About Bits

The question of whether converting colorspaces causes harm is closely related to one mentioned during the discussion of Figure 6.9: whether there might ever be an advantage in correcting files in Mode: 16 Bits/Channel as opposed to the more conventional 8 Bits/Channel. That subject is academic for us, because all techniques in the book work either way. However, the debate does offer some constructive lessons.

16-bit files are twice as large. They contain 65,536 tonal levels per channel rather than 256. It is logical to think that such a file might be more forgiving of major tonal changes than an 8-bit file would be, particularly if there are several such changes in succession. So, a number of Photoshop authorities, some politely and some imperiously, have suggested that at least major editing should be done in 16-bit mode, without ever showing a single example that suggested there was any merit in doing so. In one notorious case, a prominent photographer announced that anyone who wasn't editing in 16-bit mode was a "recreational user" of Photoshop, rather than a professional.

It sounds sensible, just as the theory that converting to LAB is damaging sounds sensible. And the result is just the same: in practice, the theory doesn't work. On images containing computer-generated gradients, yes. But on color photographs, no. Consider Figure 6.9, which has been massively corrected, seven different times. Yet the version done entirely in 8-bit *and* also converted seven times during the process to and from LAB is just as good as the one done in 16-bit all the way with no unnecessary conversions.

In the last three years, around a dozen people, including me, have made serious efforts to find anything to support the proposition that 16-bit editing might be better under any circumstances. By that, I mean any unretouched color photograph that might possibly be used in the real world, and any sequence of attempts to improve the image, however farfetched, where editing in 16-bit creates a better result than 8-bit. Images have been tortured beyond belief. Nobody has found any quality gain at all.

Neither, of course, has anybody shown that there's any loss by doing so. So, if you have the disk space to spare, and feel like wearing belt and suspenders, go ahead.

As for LAB specifically, a number of people whose opinion I respect think that because LAB is so huge, editing there in 16-bit might make more sense than it would in RGB. With the possible exceptions of nearly neutral images that have been heavily altered in the L channel and of once-in-a-lifetime images where you decide to unsharp mask the B channel, it isn't true. Counterintuitive as it sounds, for a lot of the

8- and 16-Bit: An Exception

Many digital cameras offer the option of producing an 8-bit or 16-bit file, although most consumer-level digicams output in 8-bit only. If you have the option, and are planning to work on the image afterward to any extent, you should open in 16-bit and convert to 8-bit in Photoshop at your convenience, whether you use LAB or not.

In response to a standing challenge, many users have sent me files, together with the actions that were taken, seeking to show that 16-bit corrections were better. There have only been two cases where the claim held up. In each, the user had output both types of file using his camera software and then had applied massive, but identical, corrections to both.

The first user supplied images on a gradated gray background, which posterized badly in the 8-bit version. The second had work featuring dark, rich colors: burgundies and greens. After huge corrections, which included attempting to work on a raw 1.0-gamma file in Adobe RGB, the 8-bit version exhibited ugly dark noise in these areas that wasn't found in the 16-bit.

When these corrections were repeated on 8-bit files that had been generated by converting the 16-bit original to 8-bit *in Photoshop*, however, the results were every bit as good as the ones done in 16-bit all the way.

One, with the 8-bit file prepared by Canon's Digital Photo Professional 1.5, arrived while I was drafting this chapter. I compared it to an 8-bit version generated in Photoshop from the 16-bit file prepared by the Canon software. After verifying that the Photoshop version was extremely close to the 16-bit original, I compared the two 8-bit versions before they were corrected. The variation was a ghastly 7.5 Cyrano Units in the green channel—more than enough to cause problems if the image is edited extensively.

reasons discussed earlier, RGB would need the extra bits more than LAB does. Theoretically only, I hasten to say: in real life neither one needs it at all. However, if we were forced to work in 6-bit—only 64 levels per channel—6-bit LAB would have a lot of advantages over 6-bit RGB. And with that, I think we should stop discussing 6-bit Photoshop and files that are converted 25 times back and forth, and how many angels can dance on the head of a pin, and whether Photoshop books should be written in blank verse.

Ton Nom Est Dans Mon Coeur

Lawyers would describe this half of the chapter as being an attempt to *prove a negative,* an exercise in futility. That is, there's no way of proving absolutely that converting to LAB *never* damages a file or that editing in 16-bit *never* gives better results, or that wearing garlic around the neck while at the computer never prevents shadows from plugging.

Fortunately, it's not up to me. Whoever is advocating doing something inconvenient is responsible for demonstrating why it's necessary. The purpose of this book is to suggest that you should learn an alternative way of working with color, which is certainly inconvenient even before we consider having to convert each file to LAB and then back. Therefore, I'm the one who has to make the case that you will get better results that way. So, where possible, I compare the LAB method to the RGB equivalent—if one exists.

> CYRANO. I am so in thrall to your hair
> That, like one who stares at the sun,
> And thereafter imagines shades of vermilion
>   on everything,
> When I leave your fire, your luminescence,
> My whole life develops a blond cast.
> ROXANE. [with trembling voice]
>   Oui, c'est bien l'amour…

This is not very good color theory. One who stares at a colored object sees the *complementary* color thereafter, so if Roxane's hair was all that compelling, Cyrano would have been looking at the world through B—negative glasses once he turned away from her—a blue cast, not a blond one. Nevertheless, as Roxane remarked, it is truly love, and mere matters of factual inaccuracy have seldom troubled suitors.

Cyrano was not a Photoshop user himself, but had he been, he would have been a devotee of LAB, the space that liberates color and allows the imagination to put blond casts where it will. If someone suggests you should give that up on a theory, that person should be wielding a picture, not statistics; a sword, not a histogram.

> THE FIRST CADET. [shrugging his shoulders]
>   Always the sharp, the pointed word.
> CYRANO. Indeed, the word is the point.
> And when I die, I should like it to be
> In the evening, under a rosy sky
> As I speak sharp words in favor of beauty.
> Ah! To be struck down by the noble arm
> Of a man worthy to be my enemy,
> On the field of glory, and not in a sickbed,
> A point in my heart and a point on my lips.

The Bottom Line

Most problems with LAB derive from using it on images for which it is not suited, from not appreciating that it can produce colors that are wildly out of any known gamut, and particularly, from trying too hard to get a perfect result in the L channel.

LAB should be a Photoshop-only tool. Other programs generally don't support it. Sending an LAB file to an output device is a form of Russian roulette.

There is no problem in converting files from RGB to LAB and back, unless the file contains a computer-generated graphic such as a gradient. Such graphics should always be made in the final output space—CMYK if the job is to be printed.

The L channel sometimes serves as a better black and white version of a color file than a direct conversion to grayscale would be. However, the two are close relatives. Blending channels gets superior results.

7

Summing Up: LAB and the Workflow

How do LAB's capabilities fit into your workflow? Much depends on your expertise—and on how much time you have per image. This chapter sorts out the advantages, adds a few new wrinkles, and shows why LAB is the best home for the Shadow/Highlight command.

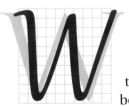e have now reached a natural resting point in our survey of LAB and its uses. The first six chapters covered the basics and gave an idea of the kinds of things that are possible in LAB and how they stack up to the alternatives in RGB or CMYK. The remainder of the book is harder, as we get into the areas where LAB can do things that are clearly out of the question elsewhere. Therefore, the chapters will no longer have separate sections aimed at an advanced audience: enter the rest of this book at your own risk.

First, however, we should try to sum up, to discuss and make suggestions as to how LAB might fit into your own workflow. Certain aspects of it are right for all users; few if any are wrong for all users. In the middle lie a slew of techniques that are appropriate for some of us and inadvisable for others.

Before getting into this middle ground, here's a preview of some of what's found in the second half—most of which is not middle ground at all, but territory in which LAB is clearly superior to any alternative.

• LAB is generally the best space for retouching. This doesn't refer to simple stuff like eliminating dust and hairs; such moves can be made with many different tools in whatever colorspace you like. But the more difficult the retouching, the more LAB has to offer.

• Sometimes we are asked to make radical changes in a product's color, such as turning a blue shirt red. If you are currently making the mistake of doing this work in RGB or CMYK, you should read Chapter 10 immediately. LAB changes colors better and faster, particularly if the desired color has a Pantone Matching System or other known specification.

- Certain types of selections and masks are easily available in LAB but not elsewhere.
- If you are involved in calibration or color management of any kind, a working knowledge of LAB is invaluable.
- Several blending techniques work well in LAB and not at all in RGB or CMYK.
- If you frequently work with portraits, LAB has several important advantages.

A Picture Is Worth a Thousand Words

To decide how much to use the techniques we've learned requires discussion of the age-old question, how much is a picture worth?

Worth refers not to a volume of words so much as to an amount of time. Let's measure how much it's worth to you, by talking about your typical image—neither the most important of all nor a throwaway—but the sort of image that you normally have to deal with. How much time are you willing to budget to improve quality?

You could, of course, not budget any time at all: just print or post whatever comes out of the camera and hope for the best. But if you have even ten seconds to spare, you can probably do better with Photoshop's artificial intelligence: Image: Adjustments>Auto Color. With a whole slew of such images, you can even set up an Action, and a Droplet, and have Photoshop apply Auto Color to a whole batch of images. If you're more conservative, you could substitute Image: Adjustments> Auto Contrast, which is less likely to make a dramatic improvement but also less likely to do something really stupid.

But suppose someone suggests a method that would improve quality substantially over either of the above methods, but which requires one extra minute per image. Would you be willing to spend that minute?

As a reader of this book, the chances are quite good that you would, although that minute may be too long for some readers. But now comes the interesting part: if it took five minutes per image, not one, to assure the extra quality, would you still do it?

I think most readers would continue to say yes, but we will have lost quite a few for whom five minutes extra is not going to cut it. Usually, these are people in high-volume operations, or those facing difficult deadlines.

Would you take 10 minutes per image? Would you accept 15? How about half an hour, if it truly made each image look better?

So far, these are real-world questions. Professionals using traditional techniques to make global corrections ordinarily need around five to 10 minutes per image, and the result is incomparably better than anything automated. Tricky images take more time, possibly as much as half an hour, rarely more. That's the point of diminishing returns, in my opinion.

But let's continue the game. If, hypothetically, you could get significantly better quality by investing an hour, would you do that? Two hours? A full day? Where do you draw the line? Obviously, certain images come along that are so important to our careers that we would hypothetically spend six months to fix them up, if that's what it took. Forget those: we're talking typical images.

I've asked this question a lot over the years, so I have a pretty good handle on where people stand. The work that I'm most familiar with, high-end agency and magazine color correction, as well as the stuff I use in my books, typically eats up 15 minutes to half an hour per image. But, if an hour per image was what it took, I'd invest that time. Two hours apiece, no.

Many photographers and in-house production departments say they're willing to go as far as I would, but I'd guess that at least a third of this book's readers would not. Then again, some might be willing to go further. Many people say that they would willingly spend a day or two per image if needed. The most extreme answer I ever got was from executives of a manufacturer of theme calendars, which feature pictures in formats up to 11 by 17 inches. They said that if, for the sake of argument, it took 40 hours per picture to get them right, they would do it.

When Speed Is All-Important

All these responses can be divided into two broad groups: those who have enough time to optimize the image, and those who are going to have to wing it. If you fall into the first, happier category, your course is clear. Analyze each image; don't assume that you will be using LAB but look for opportunities where it might be advantageous.

If you fall in the second, rushed category, however, you need to be a desperado. Although your images will doubtless look better than if you had just run Auto Color, you have to accept that they won't be as good as if you had had a more reasonable amount of time. It becomes a matter of what method gives the biggest bang for the buck, and the answer is clear. If you can only spare one to five minutes per image, an all-LAB workflow is the way to go.

If I had 15 minutes, I'm not positive I'd work on Figure 7.1 in LAB. Probably I would, because the yellow could stand more variation and more intensity, but I'm not sure—I might have a go at it with RGB curves first.

In the one-minute scenario, however, there's no time for philosophizing. I open the image, convert immediately to LAB, and look for a couple of key numbers. The top of the rail seems to be the lightest point of

the image. It measures $100^L 0^A 0^B$, no detail at all. The door frame I will guess should be neutral. Measuring a point halfway up it finds $76^L (4)^A (11)^B$, a greenish blue. I should really measure the darkest point of the image, too, but it's not obvious where it is and I am in too big a hurry to find out. Time elapsed for this investigation: around 15 seconds.

Command–M brings up the Curves dialog. I steepen the AB curves along the lines of Chapter 1. Each passes to the right of the center point as described in Chapter 4, moving away from green and toward magenta, and away from blue and toward yellow. I check the Info palette again to be sure that the door frame has become approximately $0^A 0^B$. Then, the L curve, putting space between the blue reflection and the dark trees. After clicking OK, the time elapsed is up to 35 seconds.

Finally, Command–1 to expose the L channel, and Filter: Sharpen>Unsharp Mask. No time to test alternate numbers, so I just click OK to accept whatever's there. I am now ready to convert out of LAB for final output. The total time to get to Figure 7.2 is somewhere between 45 seconds and a minute.

Figure 7.1 This raw image could be enhanced by many different methods, of which LAB maneuvering is only one. But suppose that you only had one minute to do whatever you could?

Figure 7.2 *Top, the image was created from Figure 7.1 in less than a minute, using the curves shown below plus a minor sharpening.*

With the extra time, I avoided the awkward L channel move. A set of RGB curves might have worked alone, but here I helped them out with a luminosity blend involving the blue channel, a topic to be discussed in Chapter 14.

I still did some of the work in LAB, but a bit more precisely. First, instead of just measuring one part of the door frame, I tried several—too much chance that a single area isn't typical. Also, in the one-minute correction, I took the position that the frame was gray. I'm not sure that was the correct view. With extra time, one must be alive to the possibility that, since blue sky is being reflected off the glass, the frame may be reflecting blue as well. In forcing neutrality into the door frame, I probably made Figure 7.2 too yellow.

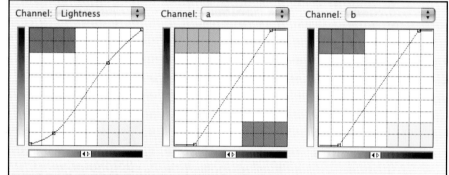

Now, let's consider the alternatives, both quicker and slower. The quick one is an application of Auto Color to the RGB file. Usually, that improves the original. This time, Auto Color made it worse, because it mistook the presence of a lot of natural yellow for a yellow cast. It therefore tried to compensate by making the image bluer, resulting in the disastrous Figure 7.3A because the image was in fact already too blue.

Instead, what would you get if you were an expert and could spare 15 minutes? A better image, presumably, but how much better?

I tried finding out, and got Figure 7.3B. It's better than Figure 7.2. The sky reflected in the doors is lighter and bluer; the sharpening more precise, the palm trees snappier; the yellow gradations subtler.

And certainly, I didn't just accept whatever value popped up in the Unsharp Mask menu. Rather, I customized the sharpening for the image. Also, after converting the image into CMYK for printing, I steepened the dark half of the black curve to try to accentuate shadow detail.

We know which of these three efforts is worst and which is best. But if Figure 7.3A, the Auto Color method, is what you get in five seconds and Figure 7.3B is what an expert gets get in 15 minutes, the one-minute alternative, Figure 7.2, starts to look attractive if you're pressed for time.

So attractive, in fact, that we should probably discuss a LAB-*only* workflow for those for whom time is at a premium.

Two types of images remain problematic in LAB with the tools we've discussed so far: those with different color balances in the highlights and shadows, and those with color casts *except* in the highlights and shadows. We'll end this chapter—and this half of the book—by showing ways of getting around these inconveniences. For now, we'll return to the recommended way for people who have the time and the inclination—and, let us not forget, the expertise—to optimize the image beyond what LAB can do alone.

The Going Gets Tough

Considering that a reader of this book could be anyone from a user of a disposable camera to a retoucher to a professional photographer, and the images could be anything from tourism shots to a candid of Aunt Hortense with the light behind her to carefully planned studio exposures, it's mildly difficult to generalize about workflow. Nevertheless, we all have a few things in common:

• At some point we have an RGB file. In past years certain scanners delivered raw files in CMYK or even in LAB, but that workflow is rare nowadays.

• At some point we have to decide whether it pays to convert that RGB file into LAB in

Figure 7.3 *Above, an alternative that takes less time than the LAB correction shown in Figure 7.2: an application of Photoshop's Auto Color command. Below, a more complete correction, involving not just LAB but some RGB channel blending plus a final adjustment in CMYK. Time: 15 minutes.*

order to work some kind of magic with it.

● Once we're done in LAB, we have to convert the file to something else.

Now, the differences.

● Some of us get the RGB files dumped on our heads, whereas others may either be forced to or have the option to acquire the RGB by some nefarious digital means, such as scanning film, opening a file into Photoshop's Camera Raw, or opening a digital capture using software supplied by the camera's manufacturer. With any of these three methods, the possibility exists of attempting to improve quality before we get to the RGB stage mentioned above.

● If we decide to work in LAB, some of us have to reconvert to RGB afterward because we're planning to send the file to some kind of output device that requires RGB, or because it will be posted on the Web. Others need to convert to CMYK because the job is destined for a printing press or because it is going to a desktop printer with a Raster Image Processor (RIP) that prefers CMYK data.

● Some of us face deadline pressure that compels us to work very quickly, whereas others can take a deep breath, decide how they want to treat each image, and then take their time in doing so.

● Finally, some of us work with Photoshop for a living, and others feel lucky when they are able to get it to boot up successfully, and still others fall somewhere between the two extremes. Some of us comprehend exactly how Figure 7.3B was created. For others, the description of how I did it might as well have been written in Sanskrit.

Before we go too much further, we need a pep talk about this last item. LAB is both simple and complex. The first halves of all the first five chapters of this book were written in, after a fashion, plain English. There isn't a step-by-step box for every picture, but you don't have to be very good at Photoshop to follow what's going on.

As for the second halves, well, as advertised, they weren't for beginners. But, starting with the second half of Chapter 5 and continuing up until now, the book has insidiously become an expert text. Even the most knowledgeable will have difficulty with some of the content on their first read.

If you're getting confused at this point, you will be pleased to know that the editing team for this book felt your pain. Upon reading the statement in the opening sentences of this chapter that things were about to get hard, beta reader Bruce Fellman remarked, "Oy, and it's been a walk in the park so far!" Several others also indicated that they threw the manuscript at the wall upon reading the same passage.

Be that as it may, please remember that the first halves of all the chapters so far have suggested the following workflow, which is not all that hard:

● Once the image is converted to LAB, see if the main focus of interest can be isolated in a narrow range in the L channel, and if so, apply a curve that steepens that area.

● Decide whether the grays in the file are really gray, or whether you see any internal indication that there's a color cast. If not, steepen the A and B curves by pivoting them around the midpoint. If yes, move the midpoint to the right or left as necessary.

● If necessary, blur the AB channels separately, and sharpen the L.

Now, it must be granted that it takes an hour or so to get used to the weird positive-negative numbering system in the A and B channels. And, certainly, the first few times you make the A and B curves steeper it feels awkward and the relation between the two isn't clear. Nevertheless, in the overall scheme of things Photoshop, that's a pretty easy workflow considering its power.

But, yes. There's no denying it. The book starts to get very hard now. The good news is, as far as I'm concerned, if you can learn how to make a peanut butter and jelly sandwich, you're able to implement a simplified LAB workflow using what we've described so far—and make a dramatic difference in the quality of your results.

Mandatory Steps, Optional Steps

The simplest possible workflow is to open an existing RGB file, find it acceptable, and hit the print button. The second simplest would be to open the file, find something objectionable and fix it then and there, and print. In either case, we've only seen one colorspace. For it to be that simple, we have to assume that the printing device wants RGB data.

The most complicated sensible workflow has four steps, in any of which there could be alterations made to the file:

- **Step One**. Acquire the file either by scanning film or by using some kind of import plug-in, like Photoshop's Camera Raw or the proprietary acquisition modules of various digital cameras. All of these methods have controls, some more flexible than others, that let us lighten, darken, or change colors before the file enters Photoshop RGB.
- **Step Two**. Having arrived in RGB, make certain changes there.
- **Step Three**. Convert to LAB and make more changes there.
- **Step Four**. Convert to the final space of the file, whether RGB or CMYK, and make further changes there.

In rare circumstances, there might be a case for even more steps. An example would be a very poor-quality file that contains a lot of colored noise. In that case, there might be a case for entering LAB immediately, trying to get the noise out of the A and B channels, then reentering RGB to get the color somewhere within reason, and then back into LAB for the usual type of moves. In real life, I think we are all more likely to add extra steps by carelessness: we do our LAB thing, move into our "final" colorspace, decide that maybe our

LAB move wasn't all that hot, and move back into LAB to cover up our own ineptitude.

Setting that possibility aside, the question is how many of these four steps should really be taken. The first may not be up to us. If we already have an RGB file, we're at Step Two before we begin. If not, then we may have to decide how much energy to put into the acquisition step, as opposed to just getting it into RGB any old way.

The second step definitely exists, because at some early point in the process we will open an RGB file. We may do nothing more than convert it to LAB, but we may try something more ambitious.

The third step is optional and leaves the most room for debate. We can do all of our work in LAB, or none of it. Step Three can therefore be all-important, or not exist at all, or any point in between. If we decide to do some work in LAB and some outside it, we could do that outside work before going into LAB, afterward, or a little of both.

The fourth step also depends on the third. It may be nothing more than a conversion to CMYK or RGB followed by saving the file. Or it could be something more.

Beta reader Clarence Maslowski, whose workflow requires a CMYK file at the end, offers a typical modification of these steps. He comments, "I generally follow your outline under the heading of Mandatory Steps, Optional Steps. I get my endpoints, neutrals, overall luminosity, subject contrast, and approximate / acceptable colors in RGB and LAB, convert to CMYK and fine-tune the above. I make a habit of saving copies of the RGB and LAB files as I complete corrections for each mode. I then go back to the LAB copy and jack the colors around, either though curves or overlay blending. I copy and paste the new LAB file on the CMYK file as a layer in Color mode. On occasion, I employ a saturation mask to maintain less saturated colors (e.g. skintones)."

It should come as no great shock to learn that the correct approach depends not merely on the image but upon your own Photoshop skill.

Which One Works Best Where?

Some of Photoshop's bewildering assortment of commands duplicate one another to some extent, such as Image: Apply Image as opposed to Image: Adjustments>Channel Mixer as opposed to Image: Calculations. Others are definitely not as good as alternative methods, such as Image: Adjustments> Brightness/Contrast as opposed to curves, or Filter: Sharpen>Sharpen More as opposed to Filter: Sharpen>Unsharp Mask.

Of what's left for the serious user, some commands always work better in certain colorspaces. Others work better under certain circumstances. Here's a quick survey, bearing in mind that several of these commands haven't yet been touched in this text.

● Curves and other commands aimed at making **gross changes in the image** work better either at the acquisition stage or in LAB. Often RGB offers channel-blending opportunities that can reduce some of the devastation, but if there's something really wrong with the image, RGB is the clear third choice to fix it and CMYK is even worse.

● Curves that aim at **fine-tuning the image** work better in CMYK than elsewhere, with RGB runner-up. Having four channels rather than three enables certain extra subtleties. Both LAB and acquisition software are blunt instruments by comparison.

● Curves aimed at **brightening, suppressing, enhancing, or changing color** generally work better in LAB than in any of the other three possibilities.

● When we **aren't sure exactly what we're trying to get,** LAB is a flexible and forgiving space to experiment in. Many acquisition modules also allow quick visualizations of the alternatives.

● The Image: Adjustments>**Hue/Saturation** command and its close relative Image: Adjustments>**Selective Color** are best saved until the end of the process. These two commands, which instruct Photoshop to make changes only to areas that are of a specified color, are necessary, but overused. They shouldn't be trotted out before you're certain that there are no major global color issues, because the presumption is that proper numbers always yield proper color. In the real world it doesn't quite work that way. If you've finished all other work, and all the numbers seem good, but the sky just plain looks like it's the wrong color, that's a good time for one of these two cousins.

● **Making difficult selections or masks** usually starts off with finding a channel that resembles what you have in mind, and working with that through Image: Calculations or by making a copy of it and editing it. CMYK is a bad choice as the source of such masks, and acquisition modules usually have limited masking features if any. In principle, therefore, we look for the start of the mask in an RGB channel. However, as we'll see in Chapter 9, LAB is very underrated in this regard. The A and B channels sometimes make the best beginnings.

● **Adjusting a shadow** that's too light without plugging its detail is a piece of cake in CMYK—we just darken the shadow half of the black channel. In any of the other three options, it causes needless gnashing of teeth. RGB is the second-best way of doing it.

● Any attempt to **blur colored noise** away will work better in the AB channels than anywhere else. Settings in acquisition models are sometimes better than their equivalents in RGB because of gamma considerations: Camera Raw, for example, does its computations at 1.0 gamma, giving better results than RGB, but still not as good as LAB.

● The most flexible space for **sharpening** is CMYK. If the image is dominated by a single color, CMYK will have two weak channels, black plus the complementary. These two weak channels can be sharpened heavily without any risk of altering color, and generally give a result superior to what's obtainable elsewhere. When sharpening an image overall, LAB is technically the best, but often RGB or CMYK is just as good. Sharpening on acquisition is a poor idea in comparison to any of the other three options, not just because the tools aren't as powerful but because sharpening is better done relatively late in the process.

• The Image: Adjustments>**Shadow/Highlight** command is most frequently used to open up excessively dark images. The command works considerably better in LAB than elsewhere in attaining that objective. As we haven't discussed S/H before, an extended example of the difference is coming right up.

• **Channel blending** to add contrast or to change color works better in RGB than CMYK, where much valuable information gets transferred to the black channel and therefore can't help the blend. There are also certain incredibly powerful blends available using the AB of LAB, which we'll be getting to in Chapters 15 and 16.

• **Retouching,** the use of blending and/or painting tools to merge new detail into an existing image, works best in LAB, which computes intermediate colors more effectively than RGB does, for reasons explained in the second half of Chapter 5. Simple cloning is equally effective in all colorspaces, but the more colorful the image, and the sharper the contrast between the colors that are being blended, the more the LAB advantage.

The Get-Halfway-There Principle

Imagine yourself transported to a time not that long ago—1990, to be exact, 15 years before this book is being written. You operate an establishment specializing in the production of digital images. Not from digital cameras, of course, because they don't yet exist. And not in Photoshop, because although it exists, it doesn't support CMYK yet, and this is a very CMYK world, since the Web hardly exists, and desktop color printers don't exist, and the only thing an RGB file is good for is continuous-tone output on a film recorder.

Even a more powerful Photoshop would be of limited utility. Macintoshes are just becoming capable of supporting more than eight megabytes (reality check, yes, megabytes) of RAM, although Photoshop isn't yet capable of using it. In any event, an extra eight megs would run around $1,500. The same money might also buy you a 180 megabyte (yes, megabyte) hard drive to store a picture or two on. So, for the time being, any color correction has to be done on a workstation costing around a quarter of a million dollars, and as slow as a three-legged tortoise on Quaaludes in comparison to the systems we work on today.

Speaking of six-figure hardware, you work with a drum scanner, since desktop scanners haven't been invented yet. It takes around ten minutes to analyze and mount each original, and a few minutes more to spin the drum and save the data.

Scanning is therefore quite expensive, but nevertheless a lot of it gets redone. You have to, because you shoot for near-perfection every time. If the highlight is a little too dark, it's cheaper to rescan than it is to transfer the file to an abhorrently expensive workstation, apply a simple curve, and then go out to lunch while the curve is executed.

It follows that the scanner operator is your highest-paid employee. If you're trying hard not to make the highlight too dark, now and then you're going to make it too light and then the scan will be worthless. There's a huge difference to the company's bottom line between an operator who has to rescan 30 percent of the time and one who rescans 20

Figure 7.4 This image doesn't need brighter colors or more hue variation, and its important objects occupy a long tonal range. It is therefore a poor choice for work in LAB.

involved as opposed to some ill-paid gnome adjusting the highlight by two points.

The same is true in the idealized workflow we're about to discuss. There are four potential steps: acquisition; RGB; LAB; final output space. We may not be using all four. But if there's going to be a next step, then the current step doesn't have to be perfect—and, in fact, trying to make it perfect is likely to be counterproductive.

percent of the time. It might even be worth it to pay the extortionate salary of a manager like myself, who would come in on a platform of reducing rescans to 10 percent.

Returning to our own century, there's much to be learned from a 1990 workflow. The things that make a good picture haven't changed. And, although the interface was hardly as user-friendly, what drum scanners did is exactly analogous to what takes place today in Camera Raw or some camera vendor's proprietary acquisition method.

A 90 percent success rate for the acquisition process was a cause for uncontrolled jubilation in a day when computers and RAM and hard drives each cost a thousand times as much as they do today. It's a cause for firing the incompetent person who can't do better today. There's no longer any need for a perfect scan, because if, say, the highlight is two points too high, it takes less time to fix it in Photoshop than it would for the scanner operator to figure out that there was a problem in the first place. Our only requirement is a scan that doesn't create undue problems down the line, like requiring an expert to get

Will There Be a Step Three?

Four potential steps sounds like too many options, but the third step (or lack thereof) is the key. When planning your approach, you don't need to know whether there will actually be a fourth step—provided that there was a third step. If you do something in LAB, you have to convert out of it eventually. And there's time enough then to decide whether the LAB move was good enough or whether you have the time and desire to do more.

The general reasons to go into LAB would be a desire to do one of the following things:
- Increase variation in colors.
- Make certain colors purer.
- Blur away colored noise.
- Use the Shadow/Highlight command to open shadow detail.
- Increase contrast in a small tonal range.
- Simplify difficult retouching.

If you're not trying to do any of these things, there's no point in using LAB at all. The color balancing and sharpening can be done elsewhere. In Figure 7.4, LAB offers no advantage. There's plenty of color variation already; the colors tend to be duller ones like

Figure 7.5 The original, top left, doesn't need brighter colors, but it could use more contrast. In the red channel of RGB, second from left, that's difficult because the flower is light and the leaves dark. The green channel, second from right, is the opposite. But both flower and leaves are in the same range in the L channel (top right), permitting the contrast-enhancing curves shown here. Lower right, the corrected version.

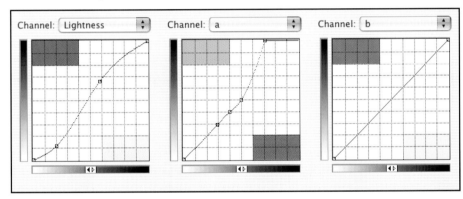

wood or brick red that shouldn't be made brilliant; there's no obvious noise; we don't need to increase shadow contrast; and there are interest objects that range from very light to very dark. So, we forget LAB. If we want to improve the picture, RGB or CMYK will give us what we want.

But we have to be careful about writing LAB off too quickly. Figure 7.5 looks like it's another picture where LAB is to be avoided. The flower is more than bright enough, and the leaves don't have to be much more green than they are. There's no important shadow detail, no obvious noise. And there appears to be a big tonal range, which would foil anything fancy in the L.

This is the second time we've looked at this image, having first seen it in Figure 2.1, where we studied channel structure of RGB,

CMYK, and LAB. That wasn't just for fun. Visualizing the channels is one of the key elements in getting the pictures to look right.

To see the individual channels, open the Channels palette (Window: Channels) and click on the one you want, clicking on the composite color icon when finished. The keyboard shortcut is Command–1 to show the first channel (red of RGB, cyan of CMYK, L of LAB), Command–2 for the second, and Command–~ (tilde character on U.S. English keyboards) to show full color.

Here, what the channels must look like should be self-evident as soon as we open the file. In RGB, the lighter the channel, the richer it makes the overall picture in that color. So, in the green, the leaves are moderately light; not extremely light, which would make them a brilliant green that would be inappropriate.

The flower, however, is about as non-green an object as there is in the world. It's magenta, green's direct opponent. Therefore, the flower must be almost a solid black in the green channel.

Contrariwise, the red channel is going to be close to blank where the flower is, but the leaves are dark, since they're not red at all. The blue channel isn't shown because the blue of RGB and its cousin, the yellow of CMYK, don't add nearly as much definition to the pictures as other channels do. But if it were here, it would be even worse than the red: leaves even darker, flower just as light.

To increase contrast in any image, any colorspace, we put the interest objects into steep areas of the curve. That won't be easy here in RGB, because the two main interest objects—the flowers and the leaves—are of very different darknesses in all three channels, since their colors are so unlike.

In the L channel, of course, colors don't matter. The leaves and the flower may be of totally different hues, but they're just about the same darkness. Therefore, they occupy the same range on the L curve, and for our purposes, the two of them constitute a canyon: a relatively narrow range that can be steepened effectively. So, by a lucky fall of the colors, this image should be corrected in LAB.

While the move in the L is key, note also the unusual A curve, accentuating the green component of the leaves while holding the magenta flower with locking points. There is no move in the B at all because we have no desire for anything in the image to get more yellow or more blue.

The Channel Structure Bites Back

That the L didn't look much like either the red or the green was a big advantage in Figure 7.5, but the shoe is on the other foot in the next example.

The Shadow/Highlight command, first seen in Photoshop CS (2002), is one of the more valuable innovations in Photoshop's history. It can revivify a seriously dark image like Figure 7.6A in seconds. Before S/H, the services of an expert were necessary.

Although S/H also has a routine that adds detail to highlights, the shadow-enhancing routine is needed more often, and that's what we'll limit ourselves to here.

The following section may make more sense if you go back two chapters and review the discussion of the sharpening of Figure 5.12. In that particular image, sharpening the L proved superior to sharpening in RGB, even when the RGB sharpening was done in Luminosity mode to prevent a color shift. The advantage that LAB offered in Figure 5.13 also applies to shadow-lightening moves, but more so. That half of the S/H command is more effective in LAB than in RGB. Smoother transitions and more detail are achievable, provided we dance around a trap or two.

To review: one might think that after converting an RGB file to LAB, the L would look like some kind of weighted average of the previous red, green, and blue channels. It's not: it's usually lighter than all three. In constructing the final color, Photoshop *interprets* the L as being darker than any of the RGB channels; to retain the same colors, therefore, the L has to be lighter than one would expect. It does, however, use the same endpoints as the RGB channels do: a white and a black. It's what's in between that's lighter.

Something that used to be a midtone in RGB thus will be lighter than a midtone in the L. As the dark points are the same, the L devotes more of its space to the range between midtone and dark than RGB does, and less to the range between light and midtone.

Consequently, any move that involves massaging what used to be the dark half of the RGB file is likely to work a lot better in LAB—and vice versa, I hasten to add. But humans are a lot more conscious of variation in dark areas than they are in light ones. With a longer range to work with, corrections (except curves, which are different animals) can be applied more precisely, and the results may seem more realistic, as Photoshop is more able to distinguish real detail from noise. These factors were decisive in Figure 5.13, and they're more important yet in the use of the S/H command.

Efforts to compare S/H in RGB against LAB are difficult because of the range issue: a given setting has less of an impact in the L than it would in RGB. Figure 7.6B applies straight default settings to an RGB file, except in the Color Correction field, which is disabled. Figure 7.6C hits the L with the same numbers, which in principle is not as strong of a correction as if the file had been in RGB.

The LAB version therefore appears darker, as expected, with the glaring exception of the woman's red jacket. To match the apparent lightness of Figure 7.6B, bigger numbers would have been needed for Figure 7.6C because of the longer range. However, even as is, it's clear that Figure 7.6C will be the better of the two when it reaches adulthood. The men's jackets and the leaves all seem lighter in the RGB version, yet

Figure 7.6 The Shadow/Highlight command has different effects in LAB and RGB. Top, the original. Center, the shadows are opened using S/H defaults in RGB, except that Color Correction is set to zero. Bottom, the same setting applied to the L channel.

Figure 7.7 The woman's jacket in Figure 7.6C fell into an awkward range in the L and was damaged by the S/H command. The RGB channels were more favorably placed. Left to right: the red and green channels of an RGB version, and the L of an LAB version, of Figure 7.6A.

snappier in its LAB counterpart, which has somehow managed to conjure up more contrast with less range, a rare phenomenon.

Before making a more realistic attempt to improve Figure 7.6A, two tech notes. First, pictures that are too dark are usually too colorless as well. I didn't try to bring up color here in the interest of a direct comparison of contrast, so both Figures 7.6B and 7.6C are too gray.

Photoshop's RGB response to that problem is to increase saturation with the Color Correction field in the S/H dialog, a slider that is on by default, as it should be, at a value of +20. LAB offers the more effective solution of steepening the AB curves.

Second, LAB failed with the red jacket for the same reason it succeeded with the magenta flower of Figure 7.5.

Figure 7.7A, the original red channel, contributes all the detail in that jacket. The green, Figure 7.7B, contributes color and that's about it; no shape to speak of.

As it did with the flower, the L's jacket in Figure 7.7C falls between the two extremes. Unfortunately, that makes it a shadow for S/H purposes. It can't be differentiated from the other dark areas, such as the background greenery, and when it gets lightened a lot of detail goes. The red channel is too light for the long arm of S/H to reach, but the L is in the wrong place at the wrong time.

This image was chosen specifically because it contains a brilliant red. A brilliant blue would have created the same havoc. If either color appears in the image, you should have a solution in mind before hitting it with S/H in LAB.

But if such colors aren't there, or if you do have a solution, you'll see the same level of difference as between Figures 7.8A and 7.8B. Color enhancement has been added this time: the default +20 Color Correction in RGB, steepened AB channels in LAB. The Amount setting, which governs the violence of the correction, has been reduced from the default 50% in both versions to 30%. The Tonal Width setting, which defines how light an area has to be before Photoshop stops considering it a shadow, was kept at the default 50% in Figure 7.8A. However, to assure a level playing field, I increased it to 60% in Figure 7.8B to compensate for LAB's longer shadow range. The Radius setting, which is the key to the use of S/H but is regrettably off-topic for this book, was kept at the default 30 pixels for both.

If you're thinking that Figure 7.8B is simply a lighter picture, look again at the men's jackets, which are lighter in Figure 7.8A. No, it's a question of space allocation, and the LAB version is doing a better job of it.

That takes care of the final missing piece of our global imaging tools, so let's try to put a recommended workflow together. Here's what goes through my mind when I open an image for the first time.

A Comprehensive Approach

● Step One: The acquisition. If I have to scan film, or open a digital file in some plug-in, then I'll try to avoid producing a really defective RGB file. Almost all such modules can make gross changes that might prevent bad casts or ridiculously flat images.

If you're using something as powerful as

Figure 7.8 *When color enhancement is added, the advantage of using the Shadow/Highlight command in LAB becomes more pronounced. Above, a version of Figure 7.6A created in RGB with S/H settings of 30 Amount, 50 Tonal Width, 30 Radius, +20 Color Correction. Below, executed in LAB with settings of 30 Amount, 60 Tonal Width, 30 Radius, followed by application of steepening curves in the AB channels.*

Camera Raw, and you're truly pressed for time, I suppose you could try to let Step One be the only step—go for a perfect file, just as the scanner operator used to. I don't recommend such an approach, because I think the one-minute LAB solution is better.

If you're prepared to make changes afterward, then trying to perfect the acquisition is not just a waste of time, but may actually cause problems down the line.

Part of the danger in trying too hard is the possibility of going too far. If you try to make the highlight perfect, at $250^R250^G250^B$ or whatever you think is appropriate, every now and then you'll do what the 1990 scanner operator did: get $255^R255^G255^B$ and a worthless file with no detail at all in its lightest areas. The obvious solution is to go for more conservative endpoints. They're easy enough to fix in Photoshop.

Similarly, if the image has an ugly green cast, it surely is right to try to reduce it in an acquisition module. What's dangerous is to try to obliterate it altogether. Some of these modules are not all that accurate. An image that's slightly too green in certain places and a bit too purple elsewhere is harder to fix than one that's simply way too green.

Even if you're careful, beautiful endpoints may not be the blessing that they seem. Something almost as light as it can get has to be *white* in RGB, which can prove awkward if the rest of the image has a cast. The 1990 scanner operator never had to deal with one of the big plagues that face us every day in the digital age: files that are correct at the endpoints and completely the wrong color everywhere else.

• Step Two starts with deciding whether there's going to be a Step Three—that is, whether LAB is going to be used at all. If it's not, then Step Two is the final step provided that an RGB file is our eventual goal. If LAB is not going to be used, and the final goal is CMYK, then I'll postpone curving and

sharpening until I get there, where I expect them to be more effective. I will, however, look for channel-blending opportunities while still in RGB, of the sort to be described in Chapter 14.

If there's to be a LAB step, I'll make one addition to Step Two. Beyond looking for blending opportunities, I may put a duplicate layer of the RGB file on top of the original, with the idea of fine-tuning the colors, something LAB isn't notably good at.

An example: clouds in an otherwise blue sky. We think of them as white, and in fact they are, at their lightest and fluffiest. As they get darker, though, they get bluer, picking up some of the color of the background sky.

The camera is more sensitive to that added blueness than our eyes are, because the camera lacks the sense of simultaneous contrast described back in the second half of Chapter 1. We break colors apart from their neighbors. If the background sky is blue, we mentally readjust the cloud's edge to be less blue.

That slight blueness at the edge of an otherwise neutral cloud is the kind of thing that can jump up and bite us in LAB. We can't move the center point of the B curve to neutralize the edge without making the center of the clouds yellow. And the impact of AB curves is to bring up existing colors, making the blue edges even worse.

Therefore, I try to address the problem in Step Two, before even getting to LAB. Lightening the red channel slightly in the quartertone region of the curve should do it.

And why do it on a duplicate layer (or an adjustment layer)? Merely to keep options open, and because once you start to think in LAB it becomes second nature to separate color and contrast in the mind. If the RGB curves to neutralize the clouds make everything look better, fine, I flatten the image and proceed to Step Three. If they help the color but harm detail, then before flattening I change the mode in the Layers palette to

Color instead of Normal. That restores the original detail while retaining the color created by the curves.

● Step Three: Now we're in LAB. You already know the drill here.

● There's little need to discuss Step Four, which is going to be a cleanup operation to make any final adjustments.

Two possible variations depend upon whether Step Four is a CMYK or RGB step. If it's CMYK, then during Step Three I'll consider where the sharpening, if any, should be done. Generally, if the image is dominated by a single color, I'll go the CMYK route, if not, the L. And if Step Four is an RGB step, then I sharpen the L for sure.

Also, if Step Four is CMYK and the shadow is currently too light, I won't fix it in LAB, because it's so much easier to adjust in the black channel of CMYK. If Step Four is RGB, then I don't much care where the shadow gets adjusted.

By the Numbers and by the Instinct

Before closing out the chapter, and with it the first half of the book, we should look at three specialized maneuvers. Two, as promised earlier, are for those people who are under such pressure to get images out quickly that they need to adopt an all-LAB workflow, never mind that they could get better pictures if they had more time. The other involves a duplicate layer like the theoretical one we just constructed in RGB to prevent the clouds from getting too blue.

A lot of color work depends on doing things "by the numbers," starting with white point and black point. The last example we discussed, a curve that was designed to make the edges of a hypothetical cloud less blue, was also a "by the numbers" correction. Experienced folk would understand the assignment to be "make the blue parts of the cloud more neutral." They would know that, in RGB, neutral colors occur when all three channels

have equal numbers. They would also know that an overly blue cloud means that the red channel is too dark, or the blue channel too light, or both. So they would try to equalize the two values, or get as close as they could without massacring the rest of the image.

On the other hand, some of what we do comes under the heading of wild guesses. We know that the canyon images of Chapter 1 should be more colorful than they were originally, but we don't know how much. We agree that Figure 7.6A is too dark, but we may not agree as to whether the proposed corrections went too far in battling said darkness, or not far enough. There's nothing "by the numbers" about that determination.

In such situations, where there is no right but there is a wrong, and where we are just experimenting to try to get something more pleasing, layering obviously excessive corrections on top of one another becomes attractive, particularly when short of time.

There's nothing overtly wrong with the numbers in Figure 7.9A, so you could conceivably vote for it as the best one of the four versions on the next two pages. Personally, I find it third best, because the dark areas in the animal's head and body are plugging, and because there isn't enough color variation. If it were only as easy to cure brucellosis as these problems, herds of bison might again be roaming the American west. The indicated medication here is S/H, followed by a dose of steepened AB. But the question is, how much to prescribe?

When to Go Too Far

As we saw earlier, Shadow/Highlight is more effective in the L channel than it is in RGB, particularly when there aren't any bright blues or reds to cause trouble. After converting the image into LAB, I activated the L channel and chose S/H shadow values of 50% Amount, 25% Tonal Range, 12 Radius, reaching Figure 7.9B.

I then tried Layer: New Adjustment Layer>Curves. An adjustment layer maximizes flexibility. It encompasses a single command (in this case, curves) but that command can be modified at any time before the image gets flattened for output. Moreover, as with all layers, its opacity can be changed at any time if we feel that the effect is too strong.

The effect of Figure 7.10B *is* too strong. The AB curves are so incredibly steep that parts of the animal became brilliant red and other parts that were originally of a similar color became blue. The result lacks contrast almost completely, because nearly the entire LAB file now consists of imaginary colors: greens, blues, and reds too brilliant for any form of reproduction. So, Photoshop lightened everything in a doomed effort to match the intensity.

By lowering the adjustment layer's opacity to a minuscule 6%, I was able to bring those wild colors back into gamut and get what I wanted, more or less, in Figure 7.10A. Or, to put it another way: the curves of Figure

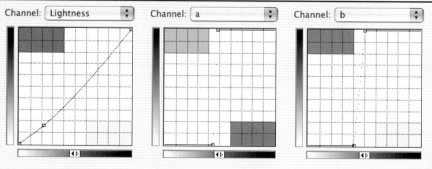

Figure 7.9 *The original, top, needs increased shadow detail, provided at center by an application of the Shadow/Highlight command. To establish color variation, the extreme curves at bottom were put on an adjustment layer before proceeding.*

7.9 were terrific, but 16.67 times too much of a good thing.

Having a layer go a little bit too far is eminently sensible. You can always cut the opacity if it's too much. But 100% opacity is as far as the slider goes. If the layer hasn't gone far enough, you have to begin again.

Making the layer 16.67 times too extreme is overkill. My first Shadow/Highlight move was also questionable, for the opposite reason.

As the Figure 7.10B inset shows, I put that correction on its own duplicate layer, so the final document actually had three layers: original on bottom, S/H layer in the middle, and the weirdly colored layer on top. Its opacity is only 6%, but the middle layer is at 100%. There's something to be said for a stronger correction on the middle layer, on the theory that if we don't like it, we can always dial down the opacity setting, whereas if we think it's not enough, we'll be put to needless extra work.

The Partial Cast and Its Cure

The final piece of the one-minute workflow puzzle connects two types of images that have large partial casts. The less common variety is biased toward different colors in its dark and light areas. The more common one is usually caused by overzealous autocorrection routines on digicams. It consists of beautifully neutral white and/or black points hitched to images with painfully bad color in the midrange.

Such images can usually be made to look just as good as if the lighting had been normal, provided you're highly skilled and have 15 minutes or so. LAB is usually *not* the first step in that case. Instead, we start with some

Figure 7.10 Top, the final version is loosely based on the bottom version, which was produced by the curves of Figure 7.9 applied on an adjustment layer. Inset, the Layers palette sets the opacity to a very low number.

sort of cast-minimizing channel blending in RGB. But that takes time, and we're talking about workflows where we don't have much. So, the question is, how do we get the biggest impact as quickly as possible?

LAB, being capable of huge color moves (see, for example, Figure 7.10B), is the likely choice. The problem is that AB curves can only drive the entire picture in a single direction, unlike RGB or CMYK, where curves can affect the highlights in one way and the shadows in another.

The solution requires a selection, usually based on the luminosity of the image. It sounds harder than it is—it requires only a single keystroke and thus doesn't knock us past our one-minute deadline.

Our first opponent is a live image from a newspaper. Therefore, it's quite relevant—in newspapers, a minute to fix an image isn't an uncommon demand. They don't hold up the pressrun if your curves aren't finished.

As a formality, we examine the numbers and verify what we already know, that Figure 7.11A has a major-league yellow cast. The

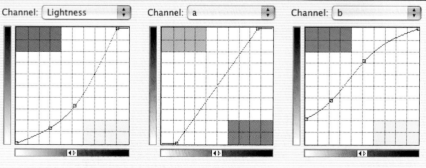

Figure 7.11 The original, top, has a strong yellow cast in its light areas, but the dark half is almost unaffected. Applying curves that neutralize the yellow in the highlights (left) creates a strange-looking dark half of the picture (center).

pile of papers in the right foreground averages an eye-popping $95^L(4)^A43^B$.

However, as the image gets darker, the cast goes away. The man's face is $49^L24^A53^B$. That's still too yellow, but not nearly as bad. If the paper is a pure white, the A and B values should be equal, but they're 47 points apart. A face is typically slightly higher in the B, and here it's 29 points higher. In the dark wood framing of the windows, the yellow's not out of whack at all: $8^L9^A10^B$, a bit to the yellow side of red, just as you'd expect. For objects darker still, we have to ignore the man's jacket and tie, which for all we know could be blue. But the woman's hair can't be blue, and it comes in at $4^L1^A3^B$.

Figure 7.12 *This version uses the curves of Figure 7.11, but applies it through a luminosity mask that makes the impact of the correction progressively less as the image gets darker.*

The B curve shown in Figure 7.11 sweeps away the yellow cast in the paper as easily as we might brush away an insect. Unfortunately, the darker parts of Figure 7.11B become too blue. The papers may be white, but the faces are purple.

Avoiding this takes only a second. Starting with a fresh copy of the original, the same curves got me to Figure 7.12, except that before applying them, I hit Command-Option–1. Yes, we can get better results than this if we have a lot more time. No, Image: Adjustments>Auto Color isn't an option; it chokes on this type of image so revoltingly that I refuse to waste space on it; even Figure 7.11B is much better.

The Minute Waltz at the Masked Ball

What we just saw was an application of a *luminosity mask*, or, more precisely stated, a luminosity selection. As most readers know, Photoshop allows us to *select* certain areas of a file, locking off all other areas so that they can't change.

In its simplest form, the selection divides the image into two completely separate parts. For example, if the area you want to select is very distinct from its surrounding, as the pink flower is in Figure 7.5, you can click it with Photoshop's magic wand tool, establishing a selection. If you now hit the Delete key, the flower will vanish from the scene, leaving a hard edge as though someone had cut it out with scissors.

It's also possible to have something *partially* selected, meaning that anything we do to it will have less impact than it does on something fully selected. For example, we could Select: Feather the flower before deleting it. The edge of the vanished flower would then be softer, because it was partially selected and therefore only partially deleted, as opposed to the flower itself, which was fully selected and therefore would be on its way to pixel purgatory.

A selection can be saved as a separate nonprinting (sometimes called *alpha*) channel, or as a distinct grayscale document. We can use the term *mask* to describe either one: something that can be turned into an active selection, by means of Select: Load Selection. White areas of the mask fully select the corresponding areas of the image; black areas don't select at all. Grays represent partial selections: the darker the gray, the less the selection.

In retoucher heaven, all objects of interest are as easy to select as a pink flower on a green background. In real life, the devil, who never sleeps, arranges for us to get stuff, particularly when a deadline looms, that's about as easy to extract from its background as a beefsteak is from a hungry lion.

Knowledge of LAB is a huge help in mask construction. In fact, it often eliminates the need for masks in the first place, as we'll see in Chapters 10, 12, and 15.

Still, there's no denying that we frequently have to save complicated selections as masks. Often enough our first try at a mask isn't perfect, and we need to retouch it just as if it were a picture in its own right. We can then load the finished mask as a new selection.

In a one-minute, all-LAB workflow, we don't have any time to save masks, let alone edit them. Fortunately, Photoshop has one already made for us, take it or leave it.

We can load an existing channel as a selection, just as if it were an existing mask channel. The long way to do it is to open the Channels palette and Option–click the appropriate channel. The keyboard shortcut is Command-Option–1 for the first channel, and so on. In my LAB file, a Command-Option–1 loaded the L.

There's a huge difference between *selecting the L,* which would make the A and B unavailable, and *loading the L as a selection.* That's why many people use the phrase *luminosity mask* to describe it.

When the L is loaded as a selection, the lightest parts of the image, the papers, are

Review and Exercises

✓In Figure 7.5, what would have happened if the bottom half of the A curve had not been locked in position with extra holding points?

✓If you are using the Shadow/Highlight command to lighten an overly dark image in LAB, what type of object may be damaged?

✓What is the normal purpose of loading a channel as a selection?

✓Why is it dangerous to decide whether an image is neutrally correct based only on reading values for the light and dark points? (Hint: this is a much bigger problem in the age of digital photography than it used to be.)

✓Experiment with sharpening two of your own images. One can be anything where the interest object isn't especially light; the other, if possible, a picture of a person with dark hair. Make three LAB copies of each for comparison (or start with three duplicate layers). On one, sharpen the L channel a bit more than you think is appropriate. Then try the same sharpening settings on the second version, but before applying them, load an inverted luminosity mask (Command-Option–1, followed by Shift-Command–I). This result will presumably look better. Now go to the third original, and see how close you can get to the second without using any mask.

almost fully selected. The darkest areas, such as the man's jacket, are hardly selected at all; and areas of intermediate darkness, such as the faces, are partially selected. That's the secret of Figure 7.12. The full fury of the yellow-busting B curve is felt in the papers that are in our face in the foreground. The faces are made less yellow, too, but thanks to the luminosity mask, the effect is only about half what it is in the papers. The faces are therefore neither too yellow, as they are in Figure 7.11A, nor insufficiently yellow, as in Figure 7.11B.

Before leaving this topic, we should discuss two other keyboard shortcuts. First, we sometimes need an *inverted luminosity mask*. Figure 7.11A was a disaster area in the highlights but not bad in the shadows. Sometimes we get the reverse. A common situation is to find excessively neutral dark areas, particularly in forests, which want to be slightly green, while the remainder of the image is fine.

To attack the shadows only, Command-Option–1 to load the luminosity mask, and Shift-Command–I to invert the selection, making darker areas more fully selected than lighter ones. That second keystroke is a shortcut for Select: Invert Selection.

Also, remember Command–D, short for Select: Deselect. You have to do this after finishing your mask move; otherwise the selection will remain active indefinitely. I always forget this step.

An Up-to-the-Minute Use of Layers

There remains only the case where *both* the highlights and shadows are correct, but the rest of the image is messed up. Images of this description are a common occurrence in the age of "intelligent" digital cameras. We can't correct them through luminosity masks, because the problem is at the center of the image, not the ends.

In the mixed-lighting horror of Figure 7.13A, the light area in the second window from the right reads $99^L(1)^A4^B$. I'd rather not have to measure a light source, and I'd rather than the A not be negative at all, but still the values are reasonable. Similarly, the darkest point, the side of the desk facing us at bottom left, is acceptable at $8^L0^A5^B$. Note that we don't measure the dark tiles. The corrected versions prove that not all of them are black.

We don't need any numbers to tell us that the rest of the picture is way too yellow and also too dark, just as Figure 7.11A was.

And, as with Figure 7.11A, we can come up with LAB curves that slice through the yellow cast, only to get a disappointing result, which, in turn, is so vastly better than the monochromous mud produced by Auto Color that it's not worth the space to compare them.

But at least in Figure 7.11B, the highlights, the papers, were correct. In Figure 7.13B all the light areas have turned blue. So this time, instead of a selection that gets weaker as the picture gets darker, we need one that's strong in the middle and weak at the ends.

Constructing a strong-in-the-middle mask can be done but it isn't easy. The more logical way is to use Photoshop's most underrated selection tool, layer Blending Options.

To proceed, the correction must be on its own layer. We can either duplicate the background layer and apply the curves to that, or, more economically, Layer: Add Adjustment Layer>Curves. Either way we wind up with, in effect, Figure 7.13A as the bottom layer and Figure 7.13B as the top.

If the palette isn't open, we open it now with Window: Layers. Now, we click and hold on its top right arrow, which brings up several choices including Blending Options, which is a subscreen of the Layer Style dialog. Or, we can get the Layer Style dialog directly by double-clicking the top layer's icon.

At the default layering settings of Normal mode, 100% opacity, the bottom layer isn't seen at all. If we choose a different mode or change the opacity, the bottom layer can play

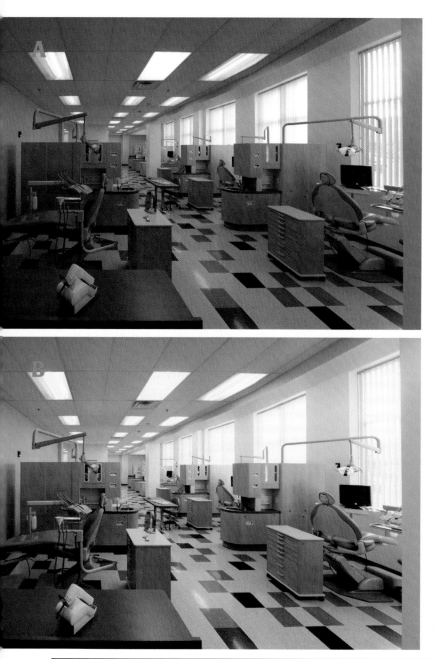

a role. In Chapter 5, we discussed Luminosity mode, which uses the detail from the top layer and the color from the bottom. Or, in Normal mode, an 80% opacity gives us a blended version, an 80-20 mix of the two layers.

We can also exclude certain areas of the top layer by constructing a layer mask—or we can do it mathematically, by describing the areas we don't want to use.

That's the function of the Blend If sliders at bottom right of Figure 7.14, which shows the two sets of L (Lightness) sliders. Similar sets exist for A and B, and they're excruciatingly powerful, as Chapter 9 will show. For this image, however, we only need the L.

By default, all sliders start at their endpoints, instructing Photoshop to use the top layer in all circumstances. But when the sliders are moved in, they impose limits. The settings in Figure 7.14 say, use the top layer, unless *either* the top layer is very dark *or* the bottom layer is very light. Observe that the sliders have also been split in half; we do this by Option–clicking as we move them. Between the two half-sliders is an area of transition, an area in which Photoshop is to blend the two

Figure 7.13 *Another yellow cast in the original, and another set of curves to kill it. But the highlights in the top version were correct, so although the bottom version eliminates most of the cast, all the light sources have turned blue.*

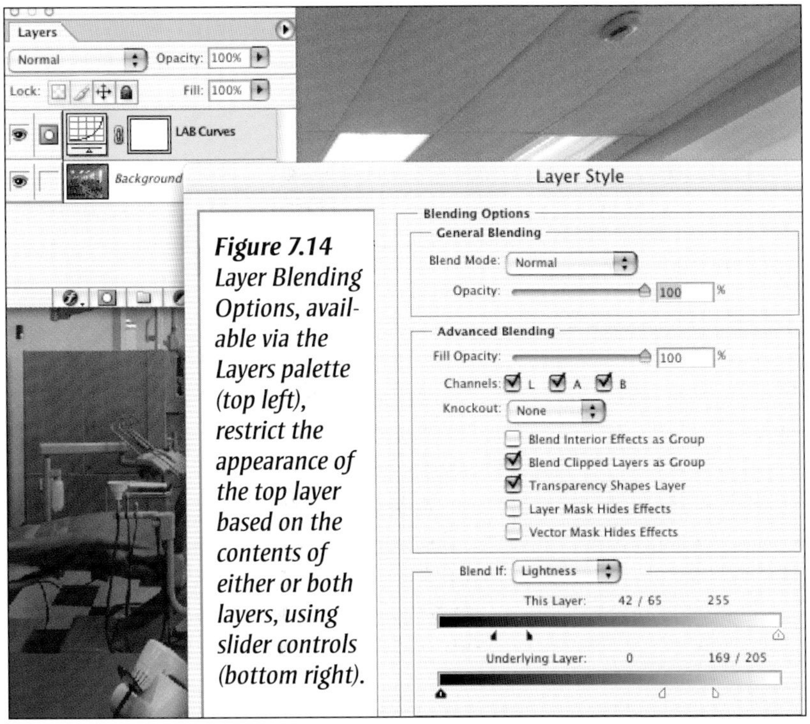

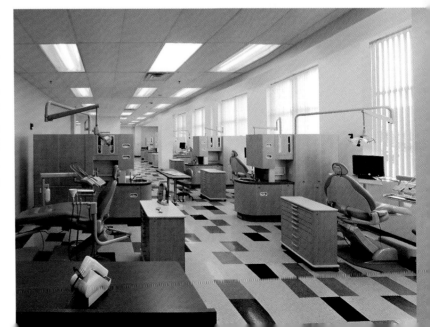

Figure 7.14 *Layer Blending Options, available via the Layers palette (top left), restrict the appearance of the top layer based on the contents of either or both layers, using slider controls (bottom right).*

to exclude (that is, use the bottom layer for) anything that measures quite A–positive.

That could also have been done in RGB, but it would have taken two channels' worth of sliders, not to mention an extra layer. If I had asked to exclude everything that was very dark in the green channel, the jacket would have been covered, but so would every neutral dark point in the image. So, the setting would have had to be modified to exclude anything that was very dark in the green and *not dark* in the red channel.

It Only Takes a Minute

Before wrapping up the first half of our journey through LAB, two quick tech notes on the last image. First, in principle both the highlight and shadow adjustments could have been done on the same line in the Blending Options menu, but it was better to split them as shown, because of range issues. The top

layers so that there's no harsh transition where it stops using the top layer and reverts to the bottom.

Applying these Blending Options produces Figure 7.15. As with Figure 7.12, it isn't the best that can be done with this picture, but there's a real shortage of alternatives if you're trying to get the disastrously yellow original into acceptable shape in a minute or less.

An even easier use of the Blend If sliders took place in Figure 7.8B, where I borrowed a red jacket from one image and put it in another.

At that time I had two images: an LAB version that was good everywhere except the jacket, and an RGB file in which the jacket was the only worthwhile thing. I converted the RGB document to LAB and pasted the other file as a layer on top of it. Then I changed Blending Options

Figure 7.15 *The final correction merges Figures 7.13A and 7.13B in the manner defined by the Blending Options.*

layer had already been lightened by the L curve of Figure 7.13. As the very darkest point stayed constant but medium grays got lighter, there was a longer distance between pure black and a gray than on the bottom layer. And, conversely, less distance between a white and a gray. Stated differently, the top layer devotes more space to shadows and the bottom layer more to highlights. It's sometimes hard to get the slider settings to precisely what we want. It helps if the range of what we're trying to home in on is relatively long, as moving the sliders a short distance will have less of an effect.

Second, we can save even more time by storing some of these maneuvers as Photo-shop Actions, or doing other things to automate the process, such as creating a Droplet, a location in which you can drop files for batch processing. You can, for example, do a batch conversion of a slew of files to LAB, and even drop a layer on top of each with the Blending Options premade to exclude the highlights and shadows, just in case.

Actions store a series of commands so that they can be executed with a single keystroke. For anyone whose workflow is somewhat repetitive, they're very valuable, whether or not LAB is involved.

The focus of these first seven chapters has been on global maneuvers that don't require much expertise but make the picture look better, sometimes a whole lot better, than more conventional methods. At the same time, I've tried to point out the types of images in which LAB falls short, and also (as in this chapter) where it's useful if you're pressed for time.

We now move on to more advanced applications. If you can make use of them, so much the better. But even if you only master what we've covered so far, the basic control of LAB curves, sharpening, and blurring, that's going to be enough to make a sizable improvement in the quality of your images, particularly if you're in a hurry. And if you're not, the best is yet to come.

The Bottom Line

How LAB fits into the workflow depends on the type of images being used and especially on how much time is allotted to each. For those in a hurry, LAB offers the biggest bang for the buck. When there's more time, each picture needs to be analyzed to see whether LAB is appropriate at all.

The chapter introduces three techniques that work especially well in LAB: the Shadow/Highlight command, the use of luminosity masking, and the use of layer Blending Options. With these three tools, it's possible to construct an all-LAB workflow, if that's what's desired.

The Imaginary Color, The Impossible Retouch

Colors that don't, can't, and could never exist sound like trouble—but LAB can call for them. What happens when it does? The monitor can't display them, the printer can't print them, but, handled with care, they can solve otherwise intractable retouching problems. When imaginary colors rear their heads, the fireworks can begin.

ine-thirty in the evening of a torrid Fourth of July. The town's residents are gathered in the park, waiting for the fireworks display to begin. It was scheduled to start half an hour ago, but was delayed to let the sky get a bit darker.

Finally, the first salvo gets launched. Appropriate whistling sounds, then a barrage of brilliant greens and magentas as the rocket explodes and sub-explodes. Five thousand people recoil in pain, turning away with hands rubbing tightly closed eyes.

A picture is only worth a thousand words if it fairly conveys the actual scene. A photograph of what I just described is worth only one word, and the word is one the publisher won't permit me to use.

A reasonable rendition of this scene, in my opinion, requires a violent assault on the viewer's senses, just as was the case in real life. If I print the picture here, I would like you to react by dropping the book as fast as if it were a notice of audit from the Internal Revenue Service. The colors of the fireworks need to be blinding, painful.

That's never going to happen, not on a printed page, and not on your monitor, either. In fact, I would like to introduce a word that has a major role in this chapter: *impossible.* It's a word we try to avoid in digital imaging, especially in color correction, as what seems impossible to one person often later proves to be nothing of the kind.

Nevertheless, *impossible* is the right response to the suggestion that we can use Photoshop to reproduce the colors of exploding fireworks. Furthermore, it's not just a matter of a dark environment in which brilliance suddenly confronts us. If it were, you could wheel a monitor into a completely dark room, pop up a fireworks picture, and hurt your eyes.

Fireworks represent an extreme case of a phrase with which color geeks often confuse the uninitiated: *out of gamut,* a fancy way of saying *impossible.* The phrase is normally used to describe colors that can be achieved on a monitor but not in print. If that's the meaning you want, *out of CMYK gamut* is more accurate. Exploding fireworks are not just out of CMYK gamut, but *out of RGB gamut* as well.

Not, however, *out of LAB gamut,* because there isn't any such animal. The complex theme of this chapter is that colors can be created (or, better stated, *specified)* in LAB even though they are impossible, unthinkable, out of gamut, in both RGB and CMYK. You can't see or reproduce such colors, but they're there, and they can have a big impact on the future of the file—and, often enough, that impact is for the better.

The universe of color can be divided into five galaxies.

● Colors that can be achieved both in RGB and CMYK. Everything in Chapter 1, with one exception—the sky in the Death Valley shot of Figure 1.1, which is too vivid in the original digital capture for a press to equal—features such relatively dull colors.

● Colors that are possible in either RGB or CMYK, but not both. CMYK has difficulty producing rich blues, and also pastel colors. The blue sky in the bottom half of Figure 1.1 is nothing like the color in the original file, which is, alas, unmatchable in CMYK. Colors that CMYK makes but RGB doesn't are much rarer, but they exist: a swatch of solid yellow ink printed on quality paper is too vivid for a monitor to display.

● Colors that definitely exist somewhere, just not in RGB or CMYK. Examples would be not only the aforementioned fireworks, but anything with a pronounced color that is simultaneously either very light or very dark. If you look in the shadowy areas of a forest, you'll be able to perceive a green so dark that it's out of both the RGB and CMYK gamuts, which require that all extremely dark areas be neutral.

● Colors that are, whether they exist or not, at least conceivable. Fireworks manufacturers have apparently not been able to create good yellows. There are no yellow laser beams. Accordingly, as far as I know, there isn't any such thing as a yellow as intense as the red of a laser beam or the greens and blues of exploding fireworks. However, we can *imagine* such a color. If it exists, it's way more yellow than can be achieved in print, which in turn is more yellow than is achievable in RGB.

● Colors that do not and cannot exist. Something as brilliantly green as exploding fireworks, but at the same time as dark as the night sky surrounding them—such a color is impossible, inconceivable, a preposterous offense against logic, a contradiction in terms. And yet it can be created, however theoretically, however fleetingly, in LAB.

The idea of *imaginary colors*—the kind you can pretend to make in LAB, but that don't and can't exist otherwise—is not new. Let's enlighten this tenebrous subject by turning to one of the great comic scenes in all of theater, courtesy of that great color theorist, William Shakespeare.

King Henry IV, Part I stars the fat, white-haired, lecherous drunkard, Sir John Falstaff, friend of and bad influence upon the young Prince Hal, later to become King Henry V. In addition to his other lovable qualities, Falstaff is a coward, a fact recently taken advantage of by the prince. Hal and friends, in disguise as bandits, had feigned an attack on Falstaff, who had immediately dropped his money and retired at high speed. Shortly thereafter, he reappears, apparently beaten and bloodied, with a cock-and-bull story of how he, heavily outnumbered, fought valiantly against overwhelming odds. The prince wants to know the details.

PRINCE. Pray God you have not murd'red some of them.

FALSTAFF. Nay, that's past praying for: I have pepper'd two of them; two I am sure I have paid—two rogues in buckram suit. I tell thee what, Hal, if I tell thee a lie, spit in my face, call me horse. Thou knowest thy old ward: here I lay, and thus I bore my point. Four rogues in buckram let drive at me—

PRINCE. What, four? Thou saidst but two even now.

FALSTAFF. Four, Hal, I told thee four.

The longer the story goes on, and the more drink consumed, the greater the number of assailants becomes. We pick up with the count having reached seven.

FALSTAFF. Dost thou hear me, Hal?

PRINCE. Ay, and mark thee too, Jack.

FALSTAFF. Do so, for it is worth the list'ning to. These nine in buckram that I told thee of—

PRINCE. So, two more already.

FALSTAFF. Began to give me ground; but I followed me close, came in foot and hand, and with a thought seven of the eleven I paid.

PRINCE. O monstrous! eleven buckram men grown out of two.

FALSTAFF. But, as the devil would have it, three misbegotten knaves in Kendal green came at my back and let drive at me—for it was so dark, Hal, that thou couldst not see thy hand.

By this time, Hal has had it. He uncorks the most devastating series of put-downs in the history of English-language theater.

PRINCE. These lies are like their father that begets them—gross as a mountain, open, palpable. Why, thou clay-brained guts, thou knotty-pated fool, thou whoreson, obscene, greasy tallow-catch—

And, in case *you* have had it by this time, the color theory part is coming right up.

FALSTAFF. What, art thou mad? art thou mad? Is not the truth the truth?

PRINCE. Why, how couldst thou know these men in Kendal green, when it was so dark thou couldst not see thy hand?

A scintillatingly on-point question. The scene should have continued,

FALSTAFF. 'Sblood, Hal, I forsooth did battle them in LAB.

Falstaff, however, was doubtless too inebriated to think of such a riposte. So, thanks to his own RGB-centricity, he has gone down to posterity as a whoreson, obscene, greasy tallow-catch.

What is it about the concept of a totally black green that's so impossible that Shakespeare could build a scene around it? To explain, let's consider the opposite: a totally white green.

If we're working in CMYK, the very brightest color we can produce is the paper itself: ink values of $0^C0^M0^Y$. That's a white. If we want to make it more green, we have to add cyan and yellow ink. The very act of doing so makes the area darker. So, a color that is green, but simultaneously as light as the paper, is by definition out of CMYK gamut.

In RGB the brightest possible color is $255^R255^G255^B$. That's a white, too. If we want it more green, we have no choice but to turn off some of the red and blue light, but doing so of course makes the result darker, too. And therefore, a green that's simultaneously as bright as when all three channels are at full intensity is out of RGB gamut as well.

Let's look at it another way, using the opposite of green, magenta, and looking at it from the CMYK point of view.

The most magenta thing possible in CMYK is $0^C100^M0^Y0^K$, a color so extreme as to be out of the RGB gamut, and therefore a member of our second category of colors, one that can be made either in CMYK or RGB, but not both. Naturally, though, it can be made in LAB: $52^L81^A(7)^B$, remembering that your numbers will vary if your color settings don't match those shown way back in Figure 3.6.

Suppose that, working in LAB, we made the A channel one point more positive; or say we even made it 90^A. Now, we've entered the third category: a magenta too rich to be made either in CMYK or RGB, but a color that we can probably imagine.

In short, although LAB allows us to specify values up to 127^A, we can't get there from a CMYK file. The best we can do is 81^A—and we can only do that if there's a 52^L to go along with it. Any other L number implies a lower A.

The further the L moves away from 52^L, the closer to zero the A will have to get. If we want a lighter magenta, and cut the ink to $0^C90^M0^Y0^K$, that equates to $56^L72^A(7)^B$. Drop to 50^M and it's $74^A38^A(6)^B$; to 25^M and it's $86^L19^A(4)^B$.

Imagine, then, an area that measures 86^L, which is to say, fairly light. We've just found out that any value higher than 19^A is out of CMYK gamut. If we nevertheless start increasing the A, we can, for a time, at least conceive of the color that we're trying to achieve, even if we can't print it or display it on the monitor. But, in the context of such a light area, once we start getting up in the 70^A or 90^A or 110^A range, when 19^A is the real maximum, then we are starting to enter the fourth category: a color that does not, could not, may not, and cannot possibly exist; an imaginary, an impossible color, yet one that LAB lets us conjure up.

I won't bother to go through all this in reverse, but you can guess the bottom line. Make the color darker than 52^L rather than lighter, and the same thing will happen. The darker we get, the lower the maximum A value. By the time we hit 10^L, the maximum A is probably in the single digits—yet we can have triple digits in our LAB file.

This is a very long introduction to a very simple question: *what happens down the line when our LAB file contains imaginary colors?*

Once we have the answer to that question, we'll also know the answer to its obvious correlary: how and why would an imaginary color ever get there in the first place, and are there ever reasons for us to put imaginary colors in on purpose?

Enter, Stage Left, the Ghost of Color

Let's start with Falstaff's folly: a pronounced green in lighting conditions so dark that thou canst not see thy hand.

No need to be doctrinaire and insist on 0^L, absolute black. A more demure 5^L is plenty dark enough to require that the AB values both be close to zero.

Kendal green isn't all that pure, but why be shy? Let's make it $5^L(50)^A0^B$. If asked to describe this, I'd call it an emerald-green black—in short, an imaginary color; a color that could no more exist than Falstaff could win an Olympic medal in any sport other than drinking or lying.

Yet, if we enter the Color Picker by double-clicking the foreground/background color icon in the toolbox, we can enter those preposterous values, as Figure 8.1 shows. And then we can open a new LAB file and, with the Edit: Fill command, create a file full of emerald-green black.

The process of converting an imaginary color into one that we can print is much like

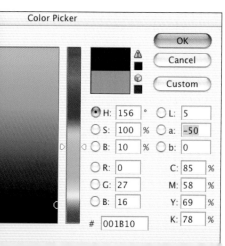

Figure 8.1 Falstaff's folly: a brilliantly green black is an imaginary color, but LAB files can ask for it. Photoshop generates its "equivalents" in other colorspaces by splitting the difference: green, but not very green; dark, but not very dark.

converting an imaginary flavor of ice cream into one that we can eat: there's a lot of room for interpretation. Photoshop's take on it is shown in Figure 8.2. The original file was made in LAB, and was then converted into CMYK to print here.

The outside box was a neutral $5^L0^A0^B$, which Photoshop has converted into $73^C67^M66^Y83^K$. The inner box was the imaginary color, $5^L(50)^A0^B$, which converted to $88^C56^M71^Y74^K$.

If we'd converted into RGB for output to some kind of desktop printer, the numbers would have been different, but the result the same: $17^R17^G17^B$ for the outer box, $0^R27^G16^B$ for the inner. Either way, the interior box is supposed to be as dark as the outer one, and it isn't. It's supposed to be emerald green, and it isn't that, either. Faced with a demand for a square circle, a giant midget, a torridly hot iceberg, Photoshop has given up and split the difference.

Figure 8.2 *Before being converted into CMYK, the outer box was defined as a neutral black, $5^L0^A0^B$. The inner box is an imaginary color: something just as dark as the top box, yet brilliantly green. It's defined as $5^L(50)^A0^B$, but no such color could possibly exist, so it can neither be printed nor displayed on the monitor. In such cases, Photoshop tries to split the difference. The inner box is neither as dark nor as green as the LAB values call for, but it's lighter than the outer box, in spite of sharing equal L values.*

The Theater of the Absurd

When the L is extremely dark or light, any seriously non-zero values in the A and/or B will create imaginary colors. When the L is extremely dark, the effect is rather subtle, as in Figure 8.2. When the L is very light, however, the fireworks begin; the magic show commences.

When Figure 8.3A was created in LAB, it consisted almost entirely of imaginary colors. Throughout, there was—but there isn't any longer—a value of 100^L. When converted to RGB or CMYK, 100^L, like 0^L, has to be accompanied by 0^A0^B. Here, however, each quarter of the graphic was a gradient, going from neutrality to the most extreme value in each of the four primary AB colors. Therefore, the

lower left corner started out at $100^L127^A0^B$. Being that this is an imaginary color, it is rather difficult to describe, but I'll try. It's a magenta so brilliant as to make a laser beam look dull, yet simultaneously as white as the blank paper printed next to it.

To get an idea of how unpredictable a process this business of portraying imaginary colors is, compare Figures 8.3A and 8.3B. One was converted to RGB first and then converted into CMYK for printing here. The other was converted directly from LAB into CMYK. By rights, these two files should be nearly identical, and they would be if this had been any ordinary photograph that wasn't full of imaginary colors. But they aren't even particularly close, setting another little trap for us.

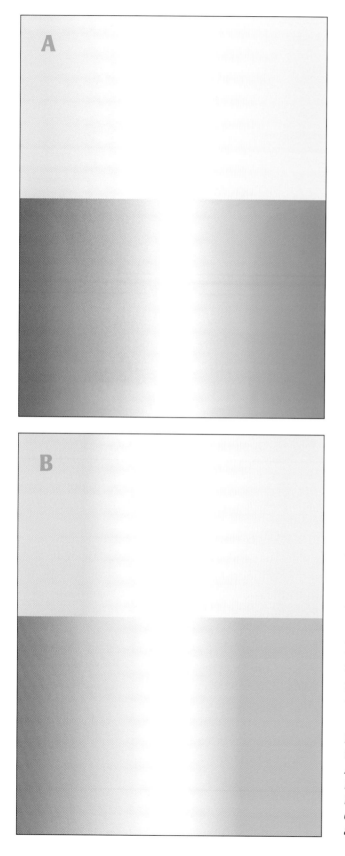

When the LAB file contains imaginary colors, Photoshop still has to display *something* on the screen. What it will display will look a lot more like what you will get if you convert to RGB than if you convert to CMYK. Therefore, if you know you are working with imaginary colors, and your final destination is CMYK, and you are reasonably satisfied with what you see on the screen, do something that seems like a waste of time: convert the file to RGB first, and then immediately to CMYK. Or, try it both ways and decide which one you like best. That imaginary color $100^L127^A0^B$ converts to $0^C79^M0^Y$ if you go directly to CMYK, but $16^C62^M0^Y$ if you take a stopover in RGB.

Convert either of these files back to LAB, and the extreme magenta corner will read around 60^L, which is not even close to the 100^L first called for.

To condense the last few pages into one sentence: Imaginary colors force Photoshop to move away from neutrality in extremely light areas while simultaneously darkening them; and to move away from neutrality in extremely dark areas while simultaneously lightening them. The whole point of this chapter is that these two effects are often desirable, particularly in light areas—and without this technique, difficult to achieve in a realistic-looking way.

These computer-generated graphics can be used to prove a point, but they don't exactly call for colors that we might ever be likely to use. It's now time to examine some real-world files that offer hints as to why you may actually wish to cuddle up to this particular porcupine.

Figure 8.3 *These two files measured 100^L throughout; the sides went up to the maximum in the four primary AB colors. The top version was converted directly from LAB to CMYK; the bottom version went from LAB to RGB to CMYK. Ordinarily, there wouldn't be a difference between the two files, but when imaginary colors are in play, chaos reigns.*

It Would Be Argument for a Week

An image on which LAB performs poorly seems like a strange start to a discussion. If you understand when imaginary colors don't work well, however, it becomes much easier to appreciate their power.

First, some definitions. A *multitone* is a file with every channel based on a common ancestor, which may have been modified by a curve. The channels are therefore not necessarily identical, but they are close relatives, as opposed to normal photographs, where the individual channels may bear little relation to one another. A multitone is intended to create some type of monochromatic effect.

The most common type is the *duotone,* a multitone containing exactly two channels. While the channels can theoretically be of any two colors, in practice one is almost always black.

While the remaining channel could also be of any color, the most common configuration is a *sepiatone,* a term with no specific meaning that refers generally to a brown, yellowish brown, or coffee-colored feel, often with the idea of creating an antique look.

The traditional way of making a sepiatone is to print it on press, using black plus some kind of dark orange ink. This is an expensive process, both because special inks like dark orange don't come cheap and because there isn't a reliable way of proofing short of a trial pressrun. Therefore, although sepiatones are now a distressingly hackneyed and overused design element, they are almost always created as duotones in Photoshop and then converted to CMYK (or RGB) for output just as any other picture would be. Those who are more interested in technicalities than quality would point out that such a converted file is no longer a duotone but a multitone, since a CMYK file has more than two channels. The rest of the world is disinterested in this semantic distinction and continues to call it a *duotone,* as will we.

Today's exercise is to create a sepiatone. For the purposes of this book we need to convert it to CMYK when finished, but it would make no difference to the following discussion if an RGB file were needed instead.

All duotones require starting with a grayscale (black and white), not a color image. The quality of that grayscale image is the whole key to success; without a snappy grayscale, any duotone will look flat.

A skilled user could produce duotones from scratch several different ways. However, the sane method is to start with some nice presets that are included with Photoshop.

A good grayscale image is always required as a starting point. For this exercise, we'll use one we created of a Venetian scene back in Figure 6.4B. Open it up, and Mode: Duotone. Up pops a menu defining the individual channels of the proposed multitone, which can be filled out from scratch if you happen to be both an expert and a lunatic. Everyone else should simply click Load and navigate to a folder called (depending on the version of Photoshop) Duotone Presets or Duotones.

The folder contains three subfolders, of which the one of current interest is Pantone Duotones. As the name suggests, it contains readymade formulas for duotones using black plus one of several extra inks defined using the Pantone Matching System, or PMS.

Three or four inks in this folder would combine with black to create what at least some people would call a sepiatone. If you want some other hue, you can load one of the presets and edit the ink color without difficulty. You can also edit the supplied curves if you are so inclined. For our purposes, there's no need to do either. I nominate and appoint PMS 159, which already exists in the folder.

Each ink preset contains four numbered pairs of curves, which regulate the balance between the black and the colored ink. Curve 1 always yields the most colorful result; Curve 4 gives almost a black and white with just a

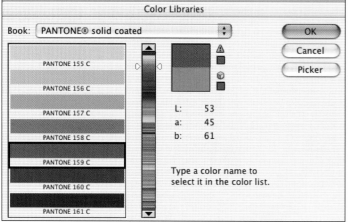

The LAB alternative seems to make sense. We can easily tint the AB channels any color we like, without damaging the detail, which lives exclusively in the L.

So, we open a new copy of the original grayscale file and convert it to LAB. At this point, being colorless, the whole thing reads 0^A0^B. All the variation is in the L.

Next, we have to figure out what color to stick in the AB channels. Fortunately, Photoshop will tell us, thanks to another unique use of LAB, one we'll be exploring more in Chapter 10, which is about how to make radical color changes, such as transforming a blue shirt into this PMS 159 color.

hint of the extra color. Curves 2 and 3 fall somewhere between the two extremes. Here, we'll load Curve 1.

That's all there is to it. In the unlikely event that we actually are printing with a dark orange ink, we save the file now in EPS format. Otherwise, we convert to our output space. To create Figure 8.4A, I simply chose Mode: CMYK and saved the file as a TIFF.

As has been noted several times, the definitions of RGB and CMYK are not fixed; yours may vary from mine. LAB has no such ambiguity: Photoshop offers only one flavor, although variants of LAB can be found in other applications. If we each take the same LAB file, we each get the same colors and the same numbers. If we each convert it to RGB, we still (in theory, at least) have the same colors, but we may have different numbers.

Since Pantone wants us to be able to create a known color just by typing in a PMS number, it supplies Photoshop with LAB equivalents for each. When you and I try to emulate these PMS colors in RGB or CMYK files on our own systems, we'll get different numbers again unless our definitions are the same—but we'll theoretically get the same colors, because we both converted from the same original LAB values. (Note: this applies only to Photoshop 7 or later. Earlier versions used a different method.)

To learn the LAB equivalent for any PMS color, call up the Color Picker by double-clicking the foreground or background color icon at the bottom of the toolbox. Click Color Libraries (click Custom in all Photoshop versions prior to CS2), verify that the dialog is showing Pantone Solid Coated colors as in the top left of Figure 8.4, and either scroll to the proper number, or type it in.

For this image, I typed in "159" and was rewarded by learning that the equivalent is $53^L 45^A 61^B$. I made this the foreground color

Figure 8.5 *Left, Figure 8.4B applied to the grayscale LAB version at 25% opacity, in an effort to match the color look of Figure 8.4A. Right, after curves have been applied to Figure 8.4B to establish neutral, as opposed to tinted, light and dark points, such as would be used in conventional duotones like Figure 8.4A.*

and returned to the LAB document. Wanting to replace the A and B channels with uniform values of 45^A61^B, I made a duplicate layer, then Select: Select All; Edit: Fill>Foreground Color. Having thus created a layer that was only a flat color, I changed the layer mode from Normal to Color. This blending mode is ordinarily most valuable when the file is *not* in LAB, because it emulates the LAB behavior of separating color from contrast. When using Color mode, the color comes from the top layer, the luminosity from the bottom. It's the reverse of Luminosity mode.

Photoshop provides at least four other ways of doing essentially the same thing. The bottom layer now ranged from around 98^L to 5^L, and the top layer contributed a constant value of 45^A61^B. Retaining one copy of this layered file, I made another, merged the two layers, and went to CMYK, producing Figure 8.4B, whose eccentricities—and imaginary colors—are the next topic of discussion.

Pantone doesn't specify any imaginary colors: it gives recipes that allow printers to mix up real-world inks. Many of these inks, however, are outside of the CMYK gamut, and some, particularly the most vivid blues, are *way* out of the CMYK gamut.

The dark orange that is PMS 159 is one of the former category. CMYK inks just aren't quite up to matching an orange that intense and that dark. If it were a little bit lighter, yes. Colors between $57^L45^A61^B$ and $68^L45^A61^B$ are, according to Photoshop's calculations, achievable in CMYK. If the L is within 10 points of these values, the color is probably imaginable. More than 20 points is something really difficult to picture. And more than 30 points is an imaginary color, period.

That's why the tower in the background is so dark. Photoshop sees $98^L45^A61^B$ and wonders how to make something intensely orange yet as white as the surrounding paper. It splits the difference, giving us something way too dark and not nearly orange enough.

Also, this effect is considerably more colorful than that in Figure 8.4A. Brilliantly colored duotones are out of the question with Photoshop's supplied curves, because as the colored ink gets darker, the black gets darker as well, killing color. A fair comparison requires something more neutral. I therefore returned to the layered LAB file, and changed the opacity of the top (Color mode) layer to 25%, moving the overall look much closer to the neutral bottom layer.

I then flattened and converted to CMYK, producing Figure 8.5A. The color doesn't quite match Figure 8.4A because Photoshop's duotone presets are rather old and don't use current values for Pantone inks. However, the two are close enough to pass judgment—and the judgment doesn't favor the LAB version.

Figure 8.4A is superior not just because it's made in the traditional style that we're used to seeing. It's better because it's snappier, because it has real whites and blacks, unlike Figure 8.5A, which was trying to accommodate imaginary colors and so didn't want whites or blacks to occur.

We Shall Have More Anon

So, if you're planning to make duotones, forget this cockamamie LAB method, with one exception. Remember, Figure 8.4A is about as colorful a duotone as you can make using Photoshop's presets. If you want something more violently colored, LAB is the way to get it. You produce something like Figure 8.5A in LAB, convert it into CMYK or RGB, and apply curves that will create a true white and a darker black, as in Figure 8.5B. The alternative, Image: Adjustments>Hue/Saturation>Colorize, can't produce anything nearly as smooth, for reasons discussed in the "Closer Look" section of Chapter 2.

You may be wondering by this point what the motivation could possibly be for spending four pages discussing duotones, something most of us don't make very often, only to conclude that LAB isn't much help in making them in the first place.

Here it is: LAB can create imaginary colors that are very light. When brought into RGB or CMYK, they won't be light any more. In this duotone exercise, that was the wrong approach: we *wanted* to have white areas pop out of a strongly colored picture.

Fine. That's duotones, which play by one set of rules. Color photographs play by another. In normal photographs, white areas in the middle of something of a pronounced color are usually bad, and usually hard to eliminate—unless you know how to deploy imaginary colors.

Figure 8.6 is the classic example. As the manufacturers of Oxy-10 are pleased to note, human skin is oily. Oil reflects light. The human visual system has a complex filtering mechanism that reduces the impact of reflections. Cameras don't.

We've all seen the result, again and again. Portrait shots often feature nasty-looking reflections that we never would have noticed ourselves. In studio work, the effect is so pronounced that photographers slather heavy matte makeup on the subject to try to cut the reflections down. But often we open a file and find big blown-out areas that cry out for digital surgery.

Tiny reflections can be handled in several simple ways, such as by using the healing brush or rubber stamp tools. Larger areas, as in Figure 8.6, are more difficult to handle convincingly. The woman's cheek has precious little detail, but there's some, so we can't paint a flat color over it. We presumably need some sort of selection

of the blown-out area but we have to expect a problem at the edge of it, no matter how soft the selection is. The existing transitions between very light and more normal skin are critical to believability. We can't afford to retouch them out.

We aren't looking to eliminate the reflection altogether, but at the very least it needs to be some shade of pink rather than blank white. When trying to change the hue of an area convincingly, retouching with Photoshop's Color mode is a likely candidate.

Color mode works using retouching tools just as it does when on a separate layer. Double-click a painting tool, change its Mode in the Options bar to Color, and it will be permitted to affect detail. As a crude example, while Figure 8.6 was still in RGB, I set up a purple-blue as foreground color, activated a wide brush tool in Color mode, and painted the purply X of Figure 8.7.

In a perverted kind of way, the detail beneath the brushstroke still looks good. The definition of the purple hair is fine, as are the sunglasses and the background.

The only place the color doesn't change is, unfortunately, the only place we really want it to. The nose has become purple but the cheek hasn't; the model has purple lips and tongue but not purple teeth.

Figure 8.6 *Reflections off faces can be a difficult retouching challenge. The woman's cheek is almost entirely washed out, but there's a smooth transition into areas of more acceptable tonality.*

Figure 8.7 *Color mode doesn't change detail. This image was created in RGB by setting foreground color to a purple and painting the crude X in Color mode.*

The light areas don't pick up color because they can't. As this chapter has drummed into you, in RGB or CMYK a very light tone always has to be white.

You can't create a color in RGB that can't be created in RGB. Color mode can't change the darkness of what's underneath it. If the affected area is as light as the paper it's printed on, then it has to be the *color* of the paper it's printed on.

That near-white luminosity value constitutes an immovable object—in RGB. What's needed is the irresistible force of LAB.

Methinks It Were an Easy Leap

We'll now introduce a proper pinkness into the blown-out area. Rather than make a selection that may be difficult to detect, however, we'll use a gross one that encompasses parts that really shouldn't change and misses others that really should.

We start in RGB by establishing some kind of fleshtone value as foreground color. The normal way of doing so is, with any painting tool active, Option–click a relatively colorful area of skin. Note that it would be a mistake to click too close to the blown-out area. That

would find AB values that are only slightly positive. We need a robust red, like that found in the center of the forehead.

Now, I create either a new layer or a duplicate layer, and make a large horizontal selection across the center. Please remember that this is *not* the way one retouches faces but rather is a means of demonstrating the basics of Color-mode blending.

On the top layer, I fill the selection with the new foreground color, arriving at Figure 8.8A.

Next, in the Layers palette, I change Mode from Normal to Color. Still working in RGB, this produces Figure 8.8B.

There's not much impact across the face, because the color that we're replacing is quite similar to the one we're replacing it with. The big changes are seen in the background, the cell phone, and the sunglasses, all of which have turned dark red.

The effort to introduce redness into the blown-out area, however, went nowhere. The selection line cuts the ear in half, and (intentionally) misses the entire bottom quarter of the blown-out area. But that part of the hard horizontal selection line is invisible in Figure 8.8B. You can see it in the hair, of course, and possibly even in the right side of the ear, but once it hits the cheek, it's gone.

When we move this layered RGB file into LAB, being careful not to accept Photoshop's invitation to flatten it first, you might expect that there wouldn't be any change, but there's a big one. The colored bar on the top layer reads $77^L27^A24^B$. The blown-out area beneath it is largely $100^L0^A0^B$. In RGB, that 100^L was a killer. It couldn't change, and without such a change, Photoshop couldn't allow any color at all.

In LAB, the file asks for a perfectly legal, if imaginary, color: $100^L27^A24^B$. If we were just to return the layered file to RGB, we'd be back to Figure 8.8B, because Photoshop would lock in the 100^L and then try to apply the 27^A24^B to it, without success. But if we Layer: Flatten Image before leaving LAB (as I had to do here, to create the CMYK file to print), we get Figure 8.8C. Since the flattened LAB file has only a single layer, color and contrast can no longer be treated separately during the conversion. Photoshop is handed the lighted rocket of $100^L27^A24^B$ and asked to figure out what it wants to do about it.

Again, the program throws up its hands and splits the difference. The new cheek isn't as red as the imaginary LAB color, but it isn't as light either. So we get a light pink, exactly what's needed. Now the horizontal line through the blown-out area is clearly visible. Yet

Figure 8.8 Color mode has a different impact in LAB than in other colorspaces. Top, a horizontal bar of a fleshtone color is placed on a separate layer in RGB. Middle, the layer mode is changed from Normal to Color, theoretically giving everything underneath the bar a pink color, yet not destroying detail. Bottom, the same layered file is converted into LAB, without flattening. The light areas of the cheeks are more strongly affected than in the center version, because the bottom file calls for an imaginary color there, one that does not exist in RGB and hence could not be created in the center version.

the transition between the artificial pink and the real skintone is undetectable. All that's needed is a simple selection somewhere in the transition area, plus, of course, redoing the bar so that it covers the entire cheek and none of the background.

The Better Part of Valour Is Discretion

Our final example will merge typical LAB curves with an imaginary-color move.

LAB's habit of avoiding blown-out white areas where we expect to see color has shown its power before. In Figure 2.3, we saw another example of how flat bars of color are more realistic when applied in LAB than elsewhere. And Figures 5.10 and 5.11 showed an advantage of sharpening the L channel rather than in RGB: when the sharpening

process forces an extremely light area, LAB will retain color even when Luminosity mode in RGB cannot.

Figure 8.9, a tourism shot, isn't all that bad, although the presence of so much greenery suggests the use of LAB. Nobody will object to greener grass and mountains; there are no dangerously bright objects that might go flying out of gamut; and if the red slide loses all detail, we won't care.

Also, it's neutrally correct. Several objects are probably gray or close to it: the curved roof in the background, the chairs on the lawn; the dark windows at lower left; the cement walls in the building at center right. All these areas measure 0^A0^B or within three points of it in both channels, indicating that there's no color cast and that the curve-steepening recipe of Chapter 1 should work well—except for one neutral area that hasn't been discussed, the one that shouldn't be neutral at all: the sky.

In Figure 8.9 there's nothing to discuss; the image ends at the top of the mountains. A hazy day, assisted by an overzealous automatic contrast enhancement in the camera, condemned everything above it to $100^L0^A0^B$.

Assuming you agree that skies in tourism shots should have color, we need to face up to

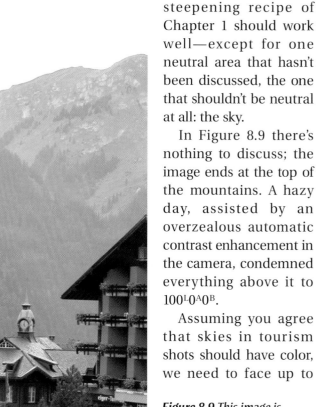

Figure 8.9 This image is neutrally correct, suggesting that the recipe of Chapter 1 should work well to emphasize the greenery. However, the sky is completely blown out.

The Imaginary Color, the Impossible Retouch   175

some problems. Any global move that makes the sky blue would also make the lawn furniture blue, among other things. And yet if the sky gets bluer, to some extent the background mountains need to also. Therefore, we have to plan on some type of selection, but we also have to worry about making the new sky mesh with the mountains.

Skilled retouchers generally hold off on doing their thing until all global corrections have been made. Otherwise, there's risk that an errant curve or excessive sharpening could emphasize artifacts that would expose some of the retouching trickery.

Imaginary colors in LAB, on the other hand, are better inserted right away. The transition between imaginary and real colors is so natural that it can't be emphasized by later moves. But if we darken the image with curves or sharpen it before creating the sky, we risk not having a believable transition into the mountains.

Accordingly, the first move is to create a duplicate layer. To it, I applied the curve, and got the result shown in Figure

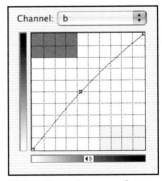

Figure 8.10 *This curve forces blueness into the entire image—and turns the sky into an imaginary color, a blue that's as light as the paper it's printed on.*

8.10. By moving the center point of the B curve to the left, I had given the whole picture a blue cast. I also made a slight darkening of the highlight in the L. The point was to define the sky as $98^L0^A(20)^B$: the imaginary color that is very blue, yet almost as light as the paper.

Naturally, the mountains have also gotten bluer, as they should. The problem will be to merge those bluer mountains into the rest of the image without some kind of telltale line showing.

That transition will involve parts of both layers. From the top of the building at right on down, however, we should be seeing the bottom layer only. To avoid any inadvertent use of the top layer, it makes sense to exclude it from the mix immediately.

With the top layer active, choose Layer: Add Layer Mask>Reveal All. This creates a layer mask, Photoshop's most potent retouching tool. Where the mask is white, we see the top layer; where it's black, the bottom; and where it's gray, we see a combination: the darker the gray, the more it favors the bottom layer.

The choice of Reveal All starts us with a white layer mask that leaves the top layer entirely visible; its opposite, Hide All, would have given us a black mask. We can start with either option.

With the new white mask active—we know this by the black border around its icon in the Layers palette—we select, and delete to black, any area that can't possibly be used as part of the transition.

Anything lower than the tree on the left shouldn't be part of the transition: it should remain as it is in Figure 8.9. So we could just activate the marquee tool, draw a big rectangle as wide as the picture from that point down, and delete to black or fill with black on the layer mask.

Instead, I used the lasso tool. Across the center of the mask I tried to imitate the drunken Falstaff's vision of a straight line, followed by a large circle to encompass the whole bottom of the image, which I deleted. Then I chose Select: Feather to create a soft edge where black meets white, as shown in the left side of Figure 8.11.

Falstaff's most misquoted utterance was, "The better part of valour is discretion; in the which better part I have saved my life." This last move, in fact the layer mask itself, demonstrates the sagacity of his concept. I really doubt that anything other than the lawn furniture and possibly the top of one building is going to be affected by what's about to happen, so I could make a tiny mask to protect those tiny areas. But what's the point? Since nothing in the bottom half of the image is supposed to change, we may as well cover the whole thing, just in case.

Figure 8.11 *The process of merging the two versions begins with a layer mask (background to this caption). Where the layer mask is black, the bottom layer appears; where white, the top layer. Inset, the Layers palette indicates the presence of the mask.*

Similarly, I have no more intention of letting the blue layer come close to the edge of the layer mask than I have of summiting Mont Blanc. But if, due to my own incompetence, some tiny piece of the soft, raggedy edge in Figure 8.11 survives in the final version, it's less likely to be noticed than if it were a hard-edged straight line.

Thou Hast Damnable Iteration

Next, we need to restrict the blue layer further. The imaginary color in the sky is fine, but we also have to have some blue left over for the tops of the mountains, as otherwise it will be too obvious that the sky wasn't there in the first place.

The tool of choice is Blending Options, first

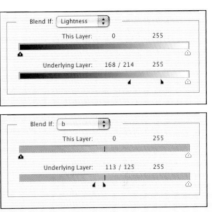

Figure 8.12 *Layer Blending Options to limit where the top layer appears. Left, the bottom slider enforces a strict darkness limit. Parts of the overly blue top layer that were visible in Figure 8.11 have disappeared, but it's still obvious where the two layers meet. Right, the luminosity slider has been split to create a transition zone between layers. Also, a slider has been added for the B channel, eliminating the top layer in all areas that were previously more blue than yellow and completing the merge. Note the split slider there as well, created by holding down the Option key while moving the slider.*

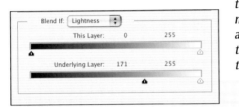

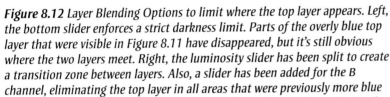

discussed in conjunction with Figure 7.13. We use this command to tell Photoshop to exclude the top layer under certain circumstances. The hard part is trying to explain what those circumstances are, because Photoshop doesn't understand skies, trees, or mountains, only numbers.

We could say, only use the top layer where the value on the underlying layer is 100^L. That, however, would create the harsh line that we want to avoid where the sky hits the mountains, which are not 100^L. Instead, we need the blueness to fade away gradually as the image gets darker. We don't have to worry about the bottom half of the picture, which has already been killed by the layer mask.

So, we access Blending Options by clicking the top right arrow of the Layers palette or double-clicking the top layer's icon. The idea is to restrict the top layer to areas that used to be light, which calls for using the Lightness slider, choosing Underlying Layer to avoid any consequences of the slight move I'd made in the top layer's L to establish a darker blue.

As the left-hand slider moves to the right, it eliminates darker areas, starting just above the tree at left, which is the darkest area above the top of the layer mask. Figure 8.12A shows the effect. There's still a harsh line where the two layers meet, but it's moved higher up in the picture.

To eliminate that line, we first need to decide whether its current location is about where we'd like the soft transition to end. There's no right answer, but I'll buy it as it stands. That is, I've decided that every area that's unaffected by the blue layer in Figure 8.12A will stay just as it was in the original image. Everything else will take on some of the blue flavor. The lighter the area, the bluer it will get.

To make a soft transition, we Option–click the Blend If slider to split it into two halves. The setup in Figure 8.12B instructs Photoshop to use the top layer at full strength in very light areas, such as the sky, and not at all in anything darker than the left half of the left-hand slider. Anything between the two halves is to be a blend of both layers.

Figure 8.13 *The final version of the image applies simple LAB curves to the original, Figure 8.12.*

This didn't make the transition quite smooth enough for my taste, so I added a slider for the B channel as well. Again, I used the Underlying Layer sliders, knowing that on that layer, the sky measures 0ᴮ, perfectly neutral, and that the mountains were always somewhat negative, meaning more blue than yellow. I therefore asked for a transition further limiting the role of the top layer wherever the underlying layer fell on the blue side of the B.

A Deal of Skimble-Skamble Stuff

Having created a version that seamlessly inserts an imaginary-color sky, we need only apply the usual AB curves, emphasizing the A somewhat more than the B, I think, just as we did in Chapter 3.

CMYK users face one remaining gotcha. If the file is being prepared for print, as this one is, we have to recall that an imaginary color is in use. The highly counterintuitive step of converting from LAB to RGB and only then to CMYK is indicated.

Remember, the LAB file is demanding a sky that's not only lighter, but far, far bluer than in Figure 8.13. Faced with that impossible demand, it's hard to predict how Photoshop will react. A monitor, however, is an RGB device. When it displays an LAB file, it uses internal Photoshop logic to translate it into the RGB data that it needs. Because the tables that govern this informal, on-the-fly conversion are similar to the ones used when we finally choose Mode: RGB, what the monitor shows us while we're still in LAB is a good prediction of what we'll have once we convert to RGB.

When going into CMYK, however, there's a complication—Photoshop looks at LAB equivalents, even when converting an RGB file. Under ordinary circumstances, there's little difference between a file that goes from LAB to CMYK and the same file converted from LAB to RGB first and *then* to CMYK. If the LAB colors are even close to being within the RGB gamut, the original LAB and the LAB-to-RGB file are indistinguishable for purposes

Review and Exercises

✓ If you are working with imaginary colors in LAB, and your final file needs to be CMYK, why should you convert it to RGB first?

✓ What common defect in images of faces is best addressed through use of an imaginary color?

✓ In what ways does Color mode create different results in LAB than in RGB?

✓ Open the original of Figure 8.9, and create a new version along the lines of Figure 8.13. Instead of creating an imaginary-color sky, however, import a sky from some other picture. If you can't find one of your own, use the original of Figure 1.2. Use layer Blending Options in LAB to create a smooth transition into the mountains.

✓ Open the original sunset image of Figure 2.8, and look at the printed results for the enhancements done in LAB (Figure 2.9) and RGB (Figure 2.10). The challenge is to remake the LAB version without the use of any curves. Re-create the RGB version by use of the Image: Adjustments>Hue/Saturation command. Then, move to LAB and attempt to duplicate Figure 2.10 by using painting tools in Color mode, and blurring the AB in areas where the Hue/Saturation command created artifacting.

of a subsequent conversion to CMYK. If imaginary colors are lurking about, however, all bets are off. An imaginary color in LAB seems to the conversion algorithm to be a very different animal from the same color that has been arbitrarily crammed into the RGB gamut.

For example, our LAB sky measured $98^L0^A(20)^B$, an imaginary color. If the file is copied and converted into RGB, it becomes $234^R250^G255^B$, a real-world one. The LAB equivalent of that new RGB value is $97^L(5)^A(4)^B$—not even close to the original, as far as a later conversion is concerned. Convert these two identical-looking files to CMYK and you'll get two different results, as we saw in Figure 8.3.

The exact result depends on what's in our Edit: Color Settings>Working Spaces>CMYK. If we convert the LAB file with today's default CMYK definition (Photoshop's SWOP coated v.2 profile, the same one this book uses), the sky won't be as blue as it is in Figure 8.13, which went to RGB first. But if we use the more traditional CMYK definitions, which aren't covered in this book, the sky would be *more* blue than in Figure 8.13.

Furthermore, my experience suggests that

Photoshop's View: Proof Colors command, which is the usual way of trying to figure out what a foreign file will look like when converted to CMYK, chokes when confronted with imaginary colors. The better part of valour suggests converting to RGB, which at least gives us what we see on the screen.

And So Ends My Catechism

Surprisingly, the part of the last exercise that's hardest to duplicate outside of LAB is the one that by now seems the simplest: those deceptively easy AB curves to emphasize the greens. There are lots of ways to put skies into empty spaces in any colorspace, although, if you don't mind a flat blue, this way is very easy. Professional retouchers often import skies from other pictures in situations like this, usually because they want to see clouds.

The problem would still remain getting the new sky in without a telltale line between it and the original image. Some of the sky's color has to affect the mountains. Even if the sky were inserted in RGB, we'd still probably use Blending Options: we could use the Gray slider of RGB as a reasonable substitute for the Lightness slider in LAB. The problem is that nasty B channel slider of Figure 8.12B, which isn't analogous to anything available in RGB or CMYK. For that reason, if we were stealing a sky from some RGB image, and if our own image were RGB, it would pay to take it into LAB to get a better transition, even if we had no other reason to be there.

That's a good introduction to our next topic, LAB's uncanny ability to isolate objects and to make selections and masks therefrom.

Meanwhile, the next time you encounter a big, blank area where detail is supposed to be, think fireworks. Think Falstaff. The color may be imaginary. The results are real.

The Bottom Line

LAB's construction allows us to specify colors that are not merely out of gamut in CMYK and RGB, but totally impossible, imaginary colors. These "colors" exist mostly in very light or very dark areas: what in the world is a bright red black, or a brilliantly green white? They don't exist, but LAB can call for them.

Imaginary colors in LAB files serve important purposes and enable types of retouching that are impossible in other colorspaces, chiefly in putting color back into blown-out or overly dark areas.

The LAB Advantage
In Selections and Masking

The A and B channels may seem blurry and shapeless, but they're often the beginnings of the best masks. Objects that can't be resolved in any of the RGB channels are sometimes clearly defined in the A and/or B. Sometimes, the strange structure of the AB channels even lets us select the ambient light.

My luve, wrote Burns, is like a red, red rose, that's newly sprung in June. While much is to be said for the creative use of flowers in romance, and while redness is ordinarily a virtue, Figure 9.1A is too much of a good thing. It's not a rose any more—all detail has vanished in an out-of-tune melody sung unsweetly in a chorus of cacophonous oversaturation.

The rose appears here because, being so different from its background, it's probably the easiest object we'd ever have to select in a photograph. But before doing so, I'd like to fill in one hole in the first half of the book.

The objective of manipulating the A and B channels is usually to increase color variation, and to make certain colors brighter and purer. Basic AB curves accomplish this when we make them steeper by pivoting them counterclockwise around the center point.

On rare occasions, of which this is one, we need to do the reverse: to suppress colors. Steepening the AB curves wakes colors up; flattening puts them to sleep. To reduce the intensity of the colors, we pivot the curves clockwise. Figure 9.1A had so many reds that were outside of the CMYK gamut that they all closed up when the file was converted. Figure 9.1B, with a contrast boost in the L channel and the AB values reduced, is a better match to what can be printed. Now, back to our regularly scheduled program.

When we *select* an object, in Photoshop parlance, we allow ourselves to change it, whereas anything that isn't selected is locked. We can also make *partial selections,* which reduce the effect of any move, applying it less than on a fully selected area but more than on an area that isn't selected at all. We used exactly such a partial selection in correcting Figure 7.11A,

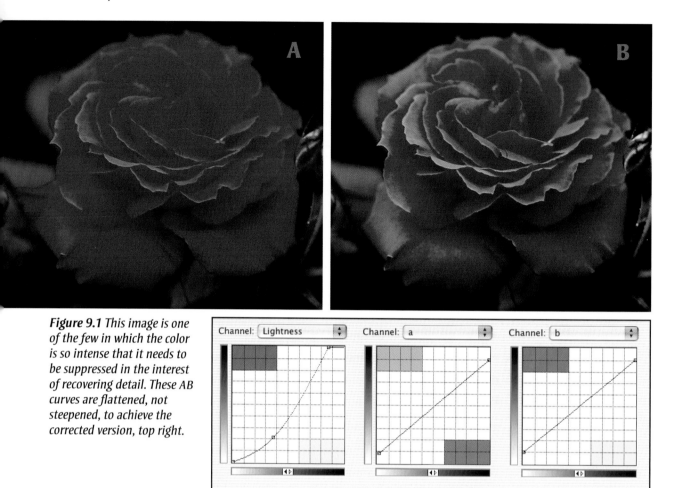

Figure 9.1 *This image is one of the few in which the color is so intense that it needs to be suppressed in the interest of recovering detail. These AB curves are flattened, not steepened, to achieve the corrected version, top right.*

which had a bad yellow cast in the highlight that grew weaker as the picture got darker. We loaded a luminosity mask that fully selected the light areas of the image but gradually lessened the selection elsewhere.

Selections become portable when we choose Select: Save Selection to store them either as a separate Photoshop document or as a nonprinting (alpha) channel in an existing one. The term *mask* applies to such portable selections. They can be edited like any other grayscale pictures and used over and over.

Too many people use selections as crutches. The better you get at image manipulation, the less you make them. Nevertheless, a selection is sometimes needed. To change Figure 9.1A into a yellow rose, or to

import it into a different picture, or to ghost it out, or to tuck some type underneath it as part of a collage—all these moves would require selections. Even in color correction, we sometimes want them. You may think that the background in Figure 9.1B has gotten too dark. It wouldn't work to select the rose and correct only that; it would look as if the flower had been cut out and pasted back into the image. But a selection of the rose and a partial selection of the background, allowing it to get *somewhat* darker, might be agreeable.

Creation of accurate masks is one of the most difficult tasks for a serious retoucher, because not every object is as ridiculously easy to isolate as the rose in Figure 9.1A is. Knowledge of channel structure saves an amazing amount of time. The purpose of this chapter is to show how the A and B channels are often the solution to otherwise intractable masking problems.

Note, please, that we are speaking only of mask/selection generation, not necessarily image manipulation in LAB. If you prefer to work on an RGB image, it's permissible to make a copy and convert it to LAB. A mask created there can be saved directly into any open RGB file that's the same size as the LAB one, as a direct copy would be.

Rose Is a Rose Is a Rose Is a Rose

First, a quick inventory of the many Photoshop methods of selecting. If we want to grab this rose, here are some of the options, listed more or less in order of complexity.

- Hit the rose with Photoshop's **magic wand** tool, which has been around since the beginning of time. It's primitive, but granting the huge difference between this rose and its background, the magic wand will not break a sweat in making this selection.
- Use the magic wand on a **single channel**, which often has greater contrast than the color composite. The red channel would be ideal, because its flower is extremely light, if not totally blank, and the background is dark. If you happen to be in CMYK, the same can be said of the cyan channel; and if you are in LAB, either the A or B will do.
- Click the rose after choosing the **Select: Color Range** command, to generate a selection of everything of a similar color.
- Trace the rose's edges with the **lasso** or the **pen tool.**
- Paint a selection by clicking into **Quick Mask** mode in the toolbox.
- Put the corrected version on a separate layer, and then use layer **Blending Options** to limit its effect to the desired areas.
- Try artificial intelligence to create the mask, using either Photoshop's **Filter: Extract** command or a **third-party masking plug-in.**
- Create a formal **mask**, usually by saving

or blending existing channels and editing them. Sometimes the result will be loaded as a layer mask; sometimes merely as a selection by means of Select: Load Selection.

Every one of these methods works perfectly for this rose. Most of them are a total waste of time, since clicking with the magic wand would work. But as selections get more difficult, the options become more limited.

The yellow rose of Figure 9.2 is only slightly harder to select than the red one of Figure 9.1A. There's more color variation. Parts of the center are significantly darker than the edges, a complication from the point of view of the magic wand.

You should be able to tell which channels might have the beginnings of the mask without actually looking at them. In RGB, the blue channel must be extremely dark, because this rose is no more blue than it is a stalk of ragweed. The green is probably light enough to work with but the red will be even better, because the flower is more red than it is green; it will therefore be lighter in the red channel, Figure 9.2B.

In CMYK, the cyan would be best for the same reasons, and LAB is the easiest to guess. The flower is only slightly more magenta than it is green, but it's way more yellow than blue. Consequently it is well defined in the B, Figure 9.2C.

Making a mask is about finding edges. Both our prospective mask channels (the red and the B) have good ones—but the two have different characters. The red gets darker as the flower does. The B doesn't give a hoot about how light or dark an object is; it becomes darker where the flower is less yellow.

Having different strengths opens up some interesting possibilities. Retouchers often make difficult masks by blending channels in some esoteric mode, using a layered file, or using the Image: Apply Image or Image: Calculations commands. There is no rule against applying a channel from a document that's in

Figure 9.2 This yellow rose's shape is well defined in the red channel of RGB (top right) and the B of LAB (bottom right).

one colorspace to a channel of a file that lives in another.

In Figure 9.3A, I applied the red channel to itself in Hard Light mode, a blending mode that we'll discuss later; the abbreviated explanation is that it lightens areas where both blending channels are light, and vice versa. In Figure 9.3B, I did better by using the same mode, but blending the B into the red.

Granted, an experienced retoucher will have no trouble creating a mask for this rose without LAB. But you can see where we're headed. RGB channels have trouble isolating a colored object as it gets darker. And there's no denying that Figure 9.3B is technically superior to Figure 9.3A.

Roses White and Roses Red

As the flowers get darker, the selection problems mount—in RGB. To see how selecting overly dark colors can become irksome, take a sniff of a second red rose. Figure 9.4 compares red and A channels. Anything red is positive in both A and B, but this flower has a

Figure 9.3 Left, a prospective mask created by applying Figure 9.2B to itself in Hard Light mode. Right, when Figure 9.2C is applied to 9.2B in the same mode, the result is technically superior.

stronger magenta than yellow component, so the A is a better choice to work with.

As redness fades into darkness, the red channel (Figure 9.4B) no longer differentiates the flower's lower left and right edges from the background. The A does, because the flower, though darker, is still magenta and the background is not. (To match the tonal variation of the red channel, contrast has been increased slightly in Figure 9.4C.)

Masks must be saved as grayscale documents, and when we save this A channel separately, we will increase its contrast even more with curves, making the flower full white and the background black. When that happens, there will be a suitable edge everywhere. Starting with the red instead would create needless work, and in our next example, it would create a *lot* of needless work.

There is no problem selecting out the white petunias in Figure 9.5A: they have well-defined edges in every channel. The red and purple flowers are a different story.

The red is again the lightest RGB channel, but not by much. The color is so subtle that, in Figure 9.5C, the purple flowers merge into the green leaves, which are equally dark.

Nor is the green a suitable option. The flowers are so utterly non-green that they're blacked out in Figure 9.5D. That differentiates them nicely from the leaves that were such a problem in Figure 9.5C. Unfortunately, the flowers now merge seamlessly with the darkest parts of the background.

The mask can certainly be made without an LAB copy of the file and without a painting tool, but it will take a while, and require a fair amount of knowledge. An expert would know how to use the Image: Calculations command to combine the red and green channels in such a way as to bring out the flowers. A multi-colorspace expert might instinctively realize that even though RGB channels almost always make better masks than CMYK ones do, this is the rare exception where the magenta of CMYK would be much better than the green of Figure 9.5D. If you know how to do these things, pat yourself on the back. But before going to the trouble of constructing a mask in such a convoluted fashion, ask yourself, what's the point? The mask is just sitting there, waiting to be extracted, in the A.

In Figure 9.5E, the flowers break easily away from both leaves and background. The A ignores darkness. It only knows that the leaves are green and the flowers magenta; that the background is neutral and the flowers aren't.

Figure 9.4 *The red channel, top right, no longer distinguishes parts of the flower's lower edges from the background. In the A channel, bottom right, the edge is distinct. (Contrast has been added to match the tonal variation of the red.)*

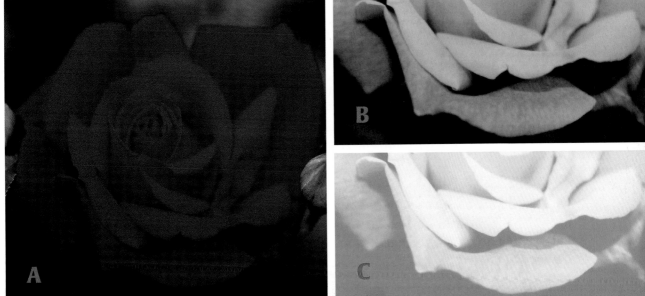

Figure 9.5 *As colors get darker, transitions retained in the A or B channel are often lost in their RGB counterparts. Right, top to bottom: a magnified color version, the red channel of RGB, the green of RGB, and the A of LAB.*

So Fair Art Thou, My Bonny Lass

The AB channels' blissful ignorance of darkness issues again provides the advantage in our final flower image. There's such a big difference between the bright flowers of Figure 9.6A and the background that it looks like the red channel might work as a mask right from the get-go.

That assumption, alas, is uprooted by the texture of the background stone. Finding nearly white flowers in the red channel would be great, if only there weren't umpty-nine million white spots behind them.

The A channel is not derailed by white or black spots in the middle of a gray area. They're all neutral, all values of 0^A, and they provide a perfectly smooth background to these heavily A–positive tulips.

Extremely fine detail often favors the use of an AB channel in masking even when, unlike that in Figure 9.6, the detail is nominally a different color than its surroundings. A photograph shot through fine netting (Figure 9.7) makes selections problematic.

Assume, then, that we wish to select the

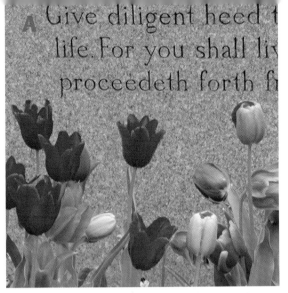

Figure 9.6 *The mottling in the stone background poses a problem for a selection using the red channel, top right. But since the background is entirely neutral, it shows up as a pure gray in the A channel, bottom right.*

face, or the lips, or the blue background, or the hair. The likeliest RGB source for any would be the red. In LAB, for a change, it would be the B, because the face is positive, more yellow than blue, and the background sharply negative.

Almost any conceivable selection would *want* to include the netting, because its color would need to change along with whatever move we were making on what's behind it.

In Figure 9.8A, the netting has picked up so much of the background color that the B channel hardly sees it. But in the red channel shown in Figure 9.8B, the netting can't be removed without some really stiff blurring. So once again, LAB is the best start for a mask.

A Rose by Any Other Name

Having established that LAB can make certain selections that are difficult to impossible elsewhere, let's look at where the principle can make a difference in practice.

Masks and soft-edged selections are often needed when there is something peculiar about the lighting, as there is in the airport scene of Figure 9.9. At first glance, it may remind you of an earlier exercise: Figure 7.6A, an overly

Figure 9.7 *The netting may be an obstacle to any attempt to select either the face or the blue background.*

Figure 9.8 The netting is less pronounced in the B of LAB (left) than in the red channel of RGB.

dark shot of an outdoor wedding. The strategy then sounds good now: Shadow/Highlight to the L channel, followed by LAB curves to add contrast and more vivid colors.

That wedding picture, however, didn't have a big ugly backlit yellow sign dominating the image. If Figure 9.9 gets a general boost in all colors, that sign will ignite and take off faster than anything currently parked on the tarmac. So we must either exclude it from

Figure 9.9 The overly dark image is dominated by the backlit signage. Any attempt to lighten and brighten the image may exaggerate the effect, as well as eliminate all detail in the signs.

the overall correction or sharply limit what can happen to it.

We've already seen this color—it's the same as the rose of Figure 9.2. Using the red channel as the base for a selection worked there, but won't here: the sign is light in the red, but so is a ton of other content. But in the B, the sign is a hermit, living in happy isolation, by far the yellowest thing in the image. Before proceeding, I verified this by comparing it to the yellow shopping bag on the right side of the image. The sign was around 95^B and the bag more like 55^B.

We now know what channel will isolate the sign; the question is how to make it happen. Creating a selection is for those who are certain they know what they want. Making a mask is for those who want room to experiment. I fall into neither category with this image. I'm not sure I want to exclude the sign totally, but neither am I about to spend 15 minutes tweaking a mask. So, I select a middle method: using layer Blending Options, allowing me to exclude the signage

altogether while offering some limited flexibility to let it change slightly.

I started in LAB with a duplicate layer, to which I applied Shadow/Highlight at settings of 25% Amount, 55% Tonal Range, and a big 65-pixel Radius, followed by a touch of the Unsharp Mask filter. This got the image about halfway to where I thought it should be.

Putting all this on a separate layer turned out not to be necessary. I was concerned that some of the moves might adversely affect the sign and that I would have to use Blending Options immediately. It didn't happen, so I added an adjustment layer and wrote the kind of curves that we've seen many times before: dropping the quartertone point in the L to make a lighter picture with more contrast in the midtones; steeper A and B to intensify color variation. Also, I moved the B curve slightly away from yellow and toward blue, to compensate for a slight yellowish cast in some of the metallic objects.

Increasing color intensity drove the sign far out of gamut. To restore it, I brought up

Figure 9.10 The sign was substantially excluded from this correction of Figure 9.9, by isolating it in the B channel.

the Blending Options dialog with the top layer still active. By default, the top layer takes precedence, but we can move sliders to exclude certain areas and restore what's underneath; we also have a limited ability to form areas that combine both layers.

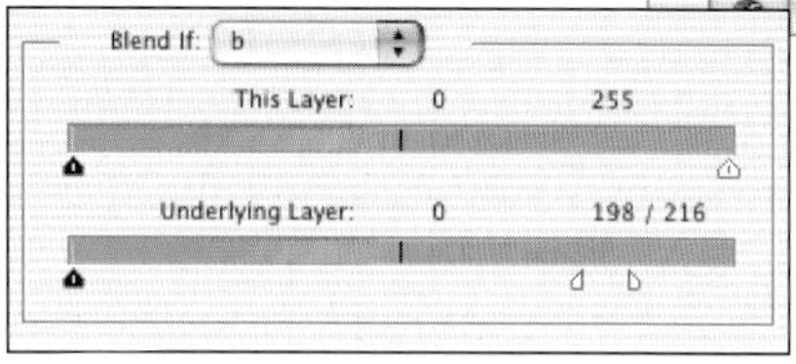

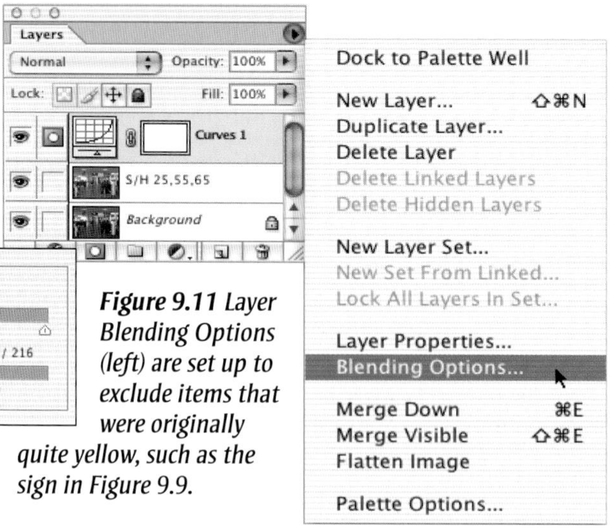

Figure 9.11 *Layer Blending Options (left) are set up to exclude items that were originally quite yellow, such as the sign in Figure 9.9.*

Here, the object was to exclude things far to the yellow side of the B channel. The tough part is making the meaning of *far to the yellow side* narrow enough to include only the sign, and not the yellow shopping bag.

After increasing color variation we would normally work with the top layer sliders, because there would be more space between the sign and the bag than there was originally, making it easier to find a point between them. Here, though, the curves had maxed out the sign to the infinitely yellow 127^B. The bag had become about 100^B, so there was less difference between the two than there was on the bottom layer.

Therefore, I moved the right-hand slider on the underlying layer to the left, until I was sure it was getting most of the sign and none of the bag. Then, feeling that the transition between the sign and the rest of the image was too harsh, I Option–clicked the slider to break it in half. The space between the two halves is a transition zone where Photoshop blends the two layers rather than using one or the other. To the left of the left half it uses the top layer only; to the right of the right half, the bottom layer(s).

Ultimately, Figure 9.10 is a lie. Not because it's lighter than the original; if we had been there, we'd have perceived the scene as lighter than the photograph ourselves. But we would have recognized the sign as being more intense than the bag, since the sign generates its own light and the bag doesn't. On the printed page, allowing a dull bag in the interest of a sign that seems brighter would not be smart. Hence, the lie, and when we lie about an image, we ordinarily need a mask, a selection, or the type of layer blend shown here.

Each Morn a Thousand Roses Brings

As noted in Chapter 1, plant life, along with light-skinned Caucasians, represents an area of disagreement between human beings and cameras. We invariably remember seeing something greener than the camera has recorded. And so, in something like Figure 9.12, we want greener, more variable grass, which is a move away from the spirit of the photograph, not to use the more invidious word found in the preceding paragraph.

There are two problems with treating the greenery the way we did the canyons of Chapter 1. Both pertain to the background.

First, as the greenery occupies the midrange of the L channel, we'd use an S-shaped curve to increase contrast. That would be too bad for the sky, which is in the light part of the L and might blow out. Second, the sky is already slightly negative in the A channel, meaning that, although blue is its dominating hue, it's slightly biased toward green. If we try to steepen the A channel, the sky may become annoyingly cyan.

These two factors suggest doing something to emphasize the changes in the lower half of the image. Not splitting the picture in half and leaving the top half untouched, mind you, as that would make the bottom half look as though it had been cut out and pasted back in. We want to use a subtle mask for maximum flexibility in editing; Blending Options is too blunt an instrument.

The color-enhancing move itself should clearly be done in LAB, because that's what LAB does best. But where should the mask come from? Remember, there's no law against using a mask derived from an RGB channel while working in LAB. But which one?

You could always check each channel individually, but the goal should be to know the answer in advance. In RGB, the lighter the channel, the more color it contributes. The red has been our best choice in all the flower images, but it won't be here. The grass and trees aren't very red, so they're dark. The other half of the image is slightly lighter, but it isn't red either.

The green channel is even worse. Both halves of the picture are rather light, since they share a green component.

The blue is the one we want. The background is distinctly blue, therefore light. The foreground isn't blue at all; it tends toward yellow, as all natural greens do. Therefore, it's dark, yielding exactly the kind of higher-contrast channel that we're looking for.

Its opponent in the LAB corner is the B. In the A, the foreground is more magenta than green, hence lighter, but the background is basically neither magenta nor green, hence of medium darkness. In the B, the foreground is sharply more yellow than blue and the background sharply more blue than yellow.

Both contenders need work before entering the ring. Masks need to be light to enable and dark to disable changes. The blue channel is the opposite; it's dark in the foreground that we want to change and light in the background that we don't. Therefore, we make a copy of it and choose Image: Adjustments> Invert. Figure 9.12B is the inverted copy.

The B of LAB, on the other hand, is too flat, inasmuch as we never find whites or blacks in AB channels. Therefore, I copied it to a

Figure 9.12 The difficulty with applying LAB curves to enhance the foreground greens in the original, left, is that they may blow out the delicate blues in the background. The solution is a mask that applies the curve more to the bottom half than to the top. Two likely contenders: an inverted copy of the blue channel of RGB, center, and a copy of the B channel of LAB to which the Auto Levels command has been applied to enhance contrast.

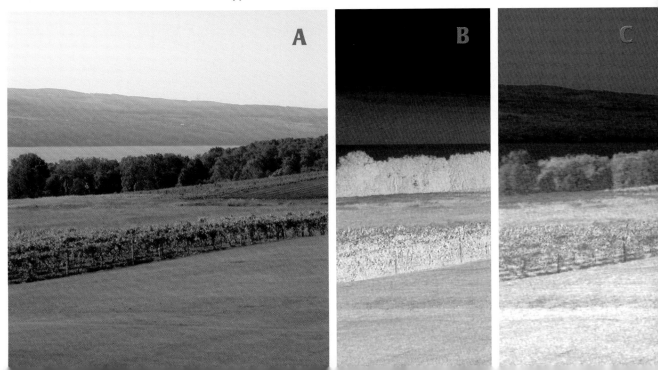

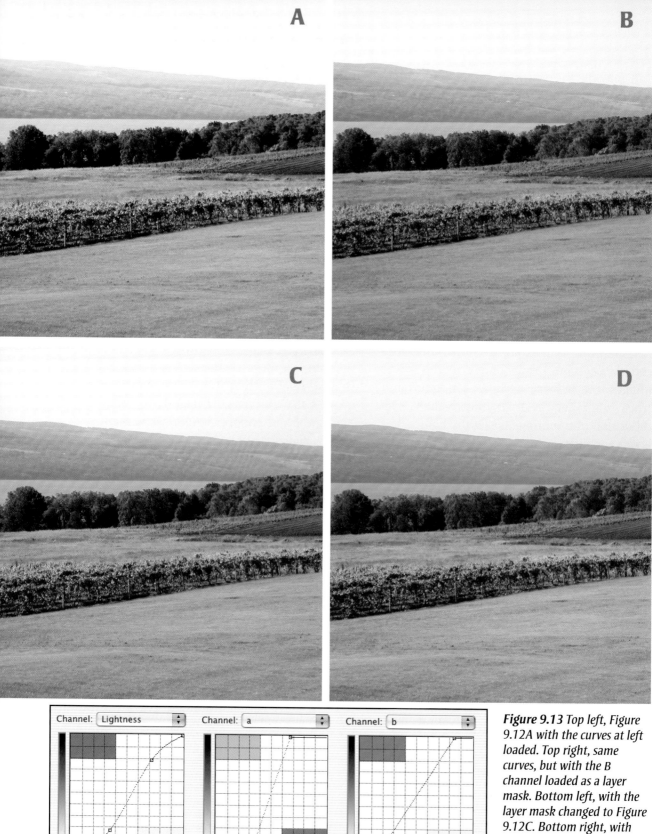

Figure 9.13 *Top left, Figure 9.12A with the curves at left loaded. Top right, same curves, but with the B channel loaded as a layer mask. Bottom left, with the layer mask changed to Figure 9.12C. Bottom right, with the layer mask edited to be almost white in the green areas and black elsewhere.*

separate document, followed by Image: Adjustments>Auto Levels to get Figure 9.12C.

Compare the two masks in the trees that are closest to the lake, and in the row of grapevines at center. In Figure 9.12B, both areas are more selected than the grass is, because originally they were darker. But in Figure 9.12C, they are *less* selected, because they originally weren't as green. That's the better interpretation, in my opinion. We would like the curves to give those grassy areas more of a pop to make them stand out from the darker, more neutral greens.

Having thus decided to use the B as the start of a mask, the experimentation begins by putting a curves adjustment layer on an LAB version of Figure 9.12A. Just to see what's what, we pretend that the background doesn't exist, and aim the curves squarely at the foreground area, without any mask or selection. The result is Figure 9.13A.

Creating, saving, and loading masks can be done with several different command sequences in Photoshop. The most common way is to establish a selection (possibly by loading an existing channel as a selection directly, as explained in the discussion of Figure 7.11) followed by Select: Save Selection. This prompts us to save either as a separate grayscale document, or as an extra, non-printing (alpha) channel. We can load as a mask any channel from our own document, any open grayscale document of exactly the same size as ours, and any alpha channel of any other same-size open document.

With this picture, I don't need to save anything at all, because I propose to use a layer mask rather than loading a mask as a selection. The reason is that I don't know yet how strong a mask to make, and I want to be able to edit it on the fly.

The layer mask defines a merge between its home layer and the layer(s) beneath it. Where the mask is white, the top layer takes precedence; where black, the bottom layer(s).

Where the mask is gray, we see a combination: the lighter the gray, the more it favors the top; darker values favor the bottom layers. All this is quite analogous to how a mask loaded as a selection works.

The layer mask isn't there unless we Layer: Add Layer Mask. An adjustment layer, however, contains a blank layer mask by default. You can see a layer mask icon on the right side of the top layer bar in Figure 9.11. Since the icon has a border, the layer mask is the current target of any move we might make.

Figure 9.13A, since it's made with an adjustment layer, has a layer mask already, but an irrelevant one because it's blank, white, meaning that the top layer always takes precedence.

One of the many ways of loading a layer mask is shown in Figure 9.14. Being sure that the layer mask is highlighted in the Layers palette, Image: Apply Image, choosing the B channel as source.

Doing so produces Figure 9.13B, in which the changes of Figure 9.13A are sharply reduced. They have to be, because an uncorrected A or B channel is very gray. Everything is close to a 50–50 blend of the two layers.

Masks and Blurring

Most masks require some type of mild blurring before being loaded. Otherwise, when the image is corrected, the line between protected and unprotected areas may be too harsh. Blurring is particularly necessary when using the A or B channel, both of which can be fairly noisy, as the base. A Gaussian blur of 3.0 pixels or less is usually sufficient.

In other types of selection, the blurring may not be recognizable as such, but it's there nonetheless. The Select: Color Range command tends to create a smooth transition on its own, as does the layer Blending Options command when the control sliders are split apart. Even when we make "hard" selections with the magic wand or pen tools, it's customary to Select: Feather afterward. In effect, that blurs the edge, creating a zone of partial selection.

There's a slight preference for the top layer in the foreground green area.

If we feel that Figure 9.13B isn't dramatic enough, we can, with the layer mask still active, choose Auto Levels, effectively making Figure 9.12C the layer mask and producing Figure 9.13C. Because the mask has been exaggerated, the correction is more intense than that of Figure 9.13B in the bottom half but less intense in the top half.

Even more radical, I applied an extremely steep curve to a fresh copy of the original B, blowing out nearly all of the grass to white and plugging the entire background to black. The only areas remaining as shades of gray were the trees, the grapevine, and limited amounts of grass. Loading the result as a layer mask produced Figure 9.13D, in which the correction is applied almost fully to the bottom half and not at all to the top.

These are only four of an infinite number of possibilities, some of which involve the use of RGB. But LAB has major advantages both for the color variation in the greenery and, if a mask is desired, for that. The key is to prevent the selection from affecting the trees and grapevines as much as the grass. An RGB mask would not do so as subtly.

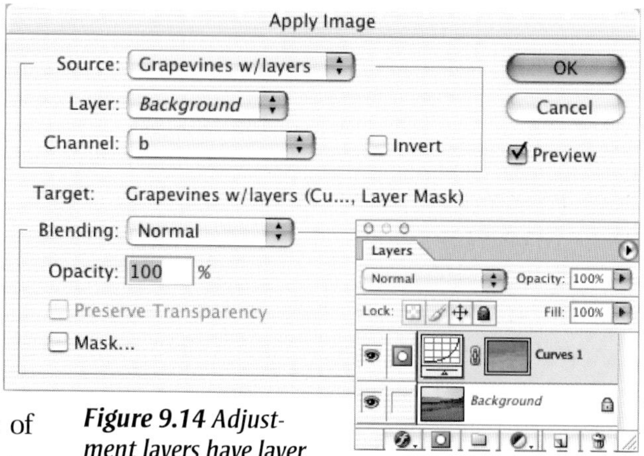

But Where Is the Rose of Yesterday?

We now turn to a more complicated, and sadder, example. The view from Hong Kong island across the harbor to Kowloon used to be one of the most dramatic and romantic in the world. No more. Rapid development in China has led to air pollution that has gotten completely out of hand in the last few years.

If you think trying to make a picture of this sorry scene look more attractive is hard, you should try breathing that air. But altering photographs in such ways is standard practice in the advertising industry, and nowadays it may be hard to find a day much better than this one to start with. As for

Figure 9.14 *Adjustment layers have layer masks by default. Above, the Apply Image command puts a copy of the B channel into the layer mask. Inset, the layer mask icon reflects the new contents.*

finding a clear picture from a few years back, forget it. Hong Kong has been adding skyscrapers at such a frenetic pace that a shot from even five years ago looks no more like today's reality than the skyline of Des Moines looks like that of New York. No, we work with what we have.

We've seen, back in Figure 3.1, how LAB curves excel at breaking through haze. The problem is the reverse of Figure 9.12A, where we wished to enhance the foreground while avoiding excessive damage to the background. In Figure 9.15A, we need to increase *background* contrast so drastically that the foreground is in mortal danger. The solution remains the same: a selection or mask to partially protect the foreground while we blast away at the background.

The curves shouldn't be difficult. They'll be very steep, and may have to be repeated because the original is so flat. The only irregularity is, since we won't be able to eliminate the haze altogether, I think we should force it to be more blue. That will make the water more attractive, and possibly fool people into thinking they're seeing sky, not smoke.

Developing a proper masking procedure requires us first to figure out what is likely to get hurt by these curves, and how we can protect it. The far bank is so enveloped with smog that it's basically entirely gray. Whites and blacks are nonexistent. Therefore, we can put our corrections on a new layer or adjustment layer, and use Blending Options to exclude things that are either very light or very dark on the underlying layer.

That's only half the battle, because certain foreground objects, particularly the large copper-colored building, won't fall in the exclusion zone. The AB curves for the background need to be very steep indeed, to try to take advantage of whatever limited color variation may be found through all the smog. Plus, I intend to force the B curve toward blue. If that foreground building gets a taste of those curves, it may turn either bright orange or bright blue, or possibly both at once! And at least one other foreground building in that darkness range starts out on the dangerous yellow side.

It sounds like another job for the B, since what we're after involves yellowness, not darkness. Furthermore, if the mask suppresses changes to things that are more yellow than blue, it permits them in areas that are more blue than yellow. That's a bonus, because it will allow both the water and the smog to get bluer.

Therefore, I followed the same procedure as in Figure 9.13C. I created a curves adjustment layer, loaded the B channel as a layer mask, blurred it, and applied Auto Levels to increase its range. This time, though, I had to invert the B to emphasize bluer parts of the image and exclude yellower ones, the opposite of what was needed in Figure 9.13C. And, for reasons I'll explain shortly, I added the Blending Options shown in Figure 9.16.

The biggest problem in masking is that in separating out parts of the image for special attention, we can separate them so much that the viewer will perceive two different pictures. That's why the mask needs soft edges, and that's why we split the sliders in the Blending Options dialog. The mask alone wasn't sufficient to protect the yellower areas from changing, so I added a further restriction in the B channel. The Blending Options applied to the L, meanwhile, partially exclude areas that were originally very light or dark,

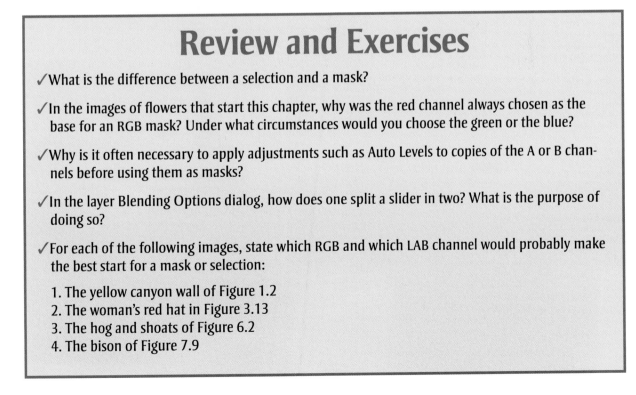

Review and Exercises

✓What is the difference between a selection and a mask?

✓In the images of flowers that start this chapter, why was the red channel always chosen as the base for an RGB mask? Under what circumstances would you choose the green or the blue?

✓Why is it often necessary to apply adjustments such as Auto Levels to copies of the A or B channels before using them as masks?

✓In the layer Blending Options dialog, how does one split a slider in two? What is the purpose of doing so?

✓For each of the following images, state which RGB and which LAB channel would probably make the best start for a mask or selection:

1. The yellow canyon wall of Figure 1.2
2. The woman's red hat in Figure 3.13
3. The hog and shoats of Figure 6.2
4. The bison of Figure 7.9

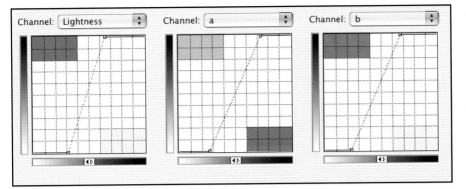

Figure 9.16 The curves, left, were applied to Figure 9.15A through a layer mask that was based on an inverted copy of the B channel (below). Blending options (bottom) further restricted the impact to smoky areas.

since our target area is a dismal gray.

Ordinarily, we work with sliders on the layer that has the most range. The curves have smashed the deepest shadows into total blackness on the top layer. We want to exclude not only those shadows, but also somewhat lighter ones. So much contrast has been added by blowing out the highlights and plugging the shadows that what's left over occupies a very long range. It's easier to experiment with the sliders, as we need not be as precise. We therefore use the This Layer line.

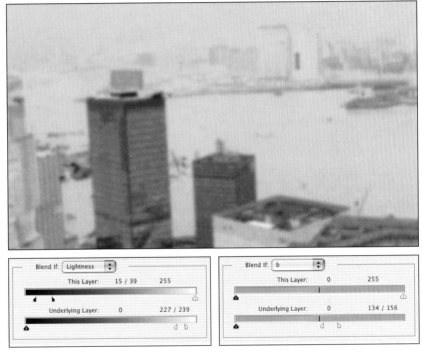

The same doesn't apply to the highlight sliders. The curves have wiped out not just anything that was originally lighter than the smog, but also some of the critical areas. So, there's no choice: we must use the Underlying Layer line, because some of what we're trying to target doesn't even exist on the top layer.

The colors were now fine, but I still wanted to increase contrast in the background. So, after flattening the image, I created a new

Figure 9.15 (opposite) The original, top, is nastily gray because of air pollution. Bottom, an attempt to create happier colors and lessen the impact of the background smoke. Inserting this added blueness required that the foreground buildings be excluded.

adjustment layer and, without a layer mask, essentially repeated the previous move, but in the L channel only: a very steep curve, limited by Blending Options that excluded very light and very dark areas of the original.

After this complicated series of moves, let's end with something just as complicated—unless you know LAB, which not only seems to make selections appear out of thin air, but sometimes can select the thin air itself.

Lighting Through Rose-Colored Glasses

Scenes with two or more competing light sources often force selections. Figure 9.17 was professionally shot for an advertisement,

Figure 9.17 *Due to different types of lighting, the right side of this image has a blue cast, but the left side is correctly balanced. Eliminating the undesirable cast in such images normally requires a mask.*

but the photographer could not compensate for tungsten lighting on one side of the image and daylight-adjusted on the other. Hence, the image is neutrally correct on its left side but has a blue cast on the right. Naturally, the client wants the cast removed.

If there were one cast in the light half of the image and a different one in the dark half, as was the case back in the office scene of Figure 7.11A, then we might be able to fix it with a single set of RGB or CMYK curves. But one cast on the right and another on the left needs a selection no matter what colorspace we work in.

Since this file came to me in CMYK, that's where we'll keep it. The procedure would be exactly the same if it had arrived in RGB. Since the only objective is to remove the cast, there's no need for LAB curves—but we still have to figure out how to, how shall I put it, select the *air* on the right side of the file.

If you insist upon making this mask in some other colorspace, you'll be in for a long day, not just in painstakingly excluding every part that isn't blue, but in establishing a believable transition between where the cast ends and the normally lit area begins. Realize that the beginnings of the mask already are stirring, however tenuously, in a B channel that doesn't yet exist, and the whole exercise can take less than a minute.

The first step is to get a copy of this hypothetical B into our CMYK file. So, we Image: Duplicate, then Mode: Lab Color. As the B is the third channel, the keyboard shortcut Command-Option–3 loads it as a selection directly into the LAB file.

Now, since the selection *is* the B, we Select: Save Selection, indicating that we want to save a separate channel for future amusement. Photoshop asks us where we would like to put it: the current document, as a separate grayscale file, or into any other open document that's the same size as the current one. That last option is the one we want: the

The Bottom Line

When a mask or selection is needed, the A and/or B channels are often surprisingly good starts. When properly handled, they produce masks that become less effective as the color becomes less pronounced, as opposed to RGB, where the mask is lessened as the color gets darker.

Before loading a mask based on the A or B, it's usually necessary to increase contrast and to blur it.

Such masks can also be used even if no other work is being done in LAB. There is no law against making a copy of an image, converting it to LAB, and transferring a copy of one of the channels to the original file.

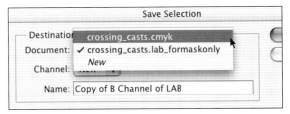

Figure 9.18 *Active selections can be saved for future use as masks either as separate documents or as alpha channels in any same-size open file.*

original CMYK file is the same size as the LAB copy, so we can drop this B into the CMYK file as a nonprinting fifth channel, as shown in Figure 9.18.

A and B channels are always rather gray, and this one is exceptionally so. A value of 50% gray represents neutrality, and this is basically a neutral picture. The slight added blueness on the right side is certainly there, but it's hard to see. This new channel's contrast has to be enhanced before the mask is usable.

Command–5 opens the copy of the B that is now the fifth channel of the CMYK document. The desired increase in contrast is too huge to be made in one step. It could be accomplished in several different ways, but, after the usual slight blur, I started by applying Auto Levels, getting to Figure 9.19A. Remember, since this is a nonprinting or alpha channel, whatever we do to it does not affect final reproduction—yet.

Although the added blueness on the right is now visible as extra darkness in the mask channel, we still have to go further. The left side should be a pure white, which it isn't in Figure 9.19A. The right side should be pure black where it's bluest. In between, there needs to be a transition. All this can be taken care of by a very steep curve.

Also, masks need to be light in the areas where change is to be allowed and dark where the file is locked. Figure 9.19A is the opposite. Upon loading a mask, Photoshop gives us an Invert check box as an option.

I find that it makes me crazy, so I always avoid having to remember to use it by applying Image: Adjustments>Invert to recalcitrant mask channels. That, plus the curve and a slight blur, produces Figure 9.19B.

We now return to the original CMYK, and Select: Load Selection. The modified B

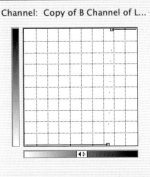

Figure 9.19 *Contrast usually must be enhanced before using a copy of the A or B as a mask. The original B of Figure 9.18 is too gray to show here. Above, after it has been blurred and Auto Levels applied. Below, contrast has been added with the curve at left, and the channel has been inverted to create the final mask.*

Figure 9.20 The final image, where the cast has been reduced by loading Figure 9.19B as a selection and cutting saturation with the Hue/Saturation command.

channel appears as an option, and we load it. At this point, we have the seemingly impossible selection of the ambient light. With that accomplished, there are at least half a dozen ways to eliminate the cast. I chose Image: Adjustments>Hue/Saturation, reducing the Master Saturation control by 50 points and producing Figure 9.20.

The Outlook Is Rosy

The removal of the cast in Figure 9.17 took longer to explain than it did to execute, yet even very experienced retouchers often take much longer to achieve an inferior result. I know this because I've used this particular picture as an exercise in advanced classes.

The ability to visualize what the channels must look like is the key to making selections of any complexity. The A and B look so foreign that many people make the mistake of ignoring them. As we've seen in this chapter, they often can provide better selections than are otherwise available. We started with objects that would be easy to select in any colorspace, but as we progressed it became harder and harder to make them without help from the A or B.

One final advantage: knowing when to use the A or B for masks is the same skill as knowing when to use them in some rather startling channel blends that are described in the final two chapters of this book. Get through that, and remember the flowers of this chapter, and perhaps your life will still not be a bed of roses. But it would be fair to say that, in image manipulation as in skillful masking, you will have found a very pronounced edge.

The Product Is Red
But the Client Wants Green

Have to make a *serious* color change? LAB can do it, not just faster, but better. It's a one-two-three process, and it doesn't get derailed when the client wants a specific PMS color.

he hungry farmer hands his wife three eggs and tells her to fry them for breakfast. In doing so, she accidentally breaks the yolks. Undaunted, she proceeds to make scrambled eggs and pretends that this is what she understood her husband to be asking for.

Usually, the farmer is smart enough not to challenge this version of the facts. Imagine what would happen, though, if, instead of merely insisting on fried eggs, the farmer were to say that he had wanted duck à l'orange, and demand that his wife produce it. His ears would certainly be ringing in that case, because there would just have been a high-speed collision between one of them and a frying pan.

In the graphic arts, similar scenes often play themselves out. The client hands us hamburger meat and asks us to return filet mignon. It happens all the time. Sometimes we can even comply. But occasionally a most vexing variant appears. We are handed eggs and told to produce Coquilles St. Jacques Mornay.

The request to completely change the color of a major component of an image isn't an everyday occurrence, but it isn't uncommon either, especially in product and clothing work.

The original Corvette of Figure 10.1A is red, but every now and then, some farmer, er, art director, will belly up to the light box and say, "Y'know, that color conflicts with the grass—don't you think the car might look better if it were green?"

Since we are not allowed to swing skillets at our clients' heads, we can only send them away and ask them to return in six hours or so, when the massive retouching that will be necessary is complete.

And, indeed, to make a car not just green but a *convincing* green, hours of work are needed—for those who don't know LAB. With LAB, it can be done in seconds. Figure 10.1B was literally done with three keystrokes, no layers, masks, selections, curves, or filters.

People who do this kind of work and are not accustomed to getting results this good—despite taking a thousand times as long—become very interested in LAB.

Before setting out the general recipe, let's admit two shortcomings, both of which we will learn how to avoid in this chapter. First, the change from red to green is so striking that it hides the undesirable color change in the background. If you've read Chapter 9, you snap your fingers at this issue, because the selection that will correct it is easy.

Second, in the real world, clients who are so concerned about product color that they order up an overhaul never use terms as vague as *green*. They ask for something more specific, often using the Pantone Matching System (PMS) to describe the desired color. If they did that, we'd need more than three keystrokes—but there'd be an even huger difference in the time it would take to execute the request in LAB as opposed to some other colorspace.

Anyone trying to duplicate even the three-keystroke result of Figure 10.1B without the aid of LAB had best be an expert with at least one of the Channel Mixer, Calculations, or Apply Image commands, if not all three. The obstacle is that the "red" car is far from being a flat color. Check out the very subtle areas of red reflections in the bottom of the rear-view mirror and in the chrome grille areas. Even on the far side of the hood, the red fades out to a near-white. These quasi-reds are just about impossible to select, so something like Image: Adjustments>Replace Color has no

Figure 10.1 *(opposite) The red car of the original, above, can be turned into a green one almost instantly with only three keystrokes in LAB.*

Figure 10.2 *While still in LAB, the car can be changed from red to green by inverting the A channel, either by the Image: Adjustments>Invert command or by applying the upside-down curve at right.*

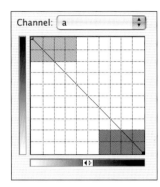

chance. We'd have to build channels from scratch to hold these transitions.

Even if you invested that much time, I don't believe you could get so natural-looking a result, due to some color factors that will be touched on when we look at this image again in Chapter 11. In any case, the discussion is pointless. When one method takes two hours and the other half a minute, we don't need to split hairs about whether the two-hour method is as good.

The three keystrokes in the LAB file that transformed the car from red to green were Command–2, Command–I, Command–S. In English, the A was inverted without touching the other two channels, whereupon the new file was saved.

Everything magenta becomes green and vice versa. Moreover, the more colorful an area was in the original, the more colorful it is in the bogus version. The reflections on the far side of the hood are barely red in the original, and barely green in Figure 10.1B. The white and black areas don't change, because they're approximately 0^A, which doesn't change when the channel is inverted. Similarly, the chrome areas seem more blue than yellow, so they're negative in the B. But they are neither magenta nor green, so they're 0^A as well, and remain unchanged.

Inverting the A by direct command is the same as applying the upside-down curve of Figure 10.2. Doing the deed with three keystrokes is spectacular, but in real life, as we're about to see, we'd use the curve. The problem

Figure 10.3 *The assignment is to transform the yellow train, above, into a specific shade of blue. Below, an overly literal interpretation of the instruction.*

to achieve, and where to try to achieve it.

• Second, we establish a new layer or adjustment layer, and apply LAB curves to implement the new color.

• Third, we figure out a way to restore everything that isn't supposed to be associated with the color change.

In Figure 10.3, the assignment is to make the yellow train blue. That can be arranged with three keystrokes just as it was with the car; we invert the B rather than the A. It will be considerably more obvious this time that the background has gotten fouled up: yellow skies are generally seen as incorrect.

As yellow is a very light color, inverting the B without touching the L would produce a very light blue. Let's complicate matters by making it a dark blue, and even further by demanding a specific dark blue: PMS 7462.

Presumably you don't know how to construct that color off the top of your head, so we have reached Step One. We have to find out what that color is, and then decide where to put it.

The first half is easy. We call up the Color Picker and click Color Libraries (Photoshop CS2) or Custom (earlier versions) to reach the treasure chest of premixed colors. The default is Pantone Solid Coated, which is what we want. We now either scroll down to the desired number or, easier, type it in. Figure 10.4 informs us that PMS 7462 equates to $36^L(8)^A(40)^B$. If we want, when we click back to Picker, Photoshop displays equivalent values in RGB, CMYK, and HSB, using our current Color Settings.

I sheepishly offer Figure 10.3B to illustrate a common atrocity. Absurdly large numbers of otherwise sane individuals, when given specific values such as those found in the right half of Figure 10.4, run completely amok and fill the entire object with them.

with the keystroke method is that if you don't like the particular green of Figure 10.1B then you're out of luck. With the curve method, you can have whatever green you like.

Three Steps to a Color Change

Just as the green car was made in three keystrokes, there are three steps to a believable color replacement:

• First, we decide what color we are trying

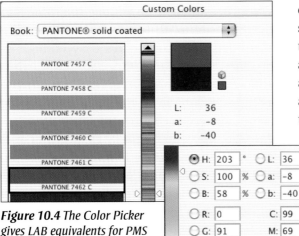

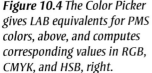

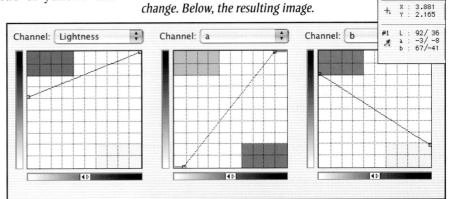

Figure 10.4 *The Color Picker gives LAB equivalents for PMS colors, above, and computes corresponding values in RGB, CMYK, and HSB, right.*

color sampler tool, which is found in the same box as its close relative, the eyedropper tool. This tool expands the Info palette by adding up to four fixed measurement points, as shown in Figure 10.5. We click a desired area to establish each point. As we modify the picture with curves or other commands, the values of the fixed point(s) change, no matter where the cursor is.

The point I chose measures $92^L(3)^A67^B$. We have now reached Step Two, which requires us to transform those values into the desired $36^L(8)^A(40)^B$. The strange-looking curves of Figure 10.5, placed on an adjustment layer, do so.

Do that, and you get a swatch from the Pantone book, not a train. The train can't all be one species of blue any more than the original was a single shade of yellow. The front of the locomotive plainly falls in shadow. It can't possibly be as colorful as the side closer to us. Also, the rear cars of the train get less colorful as they fade into the distance.

If the change is to be credible, those smooth color falloffs need to be maintained. Neither Pantone nor Photoshop explains how to do so, so the final image has to be a matter of interpretation.

The official PMS value should certainly exist somewhere in the train, but where? We should look for the spot in the original that we think most fairly represents the train's yellow color. Not too dark, not too light, not too faded. The spot marked with a crosshair in Figure 10.3A answers that description. The idea is to make that point match the definition of PMS 7462, and leave all other areas to the tender mercies of fate.

We now enter the toolbox and activate the

Figure 10.5 *These strange-looking curves drive the selected point of Figure 10.3A to the values specified in Figure 10.4. Right, the bottom of the Info palette reflects the change. Below, the resulting image.*

A value of 36ᴸ is much darker than 92ᴸ, so the bottom left of the L curve has to be raised drastically. The A is no problem, as (3)ᴬ and (8)ᴬ are pretty close. A simple steepening of the curve suffices to pick up the desired five points. Unfortunately, we next have to change the B not by five points but by 107.

Since we're looking for a very negative (40)ᴮ, but the current value is a very positive 67ᴮ, we first invert the curve as in Figure 10.2. This yields (67)ᴮ, which is too brilliant. We need a duller blue, and to get it we flatten the inverted curve, making sure, as always, that it continues to pass through the center point of the grid.

While shaping each curve, we keep an eye on the Info palette. The fixed measurement is shown in the lower left of the palette of Figure 10.5. The value before the slash is the original; to the right of the slash is the new number.

Applying these curves produces something horrifically dark, thanks to the massive move in the L channel. So, we have reached Step Three. In principle, Figure 10.5's train is correct but the rest of the picture is not. This is why the document has two layers: we need to pick up the original background from the bottom layer.

Blending Options and Layer Masks

Merging the two layers closely resembles the selection process described in Chapter 9. We can construct a channel and load it into the automatic layer mask that already lives in the adjustment layer. But the mask must be pure white and pure black except for some slight edges, as opposed to the masks we've seen so far, which usually had some gray. Such masks make for less convincing results.

A better approach is to attempt to isolate the correction with Blending Options, and then hope that only minor touchup will be needed on the layer mask. We'd like to avoid having to use some painting or drawing tool to carefully isolate an edge. If Blending

Options establishes a proper soft edge but leaves a clump of the top layer showing in some isolated area, that's easy enough to remove. For example, racing flags appear in the white fender of Figure 10.1A. In the process of turning the red car green in Figure 10.1B, the red flag was transformed as well, a mistake. However, it's trivial to lasso that area out of the layer mask, allowing the original red flag to show through.

Whether intending to use Blending Options or a formal mask, we have to take help where we can find it. In addition to the existing LAB file, we should consider whether any of the channels of a hypothetical RGB document could be of use.

The brief answer is no. The train would be so dark in a hypothetical blue channel that parts would be indistinguishable from its base. In the other two, it would be so light as to blend in with all manner of highlights.

In LAB, however, all three channels can work together to narrow down the possibilities. You might think that the B alone could isolate the train. It's true that the area near the indicated sample point in Figure 10.3A is far yellower than anything else in the file. Parts of the train, however, aren't particularly colorful. They're only yellower than the rest of the image in the mind of a layperson. As experienced LAB practitioners, we know that the key phrase is not "more yellow than" but "more yellow-as-opposed-to-blue than." The least colorful parts of the train are still more yellow than blue, but not more-yellow-as-opposed-to-blue than the left-side trees, parts of the foreground tracks, and the red logos on the side of the train.

These issues can be addressed in the other channels. The red logos are more magenta-as-opposed-to-green than any other part of the train, the trees far more green-as-opposed-to-magenta. By bringing in the sides of the A channel slider, we can exclude both. Parts of the track are darker than any yellow

area of the train and can be restored by excluding the darkest part of the L channel.

The function of Blending Options has been discussed twice before, once regarding an interior with a serious yellow cast in Figure 7.13, and at greater length with a series of images in Chapter 9. To review, we move the Blend If sliders to exclude areas of the top layer, allowing the bottom layer to show through. The crude settings of Figure 10.6A exclude everything that was more than a trifle more blue than yellow on the underlying layer. They wipe out large swaths of the sky and even parts of the dark areas on the train, but don't touch anything that used to be yellow. Ugly lines of transition appear where the top layer suddenly is cut off by the slider definition. But the top of the train begins to take shape against a restored background.

The other component of restoring the background is—if necessary—the layer mask. Trying to fine-tune it so that it defines the edges exactly is tiresome. Drawing a rough selection with the lasso tool, as I did in Figure 10.6B, takes seconds. After making the selection on the white layer mask that was automatically generated when the curves adjustment layer was

Figure 10.6 Three steps toward restoring the background. Top, a crude use of the B channel slider excludes part of the sky. Center, a crude layer mask to eliminate everything that doesn't actually hit the yellow areas. Bottom, a version using three channel sliders for greater accuracy.

formed, and making sure that it did not cut into any yellow part of the train, I did Select: Inverse, then hit the Delete key to force the layer mask to black in all areas of the background that didn't actually butt the yellow areas of the train. Once that layer mask is in place, it won't matter whether the Blending Options are accurate, except in the region directly adjacent to the yellow.

I prefer not to mess with the layer mask until finished with the Blending Options. That way, I have a better idea of how successful the Blending Options are. If all that's left is a small area around the yellow, it may be hard to spot a defect.

Figure 10.6C has no layer mask, but it does have three sets of sliders. Mild touchup may be needed in the train, and the foreground tracks and gravel will need to be excluded by a mask that takes longer to explain than to execute.

Two final reminders. First, each slider has been split into two by Option–clicking. This establishes a smooth transition between zones, rather than harsh breaks like those of Figure 10.6A.

Second, in deciding whether to use the top or underlying sliders, go for the layer that has the most range, so that the sliders can be placed more precisely. The curves of Figure 10.5 flatten the L and B channels but add contrast to the A. Consequently, we stick with the underlying layer sliders in the L and B. But the critical range in the A, the area governing things like the train that are neither particularly magenta nor green, is longer on the top layer, letting us choose more accurate placements for the sliders.

Finally, for an interesting demonstration of simultaneous contrast, which we discussed at the end of Chapter 1, compare Figures 10.5 and 10.6C. Do you perceive the two trains as being the same blue? A spectrophotometer would.

From One Channel to the Next

Suppose that the client disapproves of the off-yellow of the woman's jacket in Figure 10.7. Why this could not have been dealt with at an earlier stage is an issue that will likely be discussed once the retouching bill makes its appearance. Leaving that aside, let's just assume that we've just been asked, er, told, "Don't you think it might look better if it were brown?" and that the brown of choice is PMS 168.

Step One calls for finding out the LAB equivalent, $29^L27^A31^B$, a yellowish red more than a brown, and choosing a control point that will take on that value. The point highlighted in Figure 10.7 reads $73^L(18)^A47^B$.

Figure 10.7 The assignment is to change the woman's jacket into a specified reddish brown.

Step Two is the curves, and a variation on the previous method. In the train image, the yellow original was so light, and the blue replacement so dark, that there was little choice but to boost the light endpoint of the L curve, leaving an exceedingly flat channel.

This time, although the replacement L is still darker, there's more room to maneuver. The control point isn't practically on top of the left axis, as it was in the train image. We can shoot for a steeper start, a real curve rather than a straight line, in an attempt to gain more contrast in the jacket so that the lapels won't vanish as the jacket gets darker.

The AB curves are familiar; they're almost the reverse of the ones shown in Figure 10.6. The A is negative and needs to become positive, so the curve must be inverted. The color is to become more intense—27A as opposed to (18)A—so the curve must be steepened. The B does not need to be inverted, but the original jacket is more yellow-as-opposed-to-blue than the brown PMS color is. So the B curve must be flattened.

That brings us to Figure 10.8, and to Step Three. Peeling the background away from the newly brown jacket isn't particularly difficult with or without LAB. Some retouching will probably be necessary to prevent obvious haloing where the shoulders meet the dark background, particularly on the left side of the image, but that's routine. Because LAB is key to making the selection in many images—and because it's a lot easier than it may have seemed so far—we'll do this one the LAB way, just to make sure the steps are clear.

The jacket shares range with several other things in each channel. However, the shared objects don't stay the same from channel to channel. For instance, the gloves and the jacket share a range in the B—they're both much more yellow than blue. But in the A, the gloves are magenta and the jacket is green.

That's the chink in the armor that we can exploit—provided we do it in LAB. Other colorspaces get tripped up by the dark areas common to almost all objects. In RGB, inasmuch as the jacket and the gloves share

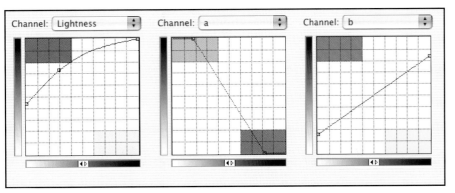

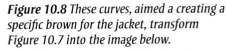

Figure 10.8 These curves, aimed a creating a specific brown for the jacket, transform Figure 10.7 into the image below.

certain dark values, they can never be isolated in any channel. But the A and B don't recognize darkness, only color, and the two objects are easily separated.

Three Sets of Sliders

With Figure 10.8 as an adjustment layer above Figure 10.7, we look at where the curves have placed the contrast to determine whether the Blending Options will reference the top or bottom layer. These curves flatten the original in the L and B but increase its contrast in the A. Therefore, we'll be using the This Layer option for the A channel but Underlying Layer for the L and B.

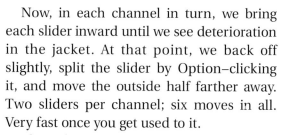

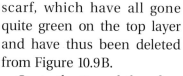

Figure 10.9 *Adding Blending Options in each channel isolates the interest object. Left, the above options, L channel only. Center, the A options are added. Right, after adding the B.*

Now, in each channel in turn, we bring each slider inward until we see deterioration in the jacket. At that point, we back off slightly, split the slider by Option–clicking it, and move the outside half farther away. Two sliders per channel; six moves in all. Very fast once you get used to it.

The jacket is originally neither particularly light nor dark, so the shirt and parts of the background can be excluded in the L channel. That gets us to Figure 10.9A.

Moving to the A (and therefore looking at Figure 10.8, not 10.7), the jacket has become magenta. The A sliders easily distinguish it from the gloves, the lips, and parts of the scarf, which have all gone quite green on the top layer and have thus been deleted from Figure 10.9B.

On to the B, and therefore back to the original. The jacket in Figure 10.7 is very yellow-as-opposed-to-blue, but not quite so much as certain parts of the scarf. But it's substantially more yellow

A

than the face, or almost anything in the background. Other than the jacket itself, the only relics of Figure 10.8 that remain in Figure 10.9C are a few pieces of scarf, plus some ugly green noise in the woman's neck.

Before setting up a layer mask to remove the remaining detritus, we should magnify and look at key areas. Figure 10.10A suggests that some of the slider settings may have been too ambitious, and its jaggedness tells us that the A and/or B should have been blurred. Fortunately, as the file is structured, it's not too late: the

original image is still on the bottom layer, untouched. Every change lives on the adjustment layer. Blurring the AB channels on the bottom layer corrects the problem.

B

The wardrobe malfunction on the edge is a piece of the original green jacket. The sliders couldn't catch it, because it had been neutralized where it hit the background. The Info palette thinks it's gray. Nevertheless, it looks greenish now for the same reason that the jacket in Figure 10.8 looks redder than in Figure 10.10C, notwithstanding the Info palette's opinion that they're the same.

Such edges are difficult to capture in any type of selection. I smoothed them out in Figure 10.10B by opening the B slider more than in Figure 10.9. I didn't retouch the edges here, but sometimes that's necessary.

To finalize the image, we click into the

Figure 10.10 Close examination of Figure 10.9C (top) shows jagged edges where the shoulder meets the background. Blurring the AB channels plus a slightly more open slider setting produce a smoother transition (center). Bottom, after addition of a layer mask to exclude the areas of background that Blending Options did not, the substitution is finished. Left, a swatch indicating the desired PMS color of the jacket.

C

Figure 10.11 This car is an unusual color, heavily negative in the A channel but near zero in the B. The lack of range in the B creates a problem when switching to a color with extreme values in the B, such as orange.

Saving a Blending Options Mask

Occasionally it is desirable to create an editable mask based on what has already been accomplished with Blending Options, so that it can be retouched and loaded as a selection or layer mask.

To do this, make flattened copies of the original and of the version with the Blending Options. Convert both to RGB and apply one to the other in Difference mode, which creates black areas wherever the two are identical—namely, everywhere except where the Blending Options are taking effect.

Inset is Figure 10.7 applied to Figure 10.9C in Difference mode. To make a mask of it, you can either convert it to grayscale or steal one of the RGB channels. Either can be saved as an alpha channel or a separate file.

layer mask, locate any areas where objectionable parts of Figure 10.8 remain (gross gloppy green blotches in the face would be an example of something considered objectionable), and, with background color in the toolbox set to black, either erase them or lasso and delete them.

Next to Figure 10.10C is a flat swatch representing Photoshop's CMYK rendition of PMS 168. The question of whether the final jacket matches that color sufficiently closely is highly subjective. If you want to change it, it's not too late. The adjustment layer curves still exist. For example, if you feel that the jacket is too red, you could shove the inverted A curve slightly to the right without affecting anything else in the picture.

When the Colors Aren't Opposites

Changing a red car to a green one, or a yellow train to a blue one, avoids a problem that we now need to confront. The green car was the direct opposite of the red one in the A channel, and the B wasn't touched. The blue train was created mostly by inverting the B, coupled with a move of no great importance in the A.

Changing a light green jacket to a brown one requires moving both channels, but it's easier to make duller colors out of brighter ones than the other way around. It's much harder to try changing to a bright color that is *not* close to the direct complement of the original.

As noted in the "Closer Look" section of Chapter 4, the LAB "green"—a strongly negative A channel with the B near zero—is comparatively rare. Almost all things we think of as green, such as the green car of Figure 10.1B, are in fact strongly to the yellow side in the B. The old car in Figure 10.11, which I'd describe as teal, is, I think, the only example of "LAB green" in the book.

If the assignment were to change this car to magenta, the direct opposite of green, it would be Figure 10.1 all over again. Irritatingly, the client chooses something else, an orange, PMS 7409.

The drill is familiar. The control point shown measures $74^L (29)^A (5)^B$. We learn that PMS 7409 is $76^L 18^A 78^B$.

The curves for the first two channels pose no problem. The two L values are almost identical. The A needs to be inverted and flattened, along the lines of the B curve in Figure 10.5. But this car has a better

Figure 10.12 *The desired color requires an extremely positive B channel, but the original B measures almost zero. Top, the B channel is replaced by a copy of the A, which is more positive. Below, after the curves at right are applied to the top version.*

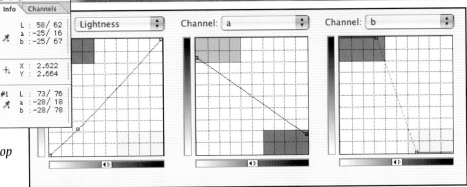

Figure 10.13 *The progression of excluding the background of Figure 10.12B. Top, working on the topmost of three layers, sliders limit the scope of the L channel. Center, the B sliders are added. Bottom, additional Blending Options are added to the middle layer, excluding areas that were originally more yellow than blue.*

chance of winning the Indianapolis 500 than we do of changing $(5)^B$ to 78^B with a curve. Making objects twice or even three times as colorful as they were is easy in LAB. Making them 25 times as colorful is another story. The original B channel is too flat to have any hope of creating some-

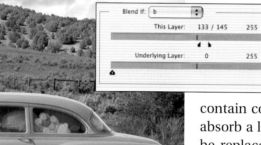

thing as extreme as that yellow. Now, if only it had started out at $(28)^B$ rather than $(5)^B$, then we might have a chance.

Since the AB channels contain color only and no detail, they can absorb a lot of punishment. One can even be replaced with the other! Figure 10.12A has a copy of the A where the B used to be.

It's important that this replacement take place on a duplicate layer, leaving the original untouched. Can you foresee why?

Now that there's a serviceable B, we add a curves adjustment layer. The file now has three layers, unlike the previous examples, which had only two. The curves that produced Figure 10.12B require little comment.

We proceed to the selection step, activating the Blending Options on the third layer, under somewhat of a handicap. As the L channels of the second and third layer are nearly identical, it won't matter whether we use the This Layer or Underlying Layer slider. In the B

Figure 10.14 *The final version, with certain areas of the background eliminated with a layer mask. Left, a flat swatch of the desired PMS orange.*

we want to use This Layer, because its range has been enhanced with the curves.

Putting a Blend If on the A, however, is a waste of time. Remember, the B is now an enhanced copy of the A. Anything this A slider can do can be done better in the B. So we operate with two sets of sliders only. For that matter, we shouldn't expect much from the L. Anything lighter or darker than the car won't be as yellow, so the B slider alone should exclude it.

When Three Layers Are Needed

We start by double-clicking the top layer to bring up the Layer Style dialog that contains Blending Options. Figure 10.13A demonstrates that, as we surmised, working with the L slider does almost no good. It's picked up some dark areas of the background trees, and that's about it.

Going to the new B channel helps a lot. The entire bottom half of the car in Figure 10.13B has cleared the background; no selection will

Review and Exercises

✓How would you find the LAB equivalent for a given Pantone (PMS) color specification?

✓Find an image that contains an object of medium darkness but reasonably strong color, such as a sports uniform. Start with one copy in RGB and one in LAB. With each, add a layer containing a flat, contrasting color. By using Blending Options, try to exclude only those parts of the top layer that will allow the object of interest to show through from the bottom layer. Why does the LAB version get a more accurate result?

✓In a hypothetical picture of a U.S. flag, you are required to change the blue background behind the stars into green. Assuming that the blue background starts at approximately 0^A, how would you proceed, and how would you differentiate your correction layer from the original using Blending Options?

✓In Figure 10.3, the assignment was to change the yellow train to blue. Why would it have been harder to change it to purple instead? What would you have done to solve the problem?

be needed. No such luck on the top half, though: the foliage remains orange.

This slider could not find a difference between the two items because this new B channel is based on the original A. And in the original image, the car was more green than magenta, and so was the background.

That's the drawback of using two channels that are based on a single one. There *was* a channel that we could have used to distinguish the greenery from the car—and fortunately we saved a copy.

In the original B, the one that we couldn't use for color, the car was slightly more blue than yellow. The background was more yellow than blue. That's enough for us to make the selection.

Therefore, we close these options, move down to the second layer, and bring up a second set of Blend If options. This time, the

The Bottom Line

LAB offers the quickest, most powerful, and most believable method of making gross color changes in isolated objects. Given also the selection capabilities outlined in Chapter 9, there is no case for doing this type of work in any other colorspace.

The change requires three steps: deciding upon the desired color (often by reference to LAB equivalents of a PMS specification) and choosing a control point where that value will be imposed; writing curves to achieve that value; and isolating or masking the area so that extraneous objects do not change color. Often this involves using an adjustment layer in LAB plus layer Blending Options in all three channels.

Underlying Layer slider refers to the original B. Excluding everything that used to be more yellow than blue results in Figure 10.13C.

Close examination of the edges reveals no reason to blur the AB. The final touchup, using layer masks, is easy. The few remaining orange trees in the background are easily lassoed and deleted inasmuch as they're nowhere near the car. I used an airbrush to paint grayness into the layer mask in the car's windows and parts of the chrome. I felt that these objects would probably still have a bluish tinge, but that they should not be quite as blue as in the original, since they might be reflecting parts of the car's new orange paint job.

Figure 10.14 is the final version. As usual with LAB color changes, it's quite convincing, more so than would be the case if the color were substituted in RGB or CMYK, both of which would have created a darker and more neutral orange.

A good chef can fake most recipes if a cookbook can't be found. Imaging isn't like that. This color-changing recipe looks complicated, but with practice it makes the changes with stunning speed. If you don't know this technique and try to muddle by, not only will you probably spend an unnecessarily long time, but the result may not be tasty.

You may never need a recipe for Coquilles St. Jacques Mornay. You may never have to change the color of garments or products. But if you think you might in the future, be prepared. Know your LAB.

The Best Retouching Space

For complicated collaging, elimination of moiré, adding color to selected areas, restoration of older images, and various painting functions, LAB has decided advantages over RGB and CMYK. Some of the magic requires fancy blends with the A or B, but most of the time you can enjoy the power of LAB retouching just by sticking with whatever tools you're used to.

ou open a file and discover a speck of dust, or a hair, or a scratch, where no dust, hairs, or scratches are supposed to be. You therefore activate the rubber stamp, the healing brush, the Dust & Scratches filter, the patch tool, the pencil, or some other painting tool, and away that dust, hair, or scratch goes to pixel heaven.

Obliterating stray garbage is the simplest aspect of the most glamorous and well-paid field in Photoshop, just as a child's fingerpainting is a simple variant of what Raphael did for a living. We would probably describe this process as *retouching out* the dust, hair, or scratch.

Retouchers are supposed to be highly skilled and highly specialized, yet there's no consensus on what *retouching* means. My definition is that retouching entails one or more of the following three things:

- Erasing dust, hairs, scratches, and other undesirable elements, such as blemishes on a model's face. In annual reports and other corporate work, a retoucher is often asked to modify a group photo to obliterate all traces of an individual who has, as Orwell put it, become an unperson.

- Putting things into the picture that weren't there previously. Inserting a rhinoceros into a photo of a cocktail party would be an example of this technique. Variations exist, such as filling a previously blank area with bogus detail.

- Completely altering the emphasis of certain areas, such as by grabbing the background of a color photo and turning it black and white or blurring it to death so as to emphasize the foreground object, or by accentuating things that already exist by enhancing their colors and/or contrast.

Retouching can also be an adjunct to *color correction*, another vague term that some consider to be a subset of retouching. Color correction employs global moves such as curves in an effort to create realism and believability; retouching generally uses selections and tools in an effort to create something unbelievable, or else to take something unbelievable and try to work it into the picture in a believable way.

The two concepts are sometimes difficult to keep straight, especially when working in LAB. Most of the examples in the first seven chapters of this book would be considered color correction, but in certain instances in Chapter 7 selections more associated with retouching are used in the context of color correction. In Figure 4.8, where red objects were turned into green ones, no selections or tools were used, but the color changes created by AB curves were so humongous that most people would consider the result to be retouching and not color correction.

It's time to raise the question of when to do retouching in LAB as opposed to RGB or CMYK. It won't matter for easy stuff. You can erase dust, hairs, and scratches equally well in all three.

On the other hand, we might

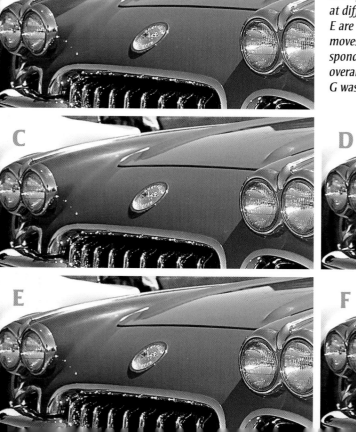

Figure 11.1 *Above, at reduced size, a green car is sloppily pasted into a red one. Below and opposite are attempts at damage control in both LAB and RGB. Versions B and J show, at different magnifications, the original merge. Versions C and E are two different blurring trials in LAB; D and F are the same moves in RGB; and the images on the opposite page are corresponding views of the rear of the car. Versions G and H are overall reduced views of the merges shown in the bottom row: G was done in LAB, H in RGB.*

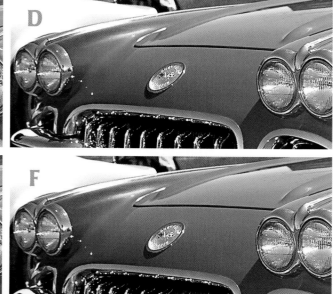

take a hint from the past. In the early to mid-1990s, before Photoshop could reliably handle big retouching jobs, the highest-end work was not done on the Scitex systems that dominated prepress at the time. Instead, the most intricate retouching work was channeled to a system known as the Quantel Paintbox. The champion retouchers of the time would work on nothing else.

Scitex systems were CMYK all the way. The Quantel box worked in HSB, a colorspace that, like LAB, employs one contrast and two color channels, sharing many techniques with LAB that can't be duplicated in CMYK or RGB.

Whatever retouching methods you use now probably work in LAB—and they may work better. Plus, certain tricks don't work at all outside of LAB. We will, therefore, tour several areas of retouching in which LAB has the advantage.

Color and Contrast, Again

For the first of the three basic types of retouching described above, erasing things, LAB is technically not the best choice. CMYK is better because of its black

channel, which often isolates the detail where it can be erased easily. In the other two areas, LAB has the edge, although it may not show up in every image.

To demonstrate, let's go back one chapter, to where a red car was made green by inverting the A channel. The background in Figure 10.1B looked odd, but the green car was great.

Let's pretend that we didn't read any of the subsequent explanation of how to restore the original background; that the only way we can figure out how to do so is to cut the green car out and paste it on top of the red one; and that we aren't real coordinated when it comes to the mouse.

Professional retouchers do the same kind of thing in a less sloppy fashion, and face the same problem: when merging two images, a hard line shouldn't appear between them; there must be some area of transition where the two blur into one another. If there are sharp differences between the two, the transition zone may need to be large.

I made a slapdash selection, and proceeded to merge the red and green cars, once in RGB, once in LAB. I then prepared two more pairs of images, one with a comparatively small transition zone, one with a larger one, for a total of four alternatives to the original sloppy cut-and-paste version.

Granted, the selection shown in Figure 11.1A and magnified in Figures 11.1B and 11.1J leaves a great deal to be desired. In fact, it's a lot worse than Figures 11.1G and 11.1H might lead you to believe. They soften the impact because they're printed much smaller than the half-page that the image took up in Chapter 10. The other eight variants, at different magnifications, compare the LAB

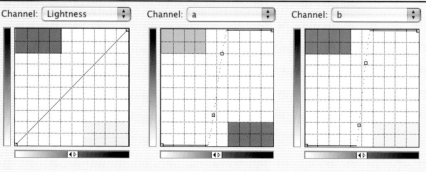

Figure 11.2 *The camera doesn't see rainbows as being as prominent as human observers do, so such images are never satisfactory in their original form.*

and RGB versions in each of two different areas for both methods of merging. The LAB versions are always on the left.

These areas of transition are supposed to be as soft and unnoticeable as possible under these absurd circumstances. The LAB versions are clearly accomplishing it better. Dark areas appear where the two colors meet in the RGB versions, but the LAB counterparts just blend green softly into red.

The technical explanation appears at some length in Chapter 5, in the discussion of blurring. During blending, Photoshop computes the new color by averaging the values of each channel. Averaging that way, it turns out, works considerably better in LAB.

The brighter and purer the colors, the more the advantage. For darker, more neutral merges where the original selection isn't done in quite so incompetent a fashion, it's questionable whether anyone would see a difference. Nevertheless, control of fringing is a big deal in this kind of blending, so I suggest that as a general rule it should be done in LAB—as, for that matter, should any retouching involving bright colors.

The Rays Are Not Coloured

Herman Melville, creator of Captain Ahab and other seamen of questionable mental fitness, used color theory to argue his view that it's difficult to know what the

Figure 11.3 Top, AB curves drastically intensify all colors. Bottom, the new rainbow is painted into Figure 11.2 through a layer mask.

difference is between crazy and sane. He wrote, "Who in the rainbow can draw the line where the violet tint ends and the orange tint begins? Distinctly we see the difference of the colors, but where exactly does the one first blendingly enter into the other?"

The answer is, *nobody* can draw the line, if all they have to work with is an original photograph. We humans find rainbows so astonishingly beautiful that they dominate the scene. Cameras are not similarly impressed.

Therefore, all rainbow pictures are retouching candidates. Someone glancing at Figure 11.2 might not even notice the rainbow. Curves in the AB channels can make it suitably brilliant, as in the eerie Figure 11.3A. But the eventual goal has to be something on the order of Figure 11.3B, which joins the two previous images via a layer mask.

The curves are fractious enough that I would suggest you open the image off the enclosed CD. The idea is, as Melville thought, to create a clear transition between colors. In the original it's hard to make out what's going on, but Figure 11.3B's rainbow has distinct regions of violet, red, yellow, green, and blue.

AB curves will wipe out one or more of these delicate colors if we are even slightly inaccurate. I used points closer than usual to the center point for greater precision in angling the curve. Also, it was necessary to move the entire image toward yellow to recover all of the rainbow's hues.

Merging the new rainbow into the original is easy. Starting with Figure 11.2, here are the steps.

- Layer: New Adjustment Layer>Curves.
- Apply the curves shown, which produce Figure 11.3A on the top layer, with the original untouched image on the bottom.
- The adjustment layer has a layer mask by default. Make sure that it is active (its icon must be bordered in the Layers palette) and that your foreground and background colors are set to white and black, respectively. Working on the layer mask, Select: Select All, Delete. This changes the layer mask from white to black and thus excludes the entire top layer, so that the original image is once again visible.
- Choose any soft-edged painting tool, set to a low opacity (around 10%). With the layer mask still active and the foreground color still white, paint into the area of the rainbow to move the image more toward Figure 11.3A. Repeat the painting steps as necessary, or change the foreground color to black and paint again if it is necessary to reverse the process.

I don't know how this retouching could have been done in RGB at all. It seems inconceivable that Figure 11.3A could be produced without AB curves, and without them there would be no way to differentiate the rainbow's colors without actually painting them in, which would be difficult to handle.

Figure 11.4 The original image.

Assuming that it could be done, the sky should be manageable, but the background hills would be a headache. It's critical that the rainbow not seem to darken the hills behind it. LAB allows that because color and contrast are separated; RGB does not. For the same reason that there are dark areas where red and green intersect in the RGB versions of Figure 11.1, the rainbow would not seem to be transparent in an RGB version, as the hills would darken behind it. Furthermore, if, as is likely, we tried to make a very vivid rainbow as in Figure 11.3A and merged it into the original through an RGB layer mask, the background hills would darken even more.

Channels That Don't Have to Line Up

When the assignment is the common one of filling in holes or areas of physical damage, LAB carries a decisive, if nonobvious, advantage: we don't have to copy and paste all channels at the same time.

Figure 11.4 is the original image. In Figure 11.5A it's been sabotaged in RGB by throwing its channels out of sync. The red channel has been moved down by 10 pixels and to the right by the same amount. The blue channel has been moved 10 pixels to the left.

In Figure 11.5B, an LAB version, the same moves were applied: the A channel went down and to the right, the B to the left.

Figure 11.5A is the type of unholy mess one would expect when three channels that each affect detail get scrambled. False shapes and outlines appear everywhere. By contrast, Figure 11.5B is surprisingly good. The red flowers have been wrecked, since the A and B

Figure 11.5 Detailing in the LAB channels doesn't have to line up nearly as exactly as in other colorspaces, a major benefit in retouching. Above, in an RGB document, the red channel is intentionally moved 10 pixels down and 10 pixels to the right, and the blue is moved 10 pixels to the left. Below, the same moves applied to an LAB copy of the file, with the A moving down and to the right, and the B moving left.

channels no longer line up, but most of the rest is acceptable. It's difficult to detect that there's been any damage to the foreground greenery or the background mountain.

It follows that if there were a major hole in the greenery, we would need to do a good job of patching the L—but the A and B might come from anywhere in the surrounding area. In fact, all three channels might come from different parts of the picture.

Contrast that with RGB, where we'd have to pick up all three channels as a group. Such patchwork always involves grabbing parts of the image and dropping them on top of the damaged areas, hoping that nobody will notice the scam. Usually, the patches have to come from relatively close to the damaged area or the detail will not match.

The problem is that if we pick up an RGB patch and drop it someplace nearby, it may be painfully evident that cloning took place, because the patched area will match its source both for color and for contrast. Not so in LAB. We patch with the L, and pick up the A and B from wherever we feel lucky.

In short, we can in effect treat the image as three retouches of grayscale documents, which is usually a lot easier and quicker than a single retouch of a color picture. Sometimes there are also LAB-only shortcuts to make the job go even faster.

Watch how quickly LAB wipes out the orange date/time stamp in the aerial portrait of Figure 11.6. The piece shown is a small portion; it's at a relatively low resolution, and you are entitled to know that several inches

of greenery have been cropped off the left side. We will be using that unseen greenery to fill in the letters. Here's the step-by-step:
- Layer: Duplicate Layer.
- Using the marquee tool, select a rectangular portion of the greenery to the left of the damaged area, and copy it to the clipboard. The rectangle has to be large enough to cover the entire date-time area.
- Paste the rectangle on top of the damaged area (Figure 11.7A), thus creating a third layer on top of the two identical ones.
- Double-click the top layer's icon to bring up the Blend If sliders of Blending Options. Exclude everything that's negative, or even slightly positive, in the A on the underlying (middle) layer (Figure 11.7B).

These last two steps wouldn't work in RGB, or at least they would require extra effort. But moving a block on top of the numbers makes eminent sense in LAB. The next step (which I hope you already have anticipated), now that the damaged area is a plausible color, is to retouch a new L channel on top of it. In RGB the effort would be pointless, since all three channels would have to be replaced simultaneously. Nor would Luminosity mode save the day in RGB: the same color fidelity wouldn't be available.

Also, don't overlook the ease of putting a big patch over the whole area and then limiting its impact to the orange parts. In LAB, it's one sweep of a single slider, because in the A channel the glyphs are emphatically more magenta-than-green than anything in the background. Whether they're lighter or darker makes no difference. In RGB, Blending Options would be able to isolate the figure *1* in the time display, because it happens to rest entirely on a darker background. In the red channel,

Figure 11.6 *The orange date and time stamp must be removed from this aerial photograph.*

the number itself would be light. Every other glyph, however, covers both light and dark areas, and can't be isolated in any RGB channel. We'd need to make and refine a conventional selection and load it as a layer mask.

In LAB, it only remains to rebuild the L where the glyphs were. I prefer to do this without a selection, although opinions vary. Therefore, I worked on the L channel of the middle layer, as shown in Figure 11.7C, using the rubber stamp tool, taking small patches from nearby and cloning them into the glyphs. When finished, I clicked back into the top layer and changed its mode to Color, meaning that only its A and B channels would take precedence, and that the L of the middle layer would remain intact.

When there is no convenient area of background to lift as a patch, it's often possible to clone into the A and B channels separately to establish a credible color, and then establish the critical L. Beta reader André Dumas suggests the sensible alternative of doing the A first, then the L, and finally not the B but the AB together. This idea recognizes that imperfections

Figure 11.7 *Top, in LAB, a rectangular piece of greenery is positioned over the damaged area. Second from top, Blending Options in the A channel restrict the impact to the orange areas. Third from top, carefully painting into the L channel to establish detail. Bottom, the final result.*

in the A channel are vastly more noticeable than in the B and therefore may require two correction passes.

In this image, there was no need for such complications. The process was speeded along by finding an easy way to isolate the damaged area, an isolation that existed only in the B and not in any channel of RGB or CMYK. That's a theme that often comes up in restoration of very old photographs.

Four Generations and Still Feisty

Around a decade ago, the last members of my late mother's family in Oklahoma passed on, and I became the owner of an outlaw gang of old photos. Among them was a picture of my great-great-grandmother, apparently taken in the 1890s, when the region was known as Indian Territory. I was so smitten by the picture that I used it in an edition of *Professional Photoshop* as a restoration exercise.

My cowboy ancestors likely contributed my panache. The Indians with whom they intermarried account for my high cheekbones and warlike disposition. That was my mother's side of the family; my father's was Russian, which accounts for my propensity to find methods that actually work, such as LAB, as opposed to those that are politically correct at any given time.

Not to be outdone, my father's side of the family produced its own great-great-grandmother, demanding equal time in the next book. I'd suspect a fake, but the woman in Figure 11.8 looks more like my grandfather than my grandfather did. Historical records from Russia are rather sketchy, but from what little I know, I'm guessing that this print dates from the 1880s. We can forgive, therefore, the deplorable state in which it has been handed down to the fourth generation.

The best restoration must be as a sepiatone, along the lines of the ones we did back in Chapter 6. Whatever color this print used to be died with the czar and his family. Anything close to a yellow feel will be acceptable.

Figure 11.8 *Images more than a century old can defy normal methods of restoration. Left, a scan of the original print. Above, converted to black and white and with contrast enhanced to show the magnitude of the physical damage.*

A sepiatone is a snap, provided we happen to have a high-quality black and white, which is as far away from what we've got now as Moscow is from Vladivostok. We can hike contrast, but the enlarged area in Figure 11.8 shows that everything is so pitted, scratched, and thumbprinted that there's no undamaged area of any significant size from which to sample the dress. I don't think we want to make the image as perfectly smooth as if it had been shot yesterday; some irregularities should be apparent, but they certainly shouldn't be as extreme as what we start with.

Photoshop has a filter called Dust & Scratches, and an army of blurring options. None work when the damage is this severe, because they all fill damaged areas with averaged values, not real detail. The patch, rubber stamp, and healing brush tools are in principle better because they in effect copy other parts of the document into the scratches. Here, they spin their wheels, because any area they could sample and copy is itself so full of damage that it isn't much use.

By now you should be wondering what this example is doing here. We saw in Chapter 6 that LAB is bad at duotoning, and also that it's an inferior way of making black and whites, which are the two things we need now. Furthermore, the usual excuse for using LAB is one of color, and this picture doesn't have any—its hue is merely a flat, featureless tint.

If those scratches could only be softened, then the healing brush or the rubber stamp might be able to do their work. But it's difficult, not to mention incredibly time-consuming, to clone over them without damaging areas other than the

Figure 11.9 *Top, applying Auto Levels to the A and B channels demonstrates that the damage can be isolated in LAB. Below, a mask created from the B channel only.*

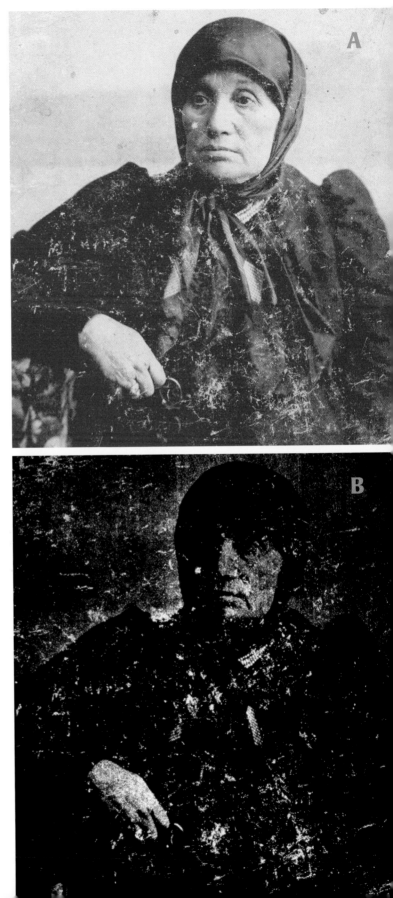

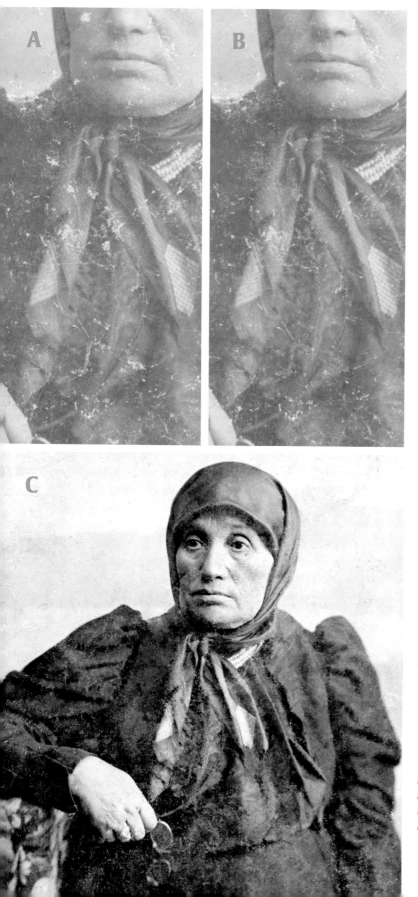

scratches themselves. Do you see how to make a selection that would limit cloning to the areas we want to affect?

It isn't found in RGB. Some of the scratches are very light, true, but so are many other parts of the image, and there's no way to distinguish noise from reality. But in LAB, there is. The emulsion of this print is decidedly more yellow than blue. Where it has vanished, the substrate is almost a neutral white.

Figure 11.9A shows how the damage can be isolated. Working with a separate LAB copy of the image, I applied Image: Adjustments>Auto Levels to both the A and B, forcing each to pure white and pure black. Now the noise is as isolated as a Siberian village in winter. There's no shortage of ways to create the needed mask in Figure 11.9B.

My method is to start from scratch with a new LAB copy of the original, and then do the following:

• With Command-Option–3, load the B as a selection.

• Select: Save Selection to save the current selection (that is, a copy of the B) as a new document, not as a new channel of the same file, which is Photoshop's default suggestion.

• Move into the new file, which is going to become the mask, and apply Image: Adjustments>Auto Levels.

• Still in the new document, Image: Adjustments>Invert. This turns the mask into a negative copy, with the damaged areas being white and the remainder black.

• A 4.0-pixel Gaussian blur to soften the edges of the mask's white areas.

Figure 11.10 *Above left, the original. Above right, rapid cloning through the mask of Figure 11.9B begins to reduce the damage. Below, the final retouched version.*

- Edit: Fade>Lighten, preventing the blur from darkening any part of the mask for the damaged areas, while allowing it to expand slightly into undamaged parts of the image.

The mask is now ready for loading. To do so, we return to the original LAB image and Select: Load Selection. The new document appears as the only possibility unless you have for some reason made other grayscale channels available.

Once the mask has been loaded, the preliminary touch-up can be done with a few long sweeps of the mouse. We simply activate the rubber stamp tool, sample an interior area of the dress by Option–clicking it, and start painting over the entire dress. Since only the damaged areas are selected, nothing else can be hurt. Where there is a big change in tonality, we Option–click a different area, as we do for the face.

Figures 11.9A and 11.9B show the progress. The painting through the mask is rapid. It's not intended to be perfect, because the selections have soft edges and because they are being partially filled with new scratches from the sampled area. But they're much better than before.

At this point, more conventional retouching methods work—in any colorspace. When the original is this ratty, CMYK is probably best, because a lot of the damage shows up in the black channel, where it can be targeted easily. But the healing brush/rubber stamp tool combination is also feasible in either RGB or LAB. Similarly, curves to combat the original's flatness would theoretically work in any colorspace.

LAB is probably the worst choice of the three. The ultimate goal is a black and white image, because the final step will be to make a duotone. Working in CMYK or RGB opens the option of channel blending prior to

applying the curves. In an RGB version of the original, for example, the red channel has the most potential. It's lightest, and an accurate curve may bring out more detail than is possible from any other channel, including the L of LAB. Also, in reaching the final version, Figure 11.10C, I built up detail in the face with some blending, curving, and layer masking, the description of which doesn't belong in this book. It would have been much harder in LAB than when there are three contrast-bearing channels to hide all the skulduggery.

Figure 11.11 *The church's dome has blown-out reflections that should be minimized. Retouching such areas is a specialty of LAB.*

The Sponge on Steroids

Before moving on to a complicated use of the unique AB channel structure as a weapon in the battle against moiré, we will remain in Russia to study a form of retouching that is difficult in other colorspaces and easy in LAB.

St. George is an iconic figure, not just to the British, but to Muscovites, to whom he is a patron. In the huge Park Plobedy, which commemorates national victories, he is sculpted slaying a Nazi dragon.

Figure 11.11, close by, is the Church of St. George the Victorious. The use of gilding as a design element is characteristic of Russian Orthodox design—beautiful to the beholder, a pain to the photographer. The large dome is so reflective that a goodly portion of it is blown out altogether, as are several less significant areas of the building.

LAB specializes in adding color to blown-out areas. We looked at the effect earlier in Figure 8.6 with a face containing a large hot spot. Such areas are a nuisance in RGB and CMYK, as painting in Color mode won't affect them: if they are that light, they can't have any color. The only solution is to darken and then add color, which is a tricky thing to handle.

LAB has no such problem. We set a painting tool to Color mode, Option–click a likely-looking gold somewhere in the dome to make it the foreground color, and brush away. Where it crosses the blown-out area, instead of rejecting any change as impossible, LAB calmly directs Photoshop to produce the imaginary color that is golden but simultaneously as light as a completely blank area. Photoshop, for its part, splits the difference between the two incompatible demands—just what we want.

Doing it this way is hard to detect. I produced Figure 11.12B with a single stroke, beginning in the sky and moving in a southeastward sweep across the damaged area. To prove it, I've left a piece of sky golden to show the progress of the stroke. You can see it in the sky, but how about the dome? I can't see it there, at least not in the area that adjoins what used to be white.

Figure 11.13A has a blown-out dome, too, but that's not the only issue. This is St. Basil's Cathedral on Red Square, the very symbol of Mother Russia. It will show us how to use LAB as a more sophisticated substitute for Photoshop's sponge tool.

Figure 11.12 Left, the original, magnified. Right, a version corrected by choosing a gold near the blown-out area as the foreground color, and then painting in Color mode in LAB. Doing this in RGB would not work, because the light area would have to be darkened before color could be added. In LAB, the brush stroke that adds the golden color is nearly undetectable in the region around the damage. To prove it, this color was added with a single stroke in the southeast direction, starting from just outside the dome. A trace of gold is deliberately left in the sky where the stroke originated.

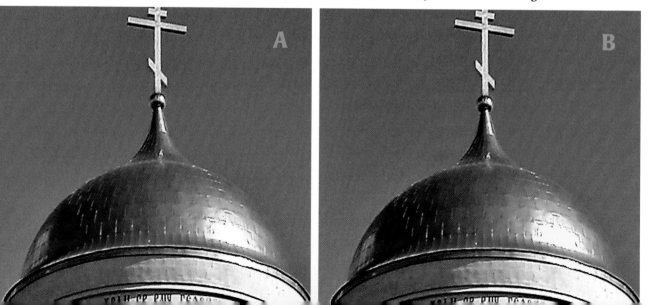

The sponge is a painting tool that either saturates (makes more colorful) or desaturates (makes more drab) whatever it touches, without changing detail, at least in theory. Saturation is closely associated with a sense of depth. Retouchers often use it to draw attention to a product or other interest area, and desaturation to persuade viewers not to look at an unimportant area such as a background.

The red brickwork of Figure 11.13A competes with the brilliant reds in the fanciful onion-shaped dome at left. I think the image would be more effective with slightly less colorful bricks. That suggests the sponge tool.

With the sponge set to saturate, most of the gilded dome on the other tower could be made more colorful—but not the blown-out area. Desaturating the towers would be achievable but somewhat unwieldy. Being neutral, the white embellishments are safe, but we'd have to be careful not to sweep over the sky or any of the green areas, so the sponging would take a while.

LAB sharply reduces the need for painting tools because of the ease of differentiating objects in the A and B channels. As we'll see in Chapter 12, where there are two objects of similar but not identical colors, such as the red dome and the bricks, we can usually write a curve that will break them apart, without any selection or painting. This particular image, however, has too much going on. Curves won't work, because the bricks have approximately the same A value as some of the yellowish domes, and about the same B as the darkest area of the bright red dome.

Therefore, we are stuck with painting. The options begin with the sponge tool, which is considerably more powerful in LAB than in

Figure 11.13 *In the original, top, the bricks are too vivid and the gilded areas not yellow enough. The version at bottom was created by using the dodge and burn tools on the A and B channels, without touching the L.*

RGB, let alone CMYK—but there are other, even more attractive options.

The sponge only allows us to move toward gray or a more intense version of whatever is being stroked. In real life, we often want to go in a third direction. I feel that the towers are not only too colorful, but too reddish and not yellow enough. Therefore, I would prefer to reduce the intensity of the A channel more than that of the B. That way, I'm diminishing the magenta component by driving it toward a neutral 0^A. I don't know how much I want to reduce the yellow component, if at all. I'd like visual feedback to help me decide.

LAB permits such experimentation even with the sponge tool. Make a duplicate layer and desaturate away, driving the towers to a duller pink. When satisfied, activate the B channel only, while leaving the composite color image visible.

Now, Image: Apply Image. The target is automatically the B on the top layer because that's the only thing open; we want to blend the bottom-layer B into it. Since the dialog uses merged layers as the default source of the blend, we need to remember to change the Layer option to Background and the Channel option to B. Opacity is 100% by default, which would restore the original B completely. We might like that, but chances are we'd want something less. As we change the number, we preview the effect we get.

That last blend would not be feasible in RGB, nor are the next trio of tricks. First, let's dispose of a method that I believe is second-best. We could create a more subdued red as a foreground color and use a painting tool to brush it into the towers in Color mode. That technique could be essentially duplicated in RGB. It's only when the items are very light or dark that RGB's Color mode falls short. However, blending in flat values takes away natural variation and makes the image less believable.

Instead, consider the dodge and burn tools, which can't be used in this context in RGB. The dodge tool lightens, the burn tool darkens, and either can be applied successfully to the A or B (not both at once, unfortunately).

Using these tools in LAB requires a certain adjustment in one's thinking. If you agree that the original tower is too magenta and that it shouldn't be so colorful, it's only natural to say that we need to move it *toward gray*. Gray, however, is merely a stop on a road that goes further. It's more accurate to say we are moving the tower away from magenta and *toward green*.

Recall that the sponge would have to be handled carefully to avoid accidentally desaturating the green areas. Actually, these objects could stand to be *more* green. So, I would be content to use the burn tool on the A for the whole tower, not just its pink areas. In fact, I didn't need to worry about staying within the towers' borders at all.

Figure 11.14 *Top, a magnified version of part of Figure 11.13A. Center, the dodge tool, set to affect midtones, is applied to the B channel, making the gilded areas much yellower but also contaminating the sky. Bottom, the contamination vanishes when blue areas are excluded with layer Blending Options, right.*

The options bar specifies whether the dodge and burn tools affect highlights, shadows, or midtones. Since the AB channels are always quite gray (anything else would be out-of-gamut colors), Midtones is always the correct setting. The Exposure option should always be set quite low in view of the volatility of the A and B; about 10% works well. And, for reasons that are about to become clear, we always work on a duplicate layer.

Creating the new towers of Figure 11.13B took less than a minute. With the A active, I simply swept the burn tool across the whole area as rapidly as I could, moving the entire area away from magenta and toward green. Because I wasn't trying to stay within the confines of the reddish parts of the tower, I created a green fringe in the sky and transformed previously white areas of the tower into light green.

Layer Blending Options made short work of these two defects, because both are found in areas of the channels that are easily distinguishable from either the green or the red parts of the towers—at least they are in LAB. The white areas are much lighter in the L than the rest of the tower is. The sky is strongly B–negative, and both red and green areas are B–positive.

After adding a third layer, I went on to the gilded domes. This time, rather than merely filling the holes, I decided to make everything more yellow. That's a B move, requiring the dodge rather than the burn tool to make the channel lighter. Again, I was in such a hurry that I brushed yellowness into the sky, as seen in Figure 11.14B. But it's easily taken out in Figure 11.14C by means of a slider that excludes anything that's substantially negative in the B.

Why was a third layer needed? The second layer's Blending Options had to exclude things that were light in the L, so that the white areas of the towers didn't turn green. If I had attempted to retouch the dome on the same layer, I wouldn't have been able to colorize the blown-out spots, which were just as light as those white areas. So, I used the burn tool on a separate layer, where I could exclude blue objects only.

The Best Way to Experiment

For a closer look at the flexibility of dodging and burning the A and B, we return to the monastery at Sergiev Posad, which we first visited in Figure 4.1A. LAB curves got rid of its disastrous cyan cast, but as we pick up where we left off, Figure 11.15A still has a kind of wintry fog about it.

My impression is that the walls need to be a warmer color. Ordinarily that would be done with curves, but here a defect in the image prevents that. Much of the foreground snow (visible in Figure 4.1B but cropped away here) measures a neutral 0^A0^B or thereabouts. The walls are variable, but $3^A(5)^B$ is typical. Therefore, the walls are bluer than the snow, which makes no sense.

Using the dodge tool to lighten the A and B (thus moving toward warmth) is a better choice than trying to paint with a flat color. The artwork is already mottled; a flat color won't look as natural as if we intentionally vary color by stroking the A and B channels separately and at different exposures. Also, there's more flexibility this way. I would prefer something more brown, but I don't know exactly what, so I would like to be able to experiment after the dodging.

Working on a duplicate layer, I activated the B and quickly stroked the walls with the dodge tool set to an exposure of 12%, making them yellower. When finished, I turned to the A, but I lowered exposure to 8%, because I thought that the walls needed less of the magenta component that the A provides. In both channels, I ran over the nearest walls and tower more than those in the distance, to make areas closer to us more colorful. After the dodging, I had reached Figure 11.15B.

Going for the garish is standard practice in such types of retouching. We deliberately overshoot the mark on a duplicate layer, knowing that we can adjust its opacity to return to something closer to the original. If we tried for perfection the first time and later decided that the image wasn't colorful enough, we'd be out of luck.

Figure 11.15C lowers opacity to 50%. I don't like it. Even though I had reduced the tool's exposure setting when dodging the A, it wasn't enough: the walls seem too pink. I should have emphasized the A even less.

What comes next is another example of LAB's ability to do things that either can't be achieved in RGB or would require several extra steps. Since the A channel of Figure 11.15A still lives untouched on the lower layer, we can use it to weaken the A of Figure 11.15C and make the walls less magenta, emphasizing the yellowness that was added by the B. I chose to apply the lower-layer A at 60% opacity, resulting in Figure 11.16. And, with a reminder that this method is infinitely flexible and that you can get whatever color for the walls you like if you don't care for mine, we will now depart Russia for our last retouching destination.

How to Eliminate Moiré

The AB channels are color only, no detail. They are supposed to be defocused, blurry-looking. If they

Figure 11.15 *Top, a portion of an original first seen in Figure 4.1B. Middle, dodging the A and B on a duplicate layer to make overly colorful walls. Bottom, layer opacity is reduced to 50%.*

```
┌─────────────────────────────────────────────────┐
│                  Apply Image                      │
│  ┌─ Source: [ SergievPosad        ▼]──────┐       │
│  │  Layer: [ Background            ▼]     │  ( OK )│
│  │  Channel: [ a              ▼] ☐ Invert │ (Cancel)│
│  │                                        │ ☑ Preview│
│  Target:  SergievPosad (Burn Layer, a)            │
│  ┌─ Blending: [ Normal        ▼]─────────────┐    │
│  │  Opacity: [60]  %                         │    │
│  │  ☐ Preserve Transparency                  │    │
│  │  ☐ Mask...                                │    │
└─────────────────────────────────────────────────┘
```

Figure 11.16 When the original A channel is partially restored from the bottom layer, the walls lose much of their magenta component and seem more yellow.

aren't, if some kind of detail is sharply defined, it's likely to be a defect. And if it is, LAB is likely to be the best way by far to get rid of it.

In Chapter 5, we studied how to eliminate noise by attacking the AB channels. Now, we'll take it a step further, by considering the noisiest image of all—the prescreened original. And, having knocked the screen out in LAB, we'll finish the chapter with a look at how to eliminate a camera-induced moiré.

Dealing with originals that have already been printed can be as time-consuming as you care to make it. Sometimes it's enough to just make it print without a disastrous moiré; sometimes the assignment is to try to improve it so much that nobody will suspect its shameful origin.

Going whole hog almost always requires selections and tools. These moves can occur in any colorspace and are off-topic for this book. However, in getting the image ready for the final retouching, LAB is the best tool by far. We'll take one image up to that last stage.

First, let's recap the problem. In presswork the illusion of continuous tone is created by a pattern of halftone dots small enough that the naked eye doesn't readily detect them. Each ink's pattern is angled differently, further to baffle the eye and persuade the viewer that the color is unbroken.

The scanner, unfortunately, is not fooled. It sees a bunch of small dots with white space between them. The dots don't line up well with the file's pixel structure, so the scan looks horrible, and usually too dark as well. Furthermore, if you try to reprint, the usual result is a moiré. The press requires a new pattern of magenta dots that is almost certain to form a disagreeable interference pattern with pattern of magenta dots in the file. The other channels will suffer from the same defect, although it won't be quite as noticeable as in the magenta.

The conventional way of compensating is to blur or to wheel out some sort of automated descreening algorithm that attempts to interpolate what might fall between the dots. Both methods either can't knock the screen out or produce overly soft images. Those dots are the only detail in the file. Leave them alone, and the image is too grainy even if it doesn't moiré. Modify them, and detail vanishes.

The better way is to do the work in LAB.

Figure 11.17 *A: the original. B: the original A channel. C: after blurring the AB and curves to enhance contrast in the L. D: a blending channel created by enhancing contrast in the A. E: the blending channel is applied to the L in Lighten mode, 45% opacity, and a curve is applied to restore contrast. F: the final version, after unsharp masking at a high radius, low amount is applied to the L. G: the blue channel of an RGB copy of the original. H: the blue channel of an RGB copy of the final version.*

The screen pattern shows up in the L, regrettably, but it's also found in the A and B, where it has no business being, where it can be easily knocked out, and where it can be used to soften the screen in the L.

Two notes at the outset. First, the magenta pattern is more important than cyan and far more important than yellow, because magenta is a darker ink. Second, we are not trying to produce something that looks like a normal digital capture. Rather, we accept that a certain amount of graininess will survive.

We start with Figure 11.17A and, as a reality check, Figure 11.18A. At each stage of the process, I make a copy and convert it to RGB, so as to show enlargements of the green channel. Screening artifacts in the green may seriously degrade the image. Such artifacts also tend to be more visible in the green even than in the L. So, generating this otherwise unnecessary green channel—which, incidentally, is the cognate of the magenta channel of RGB—is a good way to evaluate our success or lack thereof.

This type of retouching should be done on a duplicate layer for safety's sake, just in case you get a little too excited with your techniques and need to back up toward the original. However, dedicated players of Russian roulette can omit this, provided that a copy of the original A, Figure 11.17B, is saved as an alpha channel.

The A displays the kind of detail we're not supposed to find in a detail-less channel. It needs to be blurred away, as does similar noise in the B. Doing so doesn't affect the L and therefore should not darken the picture, but it does anyway. The white spaces between the dots are now in play. In the face, they are all now the imaginary color that is red but simultaneously as light as blank paper. Photoshop, as we know, splits the difference in such cases and gives us something that isn't quite white, darkening the image.

Consequently, we need to apply a curve to lighten, and hopefully add contrast to, the L. That gets us to Figure 11.17C. To see the impact of the AB blur, compare Figure 11.18B, which applies the curve without it, to Figure 11.18C, which includes it.

Next, we move to the alpha channel (the copy of the original A) and open it up with curves, producing Figure 11.17D. The white areas represent magenta dots, which were originally lighter than 50% gray. Cyan dots would have been darker than, and yellow ones exactly, 50%. This high-contrast channel is now applied to the L in Lighten mode,

The Bleeding Edge: Black and White to Color

Between the color changes of Chapter 10 and the retouching techniques of this chapter, you have enough information to undertake a mission too uncommon and too complex to warrant the two chapters it would take to discuss it. Maybe, however, it's something you could consider as a challenge.

With proper knowledge of LAB channel structure, one can take a black and white image and make pretty fair color out of it. I used to teach the technique in advanced color courses. The inset is a student effort, starting with a black and white. The hair color is problematic, and she partially missed one of the buttons, but on the whole it gives a good idea of what can be done in LAB.

Start by converting the B/W to LAB, which produces 0^A0^B throughout the picture. In areas as dark as this jacket, painting in flat AB values may possibly be sufficient, although the lighter areas of the collar should be more positive in both A and B, as they are here. Light colored areas such as the face are the biggest problem. Here, there's not enough variation; the lightest areas are a bit too pink.

If you'd like to try your hand at colorizing a picture, I'd recommend starting with a sunset image, Figure 2.8 if you don't have anything better. Such dramatic pictures don't usually require subtle AB variation, the way a face does.

When you're ready for a face, find a color image of a similar face somewhere, convert it to LAB, and study what the A and B look like. That may give you the head start you need in preparing a version from scratch. Dodging and burning the A and B can work, but better results can be had with the more complicated technique of manipulating a couple of copies of the L until they resemble the desired A and B, and then copying them into those channels for further modification.

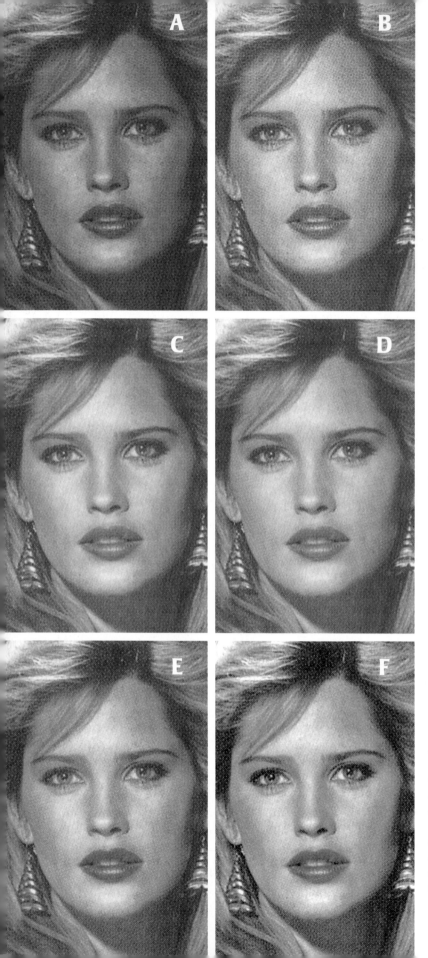

which ignores all black areas. A 100% opacity would fill the image with white noise, but applying at something like 45% busts up a lot of what remains of the screen pattern, as seen in Figure 11.18D. It also lightens the image (except in the lips, which would have been lightened so much that I painted them out of the equation by filling them with black), so a new curve needs to be applied to the L to restore contrast. The dot pattern, however, remains severely discombobulated by the earlier blend. We are now at Figures 11.17E and 11.18E.

Finally, Filter: Sharpen>Unsharp Mask to the L, which sounds crazy. However, if Radius is set high enough, the face is attractively shaped without accentuating the graininess. I chose Amount 75%, Radius 45.0, Threshold 12, getting to Figure 11.17F. You may wish to review the box on hiraloam sharpening on Page 89.

To evaluate the success of this procedure, reconvert the document to RGB and look at the individual channels. Figure 11.18F is the final green channel; Figures 11.17G and 11.17H compare the blue channel in the original and final versions.

Further improvements can be made with or without LAB. By contrast, this whole series of moves,

Figure 11.18 *These are green channels of RGB versions that were generated at several stages of the moiré removal to emphasize what happens to the screen pattern. A: the original. B: if a contrast-enhancing curve had been applied to the L without blurring the A and B first. C: with the blur applied before the curve. D: after the screen pattern is attacked by blending a modified copy of the A into the L. E: a subsequent contrast-enhancing curve to the L. F: the final version, after unsharp masking is applied to the L.*

except the curves, involves things that either don't exist at all outside of LAB (using the A as a screenbuster; blurring the A and B at different settings) or simply work better there (high-radius sharpening to the L channel).

Little modification is needed to apply this procedure to almost any prescreened original. It produces more convincing results than any descreening algorithm I've yet seen. It has implications for other types of moiré removal. Having now resurrected an image that was ripped out of a magazine and scanned, we'll end the chapter with a professionally shot digital original that nevertheless has a similar problem.

The Fabric and the Photographer

Whenever two regular patterns cross one another, interference results. If it's gross and disgusting enough, we call it a moiré, although it's sometimes hard to know where acceptability ends and moiré begins.

It takes two to tango and two to moiré, but there are several dancers on the floor, any two of whom can pair up. A pattern of dots—well, four patterns of dots, to be precise—is visible in Figure 11.17A; I suspect there is also a moiré because one or more of them may interact with the four new patterns that the printer of this book will impose. But until I get my printed copy, I won't know for sure: prepress proofs aren't terribly reliable at predicting press moiré.

There's definitely a moiré in Figure 11.17G, the original blue channel. The press may make it worse, but the problem already exists in the file, the result of a pas de deux between the scanner's pattern of horizontal sampling and the dot pattern in the original art. Careful scanning can usually avoid horrific moirés like this with respect to the cyan and magenta dots, but angling issues prevent resolving the yellow mess that is causing so much havoc in the blue channel.

Review and Exercises

✓In an LAB file with two blank layers, fill the bottom with $60^L0^A90^B$, a tan, and the top with $60^L0^A(90)^B$, a blue. Change the layer opacity to 50%. Now, convert the file to RGB, being sure not to flatten the image on the way in. Observe that both the color and darkness change. Which do you think is a more realistic blend?

✓When dodging or burning in the A or B channel, should the tool be set to affect highlight, midtones, or shadows?

✓You are given a picture that features an area of a forest in autumn. Some trees are bright yellow, some are bright red, while others are still green but are objectionably drab. The picture contains other objects of similar color, so applying curves to intensify the greens will not work. You decide to paint the color in. If you do not isolate the greens with a mask or Blending Option (meaning that your paint tool will hit certain yellow and red trees as well as green ones), describe the result of using each of the following methods:
    1. The sponge tool in Saturate mode, applied to all channels simultaneously.
    2. The same sponge tool, but applied only to the A channel.
    3. The burn tool applied to the A channel.
    4. The dodge tool applied to the B channel.
Which of these methods (or combination of methods) do you think will be most effective?

Pardon the following technical digression. Best results for scanning a pattern happen when the pattern is angled at around 30 degrees relative to the scan. In commercial printing, the cyan screen is customarily angled at 15° clockwise from the vertical, and therefore also 105°. The magenta is usually at 75°. Therefore, the two are 30° (or 60°) apart, and don't moiré with respect to one another or to the black, which is at 45°. Unfortunately, all 30-degree possibilities are now exhausted. The yellow, which is the least noticeable ink, has to be wedged in at some other angle, customarily 0°.

If you're scanning printed color pieces, you'll get better results by angling them at 45º, to be 30º away from both the magenta and cyan angles.

Figure 11.19 Fabric images are prone to moiré.

If you're a digital photographer, the angle is important, too, because a digicam is basically a scanner with a longer focal length. If the subject contains a pattern, as the man's suit does in Figure 11.19, you may be waltzing with moiré.

Yesteryear, if a file had an ugly moiré like the one by the man's right elbow, they'd rescan the film at a different angle. Today, by the time we discover the moiré, it's a little late—the guy is already in his jogging outfit.

Mini-moirés pervade the jacket. All presumably must be taken out. There are two possibilities. You can do a slap-dash job in RGB in half an hour or so, or you can delete the entire family of moirés quickly in LAB.

On the assumption that the second option is the one of choice, we start by

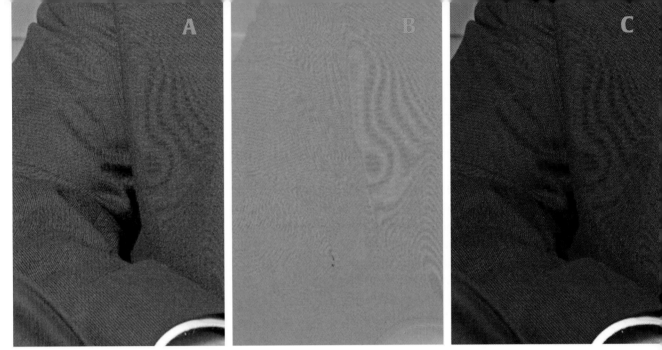

Figure 11.20 Left, the L channel of Figure 11.19. Center, the B. Right, the composite after blurring the A and B channels.

examining the LAB channels of the afflicted file. We hope, of course, that the problem is limited to the A and B, in which case we blur and head for the gym. Here, though, Figure 11.20A indicates that the music is still playing in the L. But because the moiré is blue and yellow, it's sharply defined in the B, Figure 11.20B. And, with ominous foreboding for the fate of the unfortunate moiré, please observe that the interference pattern in the B lines up perfectly with that in the L.

As usual, we work on a duplicate layer, preserving the original channels on the bottom. We select the jacket by one means or another; the method doesn't affect what comes next. And now we blur the B, and to a lesser extent the A, until the moiré is gone. That kills the garish yellow and blue, but the damage is still visible in Figure 11.20C, as it still exists in the L channel—temporarily.

As we will discover in Chapter 15, blending the A and/or B into

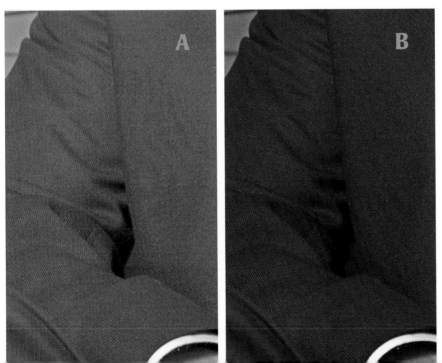

Figure 11.21 Blending an inverted copy of the original B into the L in Hard Light mode at 100% opacity not only wipes out the moiré but creates a counter-moiré (left). Right, the final version, where the blend was reduced to 70% opacity (above).

the L is one of those things that in theory sounds as crazy as an intoxicated loon and in practice is maddeningly powerful. The key is to use one of the blending modes in which values of 50% gray are ignored. The usual suspects are Overlay, Soft Light, and Hard Light. They work in different ways, but they all lighten the target wherever they are themselves lighter than 50%, darken where darker, and do nothing at exactly 50%. And exactly 50% is the midpoint of the A or B, a value of zero, neutrality. Blend the original B channel (that's why we saved the original on its own layer) into the L in one of these modes and nothing much will change except for the only area that is significantly off 0^B, namely the moiré.

The Bottom Line

LAB has major advantages in many types of retouching. Color blends are more believable. Noise can be reduced more effectively. Certain colors can be targeted for enhancement. Damaged areas are more easily filled. Most painting tools are more effective.

Using the dodge and burn tools on the A and B channels is a more sophisticated alternative to Photoshop's sponge tool.

LAB is the tool of choice for eliminating moiré. Spectacular results can often be achieved by blending with the A and/or B channels into the L in Overlay, Soft Light, or Hard Light mode.

I used Hard Light, the most violent of the three, which at 100% opacity not only obliterated the moiré in the L but reversed it (Figure 11.21A). Note that in the Image: Apply Image dialog, Invert must be checked. Otherwise, yellower (lighter) areas of the B would lighten the L, exacerbating the existing problem. We need the opposite. And inverting the channel does nothing to areas that were 0^B. I found that an opacity of 70% wiped out the moiré completely. The final result is Figure 11.21B.

Retouching is a difficult topic, and this has been a difficult chapter. The idea that a major moiré can be obliterated with a blend from a channel that looks like a gray blur is, shall we say, a foreign concept, even to experts. It's only when you visualize the A and B channels just by looking at the color composite that the fix becomes obvious.

I have tried to point out some of the areas in which retouching in LAB is superior to more customary alternatives. If you followed every example, pat yourself on the back, because most experts would not be able to. For sure, you shouldn't be upset if you didn't foresee blending an inverted B into the L to kill a moiré.

To use LAB in retouching, you don't need a ticket. Admission is free. If you want to have the advantages that we've seen in most of the exercises in this chapter, you don't have to do anything new. Do whatever it is that you've been doing so far—just convert to LAB first.

12

Command, Click, Control

Advanced LAB curving can be astoundingly effective at driving objects apart without actually selecting them. Starting the process requires only a click of the mouse—and an understanding of why we sometimes need to produce men from Mars.

eputation is an awesome thing. LAB has one, and it's justified: extremely powerful, difficult to learn. By getting this far in a challenging book, you've indicated that you're willing to make the effort to study and understand, and as a result all kinds of imaging frontiers are now open.

There is, however, another, much larger group of folk: those who are tempted by what LAB has to offer but want to be able to tame it without knowing exactly why or how it works. From time to time I drop LAB stuff into my magazine columns. It always brings forth demands for more simplification and more step-by-step, as in Chapter 1.

In early 2005, I went further, offering a recipe for a spectacular use of LAB that didn't even require learning what the individual channels do. Naturally, it involved curves and color variation. It was too blunt an instrument to introduce previously, but it's worth a look now.

In the first half of the book we stuck with one basic form for the AB curves. Now, we will look at some advanced curving that takes full advantage of LAB's power, but it may make more sense if we start with the demonstration that so impresses the uninitiated.

Introducing the Man from Mars

This strategy for the LAB-ignorant involves creating a document with the original image on the bottom layer and an impossibly colorful adaptation in an adjustment layer on the top, and then cutting the opacity to something more palatable. We've seen this method in action twice, most recently in a shot of a bison, Figure 7.9A. Our first example, the wild-looking Figure 1.15B, was a man's head and shoulders. I used that same

image to begin the magazine piece, and named the procedure after it, calling it the "Man from Mars Method." Here's the recipe, remembering that it's designed for people who don't understand LAB's structure.

- Find an image with flat-looking color, like the Venetian shot of Figure 12.1A. Convert it to LAB.
- Layer: New Adjustment Layer> Curves. The L curve appears by default.
- Locate an area that is typical of the flat color you're trying to affect— not too colorful, not too dull. Command–click there, and a corresponding point appears on the curve.
- Drag the lower left point of the L curve to the right, half the horizontal distance to the point that you clicked into the curve in the last step.
- Turn your attention to the A curve and Command–click another point—it will be called a *pivot point* from now on—into the curve.
- Drag the bottom left point of the A curve to the right until the top right corner stops being a curve and snaps into a straight line. Compare the top of the L curve in Figure 12.1 to that of the A and B to see what I'm referring to. The A and B curves hug the top of the grid; the L is still an arc.
- Go to the B channel and repeat what was done with the A. Click OK, and behold the Man from Mars, Figure 12.1B, wildly colorful.
- Reduce the top layer's opacity to taste. I chose 22% for Figure 12.1C. If you think that the yellow-sky look of Figure 12.1B is romantic, you could choose a bigger number.

Why the Recipe Works

Those who've never heard of LAB before don't understand the purpose of these steps, but they certainly appreciate that there is no simple way (if one exists at all) of going from Figure 12.1A to Figure 12.1C in another colorspace. The reason is the same striking variation in colors that made the canyons of Chapter 1 such easy pickings for LAB correction.

The key to success is choosing the right points to click into. When we look at an untamed Man from Mars version, we need to see that colors have been driven into all four corners of the LAB spectrum.

In Figure 12.1B, that goal is clearly being attained, especially in the B. At the bottom of the image the water has gotten much bluer, but the sky has turned yellow. The impact in the A channel is less obvious, but it's there: the water farthest from us is now green. Only the laundry in the left foreground can truly be described as magenta, but the buildings

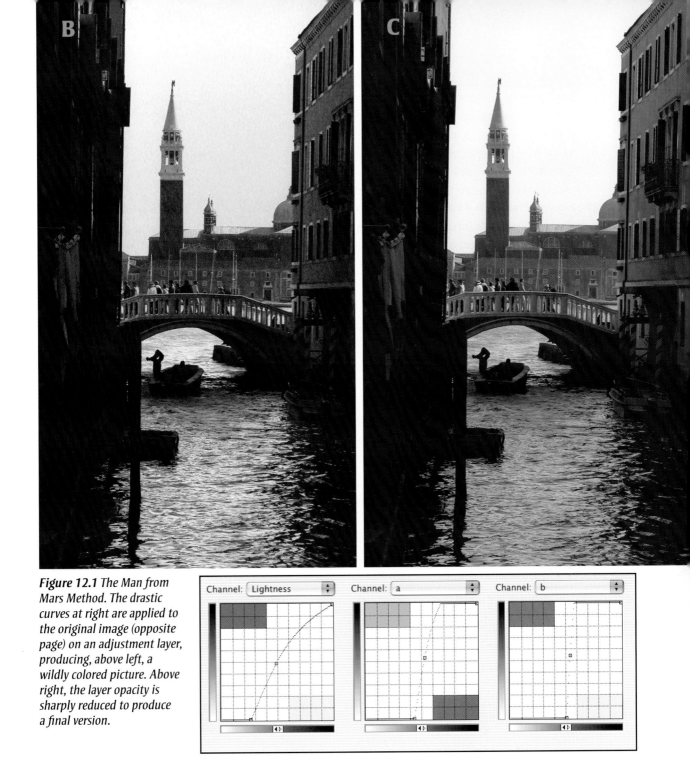

Figure 12.1 The Man from Mars Method. The drastic curves at right are applied to the original image (opposite page) on an adjustment layer, producing, above left, a wildly colored picture. Above right, the layer opacity is sharply reduced to produce a final version.

must have a strong magenta component or they would not have become so orange.

If instead of establishing pivot points by Command–clicking almost under the bridge, where the water is a dull blue, we had clicked at the bottom of the image where it's bluest of all, the entire picture would have turned

yellow. Similarly, if we had clicked low on the horizon into the sky, which isn't as blue as the water, everything would have gotten more blue. We wouldn't have needed LAB to help us do either of those stupid things. But only LAB lets us blast these very similar blues apart, making some yellow, some bright blue.

No one area of this Venetian image was vastly more important than any other. Often, though, we encounter images with two or more distinct points of interest that need to be moved apart from one another. If so, LAB can do it. The most efficient way is to Command–click some pivot points into the curve. The Man from Mars Method requires only one such point per curve. In the rest of the chapter, the images need more. We'll start with a simple example.

The Invisible Background

Figure 12.2 is a silhouetted but otherwise unedited digital capture, shot for a leading outdoorwear catalog. This merchant's design style of showing product only, without a background or a model to cause trouble, makes life much easier.

I see the jacket, which is described in the catalog as being blue, as too purple and too dark. Moreover, there's no break between the body of the jacket and the shoulder and waist areas, where there should be a significant color change, not just because the two areas are of different colors, but because our own visual systems insert simultaneous contrast when we view such things.

The action will be in the B channel, since it controls the yellow-to-blue axis. We must increase the distance between the two key areas. Possibly we may do it in the other two channels as well, but in the B for sure.

The problem is that such curves threaten to affect two innocent areas of the image. The first threat is an empty one, just like the background it covers. When the silhouetting was done in RGB, the background was deleted to a pure white: $255^R 255^G 255^B$. On conversion to LAB, it became $100^L 0^A 0^B$, and when it was without further intervention converted to CMYK it became the similarly blank $0^C 0^M 0^Y$.

Mess with the A and B curves in this image,

Figure 12.2 The body of the jacket needs to be bluer and more distinct from the grayer color found in the shoulders and waist of the jacket.

and the background may go far enough off $0^A 0^B$ to become an imaginary color—something of a distinct hue, yet defined as being as light as blank paper. If so, when it converts to CMYK there will be dots where no dots should be.

But if that happens, it's no problem—provided we've had the foresight to apply the curves to a duplicate layer and not the original file. The background is easily restored using the Lightness slider in layer Blending Options, by excluding everything that has a value of 100^L on the underlying layer.

The bigger problem is the jacket's lining, which is neutral in Figure 12.2 and should probably remain so.

With the file converted to LAB, it's sensible to begin with the critical B curve before deciding what to do with the L and A. Start with three Command–clicks, one taken in each of the three areas we've identified. The lining is essentially neutral, a value of 0^B; the shoulder/waist section is higher on the curve at around $(25)^B$; and the body of the jacket is highest of all at around $(45)^B$.

By raising the top point while lowering the middle one and holding the position of the bottom one, we achieve the goal. The body gets bluer, the shoulder/waist section less blue, and the lining stays the same.

After finishing the B, it's easier to figure out what to do with the A. In this image, it turns out that a similar three-point approach works well. The jacket body is more magenta, less neutral, than the other two points. So, just as in the B, the jacket color can be intensified, the shoulder color made more neutral, and the lining held.

The garment shows little luminosity variation, so no three-point approach is available in the L curve. Instead, we simply drop the quartertone value, making the darker half of the curve steeper and increasing contrast throughout the jacket.

After a final check of the Info palette to be sure that the background will still convert to pure white when the file enters RGB or CMYK (otherwise, use Blending Options to exclude areas that are white on the underlying layer), we have reached Figure 12.3, and the jacket is ready to wear.

Figure 12.3 The curves below force the two outside colors of the jacket apart, while retaining the neutrality of the lining.

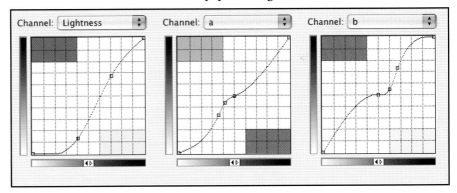

And That's No Fish Story

LAB is an essential part of the toolbox of the undersea photographer. Marine life is often so brilliantly colored as to baffle any output device. Unfortunately, the background is often strongly colored enough itself to distract from colors that have already been subdued by being brought into the CMYK gamut.

The clown triggerfish of Figure 12.4 is noted for its brilliant yellows. The impact of its mouth coloring is substantially reduced by competition from yellow areas in the background below the fish's belly and, to a lesser extent, on the fish's own back.

This picture is unmanageable in RGB or CMYK without selecting the fish. Those colorspaces have no way of reducing the intensity of one yellow while increasing that of another. In LAB, it just takes a few Command–clicks in the B channel.

The B curve in Figure 12.4 has only three points other than the two endpoints, but there should really be four, perhaps five,

Command–clicks, because there are that many areas of importance in the image. Going from the most neutral to the most yellow, they and their typical measurements in Figures 12.4A and 12.4B are

- The white spots on the fish's abdomen, $80^L(3)^A2^B$ originally, $86^L0^A(1)^B$ after the curves were applied.
- The brown body, $26^L7^A7^B$ originally, $24^L10^A0^B$ afterward.
- The yellow spots in the background, $76^L(9)^A40^B$ becoming $82^L(6)^A32^B$.
- The yellow areas on the fish's back. While

Four Tips for the Command-Clicker

Breaking colors apart can be a delicate operation, in which slight slips cause major problems. Here are three ways to minimize the chances of something going wrong.

First, apply the curves to a duplicate layer or adjustment layer. How much to move colors apart from one another is a subjective, not a by-the-numbers, decision. There's no disgrace in creating too strong an effect and then changing the layer to a lower opacity to move back in the direction of the original. Also, this type of curving sometimes creates problems in other areas of the image. By using a separate layer, you permit the possibility of excluding these areas by means of layer Blending Options.

Second, particularly when the points you have clicked into the curve start out fairly close together, be careful that you only adjust them in the north-south direction, straight up and down. Moving the control points diagonally may defeat what you're trying to achieve. You may find it useful to move a point by selecting it and then using the up or down arrow key, which forces the point to move north-south only.

Third, start with the most critical color channel. In the jacket of Figure 12.2 and the fish of Figure 12.4, the key colors are blue and yellow, so the B is the critical curve. Get that one right before progressing to the A and finally the L.

Fourth, take advantage of the option to show the curves grid at a larger size. (To toggle between large and small dialogs, click the icon at lower right.) Ordinarily, the larger size is a waste of valuable screen space, because we don't usually need extreme precision in placing points. But it makes it easier when we do—as in these examples.

these are certainly significant, I did not measure them. They appear to fall about midway between the yellowness of the background and of the mouth. As those two areas will need to be driven apart, the yellow on the back will fall into place of its own accord.

- The extremely yellow areas around the fish's lips were $88^L1^A65^B$ originally, $92^L4^A84^B$ after the curves.

As with our first two images, the idea is to drive a wedge between relatively similar colors. With this fish, we also nod in the direction of gray balance by trying to keep the spots on the abdomen close to 0^A0^B. And from that, it's an easy step to the next image, where, in addition to there being specific colors that need to be handled separately, huge areas appear that should be just about as neutral as the fish's white spots are.

The Search for the Scapegoat

When a printed job does not meet the client's expectations, it can be for a variety of reasons, such as poor ink densities, inadequate control of dot gain, bad press quality-control procedures, and the like. Printers tend to lump these issues under one inclusive technical label, namely, "bad photography." Photographers, for their part, often blame bad printing for their own foolish color-correction practices. It's a great spectacle. Color reproduction is so boring a topic that we can always appreciate any amusement, regardless of source.

Culpability for Figure 12.5A is probably shared. Many pressmen would simply blame the photographer, because, since pressmen work in the room being pictured, they know full well that it has no yellow cast. Photographers might well start blaming the pressmen in advance of the next job, since it's hard to evaluate what a printed product looks like under nonsensical lighting conditions. Fortunately, there

Figure 12.4 *Undersea life is often brilliantly colored, but the background can compete with it, as it does in the original image, top. The fish's lips are supposed to be a vivid yellow, but the yellow areas of the background spoil some of the effect. The curves at right drive the two yellows apart and result in the corrected version, bottom.*

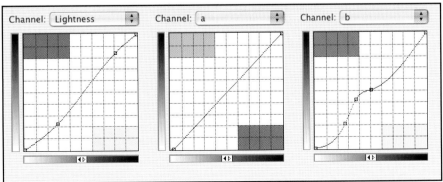

are controlled-lighting booths in the nearby pressroom for just such purposes. We hope.

Forgetting the politics, we face a gross yellow cast. In Chapter 4, we learned how to stifle such things by steepening the AB curves while moving them to whichever side of their original center point would serve to neutralize the cast.

That's not going to work this time, for four separate reasons.

● This image is like some of those shown in Chapter 7, where the digicam has "helped" us out by extending the range so far that the endpoints can't possibly have a cast because they would otherwise fall outside of the RGB gamut. The ceiling lights all measure 100^L—which, since Figure 12.5A wasn't touched after it left RGB—means that you don't need to hear about the other two channels, because 0^A0^B is automatic. The shadow areas within the equipment aren't quite 0^L, so they have positive values in the A and B, but not nearly so positive as the concrete floor and the metallic areas of the machinery.

● I think that when finished, both the metallic areas and the floor should be nearly gray. However, certain areas of the floor are around 15^B more positive than the equipment is. Steepening the B curve as a whole would drive these colors even farther apart, whereas the correct approach must be to bring them closer together.

● Critical parts of this picture are blue. The yellow cast deadens them to a certain extent. If we just steepen the B curve and move it to the left of the center point, we'll get a glowing blue that won't be appropriate.

● The bright yellow areas aren't nearly as large as the blue ones, but, being hazard warnings, they're important. Particularly that one on the delivery chute in the foreground. That ledge is right about shin height for a six-footer. A close encounter with such a thing at high speed, please believe me, causes sensations beyond all names of pain. Wiping out the overall cast by moving the B curve toward blue is likely to weaken these yellows unacceptably.

The A channel is almost meaningless because nothing important is either particularly magenta or particularly green. The L may be able to accept a minimal S-shaped curve, but almost the entire tonal range is already in use. Any drastic move would probably plug the shadows.

In such cases, I prefer to start where the action is, with the B curve. It may be possible to steepen the A afterward, but we won't know how it fits into the overall picture until the B situation is clarified.

Therefore, I commenced hostilities by Command–clicking four points into the B curve: one each for the yellow hazard signs, the blue equipment, the metallic parts of the equipment, and the yellowish areas of the floor. Because the latter two points were rather close together and therefore difficult to separate, before starting to move the points I erased the one for the floor and substituted another slightly lower on the curve.

I raised both the middle points, but the lower of the two a little more, creating a curve that looks somewhat like an inverted S. I then turned to the A curve and Command–clicked points for the yellow and blue areas, and drove them apart slightly.

After I added the L curve, the new numbers were as follows, from the bluest to the yellowest areas:

● The blue areas start at $45^L(8)^A(11)^B$ and become a significantly bluer $46^L(15)^A(24)^B$.

● The metallic parts of the equipment start at $63^L3^A14^B$ and become a nearly perfect gray, $75^L1^A0^B$.

● The yellow areas of the floor start at $62^L7^A29^B$ and become $73^L8^A8^B$—still warm as opposed to gray, but much closer to the neutral metals than they were in the original.

● The yellow hazard warnings start at $84^L(4)^A75^B$ and get more yellow, $93^L(8)^A98^B$.

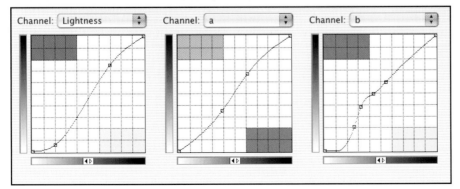

Figure 12.5 Four points were Command–clicked into this B curve. From top to bottom, they represent the blue parts of the equipment, its metallic areas, the left side of the floor, and the yellow hazard warnings. The curve forces semi-neutral areas closer to one another while allowing blues and yellows to remain pronounced.

Warm Things Are Doubly Positive

Drastic inverted S curves don't work in other colorspaces. A more subdued version is occasionally appropriate when an image has critical details in both highlights and shadows and we're willing to sacrifice midtone contrast to bring them out. But we can't make the center of the curve as flat as the one we just saw in the B curve of Figure 12.5 without blasting all detail out of the entire midrange.

There's the LAB advantage again. In the B channel, there's no detail to be harmed, and blue and yellow things land in the same location on the curve regardless of how dark they are. The curve shown retained (or even intensified) existing strongly blue or yellow areas, while neutralizing everything else. We couldn't have achieved the same result with the simpler straight-line curves that we used to kill casts in Chapter 4.

Deciding when to use the complex curve shapes described in this chapter as opposed to simple straight lines can be confounding, so there's a box on this page reviewing why this chapter's images needed special handling. In the pressroom image of Figure 12.5A, straight lines would clearly not have worked. We could have made the overall picture a lot more neutral, but certain parts of the floor would have become even yellower than they were originally.

Sometimes, though, it's hard to choose. The twilight conditions in which Figure 12.6 were shot created a coolness that the photographer could not easily control. If we start Command–clicking into every area of significance in this picture, however, carpal tunnel syndrome becomes a live possibility. Therefore, on first impression we might wish to treat it in the style of Chapter 4. The image is somewhat too dark, which can be fixed in the L. All colors are subdued, so we steepen the A and B curves, while moving them to the right of their original center point to make everything warmer.

The question is, how far to go? There are too many unknowns. Certainly the faces are not red enough, but we don't know exactly how red they should be. The man's shirt is probably gray, but it might also be a blue. The road and car in the background might both be blue, both neutral, or one of each. The woman's sweater appears to be magenta or purple, but as to the precise shade we have no clue.

When to Use This Method

The work in this chapter is more difficult than that of the first four chapters, where the adjustment curves were mostly straight lines. Both methods break colors apart, so it can be hard to know which to use.

With many pictures, like the canyons of Chapter 1 or the Venice image of Figure 12.1, straight lines are appropriate, because no one part of the picture is so important that we would be willing to suppress some other part. Plus, we want to enhance all, not just some, colors.

Command–clicking and adjusting the points up and down makes sense when we wish to drive two or more specific objects apart. Often, this entails deliberately neutralizing one area so that it doesn't compete with another.

In the fish image of Figure 12.4, consider three areas: the white areas on the abdomen, the yellowish patches in the background, and the extreme yellow around the mouth. Straight lines would create more variation than in the original, but would do so uniformly: the space between abdomen and background would increase, as well as that between background and mouth. Instead, we'd prefer to put extra space between the two yellows—in other words, to keep the white and the paler yellow at a constant relationship, or even bring them closer together.

The industrial scene of Figure 12.5 does the same thing for a different reason. Straight lines would increase the variation between the relatively neutral areas and those where the yellow cast was more violent. We'd prefer to keep them together, and to drive both toward neutrality.

To decide whether to use straight lines or a more complex shape, look on the important objects of the image as being children. If they are all playing happily together, straight lines will work fine. If they are being hostile, and competing with one another, Command–click away.

Figure 12.6 *This original image is so heavily biased toward blue that it's a candidate for the straight-line curve treatment discussed in Chapter 4. However, Command–clicking control points into the curves and adjusting them up or down may help bring out variation in key areas.*

Nevertheless, certain possibilities can be ruled out. Warm colors—reds, browns, or oranges—are positive in both A and B. Three parts of this image must meet that test: the skin, the faux-wooden bridge, and the woman's hair. The woman's sweater is very positive in the A because it's far more magenta than it is green, but we have no way of knowing whether it should be more yellow than it is blue. The man's hair could be brown, but it's dark enough that it might be black, in which case it would be 0^A0^B. The woman's hair could not. It is lighter and therefore must be some shade of brown.

The initial measurements show how far off the original is. The man's hair is $18^L0^A(10)^B$. His face is typically $69^L9^A(6)^B$. The woman's face is a little more yellow, at $65^L8^A(1)^B$.

In all of these numbers, the A and B should be a lot closer to one another. As human skin

and hair, barring visits to the tattooist and/or the beauty salon, can't possibly be more blue than it is yellow, we know that the B is hugely biased toward blue. By inspection, we see that the faces aren't pink enough, so we surmise that the A needs to move away from green and toward magenta.

To get a hint of how much, we look for other clues. The man's shirt is typically $75^L(5)^A(20)^B$, but its B value is quite variable—on our left, I'm seeing something like $(8)^B$ and on the right more like $(25)^B$. In the background, the center of the car's trunk measures $44^L(6)^A(32)^B$. Pavement of about the same darkness is $40^L(4)^A(18)^B$.

If the car is that much more B–negative than the pavement is, then it's a blue car. It can't be gray, or the pavement would be yellow. So perhaps the pavement is blue and the car even bluer, or maybe the pavement is gray and the car blue. With the man's shirt being so variable, there's no correct answer. But the B curve must move at least far enough to the right to turn $(10)^B$ into 0^B—and that's only on the dubious assumption that the man has black hair. If it's brown, we need to go farther.

The A channel seems like an easier call. I don't see why any of these three objects should be more green than they are magenta. If anything, they should be biased in the other direction. So, the minimum move makes $(6)^A$ become 0^A.

There isn't any one right way to handle this image with straight-line AB curves. The exact angles are therefore up for debate. Figure 12.7 is a reasonable shot—except for one little thing.

The colors in the original are subdued—except for the woman's sweater, which checks in at a loud $45^L50^A(10)^B$. It's a printable color in Figure 12.6, but not in Figure 12.7, where

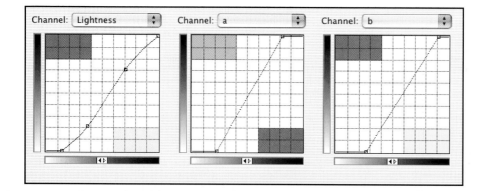

Figure 12.7 Using straight lines for the A and B curves while moving both to the right of the original center point wipes out the original cold cast while intensifying all colors. Unfortunately, the woman's sweater is driven out of the CMYK gamut, so detail is lost when the file is converted for printing.

the curves have basically doubled all A values in the interest of getting pinker faces. So, the sweater is out of CMYK gamut when the file leaves LAB. When that happens, most of the detail vanishes.

Figure 12.8 is the Command–click alternative. There are two interior points in the A curve. One establishes the fleshtones, the other the assumed neutral areas. The neutrals go slightly toward magenta and away from green. The skin goes more strongly toward magenta. Meanwhile, the lower left point is raised, suppressing the magenta component of any object that was very magenta to begin with—namely, the sweater.

In the B, the three interior points, left to right, are the light parts of the woman's hair; the skin plus the magenta sweater, which share the same range; and the background pavement. The point in the upper right is not a Command–click. It's an arbitrary point

Figure 12.8 This version uses the same general approach as Figure 12.7, but brings up the left side of the A curve to prevent the sweater from getting more colorful. Also, two points in the top of the B curve bring the background car away from the background pavement.

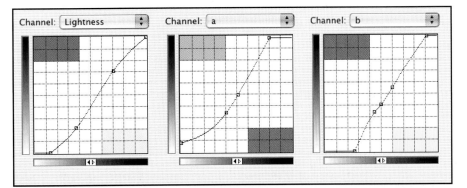

put in to accentuate the blueness of anything that falls above the third point. Check out how the car is more prominent in Figure 12.8 than in Figure 12.7.

Too Many Choices, Not Enough Time

Curving by Command–click involves not merely the most complexity, but the most creativity as well. Many options produce pleasing, yet different, results. Deadlines on this book have suffered as I've reconfigured

this chapter more times than I would have liked. Each time I redid some of these images I saw new possibilities. Figure 12.9 was supposed to appear earlier in the chapter, before I realized that it wasn't obvious what should be done with it.

This image promotes a company that specializes in Western-style fashions for women. The clothing and not the animal is therefore the prime consideration.

I don't know what the company wanted to do with this image, but if I were in their boots I would see three issues. First, admitting that the picture is about brown and brown is a dull, desaturated color, some areas seem awfully gray, particularly the face, the sky, and the sunflowers on the sleeve. Second, all these browns fall into a short darkness range, so it should be possible to add definition. Third, I think the browns are all too similar. All three of these problems suggest LAB for correction rather than any other colorspace, and these closely similar browns suggest Command–clicking.

The hard part is deciding what colors we want. Customers return merchandise at the company's expense when they don't think the advertising reflects accurate color. In making this determination, the customer does not rely on spectrophotometers, histograms, or Pantone swatchbooks. If she is a human being, she is likely to think that the pants of this outfit are considerably farther off the color of the shirt than the picture shows, as the visual system of said species is noted for the ability to see or to imagine gross differences in neighboring colors. Plus, the color of the shirt is described in the catalog text as *Chocolate.* To my way of thinking, a chocolate and a horse suggest colors more different than those found in Figure 12.9.

Also, I have doubts about the accuracy of the original. I think of horses as being brown.

Figure 12.9 Command–clicking is one of many options to break apart the browns that dominate this image.

Brown is a type of red. I therefore expect that the A and B values should be similar, if not equal. But this horse measures more like $40^L25^A40^B$. He's so dark that the cast may not be noticeable, but I suspect him of being too yellow. We may need a horse of a different color.

How Horses Look on Mars

This is the sixth image of the chapter. It resembles the first one more than the succeeding four. In each of those four, the basic goal was fairly clear and the only question was how to get there.

This one and the Venetian scene of Figure 12.1A, however, leave us with the same attitude that my wife has whenever I suggest a new destination for a vacation, an investment opportunity, or any type of reorganization of our household. To wit, a general expression of dissatisfaction coupled with a paucity of constructive suggestions for better alternatives.

When we can't visualize what we want, resorting to the Man from Mars Method, or something similar, makes a lot of sense. That is, we try a certain concept but carry it to a ridiculous extreme on a separate layer. Then, since we don't know exactly what we're looking for, we reduce the opacity of that layer until we're happy.

My first step was to add some weight to the background by using the highlight half of the Shadow/Highlight command. Without that step, some of my later L curves might have blown the background out as I attempted to add detail to the horse and clothing.

The exact settings, you'll have to work out for yourself—as you will with the sets of curves that follow. Figures 12.10 and 12.11

Figure 12.10 Four extreme variations on Figure 12.9, all emphasizing different areas of the image. In each case, the adjustment was made on a separate layer with the idea of reducing the opacity to taste.

show four ideas for improving Figure 12.9. You should be able to reproduce whichever one you favor without further help from me.

These four sets of images, the wildly colorful ones in Figure 12.10 and the reduced-opacity versions of Figure 12.11, are shown in the order I

prepared them. My first idea was that all the brown things had to become more A–positive so that they wouldn't be so yellow. But I wanted to increase the distance between the horse and the shirt. So, since the shirt was getting slightly more positive, the horse had to get much more positive, resulting in the cherry-red equine of Figure 12.10A. Also, I applied a big twist to the bottom of the B curve to get yellower flowers.

The idea of a bright red horse is so repugnant that I chose a lower opacity (25%) in Figure 12.11A than in the other three examples, which all use 35%. There's plenty of variation now between garments and animal, but it's still a horse of too different a color to suit me.

Figures 12.10B and 12.11B take a different tack. Now the variation is more equally distributed. The horse gets slightly redder, the clothing slightly more neutral. The effect seems more realistic, but the colors are tired.

Figures 12.10C and 12.11C show a literal application of the Man from Mars Method described at the start of the chapter. That is, three curves, three Command–clicks to establish a pivot point in each, three big twists. I clicked on the woman's shirt as being the most typical of the sorts of browns I was trying to separate.

The key to this method is choosing pivot points that drive large parts of the image toward both ends of the A and B. There should be visible moves toward magenta, green, yellow, and blue. Hint: to make sure

Figure 12.11 *Reduced-opacity versions of Figure 12.10. Version A is at 25%. All others are at 35% opacity.*

that this is taking place, it can be helpful to open the Channels palette and turn off the A channel while leaving only the LB visible, and then to do the same to the B to view only the LA. In this way we can closely examine two of the four AB primary colors without being distracted by the other two.

These straight-line curves create a more colorful background than in either of my first two tries. That's to be expected. The straight Man from Mars Method treats the picture as one unified composition, as the Venice scene of Figure 12.1A arguably was. My first two tries at this picture, by contrast, were aimed at improving the browns, not the background.

Figure 12.11C, in my opinion, aggravates a problem mentioned earlier. The horse seems to be too yellow, just as he's too red in Figure 12.11A. Therefore, I made Figure 12.11D by modifying Figure 12.11C's curves. In the A, I added locking points near the center and on

the shirt, and then twisted the bottom sharply to the left, making the horse more magenta. In the B, I did the opposite, locking the bottom half of the curve so that the horse wouldn't get any more yellow, but twisting the top to create a bluer sky.

You should be able to visualize the curves that created any of these four variants, but they're on the CD if you want a look. In the last two images, Blending Options were also needed in the two final versions because the hat and the fence were turning blue-green; of course, these are easily restored by using the Blend If sliders of Blending Options to exclude anything that is very light in the L.

The images beginning with Figure 12.2 are the work of five different professional photographers. I haven't asked any of them whether they liked any of the revised versions shown here, because it doesn't affect our discussion. Command–clicking points into the A and B curves and adjusting them up and down gives you the flexibility to get what you want. Have another look at the four choices of Figure 12.11. Pick the one you like, or, perhaps, imagine a better option that combines certain aspects of some of them. Now, compare it to the original image in Figure 12.9 and ask yourself: how could I have possibly gotten from that point to where I want to be, without the use of LAB?

Our final two images show how nature is both a benificent provider and a destroyer, how Command–clicking works in a real-world environment, and how having LAB in the camera bag is a must for nature photographers. Conveniently, we don't have to worry about what the photographer might want, because I am the photographer and therefore my preferences trump yours. Appropriately, we return to the place that our journey began on the first page of Chapter 1.

A Simple Field of Sunflowers

The desert sunflowers woven into the model's sleeve in our last image are duplicated in real life in our next exercise. It looks like a simple enough composition, until you find out the context—because it's a picture of something nobody now alive had ever seen before.

As noted and illustrated in Chapter 1, certain California deserts rank among the least habitable places on earth. Both Anza-Borrego and Death Valley regularly feature summer temperatures in the mid-120s. Death Valley doesn't drop much below 100 in the summer, even at night. Both parks rarely receive more than a couple of inches of rain annually. Whatever plant life survives does so by an astonishing system of water conservation, including the ability to wait patiently for years before enough rain comes to warrant expending the energy to burst into bloom.

In late 2004, about the time I was writing Chapter 1, it began to rain in the desert, and it did not stop. Storm after storm hit, each one dropping as much precipitation as usually falls in an entire year.

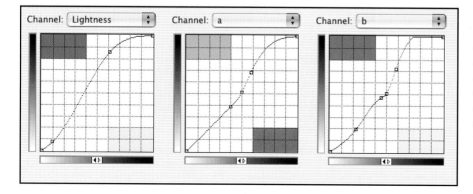

Figure 12.12 Unprecedented rainstorms in the winter of 2004–2005 created this once-in-a-lifetime carpet of flowers in arid Death Valley. The curves are designed to emphasize both the yellow and orange components of the sunflowers.

Such parched ground cannot absorb anything like that much water. Instead, there are—there were—flash floods, wiping out roads, hiking trails, and palm oases. Photographing Artist's Palette, the subject of Figure 1.1, now involves a hike of several extra miles, as the road leading to it is gone.

But not far from that desolate place, the seeds that had been lying in wait for so long found their moist reward. Carpets of golden sunflowers covered the desert, as in Figure 12.12. The purple flowers in Figure 12.13 are in a lower area, well below sea level, where only five years earlier scientists had measured a ground temperature of 200 degrees. The lake behind it had been dry for ten thousand years. In March 2005, when these pictures were taken, people were kayaking it.

Those tiny purple flowers are so shocking that they completely dominate the scene—in real life. The camera, not realizing the magnitude of what it's seeing, isn't nearly as impressed. Similarly, in real life, the small patches of sunflower that are climbing the reddish hill in the background of Figure 12.12A are unbelievably pronounced. The camera, at any rate, doesn't believe how pronounced they are.

These two areas normally resemble Mars, but we don't need the Man from Mars Method here. We need something that will radically accentuate the flowers in these two images.

The sunflower image has four interest objects: the yellow petals of the sunflowers, the orange interiors, the reddish background hill, and the stems. However, there are only three Command–clicks in the A and B curves, because two of the four objects share range in each one. The orange and yellow parts of the flowers have to be separated in the A, as they share the same range in the B. The stems need to be separated in the B, because, believe it or not, they share range with the yellow flowers in the A, both being just slightly more green than magenta.

In the L curve of Figure 12.12, the left point is the flowers, the right one the darkest point of the background. In the A, the leftmost internal point is the most magenta-as-opposed-to-green part of the picture, namely, the background. The center point is the yellow portion of the flowers; between them, unnoticed, is the orange portion. The rightmost point is a desperate attempt to create more variation in the greens, but I

Review and Exercises

✓ If you're using the Man from Mars Method described in Figures 12.1 and 12.10C, how can you verify that you've chosen good pivot points for your A and B curves?

✓ If your client asks you to merge Figures 12.7 and 12.8 to create a new version in which the sweater is more like that of Figure 12.8 but everything else is taken from Figure 12.7, what is the best way to handle the assignment?

✓ Figure 12.7 was judged inadequate because the woman's sweater was too brilliant and lost detail during conversion to CMYK. Why was there not a similar problem in Figure 12.5B, where the yellow hazard indicators were also out of the CMYK gamut before they were converted?

✓ In Figures 12.10C and 12.10D, the curves turned the woman's white hat blue. How was this problem eliminated in the final version when layer opacity was reduced? (Hint: see Figure 12.3, where the blank background also was threatening to acquire a color.)

doubt it makes any noticeable difference.

The leftmost internal point in the B curve represents both the yellow and orange portions of the flowers. The center point is the stems, being dragged toward neutrality and away from the flowers. The rightmost internal point is the background, which is neither blue nor yellow.

Yellowish things are much more common in nature than bluish ones, so the B channel ordinarily has more positive than negative values. This image takes it to an extreme: there isn't *anything* above the center point of the B curve. Nothing in this image is more blue than it is yellow.

In Figure 12.12, it's advantageous to make the background more magenta, which differentiates it from the green stems and the yellow flowers. In Figure 12.13, where most of the flowers are purple, it's a bad idea.

In the curves shown in Figure 12.14, not much can be done with the L; the image already fills much of its tonal range. In the A, the leftmost internal point is the flowers, which are far more magenta than they are green. The two central

Figure 12.13 *Curves in the A and B emphasize the purple flowers, which are rarely found in areas this desolate.*

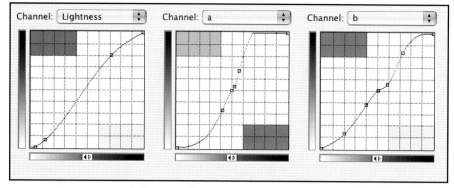

Figure 12.14 The curves that transformed Figure 12.13A into Figure 12.13B.

points are reminiscent of what was done with the pressroom image of Figure 12.5. Everything that's close to neutral—the background, and the soil in the foreground—is jammed together and made more gray, to give the colored areas greater emphasis. The right point intensifies anything that was originally more green than magenta.

The B curve has five internal points. Going from left to right, which is to say, from yellowest to bluest, these Command–clicks represent the yellow flowers, whose color is being exaggerated; the greenery in the foreground; the large rock at the very bottom of the picture, which I am taking to be a gray; the background hills, which start out somewhat blue and which I am trying to neutralize somewhat; and the sky, which is being made more blue.

With this return to a radically different Death Valley from the one pictured in Chapter 1, we close out our look at how LAB can differentiate critical colors when it has to. If you think that the flowers, whether purple or yellow, stand out better in the corrected versions of Figures 12.12 and 12.13 than they did in the original; if you see the variation in Figure 12.2 that you suspect the clothing manufacturer was looking for; if you think that Figure 12.1C is a more attractive version than the original, then you have become a convert to this school of curving.

Yes, these methods, even the primitive Man from Mars one, are more complex than the ones shown in the first four chapters. But boil them down, and they're nothing more than clicking into the critical areas of the image and then moving the resulting point up or down on the curve. How tough can that be?

Command, click, and take control.

The Bottom Line

Chapters 1, 3, and 4 introduced a method of enhancing colors by using steep, straight-line curves in the A and B channels. With slight modifications, that's the way to handle images that you wish to treat as unified compositions, where no one part is drastically more significant than another.

In certain cases, the relationship between two or more objects is more important than maintaining accurate color. Usually, the idea is to separate the objects by creating more of a color variation between them. This chapter shows how to construct the curves that do so.

13

The Universal
Interchange Standard

Because it's unambiguous, LAB has many uses in information interchange. Because its gamut is so huge, translating in and out of it offers
important lessons for other types of conversions—like RGB to CMYK,
or Pantone Matching System to RGB. And because it's based on human
visual response, it's the natural choice for all types of color matching.

Two color scientists, one emaciated, one fat, one on a rickety
horse, one on a donkey. The fat one says, *"What* giants?"

His companion replies, "Those over there. The ones
whose arms are so enormously long."

"Your grace," says the second scientist, "those things over
there are not giants, but windmills. What you take for their
arms are only their sails, which, driven by the wind, make the mill run."

"It's apparent," replies the first, much disgusted, "that you are not cut
out for adventure: those are giants, and if you are frightened, get the hell
out of here. Fall on your knees and pray during the time in which I engage
them in fiery and unequal combat."

Fast forward five hundred years. A Photoshop author and student of
Cervantes receives the following query:

> I created an illustration in two spot channels and saved it as a DCS sep-
> aration with a low-resolution composite. But I don't want a placeholder. I
> want a CMYK file to print out as a high-resolution proof. How do I do this?
>
> I converted each of the spot channels to CMYK in a new Photoshop
> document. I put a new layer over each of them with the CMYK equivalent
> of the PMS color and changed mode to Color in the Layers palette. Then I
> combined the color layer with the grayscale layer so I was back to two
> layers that I then multiplied one over the other. Would I have done better
> to do eight burns to channels? In other words, if PMS 145 uses 3% black, I
> burn 3% of that grayscale image to the black plate and then continue to do
> appropriate percentages for the other three channels and then go ahead
> and do the same for the other PMS color?

The brief response was this:
- Go to the hi-res file, copy the entire first spot channel (Select All; Copy).
- Open a new document, which by default matches the size and format of what you have copied—in this case, grayscale. Paste the spot channel into it and Layer: Flatten Image.
- Image: Mode>Duotone. For Type, choose Monotone. Double-click the color icon and insert the PMS value you want.
- Now that you have what appears to be a color copy, Image: Mode>Lab color.
- Repeat this entire procedure with the second spot channel. You should now have two LAB documents the same size, but different colors.
- Paste one as a layer on top of the other, Multiply mode.
- Convert to CMYK, choosing Flatten in response to the prompt.

Of Reds and References

These two examples introduce a chapter that seems to be the odd man out in a book that's about Photoshop technique. The subject is the use of LAB as an interchange space. In principle, if you are never involved or interested in calibration or associated issues, you can skip ahead to Chapter 14. In practice, a lot of valuable lessons about many real-world problems stem out of this chapter, including many problems that don't seem to involve LAB at all.

For example, a lot of the pain of converting from RGB to CMYK or from the Pantone Matching System to either one is merely a junior version of the problem of converting out of LAB. Understand what steps are needed to solve the problem of monstrously out-of-gamut colors in LAB and you'll have a big head start on dealing with mildly out-of-gamut colors elsewhere. And, although some of the LAB color-matching theory is exceedingly quixotic, there are many ruthlessly practical applications of LAB as an

exchange space—such as the second example given above.

To understand LAB's role in the interchange process, we have to discuss what it is, why it's needed, what it's good for, and what it can't possibly achieve, some general principles on moving files in and out of it, and some speculation on its future.

Many systems of describing colors exist. Some people use the term *color model* to describe the overall framework, as, for example, CMYK as opposed to RGB. They use *colorspace* to describe variant treatments within a color model, such as sRGB as opposed to ColorMatch RGB. In any event, Photoshop's LAB is a colorspace, because variants of LAB exist elsewhere in the world, but for our purposes it's also a color model, because Photoshop permits only this single LAB definition, whereas we can define RGB and CMYK however we like.

Several other color models exist beyond the three just named. LAB is one of those that are specifically designed to be *reference colorspaces*—that is, to be used in the sense discussed in this chapter.

Any such reference needs values that can be measured and verified against a known standard. Generic "CMYK" does not meet that requirement. 100^M100^Y, for example, is definitely red—but exactly what kind of red it is depends on the press, the paper, the platemaking equipment, the mood of the pressmen, and many other factors.

We could, however, defeat this objection, by declaring that by "CMYK" we mean the exact results obtained by the printer of this book, using this paper, at a certain hour and minute of the pressrun. We would then, provided we had appropriate sample sheets printed at that time, know precisely what kind of red is meant by 100^M100^Y. We could use that as our interchange standard, and build an image-processing program around it and try to compete with Photoshop.

Figure 13.1 Quality-oriented printers include some sort of color reference like this one.

That would be a stupid idea, for at least two reasons. First, our proposed reference space doesn't contain certain colors that we might reasonably expect to have to work with at some point. The press's red will equate to something like 70^A50^B. Lots of things in this world are redder than that, but we wouldn't be able to portray them. In LAB, no matter how red they are, they're never going to get to the maximum 127^A127^B.

Second, it would be reinventing the wheel. Several reference spaces, not just LAB, already exist. It's much more convenient just to live with what we have. But it leaves open the question: why have a reference space at all?

The Ref Needs a Pair of Glasses

You purchase a shirt from a catalog. It arrives, and you don't like the color, either because it didn't match what was in the catalog or because you've thought better of the purchase and need an excuse to return it.

No matter—when you call up the merchant to complain, they'll give you your money back. No need for any reference colorspace here. They don't want a dissatisfied client, so if you say you don't think that the color matched, then it didn't, as far as they're concerned.

If ten thousand other buyers also return the same shirt with the same story, then the traditional prepress game of finding a scapegoat begins. If the people who prepared the Photoshop file are unsuccessful in fobbing off blame on the photographer, and talk their way out of accepting it themselves, there may be a serious conversation with the printer. This time, the dissatisfied client won't be complaining about a $50 shirt but a $50,000 print job, so the vendor won't be nearly as inclined to just smile and forget about charging for it.

The argument will center around the final proof that was pulled before the job was run. The client will have signed off on that. It is referred to as a *contract proof,* because it represents the agreement between the two as to what the final job is supposed to look like.

That contract, unfortunately, isn't really enforceable. The client says that the printing doesn't look enough like the proof. The printer says that it does. Who decides which is right? What instrument can measure how close one picture is to another?

In real life, the printer, confronted by an important dissatisfied client, will take to heart a saying of Sancho Panza: whether the rock smashes into the pitcher, or the pitcher smashes into the rock, the result is bad for the pitcher. And so a concession of some kind will doubtless be made.

It is nevertheless conceivable that the differences cannot be reconciled, and some independent party must make a judgment. Going to court and leaving it in the hands of a judge and jury would be like flipping a coin. An impartial referee is needed.

Note the similarity between the words *reference* and *referee.*

In a lot of sporting events, the officiating is quite incompetent. Appointing a spectrophotometer or other color-measurement

Ink Colors

	Y	x	y	
C:	26.25	0.1673	0.2328	
M:	14.50	0.4845	0.2396	
Y:	71.20	0.4357	0.5013	
MY:	14.09	0.6075	0.3191	
CY:	19.25	0.2271	0.5513	
CM:	2.98	0.2052	0.1245	
CMY:	2.79	0.3227	0.2962	
W:	83.02	0.3149	0.3321	
K:	0.82	0.3202	0.3241	

☐ L*a*b* Coordinates
☐ Estimate Overprints

Ink Colors

	L*	a*	b*	
C:	58.3	-28.5	-42.6	
M:	44.9	75.2	-2.0	
Y:	87.6	-13.1	91.6	
MY:	44.4	67.8	42.1	
CY:	51.0	-70.2	32.6	
CM:	20.0	31.2	-43.6	
CMY:	19.2	7.1	-3.5	
W:	93.0	-0.4	1.5	
K:	7.4	1.3	-0.1	

☑ L*a*b* Coordinates
☐ Estimate Overprints

Custom RGB

Name: Simplified sRGB IEC61966-2.1

Gamma
Gamma: 2.20

White Point: 6500° K (D65)

	x	y
White:	0.3127	0.3290

Primaries: HDTV (ITU-R 709-2)

	x	y
Red:	0.6400	0.3300
Green:	0.3000	0.6000
Blue:	0.1500	0.0600

device as referee is sure to result in a lot of blown calls. After all, back in Figure 1.11, the machine misidentified two obviously different reds as being the same color.

At least, however, the machine is impartial, and if you tell it the rules, it will render a verdict.

The judgment will be rendered based on something like Figure 13.1, which printers use in process control. This particular form is complex. It allows either an instrument or a human to make the call—the small picture in the center is a great diagnostic tool for us, meaningless to a machine, which would measure the swatches of solid and 50 percent ink coverage. The other swatches have uses in diagnosing press problems, but not in determining whether the job goes to the penalty box.

The printing is presumably supposed to comply with the dictates of the Specifications for Web Offset Publications, or SWOP. To find out whether it actually does, the swatches would be tested three ways: to find out whether the inks are of the correct color; whether they reflect the proper amount of light when printed as a solid; and whether the relationship in darkness between 50 percent and solid coverage, otherwise known as *dot gain,* is appropriate. SWOP gives target values for these measurements, as well as tolerances. If all four inks are at the target or within the tolerance, there's no whistle. Otherwise, the client gets a free throw—er, a free pressrun.

The first of these measurements deals with color only; the second two with luminosity only. So, having a reference space that splits color and contrast can be helpful. LAB fits the bill, but it has competitors.

LAB's grandfather is a 1931 colorspace called XYZ, also a product of CIE, the international lighting standards group. Like LAB, it tries to relate color measurement to human foibles. It combines readings of red, green, and blue light—the so-called *tristimulus values,* these being the types of light that human vision most strongly reacts to. Also, it introduced the concept of a *standard observer,* the hypothetical typical human being. The person passing judgment on my own work is usually about as closely related to such a standard observer as The Knight of the Woeful Countenance is to Sir Lancelot.

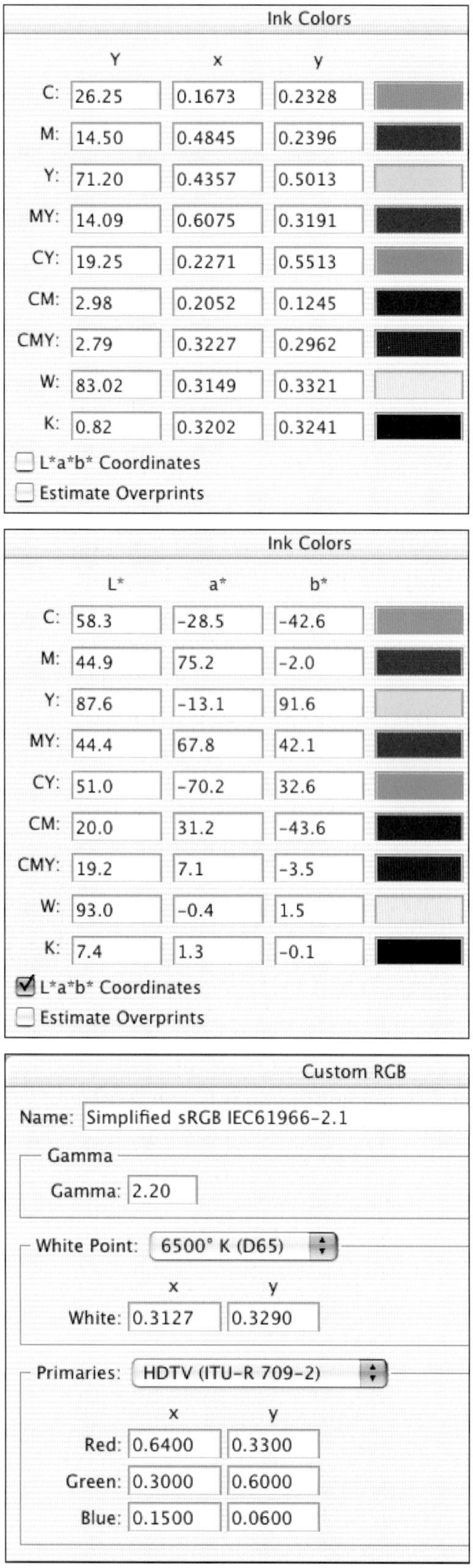

Figure 13.2 *Photoshop's internal color settings use two reference colorspaces. Top, the Custom CMYK dialog defaults to xyY. Middle, as an option, the ink values can be read in LAB. Bottom, the Custom RGB dialog defines primary colors in terms of the xy of xyY.*

Unless you're an academic or calibration specialist, you're unlikely to run into much XYZ. Photoshop does, however, use an offshoot, xyY, in formulating its definitions of CMYK and RGB. Figure 13.2 shows the Ink Colors dialog, accessed with effort, via Edit: (Photoshop: in some versions) Color Settings>Working Spaces>CMYK>Custom CMYK>Ink Colors>Custom. This dialog's default is xyY, but a check box at the bottom allows toggling back and forth to read LAB values instead. (Note: this dialog applies only to inks being defined by Photoshop's traditional Custom CMYK structure. Information for self-contained CMYK profiles, like the SWOP v.2 that is the current Photoshop default, is not available within Photoshop, although third-party software can analyze and edit them.)

The xyY structure is similar to that of LAB. The Y is a luminosity channel reminiscent of the L; the xy are opponent-color channels just as the AB are, although they are harder to decipher because they don't employ any negative numbers.

The bottom dialog of Figure 13.2 contains our RGB definition. Note that the specification of what the *primaries* (meaning red, green, and blue) are is expressed only in xy, as this is a color-only issue that isn't impacted by luminosity.

The Search for Perceptual Uniformity

While xyY is suited to this type of information interchange, it has a drawback that can show up in others. It lacks *perceptual uniformity,* a goal that can no more be achieved than Don Quijote could capture Mambrino's helmet.

In 1976, CIE introduced two colorspaces to fight the unbeatable foe nevertheless. They weren't exactly new; both had been proposed in a more primitive way some years earlier. The 1976 versions were known as CIEL*u*v*, which we don't need to know about, and CIEL*a*b*, which has the title role of this book. For purposes of remaining sane, we refer to them as LUV and LAB.

Perceptual uniformity, as a philosophy, attempts to scale all channels in the way that a human perceives them as opposed to a machine. That is, the desire is that a change of 5^L should seem to us to be a change of about the same amount whether we went from 85^L to 80^L or from 15^L to 10^L.

One of these denotes a light area and the other a dark one. If the actual amount of light (as recorded by a machine) changed by an equal amount in both, we would perceive that the dark area had changed much more. To compensate, the meaning of 50^L, the midpoint, is defined as considerably darker than just 50 percent of the available light. Therefore, something that a machine would consider to be half as light as it could possibly be will be more like 75^L than 50^L.

Creating more uniformity by making the spaces between dark values smaller is an effective use of theory. Unfortunately, it gets insanely complicated when the A and B are

Finding an xyY Equivalent

The more involved you get in matching and calibration issues, the less improbable it becomes that you may have to know the xyY equivalent of some color that you want to use. If it's a once-in-a-long-while proposition only, venturing onto the Web to download a colorspace converter is unnecessary. Photoshop already has one, if you know where to look.

Suppose we need an xyY value for a vivid green that nevertheless is within the CMYK gamut. About the brightest CMYK green is $70^C0^M100^Y$. Any more cyan than that, and the viewer will think the color is too blue. So, we call up the Color Picker, type those values in, and learn that they equate to $67^L(48)^A46^B$.

Armed with that information, we slog through the several commands needed to get to the Ink Colors dialog of Figure 13.2. We check the L*a*b* Coordinates box, and type the LAB values into any ink field. Now we click L*a*b* Coordinates off, and presto, $.3152^x.5109^y36.63^Y$. Ugly, but it works.

added. A 5^A or 5^B variation is huge if the L value is high and inconsequential if it's low. The importance of the variation also depends on what's happening in the other color channel. So, while LAB may be more perceptually uniform than xyY is, it's far from its goal.

Perceptual uniformity is not useful at all in the context of Figure 13.2; it may or may not be useful in the Photoshop techniques discussed in the rest of the book. It's most helpful in calibration.

We discussed earlier how some of the swatches of Figure 13.1 could be measured to verify whether a print run was within required tolerances in each of the four inks. Unfortunately, printing that technically doesn't comply with the standard is often better than printing that does. If the printer does not comply with respect to yellow dot gain, but all other swatches are spot on, the result will be more acceptable than that of another printer who technically complies with the full standard, but is at the edge of the allowed tolerance in each ink.

The knights-errant who tilt at such problems are understandably dissatisfied with such a state of affairs. They would prefer a method that could tell how different one composite color—not each one of four inks—was from another. Doing this requires at the very least some weighting of the channels, because what happens in the black is much more important than in the magenta, cyan is less important than that, and yellow least important of all. In RGB, the most weight would have to be given to the green, then the red, then the blue.

The most accurate way to quantify the difference is to measure both samples as LAB. That's what's going on in Figure 13.3, a screen

Figure 13.3 A color-measurement package attempts to quantify Delta-E, the difference between two greens.

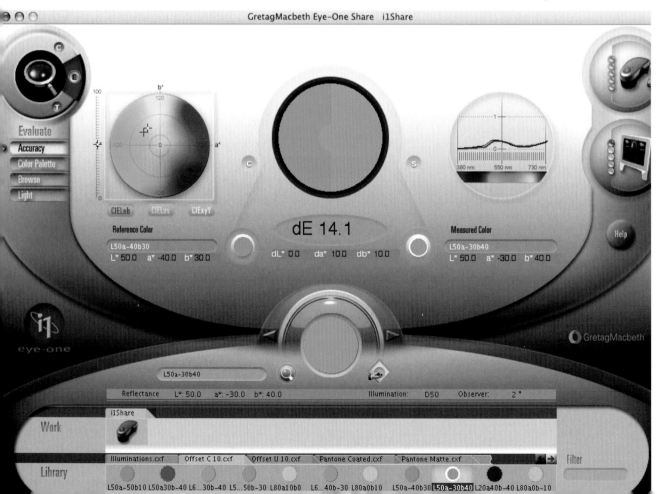

Figure 13.4 The middle row holds the reference colors. Are the colors at the top closer to the middle ones than the bottom ones are? A machine would think they are each equally far off.

shot from a product of GretagMacbeth, a leading vendor of color measurement instrumentation. It has measured $50^L(30)^A40^B$ where the desired value is $50^L(40)^A30^B$, and it wants to know how far different these two greens really are from one another.

Notice first that below the color wheel on the left, the program permits us to express these colors in xyY or even LUV, if we'd like to avoid LAB. But that's a side issue. The big action is underneath the green circle, where we find one large and three small numbers that are introduced by the lowercase letter *d*. It stands for the Greek delta, which mathematicians often use to denote the quantity of change. The asterisks remind us that the snooty name is L*a*b*. In comparing the two colors, the program notes that the L values are identical, so dL*=0. da* and db* are both 10.

To Each His Dulcinea

"A knight errant who loses his lady," Don Quijote remarked to Sancho, "is like one who loses the eyes that let him see, or the sun that shines on him, or the food that maintains him. I have told you this many times before, and now I say it again: a knight errant with-

out a lady is like a tree without leaves, bricks without mortar, and a shadow without the body that cast it."

Right above the three readings we've just been discussing in Figure 13.3, much larger type informs us that dE=14.1. That's the key, the iconic number. Pronounce it "Delta-E," and prostrate yourself before it if you believe that machines see color better than you do.

Delta-E is an attempt to quantify the three readings on the line below it to create one comprehensive number that describes how far the two colors are from one another. There are several formulas to produce it; this one involves weighting the A channel more than the B, a lot of square roots, and other fancy stuff. But whatever the formula, a dE of zero is ideal; the higher it is the worse the match; and the objective of a good interchange between two devices is to have the average dE be as close to zero as possible.

Opinions on the merit of dE are, shall we say, varied. On the one hand, certain calibrationists are so smitten that they make a Dulcinea out of dE: they believe that she embodies perfection and it is only a matter of time before we find, attain, and adore her. On the other, one color expert offers the following succinct opinion: "The original conclusion therefore remains, the CIELAB is perceptually extremely non-linear and the dE* unit of color-difference is totally worthless for all processes and uses in photographic imaging."

Personally, I am somewhere in the middle, but closer to the second view than the first. The real Dulcinea, like dE, was no thing of beauty. She herded pigs, a dirty and unpleasant task that nevertheless needs to be done. dE is like that, too. Machines can aid in calibration, and a formula like dE, however imperfect, is the only way they can come to a decision. We simply have to understand that sometimes it gives misleading results, and sometimes we deliberately want to disregard it because we get a closer visual match with a worse literal match.

Let's assume that we are trying to make output from a desktop printer match that of a commercial print shop so that we can make inexpensive proofs at home. A conventional idea is to have the print shop produce a variety of patches, which are then measured spectrophotometrically. The desktop printer spits out the same swatches, which are measured and compared to the press's. Adjustments are then made to try to get dE lower by forcing the desktop printer to get closer to the print shop's results.

There's nothing inherently wrong with such an approach, but the two greens that

Further Reading on Colorspaces

For those interested in more detailed discussion and comparison of the colorspaces described in this chapter, the enclosed CD includes six papers by Prof. Gernot Hoffmann, a color expert at the University of Applied Sciences in Emden, Germany. They include a general introduction to graphics for color science; one paper each on the structure of XYZ and LAB; a study of the question of gamut generally; and one that is specific to the question of CMYK gamut. Finally, there's one paper that has nothing to do with the topic of this chapter but does bear on Chapters 5 and 11, namely a discussion of how gamma can create certain problems when working in RGB.

I suggest starting here because Gernot does a good job of reducing technical concepts into somewhat comprehensible language. There is a fair amount of mathematics involved, but no calculus. If you don't remember what went on in your 12th-grade algebra course, however, you may find it heavy sledding.

Thanks to Google and its ilk, much more information, including the actual formulas for converting between the spaces, is available by typing in search criteria such as CIELUV, CIExyY, and so on.

The CIE is alive, well, and living in Austria. Its URL is www.cie.co.at.

we've been discussing—$50^L(30)^A40^B$ on the press and $50^L(40)^A30^B$ when we try it on our printer—demonstrate the deficiencies of any such formula, in at least three different ways.

First, humans expect greens to be greener than a machine does. If the desktop printer produces a better-looking green than the press does, we may declare that the two match, even though a spectrophotometer finds a big dE. Also, the machine thinks that misses of equal magnitude make for equal dE. Not so. If one of the misses is greener than the desired value, and the other is less green by an equal amount, humans will invariably consider the greener one a closer match to the original.

Second, how far one color channel appears to be off from the desired value depends on what goes on in the other, a fact lost on a spectrophotometer. If the desktop printer's patch had measured at $50^L(50)^A40^B$, the machine would compute the same dE, because there is still a difference of $0^L10^A10^B$ between that and what's wanted. However, we would perceive that color as being closer to the original than $50^L(30)^A40^B$ was, because, while both the A and B were each inaccurate by 10 points, both were further away from 0^A0^B than the desired value was. Were they the same 10 points off, but one channel moved toward neutrality and the other away from it, a spectrophotometer sees less difference than we do.

If you don't believe it, check out Figure 13.4. The "desired" colors are in the middle row. In the top row, both A and B were moved 15 points further from zero. In the bottom row, one channel went 15 points in one direction and one 15 points in the other. Therefore, the top and bottom rows both have the same dE with respect to the middle. (None of the original LAB squares were out of the CMYK gamut, so the conversion for printing didn't affect the relation of these colors.) Humans would see the bottom row as being much further from the middle than the top is, particularly in the context of a real image.

And third, the age of a spectrophotometer doesn't affect its color perception. The age of a human does. The measured green is more yellow than the desired one. A younger person is likely to find this fact more objectionable than an older one would. As we age, our corneas become yellower, lessening our sensitivity to that color. If you're over 40, you definitely are seeing less difference between these two greens than you would have in your youth.

Matching Unmatchable Pantone Colors

If it sounds like the machine may be right and humanity wrong, ask yourself who decides whether the match is a good one. If you want your monitor, or your desktop printer, to predict what output will look like on some other device, are you going to accept something that a machine says matches, when your own eyes tell you it doesn't?

Furthermore, many conversions are better done by ignoring numerical matching altogether. The prime example, and one that features LAB in a big way, is the handling of Pantone Matching System colors.

Authentic PMS colors are created by mixing special inks. Such custom-mixed inks can achieve certain colors, particularly pastels and blues, that aren't otherwise available on any current output device.

Unfortunately, printing with an extra ink is expensive. Clients often request that the PMS color be emulated with standard inks, no combination of which can match it. This traditional problem has a relatively modern solution.

The traditional workaround was a set of

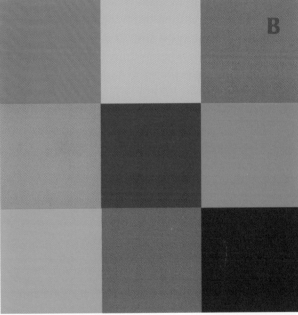

Figure 13.5 Three attempts to emulate PMS colors in CMYK. Top, Photoshop 7 and later versions use Pantone-supplied LAB values, converted to CMYK here by the default settings of Photoshop 6 and later. Middle, the same LAB values converted to CMYK using Photoshop 5's default. Bottom, CMYK values were inserted directly using Pantone-supplied tables (Photoshop 6 and earlier).

PMS 279 $56^L(2)^A(50)^B$
PMS 3385 $77^L(48)^A6^B$
PMS 1655 $63^L61^A75^B$

PMS 1775 $70^L49^A11^B$
PMS 2728 $33^L20^A(69)^B$
PMS 340 $51^L(73)^A13^B$

PMS 361 $62^L(57)^A52^B$
PMS 1787 $58^L70^A28^B$
PMS 2747 $17^L20^A(57)^B$

CMYK "equivalents" that Pantone issued for each of its custom inks. Most graphic arts applications contained a library of these "equivalents"; some still do.

By the turn of the century, the problems with this one-size-fits-all approach had become apparent. The same CMYK values produce different results in different settings. A newspaper, for example, would get darker, muddier colors than this book, which is printed on much higher-quality paper. Furthermore, desktop printers that didn't want a CMYK file at all, but rather an RGB one, were starting to make a dent in the market.

Pantone responded by issuing *real* equivalents to its inks—using LAB. They were introduced in Photoshop 7, in 2002. In previous versions, specifying a PMS color in Photoshop's Color Picker got us the Pantone-supplied CMYK value, plus a LAB value of dubious origin. Since then, we get only the new Pantone LAB value. All CMYK and RGB values are computed from it, using whatever our current color settings are.

Today's method is an improvement, but no magic elixir. When a color can't be matched, it can't be matched.

Take a look at emulations of nine PMS colors, all of which are out of the CMYK gamut. Figure 13.5A uses the post-2002 LAB values, converted to CMYK using the default separation setting of Photoshop 6 and later: the U.S. Web Coated (SWOP) v.2 profile, which was derived from machine measurements of actual printed samples. Figure 13.5B uses the same values, but the default separation method of Photoshop 5, which was put together by human observation and tweaking. And Figure 13.5C was never separated at all. The CMYK values were inserted directly, using the Pantone-supplied numbers of Photoshop 6 and earlier.

Unless you have access to a Pantone swatch book, you won't know which methods worked best. I've got one, and in my opinion,

Figure 13.5C is non-competitive in all nine colors. The current separation method, Figure 13.5A, has a better match in five of the nine colors, but a serious problem, too.

In their custom-ink incarnations, the three reddish colors are all more intense than anything you see here. The pink is lighter and purer. The color that prints as orange in the upper right is more like an angry pink, and the red at bottom center should simply be redder. I rate Figure 13.5A as the closest match in all three.

It also wins in two of the three greens, but not the one at middle right. Photoshop 5 did a better job, because the machine-generated method fell victim to the same problem that made all its blues purple, and made this green too yellow.

Ah, that problem with the blues. If a PMS blue is a key color, converting with the v.2 SWOP profile is likely to get the job rejected. The blues—and that's what they originally are, blues, not purples—are a disaster in Figure 13.5A. In the center swatch (PMS 2728), the cyan ink is 16 points higher than the magenta in Figure 13.5A, but 30 points higher in Figure 13.5B.

The atrocity occurred, I suspect, when software decided that Figure 13.5A's "blue" had a lower dE with respect to the Pantone original than Figure 13.5B's does. And why not? Any sensible dE algorithm is going to give much greater weight to fidelity to the A value than that of the B. The desired numbers are $33^L20^A(69)^B$. That $(69)^B$ is out of the question in CMYK.

Photoshop claims that $33^L20^A(53)^B$ is achievable. A machine will think that that's the best we can do, since it tries to get as close as it can to all three LAB numbers. Lowering the 20^A would, in its small mind, increase dE and therefore be undesirable.

Human graphic artists instinctively know that the A must nevertheless be lowered, because blues that are overly cyan are apt to be much more acceptable to a client than blues that are too purple. So dE goes out the window, and the artist is true to the spirit of the original blue, rather than to its numbers.

Maintaining the Distinction

The problems of converting out of LAB offer instructive points about converting out of anything else.

LAB's problems are more severe because it is capable of constructing colors that are wildly out of the gamut of the next space. However, the solutions are entirely applicable to less onerous conversions. RGB to CMYK is the case that most people think of, but it isn't the only one. Some original LAB values of Figure 13.5 were out of the RGB gamut as well as the CMYK.

Consider what happens when we approach the edge of the gamut. Yellows are a strong point for CMYK and a weak one for RGB, so they're a good example. A value of $94^L0^A90^B$ is fairly extreme. It converts to $0^C4^M81^Y$, or $255^R235^G21^B$. (The LAB "yellow" is actually slightly orange.)

Raise the original value to 91^B, and one point of yellow is added in CMYK. The RGB value also rids itself of some of the contaminating blue, dropping to $255^R235^G10^B$.

Raise it to 92^B, and CMYK adds another point of yellow. The RGB hits $255^R235^G0^B$. It can't get any less blue than that, so when we raise the stakes to 93^B, RGB has no way to call the bet.

As we continue to increase the B, CMYK continues to add yellow, for as long as it can. By the time we get to $94^L0^A99^B$, it's $0^C4^M100^Y$, and now there's no more yellow ink to add. The RGB "equivalent," meanwhile, is still stuck at $255^R235^G0^B$.

Increase the B still further, and nothing happens. Even when we max out at $94^L0^A127^B$, the "equivalents" don't change in either RGB or CMYK.

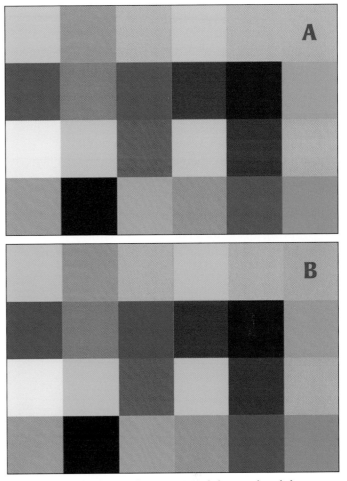

Figure 13.6 All colors in the LAB original that produced these images were within the CMYK gamut. The top version was separated using the default settings of Photoshop CS2, which employ Relative Colorimetric rendering intent. The bottom image's colors are more muted because Perceptual intent, which was previously the default, was used to separate into CMYK.

Therefore, at least 36 yellows that are all different in LAB will convert to the same color in RGB. At least 29 will convert to the same color in CMYK.

Sure, it's possible to preserve all these distinctions. But nobody with any more rationality than Don Quijote would try it. Even 90^B denotes an extremely intense yellow. To save room for 37 even more vivid flavors of yellow would be outlandish. Every yellow in the image would have to be drastically toned down so that these hypothetical brighter yellows could be distinguished from them.

But what if a picture comes along that somehow requires that such distinctions be maintained? Couldn't such a picture exist, and if so, how can we possibly handle it if all the yellows smoosh together during conversion?

If such pictures exist, they're rare. And if the distinctions would be obliterated during the conversion, then if we need them we have to act while still in LAB.

And that, it turns out, is the generalized solution to how to treat out-of-gamut colors during any kind of conversion. Namely, forget them. Just match everything else, and let the weird colors worry about themselves. Unless, of course, distinguishing the weird colors from the rest is a priority. Then, attack them before making the conversion.

This principle may seem obvious when the offending colors are so clearly out of gamut as these are, but it didn't seem that way in the late 1990s, when new capabilities were being engineered into Photoshop's separation algorithm. The theory then was that colors that were barely in gamut should be intentionally toned down, so that any out-of-gamut interlopers would seem brilliant by comparison. This was called *perceptual* rendering, and effective with Photoshop 6, it became the default way of doing things.

In 2005, the error was corrected in Photoshop CS2. Figure 13.6A converts the LAB file using today's defaults. These colors are all fairly bright but all were originally within the CMYK gamut. Therefore, the perceptual method used in Figure 13.6B toned them down, thinking to accommodate any brighter colors that might show up.

Rendering intent is set in Color Settings and can be overridden in Edit: Convert to Profile. The current default, Relative Colorimetric, takes the simple view that all matchable colors should be matched and whatever happens to unmatchable ones is our problem. (An alternative, Absolute Colorimetric, should be avoided. Many RGBs have "white points" that are theoretically not white in CMYK. RelCol remaps them to $0^C0^M0^Y$; AbsCol may turn them blue.)

The perceptual rendering intent, in any case, is too mild to be of any real use. It also is unavailable for conversions into RGB. In the previous example, it would have increased the yellowness

Figure 13.7 This image was prepared for prominent use in an advertising campaign.

more slowly, maxing out at 104^B rather than the 99^B of RelCol. When we deliberately tone down areas that we could have matched if we had wanted to, usually we want to tone them down a lot more than the perceptual intent does.

LAB is the universal interchange standard. We should use it to try to match what we can, in most cases. There are also times when we can use LAB as an insurance policy against the possibility of a bad conversion.

The Knight of the Unambiguous Transfer

"Señor," inquired the goatherd, "who is this man, who dresses in such a way and carries on in such a fashion?"

"Who could it possibly be," replied the barber, "but the celebrated Don Quijote de la Mancha, champion of the weak, redresser of injury, righter of wrongs, the shelter and refuge of damsels, the horror of giants and the victor in battle?"

"That sounds to me," mused the goatherd, "like what you read in books about knights-errant, who do all the things that your grace is telling me this man does, but as far as I'm concerned either your grace is joking, or this gentleman has holes in every corner of his brain."

While I was writing this book during a break in one of my classes, one of the students, a professional photographer, requested help in my capacity as redresser of injury and righter of wrongs, said wrong being that his job was in

jeopardy. He had just prepared Figure 13.7, full of rich browns and dark reds, for a very prestigious placement for his most important client. The printed results had been quite unsatisfactory, he explained—all muddy and lifeless.

I opened his RGB file—noting an alert as I did so—and said that it looked fine to me.

"Wait until you see what the printer did to it," he replied. But before he could bring me a printed sample, I said, "Let me guess. It looked a lot like *this*, right?" And I produced Figure 13.8 on the screen. Bingo.

This sad story has been repeated hundreds of times over the past several years, sometimes with pictures as important as this one is, sometimes not, always intensely frustrating, not just to the victims, but to all rational

Figure 13.8 When the image appeared in print, it looked like this, the result of misinterpretation of the original RGB file.

observers of the graphic arts marketplace, who are tired of watching it happen.

The executive summary of what happened is that the photographer handed off an RGB file tagged as Adobe RGB. The printer did not honor it, and assumed that the file was sRGB, wrecking the job. I'm suggesting that sometimes the photographer should hand off an LAB file, which cannot be misinterpreted.

Inasmuch as repeated episodes like this demonstrate that even many professionals have difficulty grasping the topic, we will take the scenic route through that last paragraph.

In defining a colorspace, everything is a matter of interpretation. For example, when LAB neophytes first see an L channel in isolation, they are often surprised that it appears lighter than a grayscale conversion of the document would be. This happens because the L is *interpreted* as being darker than it appears, for purposes of making a screen preview of the color image, or for converting into CMYK or RGB. You could create a different kind of LAB in which the L didn't behave this way, but you couldn't use it in Photoshop.

In RGB, though, we can use variants that are darker than others, or more colorful. Beginning with Photoshop 5 in 1998, users were encouraged to choose their own definitions of RGB, rather than having a single imposed standard. Its supporters trumpeted this concept as solving more of the world's problems than Don Quijote ever claimed to even want to. But there was one major unforeseen drawback.

Once we choose our own RGB, we needn't worry about the topic again—provided we never send to or receive files from anyone else. We've told Photoshop what "RGB" means, so our own work will be interpreted correctly. Somebody else's work may not be, if they've defined RGB differently and our copy of Photoshop doesn't know it.

That's why, before starting discussion of numbers in Chapter 2, I told you what my own color settings are. If you didn't change your own settings to match mine, then certain of the numbers I talked about would vary somewhat in your system. That would not be a tragedy. It *would* be a tragedy if you took one of my RGB files and output it in a professional context without taking account of how I had defined RGB. Fortunately, there's little chance of that, since I would sooner open a cage full of lions than I would put RGB files in the hands of strangers.

The original concept was that each user embeds a tag into each RGB file, identifying what kind of RGB is in play. The tag is recognized by the next user's system, the file is handled properly, and the knight rides Rocinante off into the sunset.

In practice, this works well among those who know what they're doing. Experienced users throw tagged RGB back and forth all the time without a hitch. Unfortunately, the world at large, and service providers especially, are protagonists in a different picaresque novel. Tagging an RGB file and giving it to a stranger on the assumption that the tag will be honored is a lot like walking into a busy intersection on the assumption that the traffic will stop, except the odds are not nearly as good.

To Run Where the Brave Dare Not Go

The question of which RGB to use is beyond the scope of this book. But how colorful the definition is makes a difference to the current discussion. The more colorful, the higher the probability that we will run into gamut problems such as the ones in Figure 13.5, where the RGB file calls for colors that can't be achieved on output. But if the definition isn't colorful enough, it may not contain colors that you might need. It would be best if the RGB's gamut matched the gamut of the output device exactly, but that can't happen for a variety of technical reasons.

The most prominent of the less colorful

RGBs is sRGB, a definition promoted by Microsoft and Hewlett-Packard in the late 1990s with considerable commercial success. For those who prefer a wider-gamut colorspace, the usual choice is Adobe RGB, although some use even more colorful spaces. Adobe RGB has become somewhat of a standard among professional photographers.

Most consumer devices now prefer or require sRGB. Most service providers now assume that any kind of RGB file coming in is an sRGB one.

A stalemate has been reached. Adoption of sRGB as a consumer standard has grown so much since 1998 that there is now no chance of dislodging it. Furthermore, vendors are less likely now even to consider the possibility that an incoming RGB file is something else. Yet a substantial group hates sRGB so much that they will never agree to use it.

Adobe RGB is quite workable, as is passing an Adobe RGB file to me or anyone else that you know for a fact won't misinterpret it. Throwing an Adobe RGB file out to strangers or to the world at large, tagged or not, is asking for Figure 13.8 to become your problem instead of my student's.

For the record, let's analyze how much color got lost in this critical image. I've measured four areas on the bearded elf, foreground left, and will give equivalencies in both LAB and CMYK.

- His purple cap measures $117^R43^G63^B$. When properly treated as Adobe RGB, it converts to $32^L43^A10^B$, or $32^C94^M64^Y29^K$. When misinterpreted as sRGB, the values are $29^L35^A5^B$ and a dismal $39^C89^M58^Y36^K$.
- A light part of the brown jacket is $165^R115^G80^B$. As Adobe RGB, that's $55^L24^A33^B$ and $24^C48^M75^Y8^K$. As sRGB, $53^L17^A28^B$ and $31^C55^M73^Y12^K$.
- The grass between his legs, $79^R86^G31^B$. As Adobe RGB, $34^L(11)^A32^B$ and $64^C46^M98^Y39^K$. As sRGB, $35^L(9)^A29^B$ and $62^C47^M96^Y39^K$.
- His cheek, $235^R197^G171^B$; Adobe RGB

$84^L16^A21^B$ and $1^C25^M30^Y$; sRGB $82^L11^A18^B$ and $7^C23^M31^Y$.

These readings confirm what our eyes tell us. The misinterpretation has turned an attractive mix of subtle colors into something dishrag dull.

Some people actually enjoy it when this happens. It gives them an opportunity to vent. They can denounce all printers as stupid. They can call up the CSR and scream. They can demand that the job be rerun and threaten to sic their lawyer on them. All this can be psychologically rewarding, and distract attention from others of life's worries.

If you would just as soon have the job done correctly without all the histrionics, and you would otherwise be sending out an Adobe RGB file to a stranger, the options are:

- You can call up the people you expect to handle your work and find out how they intend to behave when confronted with a tagged file. Problem: you may not know who they are.
- You can convert your own file to sRGB before sending it out. This is a more attractive option than it used to be. The chances of sRGB being misinterpreted as something else have gotten less as sRGB has become more entrenched, but they still aren't zero.
- If the file is going to a commercial printer, you can convert it to CMYK yourself. That was why this particular photographer was in my class. He had, understandably, decided that Figure 13.7 was the very last RGB file of his that any commercial printer was ever going to encounter. If you want to try something similar, though, you'd best have confidence in your CMYK skills.
- Finally, the one nearly foolproof method. There are many RGBs, but there's only one LAB. Convert your file before handing it over, and it can't be misinterpreted. That's why Photoshop uses it internally for most of its computations. Getting an LAB file forces the next person to convert to his own RGB or his

Figure 13.9 This two-page advertisement, trumpeting the virtues of LAB, ran in 1996.

own CMYK, eliminating all ambiguity. The worst that can happen is that you get a call in the middle of the night asking what to do with this crazy messed-up file. To that, I say that anyone who can't figure out what to do with an LAB file certainly can't be trusted to figure out what to do with tagged RGB.

Of Children and Colorspaces

This chapter opened with a problem that could be seen as either one of Photoshop technique or one of calibration. The user had two CMYK spot channels and couldn't figure out how to convert them into "real" channels, something that Photoshop doesn't make easy.

Coming up with a solution requires a knowledge both of Photoshop and of why LAB is used for interchange. We first think about how to accomplish the task while staying in CMYK (it can be done, but it's a nuisance). Then, we consider whether LAB can expedite the process, which it can. Hence, the answer: re-create the channels in LAB, just the way Photoshop does when it converts one colorspace to another.

More such hybrid uses of LAB will no doubt suggest themselves as the colorspace becomes more mainstream. Our next chapter, for example, is mostly RGB, but it's heavily LAB-flavored; the two exist side by side.

Other image-processing products have tried to promote the use of LAB, and it isn't a recent phenomenon. Figure 13.9, a double-page advertisement for scanning software, appeared in 1996. The thrust is that LAB is superior to CMYK or RGB, which it is in a lot of ways. Note the claim on the right side: "The human eye uses CIELAB." There's truth in that, too.

The company was so smitten by the LAB connection that it changed the name of its software from LinoColor to VisuaLab. And if you think that "Everything you need to know about color spaces" is a bit of overkill, you should know that the children appear next to the crayons because the theme of the advertising campaign was "Color Is Child's Play." Personally, I would like to lock the person who thought that one up in a room with a copy of Chapters 14 and 15, and see if he still felt that way after reading them.

Contrary to the implication of the advertising, all scanners operate in RGB. In fact, the software's only real connection with LAB was that it converted its raw scans internally to a form of LAB before saving them, just as drum scanners have always converted their RGB data to CMYK before saving. Lino-Color and VisuaLab software offered prescan color correction, but in a relative of LAB, not the real thing.

LinoColor, which was transferred to the German printing giant Heidelberger Druckmaschinen when it purchased Linotype-Hell, is no longer made. But, as it was once common and you may run across some of its files, we should briefly discuss two of its confusingly named colorspaces.

As we've just discussed in relation to my student's disaster, one great advantage is that an LAB file is completely unambiguous; it is the same from one Photoshop user to another. Once we leave Photoshop, however, that is no longer true. There are at least half a dozen variant versions of LAB floating around, one of them in this software. It's called LAB (LH), and is a smaller-gamut version of the LAB we know and love. Granted that Linotype-Hell's client base was heavily CMYK-oriented, the decision made perfect sense. Triple-digit values in the A and B are unprintable. Making an LAB that's closer to the boundaries of CMYK means that all objects fill longer ranges in the A and B and are thus easier to attack with curves, Blending Options, and the like.

LAB is a relative of the colorspace known

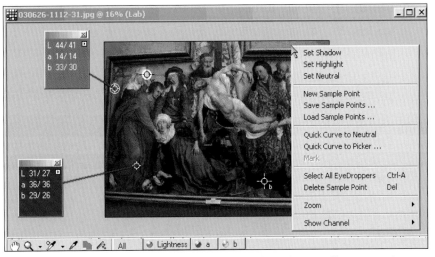

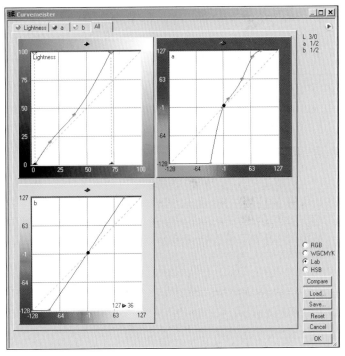

Figure 13.10 *Curvemeister, a Windows-only Photoshop plug-in, offers an LAB interface for RGB files, including the ability to use LAB curves while in RGB.*

as HSB (Hue, Saturation, Brightness; sometimes known, with a slightly different third or Lightness channel, as HSL). Like LAB, LUV, and xyY, color and contrast are kept in separate channels. The color is defined differently, one channel defining the underlying hue and the other its purity. A piece of milk chocolate, a brick, a human face, and a fire engine all have about the same H value, but each rates a higher S than the one before it.

LinoColor/VisuaLab's version of this space is called LCH (Luminance, Chroma, Hue). There are no handling differences.

To Dream the Impossible Dream

Getting back to the present, the most interesting LAB-flavored idea is a Windows-only Photoshop plug-in known as Curvemeister. The idea is to be able to write curves in whatever colorspace you like without necessarily having the file in that colorspace.

Figure 13.10 illustrates. The file itself is in RGB, but much information is available in LAB form. The curves, neatly laid out, can be applied as if the file were LAB, CMYK, or even HSB. We can even generate LAB-style imaginary colors. RGB is the strongest blending space of the four, as we're about to see in the next chapter. But it's generally the weakest for curves.

Note that both of the products we've just discussed have features that are regrettably missing from Photoshop. It would be nice if there were an option for a narrower-gamut LAB, as in LinoColor; it would be very nice indeed if all curves could be displayed simultaneously, as in Curvemeister.

As uses for LAB increase, it's likely that we'll see improvements in how Photoshop has been using it and the addition of capabilities that will enable us to push the envelope even further. That is the practical side of LAB, the side that looks for results, not theory.

As for the impractical, or quixotic side, the side of the academics and amateur theoreticians, the future is bright also, provided we understand that a hundred years from now color scientists will think that we lived in the Stone Age. It *is* possible to program a computer to analyze any image in the way that a human does, and to figure out how a human would compute dE.

Or, rather, it will be possible, because even with today's colossal rate of improvement in computing speeds, it will be a good 50 years and probably more like a century before a machine can calculate something so complex on the fly.

Like today's color scientists, Don Quijote had his heart in the right place; his error was in so believing in his own infallibility that he became ridiculous. However, for all his misadventures, he did do a great deal of good for some of the people he came across, and he serves as an example to the rest of us of the power of trying to do the right thing. Before returning to matters of LAB technique, it's only fair to give him the last word:

"To expect the world to stay the same is a waste of the mental process. Everything goes in circles, I say, in circles; the spring yields to the summer, the summer to the fall, the fall to the winter, and the winter to the spring, and thus the endless circle continues; only the human life comes to an end, sooner than time, without expecting any reprieve but in the next world, which knows no limits."

The Bottom Line

Photoshop permits an infinite number of definitions of RGB and CMYK, but only one of LAB. Its status as the one colorspace within Photoshop that is entirely unambiguous gives LAB a unique role in information interchange. Also, LAB has a stronger direct relation with how humans perceive color than CMYK and RGB do. This offers important advantages in color matching and in reconciling outputs from several different devices.

The extraordinarily large gamut causes certain problems when translating into or out of LAB. Studying how to do it properly offers lessons for other forms of conversion, particularly the translation between RGB and CMYK.

The topic of this chapter does not mesh with the rest of the book, which is less about theory and more about technique. Accordingly, it can be omitted by those not interested in the subject.

14

Once for Color, Once for Contrast

Some LAB advantages are structural. The A and B channels have no counterparts in other colorspaces, so what they do is often impossible to duplicate. But things that *seem* impossible outside of LAB sometimes prove otherwise—provided you separate color from contrast in your mind.

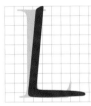anguages, like color, like Photoshop itself, become much easier to learn once you've had even a little experience. Certain concepts are impossibly difficult to fathom at first, but once you understand them, you find other situations to which they apply. As Chapter 13 indicated, LAB is a language all its own, and learning how to master it has a great deal in common with learning how to master, say, the language that Don Quijote spoke to Sancho.

Some linguistic changes make sense even when they are expressed in an unfamiliar way. I am the author, not the reader—or so the thought is rendered in English. Logically, though, the word *I* in the preceding sentence is redundant. The word *am* can only apply to the person doing the speaking. In many languages, Spanish being one, the *I* is optional. *Am the author* is a complete sentence.

The idea that a channel doesn't need to have color is no more difficult to grasp than that a sentence doesn't need to have a pronoun. So, the L channel of LAB is easy to understand, even for someone who's never heard of the colorspace before.

On the other hand, certain concepts are very hard indeed. When trying to learn Spanish, I was confounded by what grammarians call the reflexive verb. The Spanish might say, for example, *Me bought a book today*. As noted, the first word is optional. But granted that they're putting a pronoun there, I could not understand why it should be *me* and not *I*.

The answer came not out of a textbook but from experience. Spanish was my first truly foreign language, but I happen to be fluent in certain dialects that *sound* foreign to other English speakers. I speak mid-century rural Oklahoman; Standard Modern Canadian; the weird noun-equals-verb jargon of 1970s American university students; and the infamous New Jersey dialect. If I were to submit a manuscript in any one of these, the publisher would take me for being, respectively, illiterate, pretentious, incomprehensible, and obscene. So, instead, I write in Standard American (more or less), permitting the reader to take me for being all four at once.

You Ain't Seen Nothin' Yet

How that Spanish sentence makes sense dawned on me suddenly, when I translated it into the only one of my dialects that regularly employs reflexive verbs. The technically correct translation of the sentence, lexicographers of Oklahoman would confirm, is *Ah bought me a book today,* just as I might say, *Ah'm a-fixin' to have me a good ol' time in this here chapter.*

These sentences are considered substandard usage in other parts of the United States, meaning that a bunch of academics who probably couldn't put together a literate sentence themselves have decided to brand anyone who writes that way as a rube, a phenomenon that has an analog in the Photoshop world. But in Spanish, the structure is quite correct. And in Portuguese, Italian, and French, too, which were of course much easier to adjust to once I figured out that Spanish and Oklahoman are similar.

Returning to color, the grammar of LAB is also useful even when speaking a different language. Many LAB techniques work almost unaltered in HSB, which is as close to LAB as Italian is to Spanish. Between LAB and both RGB and CMYK, which are really two dialects of the same language, not so much is shared—except for the topic of this chapter.

The thing that seems most foreign about LAB was mentioned on the very first page of this book. It separates color from contrast. If you have mostly worked hitherto in RGB or CMYK, you probably have rarely tried this. But you can, and it's very powerful.

Only those who are paid by the hour are interested in spending more time than is necessary correcting or retouching an image. If color and contrast need to be treated separately, there's no problem in LAB, which treats them as distinct entities from the very beginning. If we decide to separate color from contrast in RGB or CMYK, we have to do at least some work twice and then merge it together.

This can happen in several ways. Suppose, for example, that you are impressed by some of the color variation that LAB curves created in one of the examples in Chapter 12, but you have a hunch that you could have gotten better detail by doing the work in RGB.

No problem—start with two fresh RGB copies of the image. Convert one to LAB and do what was done in Chapter 12. Return to the RGB copy and do it the way that you think creates extra detail. When finished, convert it to LAB, and use its L channel to replace the one in the other file. Presto: color done in LAB, detail created in RGB. The power of this method derives from being able to work in RGB while paying absolutely no attention to color. You can make your skintones green and your skies orange if you like, or even make the entire RGB image black and white. If the color is going to be replaced later, it doesn't matter what it is right now.

We can even speak a variant of the LAB language without ever being in LAB at all. In RGB, we can create one version for color and one for contrast, and then paste one onto the other, creating a new layer. If the version with better detail is on top, we set the layer to Luminosity mode; if the version with good color is on top, Color mode.

This chapter looks for places where RGB has such an advantage that it would pay to take the extra time to do a contrast-only or color-only version there rather than use LAB. As this could be a book-length topic by itself, we will be heavy on theory and light on step-by-step examples. We will divide the subject into four sections: when to use RGB for contrast in preference to LAB using standard methods such as curves; when to use RGB curves for color only; followed by two more variants using channel blending, a topic that we haven't addressed so far but will be featured in the next two chapters as well as this one. We won't be considering CMYK, because for technical reasons that we need not get into, RGB has decided advantages over its linguistic playmate for this kind of work.

We begin by discussing not a word, English or foreign, but rather a single letter—the *S*.

Detail, Range, and a Letterform

Most images have one or more areas of particular interest, areas that are so important that we are willing to sacrifice elsewhere if we can get more detail.

The theory is simple, the execution complex. Find the lightest and darkest points of the object, and spread them apart. Curves are the usual method, but anything that increases the tonal range will work. In curve language, we say, *the steeper the curve, the more the contrast.* Objects found in relatively steep areas of curves gain contrast; those found in relatively flat ones lose out.

That's a considerably more complex definition than the one most manufacturers and many retouchers use. Their idea of "adding contrast" is adding *midtone* contrast at the expense of the lightest and darkest areas. This is what happens when you increase "contrast" on your monitor's controls, or on your television set, or when you use Photoshop's primitive Image: Adjustments>Brightness/Contrast command.

Sometimes this blunderbuss method of adding contrast obliterates all variation in extreme lights and darks; more sophisticated variants simply reduce it in the interest of promoting more range in the midtones.

When expressed as a curve, the top and bottom sections are relatively flat and the interior part is steeper. It resembles the letter *S*, and is commonly known as an *S curve*.

S curves are not appropriate for every image, only those where we wish to add contrast to the midrange. I've illustrated this concept elsewhere with pictures of white, black, and gray cats. Apply an S curve to a white or black cat, and it yowls. Only a gray cat will purr when we stroke it with an S.

To add contrast to a white cat, we hold the lightest point constant (since we can't make it lighter than the white it already is) and darken its darkest point, which is usually around a quarter of the way up the curve, in the area that retouchers, logically, call the *quartertone*. The procedure is reversed with a black cat. The darkest point is held, and the *three-quartertone* point gets lightened.

We can't control what kind of cat we're given, but ef ah had mah druthers (that's Oklahoman), ah druther that it was a gray cat, because we're more likely to get away with drastic moves. If the cat is white, the curve we need to use darkens the entire image, which may or may not be acceptable. If the cat is black, the whole image has to get lighter, ditto. But if it's gray, and we apply an S curve, the overall darkness of the image will seem about the same—it's just that more detail will go to the cat.

S curves aren't always the answer, but they're great things when they are.

In LAB, the only way to add contrast is in the L channel, so we can temporarily forget about what's going on in the A and B. And, to save you the trouble of reviewing 13 chapters of examples, I will tell you that not only have the large majority of curves we've applied to the L channel been shaped like an S, but the percentage is much higher than if we had been working in RGB.

Let me get to the bottom line first and explain why afterward: if your work features relatively bright, pure colors, the L channel is where you should try to add contrast. If it has mostly dull colors, and you're determined to squeeze as much detail as you can out of the image, RGB is a better bet. For augmenting dull colors, of course, you'd then go to LAB.

If the picture is of rubies or emeralds, in other words, add contrast in the L. If the picture is of a human face or a forest (which are the same colors as those found in rubies and emeralds, just duller) then RGB offers more opportunities.

When to Do the Averaging

When an image is converted from RGB to LAB, Photoshop creates the L channel out of a weighted average of the RGB channels, assigning roughly 60 percent weight to the green, 30 to the red, and 10 to the blue. It then lightens the result, as discussed in Chapter 2.

If we decide to work in RGB, then we are in effect correcting now and averaging later. If we work in LAB, we average first and correct later. That's why the L channel is so apt to

accept an S curve: it averages out areas that are very light in some RGB channels and very dark in others. Those areas land in the middle of the L's tonal range.

When bright colors are present, that's a real advantage. We saw why way back in Figure 7.5, where we worked on a bright magenta flower. In RGB, the green channel was like a black cat, and the red and blue were like white cats. No S curve was possible in any of them. But when the file was converted to LAB, these whites and blacks were averaged, making the cat a gray one. The S curve became appropriate, and LAB was the most attractive way to work the image.

Figure 14.1 has the preponderance of a single color that normally suggests steepening the AB curves. But what of the contrast issue? We could use more of it in the water. The normal way, steepening the L channel in the water's range, will certainly work. But if you are determined to extract as much as possible, the RGB channels may work even better. Let's have a look.

An extremely blue sea would be nearly blank in the blue channel, and nearly solid in the red. Neither could be attacked with an S curve. But, as Figure 14.2 shows, that's not the case here. Each of the three curves (note: in keeping with all the other examples

Figure 14.1 *The dominant colors of this image are not particularly pure, implying that they fall in the midrange of all three RGB channels.*

Red

Green

Blue

L

Figure 14.2 The red, green, and blue channels of RGB each offer a more promising start than the L of LAB.

shown in this book, the dark ends of the curves are on the right, which is not the RGB default) has the desired S shape, with the water falling in the steep part of the S. As the red is the darkest of the three channels, its steepest area is farther to the right than in either of the other two. The water is basically cyan, around midway between green and blue, so those two channels resemble one another, although the green is slightly lighter in the water and darker in the sky.

When an LAB file is generated from the RGB original, the L channel resembles the green. In this image, however, it's more diffi-

cult to manage, because its sky and water are closer together. If the lightest part of water is made too light, the sky may vanish. If the darkest part is made too dark, the shadow areas on the cliff may plug.

That's not to say that improvement can't be made. Figure 14.3B shows what can be done with a mild S curve to the L channel. But we can't achieve the steepness of the RGB curves.

Figure 14.3A, the result of those curves, has developed the sort of disagreeable

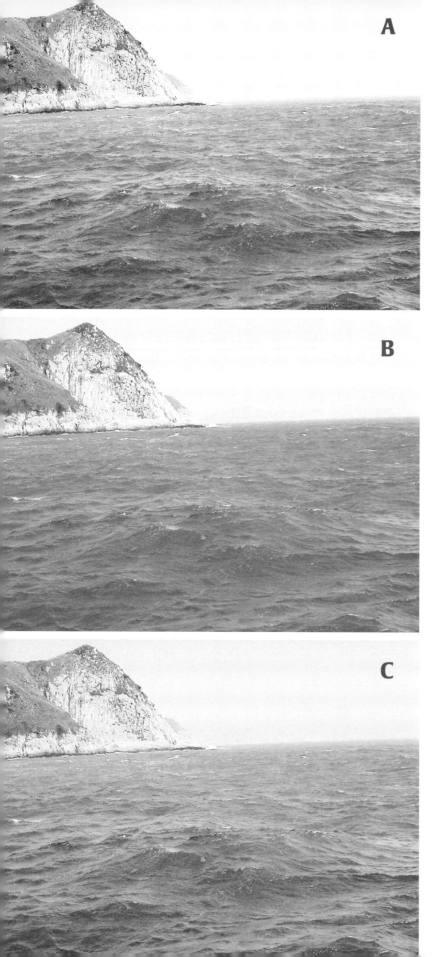

coloring that discourages people from correcting in RGB. But if you have already separated color from contrast in your mind, then you know that this bad color doesn't matter, as the original color can be restored without sacrificing this enhanced detail. If you wish to do so without leaving RGB, then the curves need to be applied to a separate layer or adjustment layer, with mode set to Luminosity.

Here, though, we don't want to stay in RGB, because, having established detail, we would like to create color variation in LAB. Therefore, we convert Figure 14.3A to LAB and substitute its L channel for that of Figure 14.3B, which can be done in several ways. For example, with both LAB images open, you could select only the L of Figure 14.3B, and then Image: Apply Image, using the L of Figure 14.3A as the source, Normal mode, 100% opacity. Doing this or something equivalent results in Figure 14.3C, and from there on it should be pretty routine. In sharpening the new L channel, since there are no hard edges anywhere in the water, I used the high Radius, low Amount method described in Chapter 5.

Then, I used AB curves to break the water's colors apart. I had to do this by neutralizing the duller colors and augmenting the brighter ones only slightly, using curves in

Figure 14.3 *Top, the strangely colored result of applying the RGB curves shown in Figure 14.2. Center, an alternate attempt to add contrast in LAB by steepening the L curve. Bottom, a combined version, in which the L channel of the center version is replaced by one from a copy of the top version that was converted to LAB.*

the style of Chapter 12. If I had used straight-line AB curves, I would have driven parts of the water out of the CMYK gamut, which would have harmed the detail I was trying to enhance.

The final result is Figure 14.4.

Older Yes, Wiser Maybe

The opposite situation—using RGB for at least some of the color adjustments and LAB for contrast—is somewhat more frequent, but usually not as dramatic.

LAB and RGB handle detail somewhat differently, as we just saw. But the techniques are basically the same; the same shapes of curves work in both. Sometimes it's better to work in the L (if there are a lot of bright colors), and sometimes it's better to work in RGB, as it was in our last example, but most of the time either one will do the job. But we often find it more convenient to do the work in the L, because we're in LAB anyway.

And the reason we're in LAB is because of how it defines color, not contrast. The AB channel structure is so different from that of RGB that each has strengths that the other doesn't duplicate. The spectacular cases—the ones where we drive colors apart to create massive color variations, or where we completely change

the color of objects as we did in Chapter 10—work better in LAB. But LAB isn't subtle. Slight color changes to achieve a particular shade, or to eliminate a cast that only exists at certain levels of darkness, can be accomplished better in RGB.

In 1994, when I wrote the first edition of *Professional Photoshop,* I had already begun to experiment with LAB but was a long way from knowing what I was doing. It was a CMYK age, because most professional work was drum-scanned directly into CMYK, and almost all output was CMYK also, as serious desktop printers did not exist.

Eight years later, I had the inspiration to show myself up, by selecting half a dozen corrected images from that book and publishing better ones based on heavy use of LAB, while making critical comments about how ham-handed the first versions were.

It was a chastening experience. By and large, I could not make the 1994 images better than I had by doing them in CMYK. Scratch some of my better-planned insults.

Figure 14.4 A final version, applying high Radius, low Amount sharpening to the L channel, and steepening the AB curves to emphasize differences between the water and the sky.

In fairness, things were quite different back then. It was very expensive to scan and correct color images. People weren't inclined to waste money trying to resurrect garbage. CMYK's weak point is that it doesn't make big moves as well as RGB and LAB do—but in 1994, there weren't that many big moves to be made.

The exception, the one image where the 1994 correction seems really lame in comparison to what's possible now, was, as you can guess, a bad original. Inasmuch as digital photography was in its infancy, this image was scanned from film, not on a drum scanner but rather on a device that did not do the auto-range and color-balancing that is common in today's digicams.

The starting point is Figure 14.5A. The yellow cast is obvious. What might not be so obvious is that it shouldn't be knocked out in LAB—even though an LAB file was what this particular scanner delivered.

The numbers: the lightest area of cloud is $93^L(4)^A19^B$, very yellow. As the clouds get darker, they become slightly less yellow, checking in at $60^L(1)^A8^B$ just above the tree-line. And the trees themselves are horrible: around $27^L3^A17^B$: an orange-yellow, not a green at all. As for the water, we really don't know whether it is supposed to be blue, cyan, or even green, so we can't use it as a guide.

Casts that vary as the image gets darker, as this yellow one does, aren't handled well in LAB. The better way is to convert to RGB and kill the cast there. Figures 14.5B and 14.5C

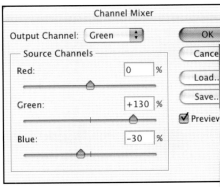

Figure 14.6 *With the curves shown followed by a touch of the Channel Mixer command (above), Figure 14.5A is transformed into the version at top right. Below, a competing LAB version falls short. Adjusting the A and B channels whitens the clouds but makes the overall scene too blue.*

show the critical green and blue channels, respectively.

Clouds should be roughly neutral: white at their lightest point, gradually taking on the color of the sky as they get darker. In RGB, neutrality is produced by approximately equal values in all three channels. (This doesn't work in CMYK!) The same highlight point we looked at in LAB measures $238^R237^G198^B$. The

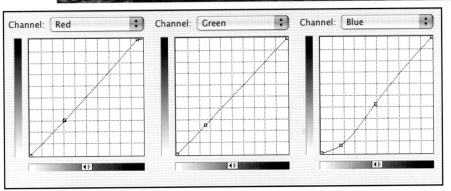

blue channel, therefore, is too dark, although as the image itself gets heavier, the issue with the blue becomes less severe.

I took two steps to change the color in RGB. First, the curves shown in Figure 14.6 removed the cast by lightening the blue channel while applying infinitesimal adjustments to the red and green. Next, while I admit that in reality this greenery is probably a rather dull color, lots of experiments have shown that viewers prefer a greener look in similar images.

An unusual application of the Image: Adjustments>Channel Mixer command in RGB can help, provided that we start with a blue channel that, like Figure 14.5C, is dark and lacking in detail in the green areas.

An area that isn't green enough implies that the green channel is too heavy. This green channel probably is about as dark as the red, although both are much lighter than the blue.

The Channel Mixer trick is to make a new green channel that contains *more than 100%* of the old green one, and to compensate by subtracting an equal percentage of the blue.

In simpler words: on opening the Channel Mixer, each channel consists of 100% of itself and 0% of each of the others. The usual procedure is to reduce the dominant percentage and add some of the other channels to compensate, but here I'm suggesting the opposite: putting in a value of, say, 130% for the green, and –30% for the blue.

Multiplying all green values by 1.3 (which is what the first half is doing) lightens the entire green channel, because in RGB, the higher the value, the lighter. And so the image gets a green cast overall. If, for the sake of argument, the trees started at 100^G and part of the clouds at 180^G, they change to 130^G and 234^G, respectively.

The second step, subtracting the blue, moves the image back toward where it

Figure 14.7 *Above, a final correction in LAB. Below, a version corrected in CMYK, as it appeared in a 1994 textbook.*

came from—in certain areas. Suppose that in the blue channel, the trees started at 10^B and the clouds at 180^B. We subtract .3 of these values from the new green. The trees now become 127^G (100^G original, plus 30^G by multiplying the green by 130%, minus 3^G by subtracting 30% of the blue). The new value for the clouds, however, is the same as the old one: 180+54−54=180. That's why the curves had to be applied prior to the Channel Mixer step. Before the curves, the clouds weren't equal in the green and blue channels, so the Channel Mixer move would not cancel itself out.

We are now at Figure 14.6A. In LAB, Channel Mixer doesn't work at all, and curves that vary in intensity with darkness only work if there's a mask. Without either, the best AB-only alternative I could come up with was Figure 14.6B. It neutralizes the clouds, but overall seems disagreeably more blue than Figure 14.6A.

Our last two exercises have both been ocean scenes. You might think that since RGB produced better luminosity results when Figure 14.1 was the original, it might do so again here. It doesn't. The sky is bluer and the water darker here. There's less difference between water and sky. Both can be attacked more efficiently in the L than was the case in the image with the lighter water.

Figure 14.7A, then, is a final version. It uses Figure 14.6A as a start point with contrast enhanced in the L and further color variation added in the A and B. Figure 14.7B, I state with some embarrassment, is what I represented as a good correction in 1994.

That, however, is par for the course in learning about color. Making the image look better than the original—and Figure 14.7B, for all its faults, is better than Figure 14.5A—is the easy part. The hard part is imagining how much better it might be. That's where LAB comes in, and, I hope, where this book comes in as well.

Finding the Right RGB Channel

Mastery of these techniques comes with the realization that in an exercise like Figure 14.1, since all the color changes came later in the AB, we were really treating the RGB channels as three separate L channels, and then averaging them together to obtain just one.

In Figure 14.1, that made a certain amount of sense, because all three channels had something to offer—a phenomenon that isn't always true. When one or two of the RGB channels don't pull their weight, there's a case to be made for not averaging them at all.

When might such a thing happen? Of course, it depends on the image. Without knowing what it's a picture of, the only possible recommendation is to look at each channel and see what's up. However, in three important categories, we can predict where the good channels are going to be.

● In normally lit portraits and other images involving skintone, the green channel is ordinarily better than the other two.

● In areas featuring natural greenery, meaning anything that grows, the blue channel is usually pretty bad, as it was in the green parts of Figure 14.5C. We don't know which will be the better of the remaining two, but the quality difference may be large.

● Figure 14.7 owes a lot of success as a photograph to its powerful sky. Unfortunately, the photographer can't utter magic words that produce such skies, and often has to work with considerably more subdued original art. Building a better sky is no particular problem—provided you know that skies are always best in the red channel. Let's see how it's done.

In Figure 14.8, the dome of St. Peter's starts out too dark. Any attempt to lighten it is likely to take what little there is of the sky with it. A look at the RGB channels reveals what we already know, that the sky is best in the red—which can, therefore, be used to beef up the other two, as long as you understand

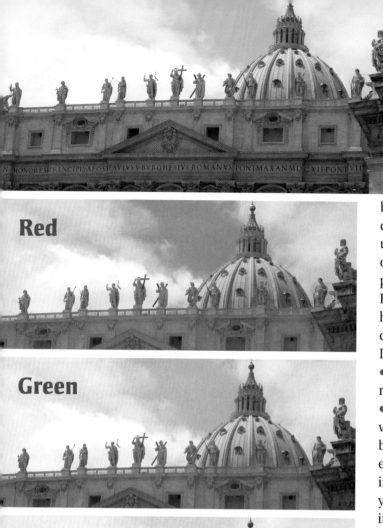

Red

Green

Blue

Figure 14.8 Skies are strongest in the red channel, which can be used for later blending.

three are always equal, and equal RGB values make a gray. But that isn't what we want, so don't click OK.

• Change the Apply Image blending mode to Darken, which disallows the blend except where the blending channel is darker than what's underneath. Here, as Figure 14.8 indicates, the red channel is darker only in the sky, which is therefore the only part that gets replaced. We have now reached Figure 14.9A. The sky is gray because the red has replaced the other two channels, producing the equal values that make neutrality. Little if anything has happened elsewhere.

• Change the layer mode to Luminosity, restoring the original blue.

• If color quality is critical, convert to LAB without flattening the image. The blues will be slightly truer in the end, due to the presence of some imaginary colors, as discussed in Chapter 9. We are now at Figure 14.9B. If you are determined to flatten while remaining in RGB, it's not a big deal.

In the real world, the fun would now begin as we started adding detail and color variation. The point, however, was to show how pre-blending can add weight to skies—and other areas—before the LAB attack commences. These blends can make a difference even when working on a shot of a canyon.

The Language of Layers

For those who enjoy driving an SUV across rivers without the benefit of a bridge, and who are undeterred by the thought of spending a chilly unscheduled night in the outdoors if the few drops of rain that suffice to make the roads impassable materialize, the Cathedral Valley region of Capitol Reef National Park has a great deal of natural beauty to offer.

Like all our other canyon images, Figure 14.10A falls in a narrow range, inviting the

blending modes and are willing to put color considerations on the back burner as you produce, in effect, a new L channel. Here are the steps:

• Create a duplicate layer.

• Image: Apply Image. As we have not selected any particular channel, the entire image is targeted. Choose the red channel as the source. If blending mode is Normal, the preview shows a grayscale image, because all three channels have been replaced by a copy of the red; therefore, the values of all

Figure 14.9 *Top, on a new layer the red channel is blended into the entire picture in Darken mode, in effect converting the sky into grayscale. Bottom, the layer mode is changed to Luminosity, picking up the original color while retaining the heavier sky.*

use of LAB. Unlike most of the others, we're interested in specific colors. The marbling pattern of red and more neutral rock needs to be accentuated. This calls for the Command–click approach of Chapter 12, rather than just steepening the curves overall.

First things first, however. The sky is so weak that it may disappear when we apply an S curve to the L channel. So, we should plan on repeating the RGB move we just saw. But looking at the channels suggests not one preliminary blend, but two.

The red channel, as we know, has the best sky. In the canyon area, however, it's light, almost washed out. The green channel is better, and it's also better than the blue.

When one channel is clearly better than the other two, why average the poor ones into the mix at all? Trash them, derail them, constrain and confound them! Sticking a copy of the good channel into each of the bad ones will make the image grayscale, but so what? The color will be restored later.

If this were a shot of a face—which is the same hue as this canyon—in all likelihood the green would be the best channel, period. Here, it's only best in the foreground; the red is better in the background. Fortunately, the two can be combined easily.

First comes a duplicate layer. I applied the green channel to create a grayscale version, and then switched layer mode to Luminosity,

restoring the original color and arriving at Figure 14.10B. The rocks have gotten better, the sky worse.

Next, I duplicated the top layer. To this third layer, I applied the red channel in Darken mode as with the previous picture. In doing so, I had to be careful to change the Apply Image command's default, which is to use a merged copy of all lower layers as the blend source. I had to specify that the blend was to be made from the red channel on the *bottom* layer, because the middle layer had lightened the sky. The layer blending mode was again Luminosity.

That helped, but I felt that the sky still

A

Red   Green   Blue

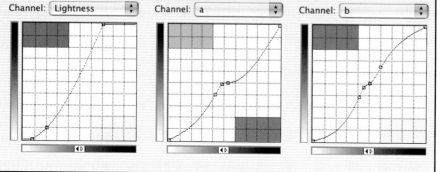

Figure 14.10 This page: the original and its RGB channels. Opposite page: top, on a new layer, the green channel is applied in Luminosity mode. Middle, on third and fourth layers, the original red is applied twice in Darken mode. Bottom, after conversion to LAB and application of the curves at left.

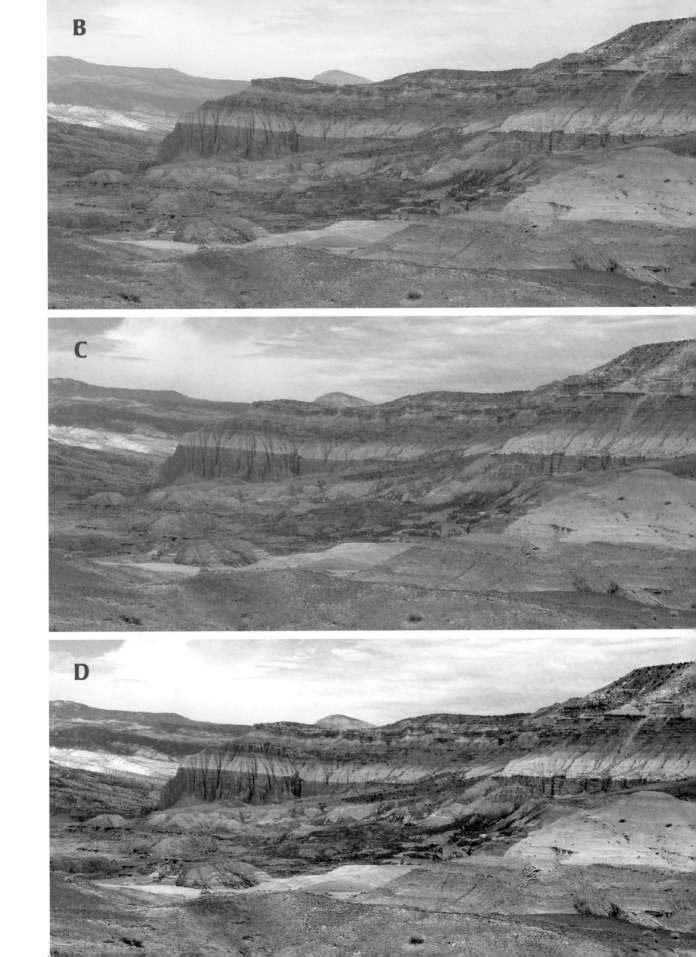

wasn't dark enough. So, I duplicated the top (third) layer, and to this fourth layer I applied the red in Darken mode again. This time, however, I used the default setting, applying the red from a merged copy of the bottom three layers. After verifying that the mode for the top layer was still Luminosity, I reduced opacity to 50%, as I felt the sky had gotten too dark. I had now arrived at Figure 14.10C.

I then converted to LAB, without flattening the file first, to permit the superior LAB method of computing color blends.

Finally, I added a curves adjustment layer, making five layers in all. Into each of the A and B curves, I Command–clicked four points: the reddish parts of the rock, the more subdued reds of the marbling, the white areas of the clouds, and the sky. The curves were like those applied to the printing facility of Figure 12.5: areas that were almost neutral were pushed toward gray; the colorful areas of both sky and rock were made even more vivid.

Channel blending to enhance only the contrast is quite a powerful tool. Figure 14.10D looks like an entirely different shot than the original, Figure 14.10A. Channel blending to adjust only color is less common, but when you see a picture with a major cast, a blend is likely the best preliminary step, as our next exercise will show.

Better Color Through Better Gray

Several times in this chapter, notably in the sky images, we have flirted with the idea of temporarily moving in the direction of a black and white image in the interest of better contrast. Moving toward black and white is, paradoxically, also sometimes a way of improving color.

Gray balance is an old printing term that describes a form of process control. The printer finds out what combinations of cyan, magenta, and yellow inks produce a neutral gray. Experimentation is needed, because equal values in CMY don't make gray, as they do in RGB. Usually, a lot more cyan and a little less yellow does the trick. But whatever the formula, once it's found the printer tries to ensure that future jobs stick to it. Impure inks, dirty press conditions, excessive dot gain, incorrect solid ink densities, and a foul disposition on the part of

Figure 14.11 *The original, near right, is too light and has a yellow cast. Opposite left, the cast is attacked in RGB by blending the red channel into the blue. Center, weight is increased by blending the blue into the composite image in Luminosity mode. Right, the image is finalized with LAB curves.*

the pressman are some of the technical factors that can throw gray balance off. When that happens, the reproduction acquires a cast that wasn't in the original file and the printer explains to the client how it was all the photographer's fault.

Similar problems can appear earlier in the process, possibly in the original photograph, possibly as a result of what we do to it in Photoshop. The good news is that it's easier to diagnose in RGB, because of the simple rule that equal values make a gray, as opposed to the lawless world of CMYK. The bad news is that getting the grays right can be more difficult for us than for the printers. It's customary for printers to measure and control gray balance, but there are alternatives: they could set up known swatches of various color combinations and measure them instead. The only reason they don't is that it's less intuitive.

We don't usually have such an option ourselves, because grays are frequently the only things we can really rely on. Figure 14.11A is too yellow, but by how much? We have ideas of what colors the wood, the face, and the flowers should be, but not nearly precise enough ones to hang our surplice on them. The only colors we know for sure are those of the priest's hair and some areas of his vestments. They should be neutral.

Ordinarily I would show the channels now, but at this point you should be able to tell what they're like without looking at them. A red, green, or blue cast means that the channel of that name is too light in comparison to its two siblings. A cast of an intermediate color indicates that one channel is too dark. If the red is the culprit, the cast is blue-green (cyan). When the green is too dark, the image gets a purple cast, and an overweight blue produces an inappropriately heavy yellow.

We could attack the yellow cast in this image in any colorspace, but since we know, even without looking, that the blue channel is currently too dark, there's a painless way to make the subsequent steps easier: blend one of the other channels into it.

Whatever kind of blend we use will help the neutral areas, because they're supposed to have equal RGB values. If they currently

Review and Exercises

✓ Suppose you like the Channel Mixer move that made the greenery in Figure 14.6A more intense, and decide that you would like to use it to make the ocean in Figure 14.1 greener. Why wouldn't it work? (Hint: check the channel structure in Figure 14.2.)

✓ Find a normally lit RGB file of a person's face. Be sure that the individual is not wearing strong red and that there is no strong red in the background. Make a duplicate layer, and, with all channels open, use Image: Apply Image, Normal mode, 100% opacity, using the green channel as the source of the blend. Now change the mode of the new layer to Luminosity. You should see a significant gain in depth and a more lifelike face.

✓ In the above example, what would have gone wrong if the model had in fact been wearing strong red? How would you modify the procedure to avoid the problem?

✓ Have a look back at Figure 7.13, an interior shot with a serious yellow cast and lots of wood. What is the RGB blend that might have made the color adjustment easier if it had been done before moving the image into LAB?

have them, a blend won't change things. If not, the blend by definition will bring them closer. Thus, the blend isn't troubled by neutrals that are wrong at some darknesses and right elsewhere.

Red objects are more common than any other kind. Any such object needs to be lighter in the red channel than the other two, but it should have roughly similar values in the green and blue. Blending the green channel into the blue is usually the best way to cut down a yellow cast. It brings closer together not only the neutral areas, but also the reds.

Not here, though. The green channel is much lighter than the blue in the priest's green chasuble, which plays a big role in the image. If he were wearing some other color, I'd use the green for the blend. As matters stand, I'll go for the red channel.

To get Figure 14.11B, therefore, I created a new layer and used the Apply Image command to blend the red into the blue, picking 32% opacity out of a hat. I used Lighten mode, which restricts the blend to areas in which the red in fact starts out lighter than the blue. Here, that comprises the entire image, so Normal mode would have done the same thing. But we certainly wouldn't want to darken the yellow in some hypothetically bright blue or cyan object, so being in Lighten mode is good practice.

With washed-out originals like this one, if you do a lightening blend to try to regularize the color, usually you should set the layer blending mode to Color, meaning that Photoshop is to pick up the detail from the bottom layer and use the top one for color only. I didn't do that, because I needed a lighter layer for the next move.

The biggest issue I have with the original is that the face scarcely exists. The whole picture needs to get darker to make any kind of credible fix. I don't mind if the flowers or the rear wall lose a little color in the process, because I think the priest is the focus.

Curving the L channel would help, but we should try to engineer extra weight into the picture first. We've done it earlier with skies; now we'll do it with the entire image.

As pointed out earlier, in faces that are normally lit, the green channel is almost always the best. This image is not normally lit. The face is much lighter than it should be, so the rule doesn't apply, any more than it would if the face were in shadow.

I made a third layer by duplicating the second, and applied the blue channel, accepting the default choice of the blue from a merged version of the bottom two layers. Choosing the bottom layer would have been a mistake, because its blue was so dark that it didn't carry detail in the green chasuble. Once lightened with the first blend, it became more usable for the second. I chose 60% opacity and, of course, Luminosity mode. That's Figure 14.11C. Then into LAB, being sure to flatten the image only after the conversion was complete, and you know the rest of the drill. Figure 14.11D is the final version.

A Vote for Fluency

This picture is not of an actual church ceremony. Rather, the priest is posing for a professional photographer using top-notch equipment. Everything is as controlled as it can be, except that it would take either divine intervention or a good knowledge of the LAB language to compensate for the ambient lighting. According to the photographer, this scene featured not just a mix of fluorescent and incandescent lighting, but also floodlights of two different colors.

In short, the picture is a tougher customer than it looks, because it's full of casts and counter-casts that are disguised by overall lightness. Yet two blends that together took less than a minute sufficed to get it on the right track. Figure 14.11C may not be attractive itself, but it's easy to fix in LAB. The original, Figure 14.11A, is another story.

The secret is to think in the foreign language of LAB even while speaking the RGB idiom. Like a new language, you have to speak it slowly at first. We've only done four images in the course of a 20-page chapter. With practice, it becomes very fast.

And, like a foreign tongue, knowing a few phrases and grammatical constructions gives only a little hint of how rich and rewarding the fully realized language can be. By necessity, this is a brief overview. We had space for only one example of each of the four major categories: using RGB curves first to change contrast only and then to change color only; and then using RGB channel blending in the same two ways. These techniques interact with one another (and with LAB correction generally) in a bewildering variety of ways.

In deciding when to use them, remember that certain things work about the same in RGB and LAB, and other things are quite different. Those radical differences are the ones you have to cater to. Trying to create extra detail with curves or some similar command may work slightly better in one colorspace or another, but you'll be able to fake it elsewhere if you have to.

The color-busting capabilities of the A and B channels, though, can't readily be faked in RGB. And the ability to use a particularly good RGB channel to strengthen an image can't be faked in LAB.

Accordingly, three final pieces of advice. First, when you open a new RGB file, start by checking out the channels to see if blending is indicated. If you don't, you may be passing up an opportunity that won't be available later.

Second, if you have decided to work on the color in RGB, just try to eliminate the impossible. Don't worry if the image temporarily looks too dull. LAB can give you far more color than you'll ever need.

A picture does not live up to its full potential unless both contrast and color are all they can be. Keep the two concepts separate in your mind, and you're well on the way to getting them to that happy point.

The Bottom Line

LAB's signature is the separation of color from contrast. It sometimes pays to do the same thing in RGB: to prepare one version to be used for detail only, and another to be used only for color. Most of the time, doing so adds several steps and doesn't deliver as good quality as LAB would.

There are, however, exceptions, where it's worth the extra time to do some of the contrast-only or color-only work in RGB. Particularly, blending of RGB channels can produce certain effects that LAB can't. This chapter discusses how to identify the situations where RGB work in the LAB style can create better results than LAB itself can.

Blending With the A and B

The final major use of LAB is as powerful as it is counterintuitive—using the A and B channels, which contain no detail, to blend into the L, which does. It's a radical way to separate objects out for treatment based on their color, and it's also the easiest way to experiment if you're not sure how much more color an image needs.

Ambitious chefs, like aspiring Photoshop authors, think they have to demonstrate their creativity by coming up with dishes that nobody has ever seen before. In both cases, the tricks can be carried to ridiculous extremes. Some years ago, it was fashionable for restaurants to marry up the most ridiculous pairs (or ménages à trois) of ingredients that they could dream up. I've had the dubious pleasure of eating liver with blueberry sauce; osetra caviar with wasabi on a tortilla; and, most recently, sausage ice cream.

None of these combinations sounds even a fraction as ridiculous as the one that's the subject of this chapter. We have just spent 300 pages emphasizing that the A and B channels contain no contrast information, only color; that they can never be portrayed as white, black, or anything even close because those would represent imaginary colors; that any detail that shows up in them is probably a defect that needs to be blurred away; and that they are, in short, dull, gray blurs.

Blending such monstrosities into a contrast-bearing channel like the L sounds roughly as appetizing as mixing 25-year-old Macallan with Diet Coke. Figure 15.1A is the original. Figure 15.1B shows what happens when you try replacing the L with a copy of the A. In Figure 15.1C, the L is replaced by a copy of the B. To make these nearly contrast-free versions, with the L channel open I chose Image: Apply Image, Normal mode, 100% opacity, with the A designated as source for one and the B for the other.

Nauseating enough, but check out what comes next. In Figures 15.1D through 15.1G, still at 100% opacity, I changed the blending mode to Overlay. In two of these four variants, I also checked the Invert box in the Apply Image dialog.

Figure 15.1 Left, the original. Bottom left, its L channel is replaced by a copy of the A, and bottom right by the B. Opposite page: four images, in a random order, show blends of the A or B into the L not in Normal but in Overlay mode. In two of the versions, the A or B was inverted during the blend; the other two are standard overlays. The A and B themselves never changed in any of the seven images, so the colors should always be the same. All variation is in darkness. Can you pick out the images made with overlays of the A, the B, the inverted A, and the inverted B? (Hint: refer to the two images below to see how darkness is being allocated in the A and B channels.)

Before discussing how such a weird concept works, let's first admit that something quite significant, and potentially quite useful, is happening, and it's something that would be difficult to achieve outside of LAB.

When Zero Equals Fifty Percent

We saw in Chapter 9 how selections and masks that would be too complex to make in RGB can often be found easily in LAB. And so it is here. The sky, the lake, the man's face, and the greenery are each clearly defined in both the A and B—but not in any RGB channel. Even if they were, we couldn't make the kind of mask that the special purposes of this chapter require, for three reasons:

• In RGB, the man's jacket, pants, and hair are three different tonalities in each channel, and would have to be selected out manually

where they intersect the greenery. In the A and B, all three objects are the same because all are neutral, and they break away from the colorful background naturally.

• Nor can you base a selection of the greenery on any of the RGB channels. The darkest, most neutral areas would be inseparable from the darkest greens. They would also be more selected than brighter greens. That's the opposite of what's needed, and the opposite of the way the A and B channels do things.

• Even if you could make the selections in RGB, you still couldn't use them for the types of trickery shown in this chapter. Those tricks require that neutral colors fall in the center of the blending channel—that is, values of 0^A or 0^B—whereas in RGB channels neutrals fall wherever they like.

The type of blending we're about to discuss

offers extraordinary flexibility to remake the image by adjusting the darkness of important objects. It can, in effect, completely change the way the image is lit.

An infinite number of variations can be conjured up. I like Figure 15.1D in principle, but think that it's gone overboard. So, I would use a lower opacity when making the Overlay blend. In Figure 15.1G, I'm fine with what happened to the lake, but the greenery is much too light for my taste. I would therefore blend the original L channel back into the new L using Darken mode, maybe at 100% opacity and maybe not.

Overlay is one of several modes using the

model that where the overlaying channel is lighter than 50% gray, it lightens the underlying one; where darker it darkens; and where it's exactly 50% gray, nothing happens. The other related blending modes would create results that were similar but not identical. Consequently they don't pertain to the basic concept. The text of this chapter will use Overlay only, but there's a box on Page 307 for those interested in the other modes.

The A and B work so well in Overlay mode precisely because values of 0^A and 0^B—neutrality, in the AB language—correspond to a 50% gray, not a white. Therefore, anything neutral won't change. The man's grayish

clothing is almost identical in all four of the overlay variants of Figure 15.1.

Where there's color, it's another story. This B channel has more decisive color breaks than the A. Anything more blue than it is yellow is B–negative, darker than 50% gray for overlay purposes. The sky is blue, therefore dark, and the lake even bluer, therefore darker.

Anything more yellow than blue is B–positive, lighter than 50%. The face is somewhat more yellow than blue, and the greenery is way more yellow than blue.

So, when the B is applied as an overlay to the L, colors don't change, but darknesses do. The greenery gets much lighter, the face slightly lighter, the sky slightly darker, and the lake much darker. Do you see which of the four variants was made this way?

By checking Invert when doing the overlay, we reverse the effect. Which of the four has the lightest lake and the darkest greenery? That one was done by overlaying the inverted B onto the L.

The two done by overlaying the A onto the L are harder to tell apart because nothing is either strongly magenta or

Figure 15.2 Overlay mode in action. Top, the original. Center, in LAB, the original is applied to itself in Overlay mode. Bottom, the L from the top version is married to the AB from the middle one.

strongly green. Nevertheless, the face is slightly more magenta than green and the shrubbery more green than magenta. The two objects move in different directions after the overlay, unlike the version done with the B, where both face and greenery were more yellow than blue. If the A is overlaid uninverted to the L, the face gets lighter and the greenery darker; inverting does the opposite. Personally, I think that both versions done by overlaying the A channel are better than the original.

The Easy Way to Brighter Color

To hammer home how the mode works, rather than apply a single channel to another, I've applied Figure 15.2A to itself in Overlay mode, 100% opacity, to produce Figure 15.2B.

Applying an entire image to another is not a composite process, but rather a channel-by-channel one. Since this is an LAB file, the L is overlaying the L, the A the A, and the B the B. Figure 15.2B's shortcomings are the fault of the L. Things that used to be light got even lighter, blowing out all the detail on the white clothing. Things that used to be dark got darker, plugging up the motorcyclist's helmet and jacket, among other things.

To correct this, I replaced this L with the original from Figure 15.2A. In Figure 15.2C, consequently, the only change is in the A and B channels. And, garish though it may be, it carries a considerable temptation.

Overlaying the A and B onto themselves can't introduce a cast, since all values of 0^A or 0^B are unchanged. Instead, it drives all colors apart, much like the curves featured in Chapter 1—with one important exception.

AB curves are powerful but not particularly amenable to experimentation. I think the colors of Figure 15.2A are basically right yet lukewarm, particularly in the faces and hair of the people on the right side. But I don't know how far to go with them. I'd like to be able to do some fine-tuning.

Constantly tweaking both ends of a curve is annoying. It's easier to have something excessively colorful like Figure 15.2C on the top layer, and adjust the opacity slider to taste. I almost always use this method when dealing with face shots.

This summarizes the two main reasons to do the improbable by using the A or B as a blending channel. We can create different effects in the L by altering the darkness of certain interest objects, and/or we can enhance color by overlaying the AB onto themselves on a separate layer and then dialing down the opacity if need be. The rest of the chapter will

The Overlay Sextuplets

Overlay is one of six blending modes in which 50% gray has no effect on the underlying image, lighter areas lighten, and darker ones darken. All six are computed in different ways. Some try to protect extreme values from blowing out, whereas others permit it. Some have relatively strong impacts and others don't.

If you just stick with Overlay for AB blending, you'll be fine. The key is knowing when this type of blending is appropriate, not which of the sextuplets to use. Or, when you set up the blend, you can toggle back and forth to one of the other modes and see if you like the result better.

For insatiably curious people, here's the executive summary of what the other options have to offer.

• Vivid Light, Linear Light, and Pin Light are, as far as I know, useless in this type of blending.

• Hard Light and Overlay give identical results when applying the A or B to themselves, but not when applying to the L. Hard Light extracts extra detail from the highlights and shadows, if that's what you're after.

• Soft Light has less of an impact than Overlay. It slightly favors darkening rather than lightening. When applying the A or B to itself, Soft Light accents subtler colors more than brilliant ones. Also, while it does increase the intensity of warm colors, it accentuates cold colors more. You may find these attributes desirable in certain images.

show examples of both uses. There will be no use of curves, filters, or selections.

Our appetizer will be Figure 15.3, which is to appear in a book titled *Palm Trees: A Story in Photographs*. That settles any question about what the important part of the picture is. Unfortunately, the lighting was uncooperative. The sky is an impressive deep blue, particularly at the top of the image. That would be great if the book were about skies, but it isn't going to cut it when we're supposed to be concentrating on the trees.

In RGB, we'd use the Hue/Saturation or Selective Color command to lighten the sky. It's somewhat difficult (we would have to select both Blues and Cyans in the dialog, as the bottom part of the sky will not lighten enough if only Blues are selected); it doesn't retain a good gradation from the top to the bottom of the sky; and it takes longer than the 10 seconds needed to produce Figure 15.4 in LAB.

We've already seen how to do this one, in Figure 15.1D, one of the variants of our first image. We have only to decide that everything in this image that's more blue than it is yellow needs to be lightened, and the bluer, the lighter.

The B channel can do this, provided we invert it when we apply it to the L in Overlay mode. If we left it uninverted, it would darken all blues, the opposite of what's needed.

Note the slight darkening of the path, the people, the beach, and the greenery, all of which have a slight bias toward yellow as opposed to blue. To me, these things are all desirable in this image's context; if you disagree, they could be removed or lessened by blending Figure 15.3 into 15.4 in Lighten mode.

If you feel that Figure 15.4 isn't colorful enough, you might wish to hit it with AB curves to make parts of it more yellow. Using AB overlays as in Figure 15.2 wouldn't be helpful. Given how light the sky now is, it can't be made any bluer. The inability to print good blues is a sad fact of life in CMYK.

Our next example deals with another gamut issue, one that requires both of the types of AB blending that we've been discussing.

Figure 15.3 *The image is to appear in a book about palm trees, but the sky is so dark that it detracts from them.*

Of Blues and Butterflies

Intense blues are hard to deal with no matter what the output destination, desktop or press. Other dark, rich colors are generally achievable. Pastel colors are problematic, especially on press. A patch of solid magenta ink, for example, like the one printed way back in Figure 1.11, is probably so intense as to be out of your monitor's gamut. Yet lighter magentas fall flat in CMYK, victims of a paper that isn't particularly white. If that paper is covered up by a lot of ink, it won't matter. But if the desired color is light, ink coverage must be light also. A lot of that ugly, contaminating paper will show through.

This problem is a common one in images of flowers, for which light magenta or pink is a favorite color. Experienced CMYK practitioners cheat by making the color darker and, often, redder, in an effort to put more ink on paper.

Even if gamut were not a consideration, I think that the flowers in Figure 15.5A are too light, particularly in comparison to the dark green leaves. I find the colors weak in both, and the beautiful butterfly that should be a focus of attention is scarcely there at all.

Figure 15.5B is more like what I think the picture should be—and

the changes are entirely the result of AB blends. Here are the steps.

● The flowers start out much more magenta than they are green, and slightly more blue than yellow. The leaves are moderately more green than magenta and sharply more yellow than blue. Overlaying the L with either the B or an inverted copy of the A will darken the flowers and lighten the leaves. A responsible person would probably try both ways and possibly combine them. Me, I thought in terms of a gross move to the flowers and a

Figure 15.4 *Applying the B channel, inverted, to the L in Overlay mode lightens all areas that are more blue than yellow.*

slight one to the leaves, so I made a duplicate layer and applied the inverted A to the L in Overlay mode at 100% opacity (Figure 15.5C). The reason for the layer was to leave room for a possible change in opacity or mode later. As

it turned out, I thought the layer was fine as it was and left it at full opacity throughout.

● On a new layer, I overlaid the A and B on themselves, sharply increasing color intensity everywhere, but not changing anything of

Figure 15.5 *Opposite page: the original and a version corrected only with AB blends. This page: top left, an inverted overlay of the A channel into the L. Top right, the A is then overlaid onto itself at 100% opacity and the B onto itself at 75%. Bottom left, the opacity of version D is reduced to 60%. Bottom right, two further overlays of the B channel onto itself. The Blend If sliders at right then restricted the brightening effect to the butterfly.*

value 0^A0^B. I thought there was a danger of the flowers becoming too blue and the leaves too green, so I overlaid the B at only 75% opacity, instead of the 100% I used for the A. I had now reached Figure 15.5D.

● Overlaying the AB channels onto themselves at such high opacities usually creates something too vivid, as it did here. That's not a problem, but an advantage. We're not looking for magic numbers or secret formulas. We're trying to make the picture look good in a trial-and-error way. We always do the overlaying on a separate layer, allowing us to move the opacity slider until we get the look we want. In Figure 15.5E, I used 60%.

● The butterfly is a special case. In the original, it's only the wispiest of yellows. No curve could make it as yellow as I want without also making anything neutral (such as the black stripes) yellow as well. Fortunately, it's easy to separate insect from background later. Therefore, having already made one overlay of the B to itself, I made another (more than doubling the effect, because the

Fighting Blend-Induced Grain

The A and B channels can be grainy enough to create artifacting in certain types of blending. The usual danger zones are relatively dark areas that are being drastically lightened, such as the sky in Figure 15.4, or where there are repeated applications of the same channel, as in the butterfly of Figure 15.5F.

The best weapon against this effect is the Surface Blur filter (Photoshop CS2 and later), applied before the blend. If Surface Blur is not available and the purpose of the blend is to enhance color, using another blurring or noise-reduction filter afterward should work. If the blend will be to the L channel, though, caution is needed. The advantage of Surface Blur is that it has a limited effect on edges. If you Gaussian blur a channel before blending it into the L, it may cause haloing around some objects. The Dust & Scratches filter can be a better choice.

For further discussion of Photoshop's blurring options, see Chapter 5.

first overlay had already put more distance between the butterfly and neutrality) and then still another, winding up with around 25^B in Figure 15.5F, where we had opened with 3^B. There was no point in doing anything to the A channel because the butterfly was at 0^A throughout and therefore would be unaffected by any overlays.

● Finally, Blending Options (review Chapter 9, if necessary) excluded everything but the butterfly. I needed only one slider (A, This Layer) to do it. It could have been done in the B as well, by bringing the left-hand slider close to the center point to exclude the flowers, which Figure 15.5F shows are more blue than yellow. Moving the right-hand B slider toward the center would exclude the greenery, which has more of a yellow component than the butterfly does. Reminder: the reason to use the This Layer slider is that this top layer has longer ranges in the areas that interest us. Its flowers are very blue, and therefore are further away from the center point of the slider, making it easier for us to find the exact point where they begin.

Doing it with the A, however, is even easier. The butterfly is found at dead center because it measures close to 0^A throughout. Everything else in this picture has a distinct color. So, just bringing both sliders in close to the center point suffices to isolate the butterfly.

The Art of Selective Lightening

When a picture is too dark, lighten it. When a picture is too light, darken it.

Simple advice, but effective. If you intend to follow it literally, you don't need this chapter. But sometimes the rule, obvious though it seems to be, isn't quite right. Sometimes the picture is too dark and we only need to lighten *parts* of it.

The most notorious such situation occurs when some knucklehead shoots a picture of a person whom the sun is directly behind. Any time the light is to the rear of the subject,

Figure 15.6 Images that are partially in shadow can be treated effectively with overlay blends.

however, will do. The Image: Adjustments> Shadow/Highlight command (Photoshop CS and later) is a good way of handling such atrocities.

Different considerations apply when a face is in *partial* shadow, as in Figure 15.6. Before discussing other options, here's the obvious one. Figure 15.7A is the Shadow/Highlight command's default settings applied to the RGB original digital file.

Let's now set that version aside for later comparison, and start again with Figure 15.6. Certainly the face is too dark. Being red, it's positive in both A and B, so either channel could be overlaid onto the L to lighten it.

The shirt and the background are green, so they're positive in the B but negative in the A. The jeans are negative in the B and near neutral in the A. If we overlay the A onto the L, the face will lighten, the shirt and the background will darken, and the jeans will stay the same. If we overlay the B, everything will lighten except the jeans, which will get darker. Which should we use?

Don't Believe What You See

When overlaying the A and B onto themselves to pep up colors, don't be deterred by what seems to be a loss of contrast. The idea of this blend is to go well beyond the intensity that you really want, and then dial it back with the opacity slider. If you are using 100% opacity for these blends, you may be creating colors well beyond what your monitor is capable of displaying accurately. If such out-of-gamut colors are there (and there's no way to know other than to look for the undesirable effect), detail will be lost when they are converted into the monitor's version of RGB, just as it would be if the file were converted into CMYK.

When you reduce the opacity of the out-of-gamut layer, bringing the colors back to something more monitor-friendly, the missing contrast will return.

When I assigned this image as a competitive exercise in one of my advanced classes, it seemed so clear to me that the A would be better that I didn't bother to investigate the alternative. Now that my own entry into the contest has gotten thrashed, something that irritates me no end when it occurs, I take the view that when in doubt we should try both ways and trash the one we don't like. To that end, Figure 15.7B is the A applied to the L in Overlay mode, 100% opacity. Figure 15.7C is the same thing, substituting the B for the A.

In judging these two, forget that the face is lighter in one version. That happened because the B is more positive than the A. If you want the two versions to match, you can apply the A a second time, or cut the opacity of the version produced with the B.

My thought was that Figure 15.7B would be better, because it would make the greenery darker, which would contrast with the lightening of the face. This theory is exploded by Figure 15.7C, whose real attraction is how it lightens the leaves to bring them out from the background. The pattern in the shirt is also more pronounced, because its green areas are getting lighter while the more neutral parts are not.

For these reasons, I favor it over Figure 15.7B, but either one will eventually be better than the Shadow/Highlight version of Figure 15.7A. The two LAB versions can't be directly compared to Figure 15.7A yet, though. When an image is too dark, it's usually too gray also. When operating in RGB, S/H therefore, quite correctly, adds saturation to all colors by default. The color enhancement step in LAB has yet to come.

Figure 15.7 Below, the Shadow/Highlight command applied in RGB to Figure 15.6. Opposite page: top, the A channel is applied in Overlay mode to the L of a fresh copy of Figure 15.6. Bottom, the B channel is applied instead.

Because this picture is so full of shadow, it doesn't need the color boost we saw in Figure 15.5, but it does have to get a bit lighter and brighter. I found a revoltingly lazy way to make it happen: I blended Figure 15.7B into 15.7C in Overlay mode, opacity 30%, producing Figure 15.8.

Overlaying a file onto itself is the same as overlaying each channel onto itself. Doing so to the A and B increases color intensity. Overlaying the L onto itself is rarely recommended because of its tendency to blow out highlights and plug shadows. In Figure 15.6, neither is much of a factor. The lightest areas are the various reflections, none of which are neutral. Doing these overlays in RGB might blow these areas out to blank white. It can't happen in the L, because even if the overlay forces 100^L, it can't force 0^A0^B. The LAB file would then be calling for an imaginary color, which would convert to something other than white when we went to RGB or CMYK. And if the deepest areas of the shadows lose detail, it isn't such a big deal.

In comparing Figure 15.8 to Figure 15.7A, the S/H version, note that the faces are equally dark—that is, if we average both the lit and shadowy areas, which are more pronounced in the LAB version. On the whole, however, Figure 15.8 seems darker, but much more contrasty. Its portrayal of lights and shadows is more realistic.

Separating Greens Conventionally...

In the foregoing example, the pepped-up color could also have been gotten by curves, though perhaps not as quickly. The blend into the L can't readily be duplicated.

To help understand why, let's end with an

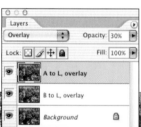

Figure 15.8 Figure 15.7B is overlaid onto Figure 15.7C at 30% opacity.

image somewhat similar to the one of the bow hunter we just worked on. This time, instead of competing with the Shadow/Highlight command, the opponent is a version done in the familiar LAB way with curves.

Figure 15.9, taken deep in a forest in Switzerland, is typical of images taken deep in forests. It's simultaneously too dark and too light, as the camera fails to make the adjustments that come so naturally to the human visual system. The colors are too muted for the same reason. Above all, the greens are too consistent because the camera lacks the sense of simultaneous contrast that we humans use to break colors apart from those of neighboring objects. This, as much as a canyon, is the classic type of image on which LAB correction works much better than any alternative.

The curves-only version is straightforward. The picture consists only of light and dark areas, with a whole range of tones missing in action. The water

Figure 15.9 *Either curves or AB blends to the L channel can lighten this forest, but the results of the two methods will show aesthetic differences.*

never gets darker than 90^L; the forest never lighter than 65^L. These findings call for an L curve in the shape of an inverted S, steep in the lightest and darkest parts, flatter in the middle.

As for color, this picture lacks prominent interest objects that need to be driven apart, so we have no need for the Command–click trickery of Chapter 12. Also, the water mea-

sures close to 0^A0^B everywhere, so we conclude that the picture has no inherent cast that would cause us to move the center points of the curves as was done in Chapter 4.

Straight lines in the AB curves would have sufficed, but I made two slight adjustments. I thought that the foreground leaves were threatening to get too yellow, so I placed a locking point at 0^A and then twisted the

Figure 15.10 A version corrected only by curves.

upper part of the A curve to intensify greens. I did not wish to simply steepen the entire curve further because I felt that the foreground rocks were getting too red and did not need more magenta.

In the B, I did use a straight line, but I made an executive decision to shift it very slightly to the left of the center point, to add a hint of blue to the water. As nothing in the image is known to be truly neutral, shifting the image toward blue breaks no rules.

These curves produce Figure 15.10. On to its curveless competitor.

...and Unconventionally

Starting again from scratch with Figure 15.9, the forest can be lightened by over-laying one of the color channels onto the L. As all natural greenery is A–negative and B–positive, we could blend with an inverted copy of the A or an uninverted copy of the B. I chose to use the B, mostly because the greenery was more positive in the B than it was negative in the A, which makes the moves more obvious and easier to control. Also, as the foreground rocks are somewhat red, an A overlay would darken them and a B blend lighten them. The latter option seems right in the context of a picture that's getting lighter overall.

To create Figure 15.11, I first blended the B channel into the L, Overlay mode, at 100% opacity (Figure 15.12A).

As this did not lighten the foreground leaves as much as I wanted, I repeated the move, overlaying the B onto the L again, this time at 50% opacity (Figure 15.12B).

Having lightened the image enough, it was time to turn to color. I overlaid the A onto itself at 100% (Figure 15.12C).

By the application of such a drastic move to the A without doing anything to the B, the picture had become unbalanced. But overlaying the B onto itself at 100% seemed to make the image too yellow. As a compromise, I did B to the B at 80% (Figure 15.12D).

Still thinking that contrast had to be added between the lightest and darkest areas of the forest, but constrained by my earlier promise not to use curves, I applied the L to itself in Overlay mode (Figure 15.12E). I did not object to the ensuing loss of detail in the shadows, thinking that it helped add depth by emphasizing the relative lightness of the foreground branches. The move blew out the water-

fall, however. So, I took the liberty of adjusting the highlights with the Shadow/Highlight command, completing the journey to Figure 15.11 and also our discussion of this weird method of blending.

The version done with curves only has a different flavor than the one done with blends. It carries better detailing in the transition to the deep shadows. It's a more

Figure 15.11 *This alternate correction employed no curves, but rather a series of blends.*

Figure 15.12 *The progression of steps from Figure 15.9 to Figure 15.11. Top left, the B is overlaid into the L at 100% opacity. Top center, the B is overlaid again into the L, this time at 50%. Top right, the A is overlaid onto itself at 100% opacity. Bottom left, the B is overlaid onto itself at 80% opacity. Bottom center, the L is overlaid onto itself at 35% opacity.*

The objects that we are trying to lighten or darken are invariably the most colorful ones. We don't want to restrict the effect only to the most colorful areas, however. We simply want it to be less in areas that are similar to the target object but not as strongly colored. Note that between Figures 15.12A and 15.12B the foreground branches, our target, are lightened more strongly than anything else, yet other green areas are lightened somewhat.

In the A and B, the more colorful the object, the lighter or darker it is with respect to a medium gray, which represents a neutral. The key is that all neutrals are of the same tonality. It seems ridiculous to group the waterfall with the darkest part of the shadows, but that's how it is in LAB, as Figure 15.13A demonstrates.

conservative take on the image. The blend version is dramatic. We seem to see a deeper picture, with more distance between the foreground leaves and the deep shadows at rear.

Whites and Blacks Are Both Grays

To review why overlay blending with the AB works (and why it *doesn't* work in RGB or CMYK), let's rehash the channel structure one last time.

Figure 15.13 *The AB blending advantage derives from a channel structure that places strongly colored areas far away from neutral ones. In RGB, neutral areas can be simultaneously lighter and darker than colored ones, making overlay blending impossible. Left, the B channel, with contrast enhanced, shows that the foreground branches are the lightest area. Right, an inverted copy of the green channel of RGB. It cannot be used for overlay blending because the shadow areas are lighter than the branches.*

Any thought of using an RGB channel in the same way is derailed by the sad reality that a colorful area is rarely the lightest or darkest area of a channel. The branches are most differentiated from the background in the green channel of RGB, but we can't lighten with it because it would blow out the considerable areas of the image that are lighter than the branches. Yet if we invert the channel as in Figure 15.13B to prevent the water from lightening, now the shadows will be lightened more than the branches will.

That's why the technique works only in LAB, and that's why the question of whether Figure 15.10 or 15.11 is preferable is ultimately irrelevant. The competition was meaningless because the rules were absurd. Overlay blending does not invalidate everything we've

Review and Exercises

✓ In preparation for the exercises of the next chapter, find some face shots and, on a separate layer, apply the A to the A in Overlay mode at 100%, and the B to the B likewise. Practice adjusting the layer opacity slider to get approximately the desired effect. Now, try cutting back the intensity of magenta by blending the A from the underlying layer into the A on the overlay, at 25% opacity. If you don't like it, cancel it and try again with the B. Can you generalize as to which kind of face images look better with more attention to the A, and which with more to the B?

✓ If you are using overlays to the AB channels to enhance color, why must the image be neutrally correct before you do it? What would happen if there were a color cast?

✓ In Figure 15.11, more intense colors were brought about by overlaying the A and B onto themselves, on a separate layer. Suppose the client feels that the greenery is now good, but that the foreground rocks have become too red. If the assignment is to restore all reddish areas, not to their original color, but rather to a point halfway between Figure 15.9 and Figure 15.11, how would you proceed, without affecting the green areas?

learned in the previous 14 chapters. Showing how we *could* fix poor images using nothing but blends gives some idea of how powerful these tools are, but in real life nobody in their right mind would ever adopt a workflow of no curves, no selections, no way, no how. Particularly, overlaying the L channel into itself was just posturing—curves would have done a better job.

I suspect that there'd be a hung jury with

respect to our two alternatives, but that a combined version, splitting the difference between the two, would probably take all the votes. Even if you're a pure-curves type of person, a small blend into the L before applying them should yield a better result in this forest image.

The real question would be, how could you get to *either* version without the use of LAB? As far as I know, the answer is that you can't.

Overlay blending is the last ingredient, the last spice one can add to the LAB cabinet that we began to describe in Chapter 1, back when life was simpler. These last two chapters on blending have introduced an entirely new angle from which to view LAB. The bad news is that it's quite bleeding-edge and that in only two chapters there's no time to do more than hint at its power. The good news is that you now have seen all the major tools that LAB has to offer.

Or, at least, that I am currently aware that it has to offer. Presumably, the process of discovery is not over, and this most powerful of colorspaces will yield up even more secrets. With that, let's proceed to wrap up what we've learned with a final chapter on how to apply it to a very common and very important class of images.

The Bottom Line

The blurry looking A and B channels seem like unlikely candidates for blending. Nevertheless, there are two major applications. First, the A or B can be blended into the L in Overlay mode. The purpose would be to lighten or darken the most prominently colored areas of the image without leaving telltale signs of a selection.

Second, the A and B can be overlaid onto themselves to intensify color. The effect is similar to applying the straight-line curves discussed at the start of the book. The disadvantage of doing so is less flexibility than in curving; the advantage is that it can be taken to an extreme on a separate layer, followed by adjusting the opacity downward. This allows quick visual feedback when you are unsure about how much color to engineer in.

A Face Is Like a Canyon

This chapter introduces a recipe for drastically improving believability in portraits. It uses many of LAB's more complex techniques, yet is easily understandable, and it works in nearly every face shot, professional or amateur, young or old.

After a prolonged period of exercise, the conventional wisdom calls for a cool-down period. If you've been riding a bicycle at top speed for half an hour, for example, they'll tell you not to stop suddenly, but rather to slow down to a sedate pace for a few minutes before dismounting.

Something along those lines is appropriate here, too. The last two chapters were a sprint. Now that the end is in sight, it's time to slow down. So, our last chapter will be in the same format as the first: a general-purpose recipe that doesn't require a whole lot of mental exertion to produce some really striking results.

You may not work on many canyon images like the ones shown in Chapter 1. Pictures of the human face should be a bit more familiar. The recipe for improving them is based largely on the techniques shown in the last two chapters, but isn't nearly as complicated. To prove that it's almost universally applicable, we'll repeat it with a series of images of people of different ages and ethnicities. Some are professionally shot and others not. Some models wear makeup; others don't. But the recipe works for all of them.

The formal recipe appears in a box on the next page. We'll go very slowly through one example, with lots of intermediate images plus a thorough explanation of the purpose of each step, possible alternatives, and what may go wrong. Thereafter, we go on cruise control.

The first opponent smiles at us in Figure 16.1A. According to the recipe, prior to Step One we have to examine the original image to see if there is an existing color cast, and correct it if there is. This preliminary RGB step is needed because the recipe later calls for using overlay blends in

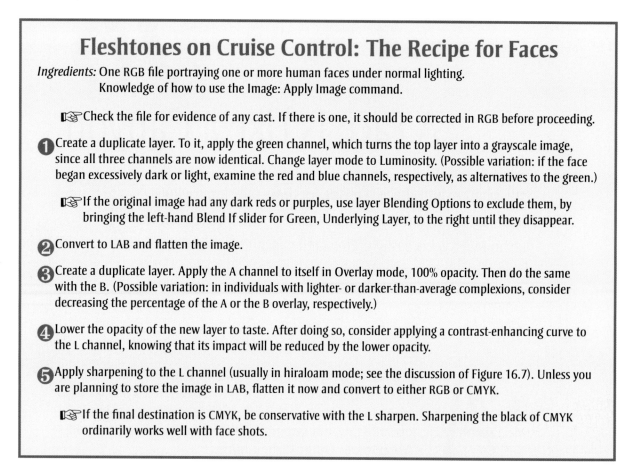

Fleshtones on Cruise Control: The Recipe for Faces

Ingredients: One RGB file portraying one or more human faces under normal lighting. Knowledge of how to use the Image: Apply Image command.

☞Check the file for evidence of any cast. If there is one, it should be corrected in RGB before proceeding.

❶ Create a duplicate layer. To it, apply the green channel, which turns the top layer into a grayscale image, since all three channels are now identical. Change layer mode to Luminosity. (Possible variation: if the face began excessively dark or light, examine the red and blue channels, respectively, as alternatives to the green.)

☞If the original image had any dark reds or purples, use layer Blending Options to exclude them, by bringing the left-hand Blend If slider for Green, Underlying Layer, to the right until they disappear.

❷ Convert to LAB and flatten the image.

❸ Create a duplicate layer. Apply the A channel to itself in Overlay mode, 100% opacity. Then do the same with the B. (Possible variation: in individuals with lighter- or darker-than-average complexions, consider decreasing the percentage of the A or the B overlay, respectively.)

❹ Lower the opacity of the new layer to taste. After doing so, consider applying a contrast-enhancing curve to the L channel, knowing that its impact will be reduced by the lower opacity.

❺ Apply sharpening to the L channel (usually in hiraloam mode; see the discussion of Figure 16.7). Unless you are planning to store the image in LAB, flatten it now and convert to either RGB or CMYK.

☞If the final destination is CMYK, be conservative with the L sharpen. Sharpening the black of CMYK ordinarily works well with face shots.

the A and B channels to enhance color. As discussed in Chapter 15, such blends can't compensate for an existing cast. The recipe calls for overlay blends rather than curves because many viewers object to even slight variations in what they consider proper flesh-tone color. Blending on a layer is the most flexible approach because it permits us to make slight changes in opacity later on.

I think this original is too gray, but there is no evidence of anything being wrong with its color balance. On to the recipe.

Building Contrast with the Green

Step One starts with a duplicate layer. Now, Image: Apply Image. The target is automatically the open channel(s). As no channel has been singled out, the target is all three at once. Choose the green channel as source, Normal mode, 100% opacity.

This procedure copies the green channel into the red and blue. Since all three channels are now identical, their values are equal everywhere. Equal values in RGB make a gray. Therefore, this is now a black and white image, but not for long.

Changing the mode to Luminosity instructs Photoshop to use the color from the original on the bottom layer. We haven't entered LAB yet, but we're behaving as if we had. We have separated color from contrast. The two are reunited in Figure 16.1B.

This step works because, just as skies almost always show most contrast in the red channel, normally lit faces almost always have their best detail in the green. Have a look at Figure 16.2. Considering the three channels as separate black and white images, the green seems best. As is sometimes the case with light-complexioned individuals,

Figure 16.1 *Step One of the recipe. On a duplicate layer, the green channel is applied to the composite image, and layering mode is changed to Luminosity.*

there is a case to be made for the blue, but the hair is too dark.

The contrast information in these channels gets averaged together to make the L when the file gets converted to LAB.

But if one of the three channels is incontestably best, why do any averaging at all? Why not throw the other two away and just use the good one? The color can always be resurrected from a copy of the original.

Next, an intermediate step. The recipe tells us to look for any dark reds or purples. We look for such areas because they start out grossly darker in the green channel that we are intending to use in Step One for a luminosity blend.

Refer again to the channels in Figure 16.2. The fleshtone is slightly darker in the green than in the red. The lipstick, however, is *much* darker. It's not as bad as if she were

wearing red clothing, which might be almost a solid 0^G. In that case, the luminosity blend would turn the clothing black. The lips are acceptable in Figure 16.1B, but remember that we are still planning to add color variation, which may turn them garish. LAB will help us make the cheeks redder than the rest of the face. No assistance from LAB is required to make the lips redder than the cheeks—the woman took care of that part for us, in front of the makeup mirror.

The recipe suggests using Blending Options now to restore the lips by excluding objects that are very dark in the underlying green channel. That works, but there's an easier way in this particular image. The blue channel, as usual, is the darkest of the

Figure 16.2 *The channels of Figure 16.1A show that, as usual with fleshtone images, the green is the best rendition.*

three—except in the lips and eyes. By applying it to the luminosity layer in Figure 16.1A in Lighten mode, we get to Figure 16.3.

Making the Jump to LAB

With the extra snap that the luminosity blends gave us, but still with somewhat tepid color, we go to Step Two by entering LAB. Repeating a recommendation from early in the book: use the Edit: Convert to Profile (Photoshop CS2; Image: Mode>Convert to Profile in Photoshops 6–CS) command rather than a simple mode change.

Layered images generally should be flattened during the conversion to

another colorspace. Adjustment layers, for example, don't survive the conversion from, say, RGB to CMYK. Blending modes other than Normal may be recalculated in an

Figure 16.3 *Applying the original blue channel in Lighten mode to the luminosity layer in Figure 16.1B lightens the lips and eyes.*

unexpected way in the destination colorspace if the layers aren't merged first.

When the file's layers include only Normal, Luminosity, and Color modes, though, it's better to let LAB handle it, as shown in Figure 16.4, because of the advantage in calculating colors that was described in the second half of Chapter 5.

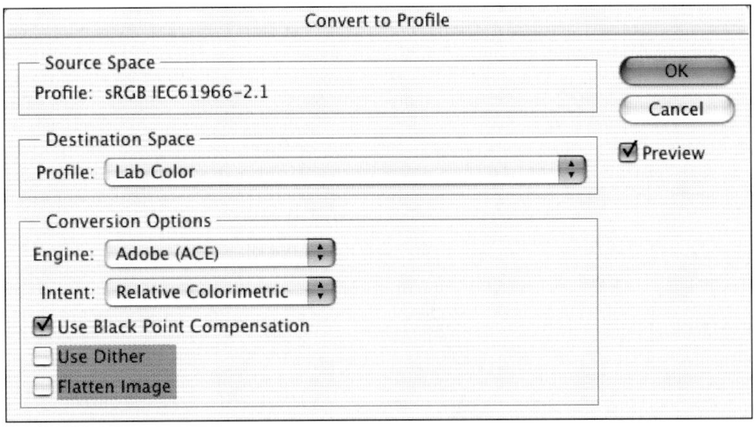

In the present image, the difference is visible but not significant enough to bother showing. The lips are slightly better defined, and the hair a bit purer yellow. In other images, however, the effect can be greater, so I recommend flattening the image *after* it gets to LAB.

Having reduced the image to a single LAB layer, we immediately put a duplicate layer on top for Step Three of the recipe. There's nothing wrong with adding color variation with curves instead, but I find that the overlay blend method described in Chapter 15 is somewhat faster and more user-friendly when it comes to faces.

The idea is to make the top layer more colorful than we want, allowing us to fool with the opacity slider later. In principle, we should apply the A and the B to themselves in Overlay mode at 100% opacity. In practice, the subject's complexion may dictate using differing percentages in the two channels.

Everybody who's ever studied how humans react to pictures knows that almost everyone prefers "healthy-looking" fleshtones. The phrase is sometimes interpreted to mean that we are supposed to make everyone look as if they just got out of the tanning parlor. There's some truth in that—provided that the subject is a light-skinned Caucasian.

Fleshtones are red, but neither the A nor the B can create that color without help from the other. Enhancing the A makes the skin more magenta, or purple, or pink, or however you like to say it. Augmenting the B makes

Figure 16.4 *In converting color or luminosity layers from RGB to LAB, the highlighted boxes are best left unchecked.*

the skin more yellow. Do both and the skin becomes redder.

In fashion work, as in James Bond novels, there is often a demand for "golden" skin. That word certainly suggests that we should apply the B with a heavier hand than the A. I agree that this approach makes sense when the subject has blue eyes and light hair. Photographs of such persons often look deathly pale. Almost every observer would prefer not just a stronger color but one biased toward yellow.

With darker-skinned persons, particularly men, a "ruddy" complexion connotes health. Throwing in extra yellow would be counterproductive. And for unusually dark-skinned Caucasians, or any ethnic group with similar or darker skintone, even adding the same amount of magenta and yellow can cause the impression of jaundice.

My advice, therefore, is to consider the individual. Unusually light skin suggests a bigger move in the B than the A, unusually dark skin the opposite. This woman has light skin, blue eyes, and blond hair. So, on the duplicate layer, I blended the A into itself in Overlay mode at 80% opacity, creating the overly pinkish Figure 16.5A.

I chose 80% because I wanted to leave room to use a higher percentage in the B. If doing so turned out badly, I could always set the B blend to 80% as well and still have something more than colorful enough for the next step. As it happened, 100% was fine. It left me with Figure 16.5B.

As the recipe foresaw, the image is now too colorful. That's why it went on a separate layer, the bottom layer being Figure 16.3. Step Four calls for reducing the opacity of the top layer until satisfied. For Figure 16.6A, I chose an aggressive 70%, knowing that the skin was about to get somewhat lighter.

The recipe now calls for consideration of an L curve. If we use one, it should be fairly subtle, because applying the green channel to the composite in Step One has already added snap to the image. Consequently, it makes sense to apply any L curve to the same layer we were on, one at lower than 100% opacity.

Here, in spite of the darkening created by the earlier green-channel blend, the face still resides entirely in the light half of the L, roughly between 85^L and 55^L. The curve shown simply steepens that range, producing Figure 16.6B. There's no danger in moving the lower left point so far right, which would usually risk blowing out some highlight areas. It can't happen when the curve is applied to a layer with an opacity of less than 100%.

The Question of Sharpening

The final step of the recipe is the most subjective. Fleshtones are unique. In almost every other image category, we strive to bring out as much subtle detailing as possible. Not with someone's face, especially not a female's. It so happens that the trend in fashion work that irritates me the most is that of going too far in the opposite direction. This woman is no longer in her teens. I don't think her skin should be made to suggest otherwise.

Figure 16.5 *Left, the A channel is applied to itself, Overlay mode, at 80% opacity, using Figure 16.3 as a base. Then, right, the B is applied to itself, Overlay mode, at 100% opacity. The higher B opacity is used to make the skintone more golden.*

A

B

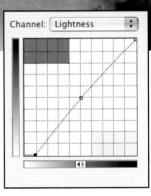

Figure 16.6 Left, the top layer of Figure 16.5B is reduced to 70% opacity. Right, still on the same reduced-opacity layer, the curves at right are applied to the L channel.

On the other hand, I could bring out so much detail in this woman's skin that she might come after me with a pistol. Some reasonable compromise between the two extremes must be found.

Conventional sharpening finds and enhances edges. That's desirable in the hair, jewelry, and eyelids and eyelashes, but we want to keep it away from the skin. Hiraloam (high Radius, low Amount) sharpening can add apparent depth to the face. There's room for both types of sharpening in this recipe.

If the image is headed for CMYK, sharpen hiraloam in LAB, then convert to CMYK and sharpen only the black channel, which typically has no detail in the skin. It can therefore be conveniently used to sharpen the hair and eyes without risking turning the subject into a reptile.

That's the way we'd normally do it for this

book, where the printer is asking for CMYK files. Let's assume, however, that we need RGB files, and would therefore like to do all sharpening in LAB.

The conventional sharpening should come first. To restrict most of the sharpening to the darker areas of the image (and thus keeping it away from the flesh), load an inverted luminosity mask (Command-Option–1; Shift-Command–I). Now, *being sure that you are sharpening only the L channel, not the AB*, see what happens with Filter: Sharpen> Unsharp Mask at Amount 500%, Radius 1.0, Threshold 0.

Those settings seemed to work here (remember, we're still on a layer that's set to 70% opacity), leaving the skin unaffected. However, noise developed in the dark areas on the

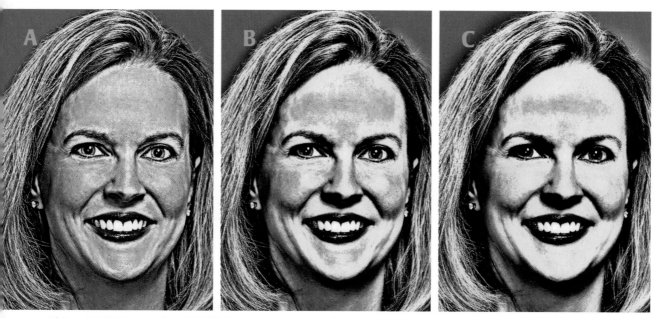

Figure 16.7 *Using an absurd 500% Amount setting initially is an easy way to visualize what the effect of sharpening with a wide Radius and lower Amounts will be. Left to right, these versions used Radius settings of 10.0, 25.0, and 40.0.*

woman's neck, which weren't excluded by the mask. Therefore, I increased Threshold to 8.

The sharpening added sheen to the hair and definition to the eyes, but overall the effect was so slight that there is no need to take the space to show it.

Deselecting the mask, but leaving only the L channel open, we now proceed to the hiraloam step. The key is to get the Radius right, and the best way to do that is to watch what happens when the Amount is set ridiculously high.

I reopened the Unsharp Mask filter. Leaving Amount at 500% and Threshold at 8, I tried several different Radii, looking for one where the sharpening halos would add shape, never mind that for the time being the preview looks appallingly bad.

The 10.0 Radius shown in Figure 16.7A would just age the woman, as far as I'm concerned. The halos around the lips and eyes aren't large enough to suggest depth. Figure 16.7B, at 25.0 Radius, is a lot more like what we're after. The eyes move deeper into the face as the cheeks get darker. This setting can add life to the picture. But at 40.0 Radius

(Figure 16.7C) the pleasing effect is gone. The halos are so big that they lighten the entire face.

My final settings were Amount 55%, Radius 27.0, Threshold 8. Recipe complete. The final result is Figure 16.8B, shown next to the original as a reminder of where we started.

Three Faces, One Recipe

That was a very slow-motion look at the recipe. In real life, it goes much faster. This time, we'll try it with three images at once. The subjects of Figure 16.9 vary in age, darkness of skin, and amount of makeup. Two, like our last image, were professionally shot; one is a candid image from an amateur photographer. Let's cut to the chase by showing the final results in Figure 16.10, and then go over the steps that got us there.

The preliminary step, in RGB, is to look for casts. None of the pictures show anything obvious, but all three should have neutral hair. We know this in two cases on grounds of ethnicity (persons of Asian or African descent generally have black hair) and in one on grounds of age.

Figure 16.8 Left, the original (Figure 16.1A) repeated for convenience. Right, the final sharpened version.

The image of the younger woman measures as having a slight red cast, on the reasonable assumption that both the hair and the background should be neutral. In glamour photography like this, a warmer feel is often desired, so I suspect the photographer did this on purpose. Nevertheless, the recipe calls for taking it out.

The man's hair has a slight bias toward magenta, but the image's midrange seems fine. Therefore, I lightened the darkest areas of the green channel with a curve.

There appears to be no color problem with the older woman. So, we proceed to Step One of the recipe, applying the green channel of each to the composite image on a new layer set to Luminosity mode. The results are shown in Figure 16.11.

As expected, all images have increased contrast, and are somewhat darker, which we'll take care of later in LAB. You should be able to see the adjustment in the man's hair color that occurred between Figures 16.9 and 16.11. And the color change in the younger woman is obvious, and disagreeable—muting the red cast has made the skin too gray.

Fortunately, working in LAB means never having to worry about tepid colors.

Next comes the intermediate step of looking for strong reds. I see none in any of the three. On to Step Two, converting to LAB and flattening the images, and to Step Three, the creation of a duplicate layer for overlay blends to the A and B.

The paths diverge here, because we have three sharply different complexions. As noted earlier, the lighter the complexion, the more it should favor use of the B; the darker, the A. The three results of the overlay step are in Figure 16.12. They're all intentionally too colorful, and all made with different overlay percentages.

● Light-skinned Caucasians, such as the older woman in this set and the earlier subject of Figure 16.1, generally need the yellow component of their flesh emphasized more than the magenta. These individuals often can be identified by their light hair and blue eyes. To make the version in Figure 16.12, I used overlay percentages of 100% in the B but only 75% in the A.

● Moderate- to dark-skinned Caucasians and other groups of similar skintone don't require the sort of artificial suntan we just manufactured. Some persons of Asian ancestry have skin darker than almost all Caucasians, but the younger woman shown here isn't one of them. I used 100% overlays in both A and B channels.

● In Caucasians with unusually dark

Figure 16.9 Three original portrait files.

skin or other individuals who are at least that dark, and particularly in African-Americans, excessive yellow in the fleshtone is objectionable. For the man pictured here, I reversed the ratio used for the older woman. I accentuated the magenta component of his skin more than the yellow, by using overlay opacities of 100% for the A and 75% for the B.

Step Four consists of choosing how to split the difference between each of the bland versions of Figure 16.11, which are on the bottom layer, and the exuberantly saturated ones of Figure 16.12 on the top. For the young woman, I chose an opacity of 70%, which is to say, a lot closer to the colorful version than to the dull one. For the older

Figure 16.10 *The same images after application of this chapter's recipe.*

woman I went to 60%, and in view of the fact that it is supposed to be a picture of a businessperson and not a cooked lobster, only 45% for the man. What would your choices have been?

From this point the steps are substantially the same as shown earlier between Figures 16.6B and 16.8B. There is no need to rehash them here.

In comparing the corrected versions of Figure 16.10 to the originals of Figure 16.9, look around the noses and chins. The greater depth stems from the original blend of the green channel in Luminosity mode, aided by the final curve applied to the L channel. Together, they are responsible for adding

Figure 16.11 *The green channel of the RGB originals has been applied to each composite image in Luminosity mode, a step analogous to that shown in Figure 16.1B. The two right-hand images have had slight color adjustments prior to the luminosity blend.*

contrast in a recipe that, being LAB-oriented, keeps color and detail in separate compartments. For the color part of the equation, see how the lips in all three individuals break away from the rest of the face in the corrected version far more than in the original. That's the AB influence, something that can't be duplicated by increasing saturation in other colorspaces.

But Here Is the Best Part

As LAB is the choice of those who are young at heart, it is appropriate that we end our discussion with the face

Figure 16.12 The images shown in Figure 16.11 have been converted to LAB, where, on a separate layer, the A and B channels were applied to themselves in Overlay mode. These versions are intentionally made too colorful so that a final choice of color can be made by finding a suitable point between each version and its counterpart in Figure 16.11.

Figure 16.13 The harsh sunlight coming in from the left side is an obstacle to the use of this chapter's recipe.

of a child. And, as LAB is the choice of the creative, it is appropriate to recall that recipes lay an important foundation but that superior dishes are prepared by those who can improvise.

A smiling little girl surrounded by flowers can make almost any photographer look good. Indeed, Figure 16.13 is passable just the way it is. A characteristic of those who use LAB, however, is the gnawing suspicion that the original image is never good enough.

The recipe we've been working with so far won't work here, at least not without some preparation. It assumes normally lit subjects. This one isn't. The sun is too strong. The right side of the face is heavily in shadow, while the left side is almost gone. Applying the green channel in Luminosity mode, as we have been doing, darkens the face, which would be good for the left side but fatal for the right.

As we near the end of a book about LAB technique, the bag of tricks that we can reach into has become rather large. It would be absurd to pretend that there's one right way to handle this picture, particularly since, as you're about to see, the first time I tried it I screwed it up. One day I'll give it out as a class exercise and see what others can make of it. For now, it might be useful to explain what I see in this original and what I think the choices are.

First, the image is full of bright colors, which constitute an argument against using LAB. Anything that intensifies the flowers or the sweater will drive them out of the gamut of whatever our final output space is.

As against that, in LAB, unlike RGB, it's a snap to exclude those areas from any other work being done on the image. Nothing is remotely close to being as A–positive as the flowers are. I can enhance the girl's face on one layer, and if it wrecks the flowers I can restore the originals with one sweep of a Blending Options slider.

The image reminds me of two that appeared in the last chapter. Another species of purple flowers graced Figure 15.5, but they were the most important part of that picture. Here the girl is the focus of attention. However, darkening the flowers and lightening the greenery worked well there. Blending an inverted copy of the A channel into the L in Overlay mode is therefore an option.

Second, the combination of sun and shade in the face is reminiscent of the hunter of Figure 15.6. Unfortunately, the light parts of the girl's face are much lighter than the man's were. Any effort to lighten the dark parts of the face by blending with the A or B will wipe out the light parts.

The Shadow/Highlight command, normally quite potent, was ineffective against the hunter image, and can't be expected to do well here either. We need a trick that will lighten the right side of the face (and, if possible, the hair) while darkening the left side. Chapter 15 hinted at how.

Overlay mode uses 50% gray as a dividing line. Where the overlaying image is lighter than 50%, it lightens the underlying one; where darker, it darkens. If we can find a channel where the two halves of the face fall on different sides of 50%, we should be able to make a significant improvement.

Once the file gets to LAB (it starts in RGB, of course), we won't find such a channel. In both A and B the entire face is positive because even in the darkest areas, it's still a distinctly warm color.

The L would also not be of use. It's lighter than any RGB channel, so both halves of the face would probably be lighter than 50% gray.

Figure 16.14 *Left, the blue channel of Figure 16.13. Right, the channel is blurred and inverted to prepare for a blend.*

Figure 16.15 *Figure 16.14B, a separate channel, is applied to Figure 16.13, Overlay mode, on a new layer.*

Unless there's some major color balance problem, any face, any race, any age, any page, any pose, any nose will be lightest in the red channel and darkest in the blue. The blue (Figure 16.14A), is where we should look because that's the one where the right side of the face is certain to be darkest. The left side can't possibly be close to 50% in any channel.

I propose to overlay this blue channel onto the composite image. It needs to be blurred heavily first, as otherwise there will be weird artifacting in sharply defined areas such as the eyes and eyebrows. Therefore, we'll need a separate copy of the blue, as we can't afford to destroy the existing copy.

Also, during the overlay the channel needs to be inverted. Otherwise, the light areas will get even lighter and the dark ones will plug. In real life, we check the Invert box in the Apply Image dialog when popping the blurred blue into the composite. For ease of visualizing what is about to happen, however, I've inverted Figure 16.14B already. Once you get your bearings—it's cropped exactly as Figure 16.4A is—you can see that it is about to darken the left half of the face plus the flowers, and lighten almost everything else. Applying it to the composite RGB of Figure 16.13 in Overlay mode, 100% opacity, produces Figure 16.15.

The face and hair are greatly improved. The background is interesting, possibly better and possibly not. Bad things have happened to the sweater and the red ribbon.

Figure 16.16 *Top, the layer is changed to Luminosity mode, restoring the color of Figure 16.13. Bottom, the green channel of the top version is now suitable for further blending.*

There isn't a convenient way to revert to the original sweater in RGB. Try to exclude things that are dark in the blue channel, as the sweater is, and you get the hair also. Exclude things that are light in the red, and kiss the left half of the face goodbye.

If the file were in LAB, the problem would go away, because nothing is nearly as B–positive as the sweater and the ribbon are. The flowers are magenta, not red; they're actually B–negative. The face and leaves are B–positive, but far less so than the sweater.

When I first prepared this part of the chapter, I fell into a trap right here. Seduced by the great improvement in color between Figures 16.13 and 16.15, I moved briskly and stupidly into LAB so as to exclude the sweater and ribbon there with layer Blending Options.

We have spent almost 350 pages learning that LAB is the best way to enhance color. Blending in Overlay mode in RGB is one of the worst. That it accidentally produced many good colors to go along with the ones that it wrecked should not have blinded me to the principle that overly gray colors are an utter, complete, total, and absolute non-issue when LAB is right around the corner. I should have (and I did, the second time around, having wasted about a day preparing these pages with an inferior method) changed the layering mode to Luminosity while I was still in RGB, producing Figure 16.16A. It's grayer than it was, but it retains the excellent detail that the overlay manufactured in Figure 16.15. Moreover, its new green channel—Figure 16.16B—is eminently suitable for further blending. The recipe is back on track. We're at Step One.

You Have a Head Start

On a new layer, I applied Figure 16.16B to Figure 16.16A in Normal mode, changed layer mode to Luminosity, and then trashed it because it looked terrible. It had darkened the face, appropriately

enough, but it had disagreeably weakened the leaves and the sweater, both of which are light in the green channel. I therefore redid the layer, this time applying Figure 16.16B in Darken mode, preventing anything from getting lighter and producing Figure 16.17A.

The recipe calls for checking for dark reds and purples, which this image has in abundance, and for taking them out of the mix by using the Blending Options slider to exclude things that are dark in the green channel. While that method works, a more easily controllable one is available, one that permits me to disallow the darkening of the flowers only partially, something I would like to do.

By going to Step Two of the recipe, converting to LAB without flattening the file first, not only do I get slightly better color, but I can take advantage of the ability to isolate colored objects in Blending Options. To make Figure 16.17B, I used two sliders, both of which I split by Option–clicking to create a zone of transition where Photoshop would average the two layers rather than choosing one or the other.

The L channel slider restores Figure 16.16A fully in the hair, which is very dark, and partially in the red ribbon, sweater, and darkest areas of the face. There is no impact on the leaves, which are identical on both layers, thanks to the darken-only blend I used to make Figure 16.16A.

The second slider is intended to catch the flowers. They are so strongly magenta-as-opposed-to-green that you might instinctively reach for the A sliders to deal with them. That would be a mistake.

You could definitely isolate the most colorful areas of the flowers, which are far more A–positive than

Blend If:	Lightness
This Layer:	69 / 113	255
Underlying Layer:	0	255

Blend If:	b
This Layer:	122 / 131	255
Underlying Layer:	0	255

Figure 16.17 Top, Figure 16.16B is applied, Darken mode, to a new layer of Figure 16.16A, set to Overlay mode. Below, the file is converted to LAB without flattening, and portions of the top layer are excluded with layer Blending Options.

Figure 16.18 In a flattened version of Figure 16.17, the A channel is applied to itself in Overlay mode, 80% opacity, and the B to itself at 70%.

whatever darkness we like. (For more discussion of this color phenomenon, see the box on Page 343.)

After making that decision, and flattening the image, I had reached Step Three of the recipe, the color boost. The idea of the step is to create something more colorful than what we want and then back off; hence, we usually overlay either the A or B onto itself at 100% opacity on a new layer, balancing it with an appropriate amount of the other, and then back off the overall color to taste by reducing layer opacity.

This image is so colorful to begin with that I saw no point in going overboard. I started by overlaying the A onto itself at only 80% opacity. Then, perceiving a slight imbalance toward yellow, I overlaid the B onto itself at 70%, reaching Figure 16.18.

I then reduced layer opacity to 45% and took care of the remaining recipe steps, which require no comment, except for one final fillip.

anything else in the picture. The problem is that parts of the flowers aren't all that colorful, and the face, the sweater, and the red ribbon are all A–positive also. You can't get all the flowers without picking up pieces of the other things as well.

If you want to make extensive use of LAB blending options, keep your eye peeled for B–negatives—objects that are more blue than yellow. Outside of outright blue things like the girl's ribbon and a sky, you won't find many. The LAB green is already quite blue; to find something on the blue side of that green is unusual. Things on the blue side of magenta are also rare, but these flowers qualify. They, and the blue ribbon, are the only B–negative objects in the entire image. It's a snap to target them with the slider, and, with nothing else to get in the way, we can widen or narrow the transition zone to make the flowers

It seemed to me that the leaves were too light. LAB presents ways to correct this that give more realistic results than those available in other colorspaces, but it's at least a two-step process that always involves an extra layer and exploits the fact that the leaves are the only A–negative objects.

I could apply curves to the top layer and then exclude everything but the leaves using Blending Options in the A, but that would require care to avoid creating obvious transition lines. The foolproof method is to blend the A into the L in Overlay mode. Doing so darkens the leaves, but it also lightens everything A–positive—to wit, the rest of the picture. Blowing out the fleshtones that I had been at such pains to develop was unfortunate. Happily, it is easily reversed by Image: Apply Image, again with the top layer's L as target, but using the underlying L as source

Figure 16.19 *The final version, after the colors of Figure 16.18 were toned down by reducing layer opacity to 45%, and the leaves were darkened by overlaying the A channel into the L (but restricting its effect to A–negative items).*

in Darken mode. This restores everything that the first blend lightened while permitting the leaves to maintain their added darkness. With that, we have a final version, Figure 16.19, and with that it's time to sum up.

If You Are Among the Very Young at Heart

LAB is often characterized as a desperation strategy best left for use in disastrously defective images. Not true. Every original in this chapter is first-rate—until you look at how it was improved.

These improvements could not have come about without LAB. However, unlike most of the examples in the rest of the book, they couldn't have come about *entirely* in LAB, either. In this last performance, fittingly, LAB played a supporting role—an important one, for sure, but subordinate to the star of the show, which was the overlay blend and

reversion of Figures 16.15 and 16.16, which can't be duplicated in LAB as far as I know.

It's easy to appreciate how powerful LAB can be, but we shouldn't ignore its limitations. It makes massive color changes easily, yet its retouching capabilities are subtler than those of other colorspaces. For all that it does, certain curves are awkward, as we saw in the last two chapters, and so are some types of blends, as this chapter has pointed out.

We started this book with a series of canyons, because we saw that canyons have characteristics that play into LAB's strengths. We end with faces, another strong point. Or, better put, another facet of the same strong point. Faces and canyons present similar issues. A person's flesh, like a canyon's walls, falls in a short darkness range, ideal for exploitation in the L channel.

Also, our last exercise was full of brilliant

colors, but none of them were in the girl's face. Faces and canyons are not gray, but their colors are dull in comparison to other common objects. Easy fodder for the A and B, as the colors can be livened up without any chance of driving them out of gamut, the way careless use of LAB might do with the background of the last image.

Above all, faces and canyons invite concentrated study on the part of the viewer. We find them interesting, and we look at them carefully. When we do, we perceive, and our minds enhance, subtle color differences. We find brilliant greens and magentas in the Artist's Palette of Figure 1.1 even though the camera assures us that no such colors are present. We perceive that the lips and cheeks of the little girl we just worked with are significantly redder than the rest of her skin, although she wears no makeup.

Recognizing such similarities is the key to making the proper use of LAB. If you understand why it is so much better to blur the A and B than to do the same thing in Color mode in RGB, then LAB's great superiority in color blending in other areas of retouching seems only logical. If you grasp why shadow detail is more effectively sharpened in the L channel than in RGB/Luminosity, then it becomes obvious that it also will do better with the Shadow/Highlight command. And if you now realize why LAB—in combination with RGB, let it be said—handles faces extremely well, then you have solved the canyon conundrum.

*   *   *

Before you set out to perfect the techniques developed in this book, and to search for LAB solutions that are as yet undiscovered, we'll close with another illustration of LAB's flexibility, its power to let different people do different things with the same image. In keeping with the theme of the chapter, it will be another excellent original. In keeping with the theme of the book, it will be a canyon.

First, Analyze the Image

Our destination is North Coyote Buttes, on the Utah-Arizona border, near Zion National Park. The formation shown in Figure 13.20 is known as The Wave, in view of the weird swirling patterns in the rock. The original digital image was provided by one of the country's leading commercial photographers, Lee Varis.

Lee, who is no slouch at LAB correction himself, uses this image as an instructional tool, not about LAB proper, but about the

The Tilt Toward Yellow

B–negative (more blue than yellow) objects are comparatively rare, skies excepted. The B channel is therefore usually biased toward yellow, not the neutrality one might expect. Noticing when an object is unexpectedly B–negative, as the flowers of Figure 16.17 are, can be useful, as the discussion of Blending Options for that image indicates.

If a picture is properly color-balanced, you might think that the average color would be a gray—0^A0^B. Not true. As I've never seen a study of the subject, I analyzed about a billion pixels myself. Not in this chapter, of course—close-ups of faces are very positive in both A and B. But I grabbed all the corrected (so as not to be influenced by inadvertent casts), uncropped LAB images from Chapters 12, 14, and 15, which portray a variety of subjects. Weighting all images equally so that size wasn't a factor, the average pixel value was 0^A7^B (mean), 1^A8^B (median). That's a substantial tilt toward yellow.

Also, there's a strong bias toward the channels pairing up, not one positive and the other negative. Of the images I looked at (excluding the wildly atypical blue jacket of Figure 12.3), the only exception was the forest scene of Figure 15.11, which averaged $(10)^A19^B$. The most A–positive picture was also the most B–positive: the church scene of Figure 14.11D, 11^A28^B. And the most A–negative was also the most B–negative: the ocean scene of Figure 14.4, $(29)^A(17)^B$.

For those interested in such trivia, Figure 16.17 would have won the most A–positive award, in spite of the presence of so many green, A–negative leaves. Its mean pixel value is 14^A9^B.

Figure 16.20 *An original image of a canyon noted for the unusual red and yellow swirling effect in the rocks.*

heavily LAB-flavored luminosity blending described in Chapter 14. He has his own sequence of suggested moves and has published his rationale for treating the image in this way. I thought it would be fun to compare how two people with LAB experience might approach the same challenging image. I had seen Lee's strategy when he published it in 2002, but, to avoid being biased by it, I didn't review it before proceeding.

First, let's get an idea of what's wanted. The National Parks Service describes The Wave as "a gallery of gruesomely twisted formations of Chinle shale resembling deformed pillars, cones, mushrooms and other odd creations. Deposits of iron claim some of the responsibility for the unique blending of color twisted

in the rock, creating a dramatic rainbow of pastel yellows, pinks, and reds."

The file arrives in RGB, tagged with Lee's custom definition that is more colorful than the sRGB used in this book but less colorful than Adobe RGB. As it seems to have captured a lot of color variation in the canyon without going overboard, I see no reason to ignore or override this profile.

The image starts off too flat. The lightest clouds measure an overly dark $204^R202^G239^B$. The darkest area of canyon is also slightly light. Moreover, that's not a good color for clouds, which are supposed to be white, meaning equal values in all three RGB channels. The red and green are acceptably close, but the blue is too light.

In addition to correcting these peccadillos, we must bring out some of the beautiful reds and yellows that the Parks Service says are there but the camera is suppressing, and to add the depth that our eyes would have seen but the camera didn't.

Before sweating the details, it pays to figure out what the big moves are going to be. How will we create the color variation? How will we add this contrast? The default answer to both is given in the first chapters: steep straight-line curves in the A and B; in the L, an S curve whose most vertical part catches the canyon.

I think these default answers are wrong for this particular image. Most canyons, like the faces we've been working with, have smooth transitions of color and no specific colors that need to be driven apart from one another. Here, though, there are four key colors, to my way of thinking. The lighter marbled areas of the rocks are red, but not nearly as red as the darker areas. The two need to be driven apart. Similarly, the clouds are blue, but not as blue as the sky. They need to be spread apart.

This calls for an approach along the lines developed in Chapter 12. There is little room to make the canyon redder, so the lighter areas will have to become more neutral, as will the clouds. The curves to the AB will thus be in the shape of an inverted S, similar to the ones we saw in the pressroom image of Figure 12.5.

While the L curve, when we get there, will doubtless add a great deal of contrast, I question whether it will bring out the marbling enough. So, I thought in terms of separating color from contrast, of doing some preliminary blending along the lines of that done in the last half of Chapter 14, particularly the very similar canyon image of Figure 14.10.

Figure 16.21 *The RGB channels of Figure 16.20.*

I originally planned to show my way first and then Lee's. The two of us wound up with different results, but our thought processes were so similar that we can do a side-by-side comparison throughout, especially since we each used the same number of steps.

Second, Set the Contrast

In examining the RGB channels (Figure 16.21), it's clear that the red is, as always, best in the sky, but that in the rocks it's approximately as useful as the Brightness/Contrast command. We both resolved to rid ourselves of its evil influence, but we proceeded in different directions.

Lee took the straightforward approach of working with what looks the best. Seeing how sharply defined the whorls were in the blue channel, he applied it to the composite image on a luminosity layer and arrived at Figure 16.22A. He did not give a hoot about what happened to the sky, as he already had plans to manufacture a new one.

I thought about the same move, but decided to use the green channel for blending instead. I reasoned that using the blue might make the image too dark, and that I had plenty of opportunities to get it darker later without risking a loss of detail now. In fact, after the blend I lightened the layer somewhat, applying a mild S curve to enhance midtone contrast. That put me at Figure 16.23A.

Back over to Lee, who now went for broke. He had noticed that the original

Figure 16.22 Correction steps of Lee Varis. All steps went on separate layers set to Luminosity mode. Top, the blue channel is applied to Figure 16.20 in Normal mode. Middle, the green channel shown in Figure 16.21 is applied to the result in Overlay mode, followed by Blending Options to exclude dark areas. Bottom, the red channel of Figure 16.20 is applied to the result in Darken mode, and a curve darkens the sky even further.

green channel—the same one I had just used for my own luminosity blend—is almost a 50% gray, except for the swirling patterns, which are much lighter. That suggested the audacious move of blending it into his image in Overlay mode. The marbling got much lighter; the rest of the rock got slightly darker on the whole but picked up a lot of interesting variation, which struts its stuff in Figure 16.22B.

He limited this move to changing contrast and not color by placing it on a luminosity layer. And because overlaying in this fashion plugs shadows as well as lightening light areas, he had to use Blending Options to exclude some of the darker parts of the picture. Using the gray slider, which RGB offers in addition to red, green, and blue ones, he created a transition zone similar to the one in the L slider of Figure 16.17.

At this point, we each attacked the sky on a luminosity layer, by blending the original red channel of Figure 16.21 into the composite color image in Darken mode, exactly as shown twice earlier in Figures 14.9 and 14.10.

An aesthetic disagreement now surfaced. Lee felt that the sky was still not dark enough, and applied a curve to his luminosity layer. The sky in his Figure 16.22C is therefore heavier than in my Figure 16.23B. I, in fact, lightened my sky with the next step.

To make Figure 16.23C, I had a different overlay blend up my sleeve. I took a lesson from Chapter 15, moving the file into LAB

Figure 16.23 *Correction steps of Dan Margulis. All steps went on separate layers set to Luminosity mode. Top, the green channel is applied to Figure 16.20 in Normal mode, and a curve lightens and adds contrast. Middle, the red channel of Figure 16.21 is applied to the result in Darken mode. Bottom, the file is converted to LAB, and an inverted copy of the B channel is applied to the L in Overlay mode.*

and blending an inverted copy of the B into the L in Overlay mode. Since much of the canyon was strongly B–positive, it got darker. The swirls, however, were around 0^B and stayed constant. And the sky, being B–negative, got a little bit lighter.

Third, Add the Color

Figures 16.22C and 16.23C aren't directly comparable. Lee's violent overlay blend had created all the detail that he wanted. I was still planning to add bite by a curve to the L, so my version remains a little flat.

Lee, however, had closed the book on contrast and was ready to turn to color. Not wishing to confuse his students with LAB, he trotted out Image: Adjustments>Hue/ Saturation. He tried to create the needed color variation by sharply increasing saturation in all yellows, breaking them away from

the more reddish areas of the rocks. He also decided that he wanted the sky more colorful, so he saturated all blues and lightened them slightly. His final version is Figure 16.24.

AB curves, as we should know by now, are a more powerful way of introducing variation than Hue/Saturation is. My final version, Figure 16.25, isn't as red as Lee's is, but that's just a difference of taste. Either of us could have adjusted ours to be closer to the other's color. The AB curves, however, had a big advantage in two areas. First, the flatness in the B curve whitened the clouds but made the background sky bluer, less purple. In RGB, it's tough to saturate one kind of blue while desaturating another. Consequently, the clouds in Lee's version got too blue/purple.

Second, remember that the official description of this scene calls for a *dramatic rainbow* of colors.

Figure 16.24 Lee Varis's final image, after an application of the Hue/Saturation command to correct color.

Figure 16.25 Dan Margulis's final version, after the application of the LAB curves shown at right.

It wasn't all that long ago that we were facing a real rainbow, in Figure 11.3. The conclusion then was the same as now: look to the color-space that has a home-field advantage. LAB is where the rainbow sleeps, waiting for us to rouse it.

Fourth, Save and Close

Some LAB techniques are both easy and effective: the Man from Mars Method of Chapter 12; the simple curves of Chapters 1–4; the blurring and sharpening of Chapter 5; and even the face recipe we've just covered. Others, like almost all of Chapters 12, 14, and 15, are quite complex. Sometimes the techniques have a huge advantage over their RGB or CMYK equivalents; sometimes the advantage is slight but present; and in some cases using LAB is not just a waste of time but actually counterproductive.

The ball that Lee and I have been batting back and forth now lands in your court, as you decide how much LAB to incorporate into your own work. If you want to save it for canyons and faces, so be it. There's a strong case to go further.

In his teaching materials, Lee Varis makes it. He describes his original (Figure 16.20) as "not too bad—but why stop at good enough when we can have spectacular!"

You don't need to be a famous photographer to feel that way. The theorist who fleshed out the law of simultaneous contrast, the father of the impressionist school of painting, and thus of retouching and correction in LAB mode, was a chemist. Here is what Michel Eugène Chevreul had to say:

> If any subject exists that is worth being studied critically because of the frequency and variety of example and opportunities it offers, it is unquestionably that upon which I am now engaged; for whether we contemplate the works of nature or of art, the varied colors that they present is one of the finest spectacles man is permitted to enjoy. This explains how our strong desire to reproduce color images of objects we admire, or which have features that interest us, has produced the art of painting; how the imitation of the works of the painter, by means of threads or small building blocks, has given birth to the arts of weaving tapestry and carpets, and of mosaics; and how the need to reproduce multiple copies of certain designs economically has led to printing of every description, of every type, using every shade of color.

As this chapter has revealed, I'm still struggling with some of the complexities that arise when LAB meets Photoshop. I had to redo the image of the little girl, and I would certainly have done this last image differently had I reviewed Lee's approach first.

Many of the examples in this book are second tries as well. I do grasp LAB's incredible potential and, I think, most of the basic ways to use it. But with disturbing regularity, I would prepare demonstration files that didn't show what I thought they were going to. Then I had to stop and figure out what I hadn't understood, and rework entire sections or even chapters. For example, I had misconceptions about the blurring and sharpening topics of Chapter 5, which were only revealed by working on images you haven't seen and receiving a series of nasty surprises.

Naturally, I corrected that chapter and others where similar things occurred, but *corrected* just means bringing them into sync with my current state of knowledge. Because working in LAB is bleeding-edge, the odds are good that some of what appears here will eventually be shown to be wrong, or at least inefficient. So, while I think Chapter 5 is in good shape now, I can't be certain.

One thing that *is* certain is that we will continue to be confronted by images whose contrast and whose color leave much to be desired. Dealing with them will be easier if we know how and when to use the most powerful of colorspaces, the one that sees color the way we do, the one that is best for retouching, best for sharpening and blurring, and best for adding realism—the one where the rainbow makes its home.

Notes & Credits

The images in this book, with only six exceptions, derive from one of three sources. First, there are the ones I've shot myself in various parts of the world. Second, 14 images come from what used to be known as the Corel Professional Photos collection of royalty-free stock photography. This 80,000-image library was marketed around a decade ago at obscenely low prices. The series is no longer marketed as such, but individual images are still available for purchase through a successor, Hemera Technologies Inc. (www.hemera.com).

Third is the real-life category, consisting of pictures offered by my students and by members of the Applied Color Theory online discussion group. Most of these images are from professional photographers who were shooting on assignment.

Two images come from other vendors of royalty-stock photography, and four date from a unique 1992 release. Kodak created a CD of interesting photographs and generously allowed unlimited use for any purpose pertaining to digital imaging. The purpose was to promote the new Kodak Photo CD product. Consequently, although the photographic concepts themselves are spectacular, they have suffered a bit on the way into Photoshop, for technical reasons that are not the fault of the photographer. Just like your pictures and mine, right? Fortunately, knowing LAB means never having to write off poor captures: if the idea was good, the original pixels don't have to be.

About the CD

The CD enclosed in this volume is for your private use in practicing and perfecting the techniques discussed here. You are permitted to manipulate the images however you like for your own edification, including printing them to test how well you did. However, these images are copyrighted. You may not publish them, post them, share them with others, or allow any reproduction other than what you yourself need for learning purposes.

Many images on the CD have been down-sampled, which will not affect the exercises. All files are in LAB, Photoshop format, except the final canyon exercise of Chapter 16, which is tagged RGB; one image in Chapter 9 in which a CMYK file was supplied in real life; and the actual CMYK output files for the bit-depth comparisons of Chapter 6.

Chapter One

The images of the three canyons and Yellowstone Lake are all mine. The picture of the man is from the royalty-free collection of Liquid Library (www.liquidlibrary.com).
* *What's on the CD:* Original files for the Artist's Palette, Yellowstone Canyon, Yellowstone Lake, and Anza-Borrego images.

   Review and Exercises Section:
* If any of the images had started out with an obvious color cast, the method used in Chapter 1 would have exaggerated it.
* The images have a common element in that the most important areas of each one fall in a narrow darkness range and don't have much color variation.
* The impact of making the AB curves more vertical would be to increase color variation and make the pictures look more vivid.
* If the AB curves were made more horizontal, all colors would get duller. If the AB curves were completely horizontal and still passed through the original center point, the picture would become a black and white.

Chapter Two

All pictures in this chapter are mine.

● *What's on the CD:* The sunset image; the three LAB graphics of Figure 2.6 so that you can experiment with what happens when you convert them to other colorspaces; and one layered file of the still life of Figure 2.3, in which the intensity of the colored bars may be adjusted to taste. For the original rose image of Figure 2.1, see the Chapter 7 folder.

Review and Exercises Section:

● Neutral colors occur in RGB where the values of all three channels are equal.

● Neutral colors occur in LAB where both the A and B channels have values of zero.

● The L channel of LAB resembles a direct conversion of the color file to grayscale, but the L is somewhat lighter.

● In the A and B channels, positive numbers denote warm colors—magenta in the A, yellow in the B. Negative numbers are cool colors—a green tending toward teal in the A, blue in the B. Values of zero are neutral.

Chapter Three

In the first section, the picture of Sequoia National Park is mine. The woman (photograph by Jack Cutler) and the rain forest shot come from the Corel library.

In the section discussing color-blindness, the woman in the red hat, as if you didn't know, is from Kodak, but you may not know that the photographer was Bob Clemens. The hockey game is from the Corel library, and the river and Halloween scenes are mine.

● *What's on the CD:* The hazy scene, the rain forest and waterfall, and the young woman in the white sweater.

Review and Exercises Section:

● In Figures 3.2 and 3.3, the most significant move was the curve applied to the L channel. The haze in the original shot meant that the L fell in an extremely short range, and that contrast could be drastically increased.

● If a client liked the added blueness in Figure 3.1A but objected to the added yellowness in green areas, the solution would be to redo the curves, placing a locking point in the center of the B curve and angling the top half more steeply than the bottom half.

● The two categories of image that often require different slopes for the A and B curves are, first, pictures of natural greenery, where we usually want to emphasize the A, and second, pictures of light-skinned individuals, where we often wish to emphasize the B.

● If you set the highlight and shadow to their extremes of 100^L and 0^L, they won't hold detail. Theoretically there is a distinction between these values and 99^L and 1^L, but few if any output devices will hold it.

Chapter Four

The wintry images of Sergiev Posad and of the Québec forest are from the Corel library. The pictures of Boston Common and of the Puerto Rican pool scene are mine. The image of the young woman is by Chris Szagola.

Beta reader Les De Moss prepared the useful schematic that appears as Figure 4.9 to help him as he learned how LAB works.

● *What's on the CD:* Les's graphic, plus the Sergiev Posad, Québec, Boston Common, and Puerto Rico images. The Death Valley scene can be picked up from the Chapter 1 folder.

Review and Exercises Section:

● The strange A curve of Figure 4.8 changed red objects to green ones by being shaped something like a letter V. Since the base of the V was at the center point of the curve, values of 0^A—neutrals—did not change. But with the left side of the curve rising rather than falling, areas that previously were A–positive (more magenta than green) became A–negative. The B channel had no great impact, because both greens and reds are B–positive (more yellow than blue).

● The Image: Adjustments>Threshold command is useful for finding highlights and shadows. Threshold divides the picture into pure whites and pure blacks, with a slider controlling where the break occurs. When the slider is brought almost all the way to the right, everything in the picture except the very lightest areas becomes black. Click OK, and toggle back and forth to the original picture with Command–Z. The highlight should be the most significant of the points that the command leaves white. The shadow can be found by reversing the process, moving the Threshold slider to the left until almost all of the picture is white.

Chapter Five

The indoor and outdoor images of the Johnson Space Center are courtesy of the National Aeronautics and Space Administration. The woman used to demonstrate the function of the Surface Blur filter was photographed by Ron Brickey.

The gymnast is from the Corel library. The scene of palm trees is by David Leaser. The image of the hand-painted yellow sign is mine.

• *What's on the CD:* The flight operations director, the woman demonstrating the Surface Blur filter, the yellow sign, the palm tree, and the horrifically noisy Figure 5.19A. The grid that produced Figure 5.18 is included for testing blending. Also, there's a PDF of the lengthy thread on the Applied Color Theory list discussing the political ramifications of how to refer to keyboard shortcuts in print.

Review and Exercises Section:

• In RGB the noisiest channel is ordinarily the blue. If the file is converted into LAB, the noise will find its way into the B, and, if it ever gets to CMYK, into the yellow.

• The major negative consequence of Gaussian blurring the A and/or B channels is that if the Radius setting is too high, sharp color transitions may become sloppy. This problem is avoided by use of the Surface Blur filter, which tries to avoid blurring edges.

• The Amount setting of the Unsharp Mask filter governs the intensity of the sharpening halos. Higher Amounts create whiter and blacker halos. The Radius setting makes the halos wider or narrower, not more intense.

• Sharpening the L channel avoids the possibility of a color shift, since the L contains no color information.

• When it is necessary to sharpen in RGB, it should be done in Luminosity mode, either by using the Edit: Fade command or by doing the sharpening on a separate layer.

Chapter Six

The bicyclists are from Kodak, photographed by Steve Kelly. I shot the hog and shoats on a trip to Guilin, China. The shot of the lobby of the Hotel San Marcos in León, Spain, is by Sylvia Kwong. The Venice canal scene is mine.

Beta reader André Dumas offered improved versions of some of the lines in my translations of Rostand's *Cyrano de Bergerac.*

The picture of the horsewoman in Figure 16.8 is by Jim Bean. Versions B, C, G, and H are the ones that went back and forth between LAB and RGB 25 times.

In the original double-picture collage of Figure 16.9, the German marketplace is from Kodak, photo by Alfons Rudolph. The car was photographed for advertising use by Aldas Minkevicius.

As for identifying the various pieces of Figures 16.9 and 16.10:

• The politically correct method, 16-bit RGB all the way, is in versions C, S, F, Q, and R.

• Doing the same thing in 8-bit all the way were versions B, N, P, U, and H.

• The method of converting to LAB and back to RGB after each one of the seven correction steps, while remaining in 16-bit at all times, is shown in versions D, E, K, G, and V.

• The least palatable method, working in 8-bit throughout and converting back and forth from LAB after each correction step, is versions A, J, T, L, and M.

If you're curious as to how well somebody else might do at picking out which was which, I can be the guinea pig. After the text of the book was finalized, I received final contract proofs from the printer. Since I had long forgotten in which order the versions appeared, I took 20 minutes and carefully examined each variant under controlled lighting conditions. I permitted myself reading glasses, but not a loupe.

In the horsewoman shot, I could see no difference at all either at 100% or 400%. In the two intermediate sizes I thought I saw enough to take a guess at which was which, and was correct in both.

I was less successful with the collage. Of my 20 answers, only three were right. Considering that someone who answered the questions on the basis of coin flips would average five correct answers, this was not particularly impressive evidence of a detectable difference between the four variants.

I was most accurate where it could be expected—at the highest magnification, looking at a single channel. In that set, I correctly identified both 8-bit versions. However, I mixed up the 16-bit versions, declaring that the one converted to and from LAB at seven different points in the process was actually the one that had never been converted at all. With respect to the four sets at lower magnifications, my responses appeared to be completely random—no discernible relation to the true order of the images.

● *What's on the CD:* The hotel lobby, the Venetian canal scene, plus the six CMYK files that produced the variant images found in Figures 6.8–6.10. As these are at high resolution, they have been cropped to prevent republication, but they are ample for studying the effects of the earlier conversions to LAB.

Review and Exercises Section:

● The L channel is somewhat lighter than a direct conversion to grayscale and has slightly less contrast in extreme highlights and shadows.

● Most layered files should be flattened during the conversion from RGB to LAB. Adjustment layers are discarded if the file is not flattened. Some blending modes have different meanings. A standard layer in Normal mode is unaffected. Standard layers in Color or Luminosity mode generally produce better results if they are *not* flattened until you get to LAB. However, you have to be careful that the file does not contain some other type of layer that will not survive the transition.

● Computer-generated gradients should be created in the final output space where possible. Otherwise, their smoothness may be interrupted by Photoshop's efforts to fit them into a new gamut. The problem is particularly severe with blue gradients that are being converted into CMYK.

Chapter Seven

The office scene with the yellow paperwork in the foreground was provided by the *Knoxville News-Sentinel.* The yellowish interior scene is by Boris Feldblyum. The Miami Beach hotel; the covered bridge in Lucerne, Switzerland; the Hong Kong wedding; and the Yellowstone bison are all mine.

● *What's on the CD:* The rose, the hotel porch, the wedding, the bison, and the dental classroom.

Review and Exercises Section:

● If the bottom half of the A curve in Figure 7.5 had not been locked, everything that was more magenta than green would have become more vivid. As the flower was already very pink, this mistake would have driven it far beyond what can be printed, and much detail would have been lost.

● Applying the Shadow/Highlight command to the L channel may damage detail in dark greens and reds.

● The usual purpose of loading a channel

as a selection is to apply a curve or other correction that needs to emphasize areas that are light in the selection channel (or dark, if the selection is inverted).

• An RGB image cannot contain color in extremely light or dark areas. Therefore, in high-contrast RGB images, neutral highlights and shadows don't prove that the image is neutrally correct. Extremely light and dark areas can't be anything *but* neutral in RGB.

Chapter Eight

The Venetian image used to make the duotone is mine. The woman with the blown-out skin tone is a royalty-free photo from Comstock Images (www.comstock.com). Before raising your eyebrows, you should know that this is the only image in the book that has been sabotaged to prove a point. The original image does have tonality in the woman's cheek, but I killed it with a curve in order to be able to demonstrate some LAB magic to restore it.

I did not have to resort to any artificial measures to blow out the sky in the Swiss landscape image of Figure 8.9; my own photography skills took care of that part.

• *What's on the CD:* Only the Swiss village and mountain scene. The image of Venice used to create a duotone can be found in the Chapter 6 folder.

Review and Exercises Section:

• When a LAB file contains imaginary colors, a direct conversion to CMYK has unpredictable results. A direct conversion to RGB, however, generally produces something that looks like what the monitor was displaying while the file was still in LAB. Normally going from LAB to CMYK would yield a nearly identical image to one produced by going from LAB to RGB to CMYK. When imaginary colors are in play, however, this is no longer true.

• The common defect in faces that imaginary colors can help solve is areas that are nearly completely blown out. Painting in an imaginary color in LAB will fill the damaged area undetectably.

• Color mode produces different results in LAB than in RGB: first, because LAB can produce imaginary colors in areas that are so white or black in RGB that they have to be neutral. Second, the method by which the new colors is computed is generally superior in LAB. It yields lighter and purer colors.

Chapter Nine

All three of the rose images at the start of the chapter are from the Corel library, as is the woman with the netting in front of her face. The pictures of purple and white petunias and of tulips against a granite background are mine, as are the images of Amsterdam's Schiphol Airport, Kowloon, and the Finger Lakes wine district of New York State.

The image of the interior with the challenging neutral-to-blue cast that increases from left to right was shot by Dennis Hearne.

• *What's on the CD:* All files except the woman's face. Figure 9.17, which features a cross-cast that affects only one side of the image, is provided in CMYK, as it came to me in real life.

Review and Exercises Section:

• A selection is a temporary isolation of certain areas of the image so that they can be altered while all other areas are locked. Partially selected areas can be altered, but not as much as fully selected areas. A mask is a portable selection: it is a selection that has been saved as a separate channel or grayscale document and can be loaded as a selection when desired.

• RGB channels impart more of their color in their lighter areas. In the pictures of red roses opening the chapter, the flowers were very light in the red channel. They therefore were well defined against the background and were a more logical choice than either of the other channels, where the flowers would be darker. The green channel would be indicated for selecting something like an emerald, and the blue for a sky.

• The A and B channels are never white or black, or even close. If they were, their values would be close to +127 or –128, which are far too brilliant for any output. Instead, the channels are quite gray. Since a mask generally requires areas that are nearly white or black, we often must apply Auto Levels or a similar adjustment to a copy of the A or B before using it in that way.

• The Blend If sliders in Blending Options are split by Option–clicking them. The purpose is to establish a smooth transition zone that averages values from both layers, rather than totally excluding one.

• A yellow object like the canyon walls of Figure 1.2 is lightest in the red channel, which should be the best start of a mask in RGB. In LAB, the B channel would be best because the canyon is much more yellow than blue. In the woman's bright red hat in Figure 3.13, the red and the A would be the best start. The hog and shoats of Figure 6.2 are much lighter and less saturated, but they're still the same color as the hat, so the red and the A would again be the choices. The bison of Figure 7.9 is an even less saturated red, so the same answers would apply.

Chapter Ten

The red car, the train, and the woman wearing the green jacket are all from the Corel library. The teal car is mine.

• *What's on the CD:* All the original images in the chapter.

Review and Exercises Section:

• LAB equivalents for Pantone Matching Systems are found in the Color Picker. Click Color Libraries (Photoshop CS2; Custom in earlier versions). Type in the PMS number, and the values will come up as shown in Figure 10.4.

• Given a strongly colored object on the bottom layer and a contrasting flat color on top, it would be easier to isolate the object with Blend If sliders in LAB than in RGB. The A and B sliders exclude pure color, whereas in RGB as the object gets darker it becomes more difficult to differentiate from other parts of the image.

• Transforming the blue background of a U.S. flag into green would require making a new A channel, because the original value would be close to 0^A and thus could not be changed without drastically changing color balance as well. A reasonable procedure would be to make a duplicate layer; copy the B into the A (making the overall color temporarily cyan); and then invert the B to create a green. After applying curves to obtain the desired shade of green, use Blend If sliders to exclude anything that is not substantially B–negative or that is any significant distance away from 0^A on the underlying layer.

• It was easy to change the yellow train of Figure 10.3 into blue because it required only inverting the B. To create a purple would have required constructing a positive A. This would probably be achieved by blending an inverted copy of the B into the A.

Chapter Eleven

The Corvette and Sergiev Posad images are drawn from previous chapters. The pre-screened image appeared in one of my columns in *Electronic Publishing* magazine. The original color image that was converted to black and white so that my student could colorize it in LAB came from the Corel library. The aerial photograph is courtesy of Hiram Vega. The man whose suit has a pronounced moiré was photographed by Darren Bernaerdt. The images of the rainbow, Mt. Rainier, and the two Russian cathedrals are mine.

• *What's on the CD:* Layered files of the front and rear of the car with the very bad transition between red and green, for studying the difference between LAB and RGB methods of blending; the rainbow image; the orange date-time stamp on the background of greenery; my great-great-grandmother; the two Russian cathedrals; the prescreened original, and a section of the man's suit with the disagreeable moiré. A mask for the suit is included as an alpha channel.

Review and Exercises Section:

● When dodging or burning the A or B channel, the tool must be set to midtones, because the two channels always consist of grays, never whites or blacks.

● In a picture of an autumn forest, the sponge tool in Saturate mode will make all colors purer. If the sponge is applied to the A channel only, reds will become purer and less orange; greens will become purer and less yellow. If the burn tool is applied to the A, the greens will become purer and less yellow, but the reds will be muted and will seem more orange; also, the yellows may become more green. If the dodge tool is applied to the B, the reds, greens, and yellows will all get yellower. (In such a forest, there would probably not be any B–negative objects.)

Chapter Twelve

The Venetian scene is mine. The jacket is from the catalog of Sierra Trading Post (www.sierratradingpost.com). The clown triggerfish image is by Fred Drury. The scene of the printing facility with the yellow cast is courtesy of the *Knoxville News-Sentinel*. The couple on the bridge was photographed by Jim Bean. The horsewoman wearing western clothing was photographed by Michael Vlietstra for Hobby Horse Clothing Co. (www.hobbyhorseinc.com). The two flower-strewn 2005 Death Valley images are mine.

The "Man from Mars Method" was introduced simultaneously in the March 2005 edition of *Electronic Publishing* and the April 2005 edition of *Photoshop User*.

● *What's on the CD:* The Venetian image, the clown triggerfish, the couple on the bridge, the woman and the horse, and the two Death Valley images. The Venetian image has the original Man from Mars adjustment layer, so you can alter the curves or change the opacity to view the effect. As promised in the text, the curves that produced the four variants of the horse image are here—but remember that I also applied Shadow/Highlight to the original before using them. And *that* move isn't enclosed.

Review and Exercises Section:

● The key to knowing whether the pivot points are chosen correctly in the Man from Mars Method is that it should be clear that significant parts of the image are being driven to the extremes of both the A and B channels: objects both strongly magenta as opposed to green and strongly green as opposed to magenta must be found in the A. In the B, both blue and yellow objects must be readily visible.

● To insert Figure 12.8's sweater into Figure 12.7, paste Figure 12.8 on top of Figure 12.7 as a new layer. Use the Blend If sliders of Blending Options to exclude anything that is extremely A–positive on the underlying layer. Be sure to break the slider apart by Option–clicking it to ensure a smooth merge.

● When strongly out-of-gamut colors are brought into CMYK, there can be a big loss of detail. This was an issue with the woman's sweater in Figure 12.7. There was no such problem with the yellow hazard warnings in Figure 12.5B, because they didn't have any detail to begin with, so appearing as essentially flat colors in the CMYK version looked natural.

● In Figure 12.10, certain moves in the B channel might turn the woman's white cowboy hat blue. To avoid this, the curving is done on a layer or adjustment layer. Then, use the Blend If sliders to exclude anything that is extremely light in the L channel. Either the This Layer or the Underlying Layer slider will work.

Chapter Thirteen

The process control bars of Figure 13.1 are available from the Graphic Arts Technical Foundation (www.gain.org).

Information about the Specifications for Web Offset Publications (SWOP), including a downloadable copy of the 10th revision of the full SWOP standards (June 2005), is available at www.swop.org.

The comment about the worthlessness of Delta-E is found at www.aim-dtp.net. Readers are cautioned that the author and site proprietor, Timo Autiokari, is frequently at odds with conventional color wisdom. I would recommend Googling his name before blindly accepting his advice. There is, however, a large amount of valuable and sophisticated technical information available at the site, along with some dubious recommendations and some overstatements, like the one I quoted. Delta-E is not accurate, but it isn't worthless either—it's the best of a bunch of bad alternatives.

Information about the Curvemeister plug-in, including a demo version, is available at www.curvemeister.com.

The unfortunate photographer who was victimized by a profile misunderstanding in Figure 13.8 is Patrick Chuprina.

● *What's on the CD:* The original LAB file for the PMS colors of Figures 13.5 for studying conversion of out-of-gamut colors, plus the six PDFs by Gernot Hoffmann described on Page 272. The checkerboard of Figure 13.6 also appears in Chapter 7. The original LAB file can be found in that folder.

Chapter Fourteen

The picture of the island, which I did such a terrible job of correcting in my 1994 book, came from Kodak, photographed by Don Cochran. The priest is by Mike Demyan. The images of the South China Sea, Cathedral Valley, and St. Peter's Cathedral in Vatican City are all mine.

● *What's on the CD:* All the original images in the chapter.

Review and Exercises Section:

● Using negative percentages in the Channel Mixer only works when the area is nearly solid in the channel being subtracted. In Figure 14.6A, there was no detail in the trees in the blue channel, so it could be subtracted from the green. In the ocean of Figure 14.1, the color is not pure enough for the blue channel to lose all detail. Subtracting it from the green would cause the darkest areas of the water to get precipitously lighter.

● In a normally lit picture of a face, it usually pays to copy the green channel to a new layer set to Luminosity mode. If the model is wearing strong red clothing or lipstick, however, the green channel may be so dark that all the color will be lost when the layers are merged. The solution is to use the Blend If sliders of layer Blending Options to exclude all areas that are extremely dark in the green channel of the underlying layer. The face itself will not be excluded because it is only moderately dark in the green channel.

● In Figure 7.13, an interior shot with a yellow cast, a preliminary RGB blend to reduce the cast would help the subsequent correction. You could blend the green channel into the blue at between 50% and 70% opacity. For safety's sake, it should be done in Lighten mode, although it probably would make no difference. 100% opacity for the blend would be undesirable as otherwise the picture would become too pink.

Chapter Fifteen

The opening overlay blends into the L channel are: Figure 15.1D, the B channel inverted; 15.1E, the A; 15.1F, the A inverted; and 15.1G, the B.

The photograph of palm trees against the dark sky is by David Leaser. The portrait of the bow hunter is by Lee Varis. The photographer by the water, the Italian street scene, the flowers and butterfly, and the Swiss forest scene are all mine.

- *What's on the CD:* All the original images from this chapter.

   Review and Exercises Section:

- When adding color to faces, as a general rule emphasizing the A is appropriate for persons with unusually light complexions, the B for much darker complexions, and neither one for persons falling between the two extremes. This topic is discussed further in Chapter 16.

- The image has to be neutrally correct before applying AB overlays to themselves because otherwise it would aggravate the color imbalance. Occasionally the A or B can be overlaid on the L even when the picture is not properly balanced.

- When the assignment is to remove some of the additional redness that an overlay blend has created while retaining the enhanced greens, you need a copy of the original A, and possibly B, channels. Blend the original A into the enhanced A at around 50% opacity, but use Darken mode. That will prevent the greens from getting lighter (less negative) while permitting some darkening of the reds (less positive). If necessary, do the same thing with the B channel.

Chapter Sixteen

The blond woman who starts the chapter was photographed by Hunter Clarkson. In the trio of portraits handled together, the younger woman is by Mark Laurie, the older woman by Marty Stock, and the man by Jim Bean.

Olga Valerovna, the daughter of my Russian publisher, is the little girl among the flowers. Even I get good pictures with a subject like that.

Lee Varis's shot of the canyon known as the Wave, plus his tutorial on how to use luminosity blending to improve it, are on his Web site, www.varis.com.

- *What's on the CD:* Four of the five original face shots, plus Lee's original canyon (please note that it is an RGB file with an embedded tag that must be honored on opening the file if you are to duplicate what either Lee or I did with it).

Applied Color Theory, the Course

In 1994, a chain of department stores bought some very expensive hardware (not personal computers, which weren't nearly powerful enough in those days) to bring advertising work in-house rather than sending it to prepress houses at a cost of millions of dollars per year. This was done based on a vendor's assurance that all the chain had to do was retrain its secretaries and receptionists to run the new equipment, and all would be well.

In real life, it turned out to be a little more difficult than that, as the vendor learned when the buyer asked to return all the equipment. In desperation, the vendor offered to arrange training in color correction for the buyer's staff. This also turned out to be more difficult than the vendor thought, as most Photoshop trainers then tended to specialize in demonstrations of fancy filters rather than how to fix pictures, and it was not feasible to Google up somebody with more practical knowledge, as Google did not exist.

The vendor learned by word of mouth that I had a reputation for being able to teach people how to get good color (I was running a plant in New York City at the time) and, in desperation, brought me to Atlanta. For three days, I sat with six members of the store's staff, learning in what I was already convinced is the best way: everybody works on the same images, then we compare results and decide whose work is the best. Then, the inquest: what did the people who were successful do right, and what did the losers do wrong?

The improvement in quality was so immediate and so dramatic that a second session was scheduled, but a couple of seats were sold to other companies to defray expenses. Suspecting that there might be a broader market for this type of color correction knowledge, the vendor scheduled a third session, open to the general public, and then a fourth, and on and on.

I have now taught this class nearly 200 times, never the same way twice. The first class used Photoshop 2.5, and everything was scanned from film. As technology has changed (and, more important, as I've learned more tricks), so has the curriculum. It's still three brutally long days, still heavy on comparisons of different versions, still limited to seven students. It usually sells out months in advance, catering to professional photographers, in-house retouchers, serious hobbyists, and anyone else who simply wants to make their pictures look a lot better. Naturally, LAB techniques are incorporated, but the scope is much broader than any one colorspace.

For a fuller description of the course, along with current scheduling, pricing, and locations, visit www.ledet.com/margulis. The site also features dozens of my magazine articles and edited, advertising-free threads from the Applied Color Theory newsgroup.

Sterling Ledet & Associates

In the United States, my color correction courses have always been marketed by Sterling Ledet & Associates, originally a tiny Atlanta operation that has grown into one of the largest providers of graphic arts training services in North America, with classrooms in many major cities. Its extraordinarily deep course list is found at www.ledet.com.

Other Countries, Other Languages

As the pictures in the book indicate, I enjoy traveling the world. I have taught classes in many countries, in, so far, Spanish, German, and Italian as well as English. If you would like to arrange an engagement outside of the United States, contact me directly.

The Applied Color Theory Newsgroup

In 1999, Sterling Ledet & Associates launched a newsgroup to support those who had attended or were thinking of attending my color correction course, or who are interested in my writings. It currently has 2,500 members and averages 250 messages per month. The emphasis is on discussions of practical applications of color knowledge using Photoshop.

Signup for the list is currently available at http://groups.yahoo.com/group/colortheory or at www.ledet.com/margulis.

Reaching the Author

My address is dmargulis@aol.com. While I do try to reply to all correspondence, a three- to six-week delay has regrettably become the norm. If you need a quicker answer to a technical question, I recommend joining and posting it to the Applied Color Theory group (details above). Please note that due to the volume of e-mail I receive, I cannot accept images or any other form of attachment.

A Note on the Type

The text type of this book hasn't been seen in print for more than a decade. I prepared it for the first (1994) edition of my book on color correction, *Professional Photoshop.* Each subsequent edition, however, featured a new text face, this tactic being a good way to force me to read every single line again instead of blithely assuming that all was well.

The letterforms are those of Utopia, designed by Robert Slimbach of Adobe in 1990. I stripped out all the width and kerning information and substituted my own, because I believe in relatively large type and I write in a two-column format, a deadly typographic combination if the letterspacing isn't well controlled.

Index